General E.A. Paine
in Western Kentucky

ALSO OF INTEREST

*Unconditional Unionist: The Hazardous Life
of Lucian Anderson, Kentucky Congressman,*
by Berry Craig and Dieter C. Ullrich (McFarland, 2016)

General E.A. Paine in Western Kentucky

Assessing the "Reign of Terror" of the Summer of 1864

DIETER C. ULLRICH *and*
BERRY CRAIG

McFarland & Company, Inc., Publishers
Jefferson, North Carolina

LIBRARY OF CONGRESS CATALOGUING-IN-PUBLICATION DATA

Names: Ullrich, Dieter C., 1964– author. | Craig, Berry, author.
Title: General E. A. Paine in Western Kentucky : assessing the "reign of terror" of the summer of 1864 / Dieter C. Ullrich and Berry Craig.
Other titles: General Eleazer Arthur Paine in Western Kentucky
Description: Jefferson, North Carolina : McFarland & Company, Inc., Publishers, 2018. | Includes bibliographical references and index.
Identifiers: LCCN 2017048125 | ISBN 9781476671437 (softcover : acid free paper) ∞
Subjects: LCSH: Paine, E. A. (Eleazar A.), 1815–1882. | United States—History—Civil War, 1861–1865—Biography. | Kentucky—History—Civil War, 1861–1865—Biography. | Paine, E. A. (Eleazar A.), 1815–1882—Trials, litigation, etc. | Generals—United States—Biography. | Abolitionists—United States—Biography.
Classification: LCC E467.1.P23 U45 2018 | DDC 355.0092 [B]—dc23
LC record available at https://lccn.loc.gov/2017048125

BRITISH LIBRARY CATALOGUING DATA ARE AVAILABLE

ISBN (print) 978-1-4766-7143-7
ISBN (ebook) 978-1-4766-3098-4

© 2018 Dieter C. Ullrich and Berry Craig. All rights reserved

No part of this book may be reproduced or transmitted in any form or by any means, electronic or mechanical, including photocopying or recording, or by any information storage and retrieval system, without permission in writing from the publisher.

Front cover: photograph of General Eleazer A. Paine (Library of Congress)

Printed in the United States of America

*McFarland & Company, Inc., Publishers
Box 611, Jefferson, North Carolina 28640
www.mcfarlandpub.com*

Table of Contents

Preface	1
Introduction	5
One. "I am compelled to be severe"	9
Two. "This district is intensely disloyal"	26
Three. "Treason was no more"	38
Four. "A Reign of Terror"	62
Five. "Conduct to the prejudice of good order and military discipline"	79
Six. "Witnesses of known disloyalty"	99
Seven. "Unity of the Spirit"	112
Eight. "Served the Union Army and did his duty"	119
Epilogue	128
Timeline	131
Appendix I: Charges and Specifications Preferred Against Brigadier General E.A. Paine, United State Volunteers	143
Appendix II: The Men Who Worked on the Fortifications at Mayfield, August 17 to September 13, 1864	149
Chapter Notes	161
Works Cited	177
Index	183

Preface

Down in old Kentucky
They're true and plucky
They know that the Union is their Shield
And they'll do their duty
In all its beauty
—Stephen Foster, 1862

In February of 1995, I began a job as a special collections librarian and archivist at the University of Tennessee at Martin and leased a duplex about forty miles north in Mayfield, Kentucky. The town was conveniently located between Martin and Paducah, where my spouse worked at the time. Once settled in, I toured the town and nearby historical sites. One of those sites was the Wooldridge Monuments at the Maplewood Cemetery. While I gazed at the life-sized carved stones behind Victorian iron railings, I noticed a nearby tombstone with a small Confederate flag planted beside it. Drawn to the grave, I walked over and read the inscription. It began, "To the memory of Henry Bascom Hicks who was shot by order of the Federal tyrant General A.E. Payne [sic] on the streets of Mayfield, Kentucky, August 21, 1864." The impact was immediate, and my quest to learn more about this tyrant General Paine began.

Soon afterward, I ventured to the Graves County Public Library where I browsed through the local, regional and state histories. Each of those publications contained a few paragraphs or a brief chapter that mentioned the atrocities committed by General Paine while he was commander of the District of Western Kentucky in the summer of 1864. Citations were a rarity, and those that were listed could be traced back to *Collins' History of Kentucky*, published in 1874. It was this book that most historians referred to when they wrote about Paine. The brutal barbarities attributed to Paine at first appeared to be factual since they fit so well into the broader story of Union oppression in the Jackson Purchase during the Civil War. There were, however, gaping holes in the narrative that lacked any evidence or creditability.

Over a decade passed before I returned to Paine's brief stay in the Purchase. By this time, I was working at Murray State University as the director of special collections and archives. One of my primary responsibilities was to catalog and document the many manuscript collections housed in the library's repository. My desire to know more about Paine's story was reignited when I came across letters and documents that related to the banishment of citizens from Paducah and Columbus to Canada. From that point on, I sought to acquire what I could on his command in Western Kentucky. What began as a trickle soon turned into a river.

I started with the commonly cited sources from the Civil War era, such as the *Official Records of the War of the Rebellion*, regimental histories, and the published diaries, journals and memoirs of participants. I next scoured the many newspapers associated with the events during Paine's command. Newspapers from Louisville, Lexington, Frankfort, Evansville, Cairo, Chicago, St. Louis and other major cites offered numerous articles on the Jackson Purchase during the war. The *Kentucky Digital Library* and the Library of Congress' *Chronicling America: Historic American Newspapers* were of great assistance in filling in holes left by earlier histories. Published records from the Commonwealth of Kentucky and the federal government yielded documentation on Paine from the state legislature and United States Congress. The National Archives had official correspondence and orders sent and received by Paine, along with the testimonies and affidavits of Purchase citizens seeking restitution from the federal government on reels of microfilm. They also had over several hundred pages of transcripts from General Paine's court-martial, which contained a wealth of information related to his decisions as district commander. The internet opened many other avenues to unpublished materials, which added a new perspective to the story. Sadly, the personal papers of E.A. Paine have yet to be located. Members of the Paine family were contacted, but the response was always that they did not exist.

What I found most intriguing while conducting the research was that the folklore was far less fascinating than the factual story. The pieces of this intricate puzzle took years to put together, and what had previously been considered gospel evolved into something completely different. Folklore and myth had been supplanted by fact and truth.

—Dieter C. Ullrich

I was eleven years old when I met Brigadier General Eleazer Arthur Paine in the pages of *Center of Conflict: A Factual Story of the War Between the States in Western Kentucky and Tennessee*. The little paperback was the first Civil War book I ever read. Its author was Hall Allen of the *Paducah-Sun Democrat*, which published the book in 1961—fifteen years before I hired in as a reporter at the paper and stayed on the staff for almost thirteen years.

Allen titled his main chapter on Paine "Fifty-One Days of Violence." He based it on Lewis and Richard Collins' well-known *History of Kentucky*, which described the general's tenure as "a fifty-one days' reign of violence, terror, rapine, extortion, and military murder."

That was pretty lurid stuff for a sixth grader. Allen, who barely disguised his Confederate sympathies, added his own indictment: "During his brief reign, Paine seems to have tried to wreak vengeance for all the blasted hopes of the Federals since the outbreak of the war. But it was not only the Rebels who felt his ire. He assumed a violent and abusive attitude toward loyal and disloyal alike. He had no time to investigate the political beliefs of any man or woman."

The author reloaded and fired again: "All were suspects in the eyes of General Paine. In some respects his rule of Western Kentucky was more corrupt, more stringent and generally more objectionable than the reign of General Ben (Beast) Butler in New Orleans."

As I grew older, my interest in the Civil War, especially in my native Kentucky, increased exponentially. When I attended W.J. Webb Junior High, I learned that Paine had a plank and earthen fort and a dry moat built around the court square in Mayfield, where I was born, reared and still live. In high school, I discovered that another Yankee brigadier, Solomon Meredith, ordered the fort flattened and had a smaller earthen work, called a redoubt, erected at what was then the southwestern edge of Mayfield. My mother was born in 1921 in a small house on Walnut Street, a few feet from the fort site. When I was at Mayfield High School, I came across a faded copy of a drawing of Paine's fort, not a trace of which survives. The steep-sided base of the redoubt remains where Tenth Street "T's" into Walnut.

I guess it was natural that I wrote my history master's thesis at Murray State University on the Civil War in my native Jackson Purchase, that section of the Bluegrass State west of the Tennessee River. In 2012, almost forty years later, I decided to expand my thesis into a book. I headed back to the Forrest C. Pogue Special Collections Library, my old grad school haunt. There, I met Dieter C. Ullrich, the principal author of this the first Paine book.

His research assistance was invaluable for *Kentucky Confederates: Civil War, Secession, and the Jackson Purchase*, which the University Press of Kentucky published in 2014. Dieter went well above the call of his duties in helping me. He has since migrated east to Morehead State University, where he is chief of special collections at the Camden Carroll Library.

My book mostly focused on the Purchase during the secession crisis of 1860–1861 and on the Confederate occupation of the region, which lasted from September 1861, to the end of February 1862. But Paine is in the book, as is Congressman Lucian Anderson. An Unconditional Unionist from my hometown, he was one of a quartet of Kentucky House members who voted for the Thirteenth Amendment, which ended slavery.

Dieter and I collaborated on *Unconditional Unionist: The Hazardous Life of Lucian Anderson, Kentucky Congressman,* the first book written about Anderson, which McFarland published in 2016. Paine, Anderson's close friend and ally, got more ink in *Unconditional Unionist* than he got in my *Kentucky Confederates*.

Dieter had been researching Paine for years. He generously shared his research with me for *Kentucky Confederates*. But after *Unconditional Unionist*, we agreed that Paine merited his own biography. We decided it was time to set the record straight about this much-maligned Yankee brigadier.

Beginning with Collins, almost all historians vilified Paine. Patricia Ann Hoskins was the exception. She gave Paine a fair shake in "'The Old First Is with the South': The Civil War, Reconstruction, and Memory in the Jackson Purchase Region of Kentucky," her outstanding 2008 doctoral dissertation at Auburn University. She, like Dieter and I, turned up no evidence that proved the general was the monster his detractors made him out to be. He was not a mass murderer; he executed a handful of guerrillas, some of whom confessed to murder. His policies, while strict, were within the accepted rules of war outlined in Lieber's Code. Too, they were similar to policies carried out by generals Ulysses S. Grant, William T. Sherman and Philip Sheridan.

It became obvious to us that Paine's "crimes" were mostly rooted in his politics. The Purchase, dubbed "the South Carolina of Kentucky," was Kentucky's only Confederate-majority region. To local "secesh," Paine was the worst kind of Yankee: He was a Republican, a friend of President Abraham Lincoln, an abolitionist and a supporter of making soldiers of slaves. On a personal level, he treated African Americans as equals, a practice galling and incomprehensible to virtually every white person in Kentucky, even ardent unionists.

Politics can indeed make strange bedfellows. Not only did secessionists hate Paine; conservative Union Democrats, who dominated state politics, turned against him. Union Democrats saw the Civil War as a conflict to preserve the Union, not to end slavery. Governor Thomas E. Bramlette, a Union Democrat, pressured Lincoln into firing Paine and ordering his court-martial. Bramlette sent commissioners to Paducah to trump up charges of corruption and abuse of power against the general. Nonetheless, a court-martial exonerated him on all but a minor charge: publicly cursing Henry W. Halleck, the army's general-in-chief. The sentence was remanded. (Bramlette's commissioners charged Anderson, an Unconditional Unionist, with being in cahoots with Paine. Congress completely cleared Anderson, who was almost as unpopular in the Purchase as Paine was. Seemingly, his "crimes" were his politics.)

"Paine certainly was no saint, but he was far from the devil," I quoted Dieter as saying in my book. Dieter pointed out that the general cut Rebels no slack and equated all but unconditional unionism with treason. He said Paine seemed to relish "the headlines he received in the North as being feared and despised by Rebels and Southern sympathizers."

Dieter said Bramlette and George D. Prentice, editor of the conservative and unionist *Louisville Journal*, the state's most important Civil War paper, set the table for Paine's condemnation by Collins and later historians. "This image was magnified after the war and became embedded in local culture and in history books," he explained. "However, the facts have been greatly distorted and the man's name severely and unfairly tarnished. Proof can be seen in his court-martial records and in the diaries and letters from Union soldiers. Many of these documents have only recently come to light, and more will follow as technology opens new avenues to researchers. Like I've told my friends in the Sons of Confederate Veterans—keep an open mind, and search for the truth," Dieter said. Doing his best to find the truth was Dieter's goal in his research and writing about Paine. I was happy to help with editing and encouragement for which he graciously agreed to put my name on this book. But without Dieter Ullrich, the truth about Eleazer Arthur Paine would remain absent from history. I am grateful in assisting my friend in righting this historical wrong.

—Berry Craig

Introduction

Brigadier General E.A. Paine arrived at Paducah, Kentucky, to take command of the newly formed military District of Western Kentucky on July 19, 1864. What followed has become a matter of both contention and debate in recent years. Within the past few decades, diaries, correspondence and government documents have surfaced that shed a new light on the events that became known as Paine's "reign of terror." Implanted within these uncovered documents are accounts of an officer greatly admired and respected by his men and the loyal citizens he was assigned to protect. Current research has proven Paine may have been ahead of his time on civil rights issues and counter-terrorist tactics. On the issue of emancipation and equal rights for African Americans, Paine was at the forefront of the abolitionist movement. As a military strategist, he was innovator in both economic and psychological warfare. For over a century and a half, Paine has been misrepresented by historians, demonized by folklorists and reviled by generations of west Kentuckians. His legacy was unjustifiably tarnished by contemporary political antagonists and propagated by proponents of the "Lost Cause."

What has often been overlooked by many historians was Paine's notable and distinguished career prior to the Civil War. He was a decorated militia officer in the state of Ohio and a successful businessman, farmer and attorney in Monmouth, Illinois. He was a graduate of the United States Military Academy at West Point and achieved the rank of brigadier general in the Ohio State Militia before the age of thirty. He was an upstanding member of the Monmouth's Presbyterian Church, a prominent leader in the Illinois temperance movement, served in the state legislature and was a political ally of Abraham Lincoln. Paine was a confident, passionate and outspoken man with seemingly limitless energy and zeal. While these personal qualities attracted many business partners and clients to his law office, they annoyed and distanced others. His early critics claimed he was self-righteous and arrogant but found him to be an honest and fair man. Once the war commenced, Paine was appointed military advisor to the governor of Illinois. Wishing not to serve behind a desk, he resigned after a few weeks and enlisted in the Army. He was soon elected colonel of an Illinois infantry regiment and six months later promoted to brigadier general by President Abraham Lincoln. Notification of his promotion came the evening before his first assignment to western Kentucky.

The Jackson Purchase, Kentucky's westernmost region, embraced secession in early 1861. Paine first arrived in Paducah with Brigadier General Ulysses S. Grant's troops on the morning of September 6, 1861. Unlike other regions in the commonwealth, the majority of people residing in the Jackson Purchase supported their Southern neighbors and favored the Confederacy. This became quite evident to Paine soon after he disembarked with Grant's troops at Paducah. The inhabitants considered Grant's actions to be an invasion followed by an occupation rather than a security force to protect the region from an encroaching enemy. Paine recognized immediately that winning the hearts and minds of those in the Purchase was going to take more than longwinded political speeches, futile concessions and imbalanced compromises. Paine had a more direct approach of converting adamant minds, but his initial plans for the Jackson Purchase would have to wait.

Paine was transferred from Paducah in December of 1861 after a month-long dispute with Brigadier General Charles F. Smith, Grant's handpicked choice for post commander. In March of 1862, he was given a field command under Major General John F. Pope. It was during the Island No. 10 campaign that Paine fully displayed his ability to lead men and manage a battlefield. At the Battle of Tiptonville, Tennessee, Paine's division outflanked a Confederate force and captured over 4,400 men. At the Siege of Corinth, Mississippi, his men held off a Rebel force twice their number, and he personally led a counter attack. His days as a field commander ended soon afterwards as he was exposed to a life-threatening virus that left him debilitated for several months. Paine returned to the army but was physically unable to stand the rigors of a military campaign. He was relegated to commanding an outpost north of Nashville, Tennessee, that guarded the Union supply line into Tennessee's capital. It was here that Paine witnessed the brutality of guerrilla warfare and the prejudice faced by emancipated slaves. He attacked both with his usual vigor and persistent determination. His policies were praised by Radical Republicans but denounced by Democrats and conservative Republicans. Though his efforts were frequently obstructed by politicians and higher-ranking officers, Paine continued his uncompromising tactics against partisans and further pressed for African American equality.

Paine returned to Paducah after influential Unionists from the Jackson Purchase requested that President Lincoln appoint him post commander. The region had suffered through Confederate invasions, numerous guerrilla skirmishes and several command changes since Paine's departure. Most of his predecessors had been removed from command under allegations of misconduct and corruption. Three months earlier, General Nathan Bedford Forrest invaded the Jackson Purchase and drove the Union defenders into earthwork fortifications at Columbus and Paducah. The property of Unionists was either confiscated or destroyed during the attacks or by frequent guerrilla raids that followed. The black market at Paducah boomed, and the trade in contraband was widespread. The majority of the region's populace was defiantly secessionist. Southern sympathizers openly criticized the national government, the Lincoln administration and the United States military. The troops stationed at Paducah lacked discipline, and low morale prevailed throughout the ranks. Paine was given the monumental task of restoring morale, stopping illegal trading with the enemy, pacifying the population and defending an area of more than 2,300 square miles. For fifty-one days, Paine labored endlessly and made enormous strides to fulfill this mission before being unceremoniously relieved of command.

Five months after his removal from command, he was tried before a court-martial. Numerous specifications were attached to the charges, which stemmed from testimonies acquired during an investigation without Paine's knowledge. The trial lasted four weeks; the court entertained over 200 affidavits, reviewed scores of military and financial records and heard the testimony of seventy-seven witnesses. Paine would be found innocent of all charges but one, that of denouncing a superior officer, which the court later recommended be remitted. The verdict was condemned by Paine's political enemies and ridiculed in the conservative Republican and Democratic Party presses. He hoped the verdict would end the mendacities and persecution, but it was only the beginning of a lifelong defense of his military record and integrity.

After the war's conclusion, Paine's "reign of terror" resurfaced as an example of Northern atrocities committed during the Union occupation. In the decades that followed, the myth evolved and became deeply engrained in the history of the region. What the research will prove is that the facts were intentionally distorted to fit a narrative of Northern oppression and Southern justification. Paine was no saint, but he was far from the fiend he was portrayed to be by generations of historians.

ONE

"I am compelled to be severe"

The wharf at Cairo, Illinois, was bustling with activity during the late evening hours of September 5, 1861. Dozens of longshoremen and dockworkers hurried across gangplanks hauling crates, loading artillery pieces and leading horses onto three large steamboats hastily converted to troop transports. Along the shoreline, the glow of hundreds of oil lamps, candles and torches illuminated the faces of of onlookers gathered to witness the uniformed men preparing to depart. In the middle of this momentous scene was Colonel Eleazer A. Paine, regimental commander of the Ninth Illinois Volunteer Infantry. He was a stern-looking man of average height, slim with white hair and dark beard. Hours earlier, he had received a telegram from President Abraham Lincoln informing him of his appointment as brigadier general. Paine's regiment, along with the Twelfth Illinois Volunteer Infantry Regiment and a section of Smith's Chicago Artillery, were given the privileged assignment to lead Brigadier General Ulysses S. Grant's invasion force to Paducah, Kentucky, the next morning. The small armada of two gunboats and three troop transports departed at 10:30 p.m. to the cheers and waves of well-wishers. This would be Paine's first voyage to Paducah but not his last.[1]

Eleazer Arthur Paine was born at Parkman, Geauga County, Ohio, on September 10, 1815, to Hendrick Ellsworth and Harriet Phelps Paine. His father was a farmer and businessman. His grandfather, on his father's side, served as a drummer boy during the Revolutionary War. His family relocated to Painesville in 1816, where his father built a successful forge and furnace in 1827. Not much is documented on his childhood or early adulthood except that he was educated at home and worked on the family farm. Paine was accepted into the United States Military Academy in 1835 and arrived at West Point in June of that year. His classmates included future Union Generals Henry Halleck, Edward Ord, Edward Canby and future Confederate general Alexander Lawton. His instructor of infantry tactics was Charles F. Smith, whom Paine later served under at Paducah. He was not a stellar student, graduating twenty-fourth out of a class of thirty-two. During his four years at West Point, he accumulated 187 demerits. In comparison, Halleck received only one. His experience at the academy was not an enjoyable one; he later remarked that the "institution is a hotbed of aristocracy and is a curse to the nation." Paine graduated on July 1, 1839, was commissioned a second lieutenant in the First Regiment of Infantry and stationed at Fort Pleasant in Florida. Though the Second Seminole War was in progress, Paine saw only post duty, serving on the staff of General Zachary Taylor. On August 24, 1840, he submitted his resignation, stating his father's health was in decline and that he must return to Ohio to assist with the family businesses. Paine left Florida and the army on October 11, 1840.[2]

United State Military Academy at West Point, 1828 (engraving from a painting by George Catlin).

On his return to Painesville, he studied law and passed the state bar in 1843. On May 23, 1843, he married Charlotte Phelps, a widow with a child, at Perry, Ohio. She was the daughter of Samuel W. Phelps, an attorney, probate judge and two-term legislator from Painesville. She was the granddaughter of General Edward Paine, Painesville's namesake and uncle of Eleazer's father. The union would produce four more children. Paine served as deputy United States marshal for Ohio from 1842 to 1845 and was an officer in the Ohio State Militia. He wrote the drill manual for militia and was promoted to brigadier general before his resignation in 1848. At the outbreak of the war with Mexico, he was in command of a brigade of volunteers whose service he tendered to the army. The army declined, explaining that accepting a militia brigade would be "inconsistent with the plan for accepting volunteers." Paine moved his family and law practice to Monmouth, Illinois, in late 1848. A Whig, he served in the Illinois state legislature from 1852 to 1853 and was one of the founders of the Monmouth Republican Party in 1856. Paine was active in the temperance movement, having led a crusade against the sale of liquor in Monmouth in 1853 and serving as the first president of the Monmouth Temperance League in 1858. He was Monmouth's justice of the peace from 1853 to 1857 and performed dozens of marriages in the community. He was also a business leader, having established the first insurance company in the city and backing the construction of the railroad.[3]

Paine and Lincoln crossed paths. They met in 1854, when Lincoln campaigned as the Whig candidate for the United States Senate. Lincoln's opposition to slavery and its spread into the western territories aligned very closely to Paine's political ideology. Four years later, Lincoln ran again for Senate, this time as a Republican. Paine renewed his support by canvassing the state to drum up votes for Lincoln. Lincoln lost, but Paine's devotion was rewarded when Lincoln visited Monmouth during the campaign. In 1860, Paine once more stood by Lincoln as he ran for the presidency.[4]

Paine was at Monmouth when news arrived that the Civil War had begun with the

Monmouth, Illinois (Monmouth College Archives).

Confederate bombardment of Fort Sumter in Charleston, South Carolina. The next day, April 13, he volunteered as a private in Company F of the Seventeenth Illinois Volunteer Infantry. On April 15, he wrote a friend in Springfield to inform Governor Richard Yates that he wished to raise a regiment. A few days later, he was appointed to the governor's military staff to organize volunteers converging on Springfield, the state capital. Seeking a field command, Paine resigned after a week. On April 23, he was elected colonel of the Ninth Illinois Infantry Regiment at Springfield. One week later, Paine and the Ninth Illinois were ordered to Cairo. There, along with other Illinois regiments, they set up camp and trained. On May 24, Paine and several officers at Cairo wrote President Lincoln that strategic Columbus, Kentucky, could be occupied in three days with six infantry regiments. Lincoln did not reply.[5]

When Major General George B. McClellan arrived to inspect the troops on June 13, Paine made such an impression that "ladies on the ground declared that their [9th Illinois'] gallant commander was the model of the officer and soldier." A correspondence from the *Daily Illinois State Journal* of Springfield wrote of Paine:

> In regard to this distinguished gentleman [Paine] I wish to make a prediction, and that is this: If he should happen to get into a fight (and he is praying for one night and morning) he will satisfy to the full, the high expectations which the people of Illinois have formed in regard to him and his regiment.

Another correspondent wrote that Paine appeared "calculating and ever ready" to serve his state and country. The Ninth Illinois' three-month term of service ended on July 25, but most of the troops reenlisted and mustered in for the second time on the twenty-sixth. Although he was a strict disciplinarian, Paine's men had confidence in his decision making skills and leadership.[6]

Governor Richard Yates, Library of Congress).

The majority of Paducah's residents supported the Confederacy, yet there was a vocal pro–Union minority. The majority, however, oppressed the minority. The Union candidate in a June 20 special congressional election, Lawrence S. Trimble, fled the city. Trimble lost to the incumbent Henry C. Burnett, a Democrat-turned-secessionist. After news of the Confederate victory at the Battle of Bull Run, or Manassas, Virginia, reached the city in late July, celebrations broke out. A group of citizens tried to raise the Confederate flag over the United States Marine Hospital but were thwarted by hospital administrators loyal to the Union. One person recalled that a "flood of secession fanaticism" overtook the entire region. This fervor was at its peak when Grant's troops landed at Paducah on September 6.[7]

Shortly after dawn, the gunboats followed by the transports broke through the morning mist below Paducah. The pulsating sounds of the steam engines and the echo of paddlewheels striking the river were heard in town. Citizens ran to the shore and gazed downriver, spotting the boats. Those with spyglasses observed the flag of the United States fluttering atop the vessels. Some citizens scurried through town shouting warnings. A company of Confederate soldiers and a few officers recruiting in the city quickly boarded a southbound train taking whatever supplies they could rapidly load on cars. Carriages and wagons loaded with personal belongings soon began to clog the avenues as people fled their homes, fearing the gunboats. On September 3 and 4, Confederate troops seized Hickman and Columbus; Kentucky's neutrality, proclaimed in May, was over.[8]

Grant arrived at 8:30. Confederate flags fluttered over the city at the confluence of the Ohio and Tennessee rivers. Grant expected, and most locals hoped, the Confederates were Paducah bound. Grant ordered Paine's regiment to the railroad depot to seize any

Puducah, Kentucky, from the Ohio River (*Frank Leslie's Illustrated Newspaper*).

supplies left by the Confederates. As his men marched up Broadway, women cheered for Confederate President Jefferson Davis. When he reached the depot, Paine found flour, coffee and lard, goods and rations ready to be moved south. Paine noticed a large Confederate flag atop the St. Francis Hotel. Taking several officers with him, Paine went to the hotel and told the proprietor, John Shields, to remove the Rebel flag and raise the national flag. Shields agreed to remove the Confederate flag but defiantly refused to have the stars and stripes flown over his establishment. Paine responded that he was not sent to negotiate terms and that the flag would be displayed with or without his consent. Once the stars and stripes flew atop the hotel, he told Shields and a crowd that gathered that if "he or any other Rebels interfered with that flag of pulled it down, they would be led out and shot down." This act of resistance and Paine's determined response would be replayed throughout the war.[9]

As Paine's troops carried away the Confederate flag, Grant read an occupation proclamation in which he promised the locals: "I have come among you not as an enemy, but as your fellow citizen; not to maltreat or annoy you, but to respect and enforce the rights of all citizens." Apparently, Grant's pledge of protection was less than convincing. "The citizens did not appear to appreciate the favor," mused the *Cincinnati Enquirer's* Cairo correspondent. In any event, Grant also dispatched part of his force upriver to capture Smithland, at the mouth of the Cumberland River. While the Civil War was America's bloodiest war, the occupation of Hickman, Columbus, Paducah and Smithland was accomplished without bloodshed.[10]

Just before noon, Grant's aide-de-camp, Captain William S. Hillyer, handed Paine instructions from the general to assume command of the troops and "retain possession and control of the city." It also stated that Paine was to "take care and precaution that no harm is done to inoffensive citizens" and "exercise the strictest discipline against any soldier who shall insult citizens or engage in plundering private property." Grant also ordered Paine to construct a "substantial field work or fort" without delay. Before Grant returned to Cairo, he gave Paine further instructions to "seize all the money in the banks" if an enemy attack upon the city was imminent.[11]

Grant departed Paducah, the seat of McCracken County, early on the afternoon of September 6. To reiterate Grant's instructions, Paine issued the following order to his officers later that day.

General Ulysses S. Grant (Library of Congress).

Captains of companies will keep their men together, and under no pretense permit them to straggle from their commands.

They will not permit any soldier to enter any private dwelling, or take and, destroy any property unless by command of an officer. Company officers will be considered guilty of disobedience of orders if this order is not strictly complied with.

No officer of soldier will be permitted to hold conversation with any slave or colored people of this town, nor insult of abuse any person.[12]

The next morning, Paine received reports of 2,000 Confederate troops within twenty-four miles of the city and that an additional 4,000 men were marching in support. Paine wrote Grant to send at least five infantry regiments and all the artillery and cavalry that could be spared. He claimed that if "armed with a sufficient force [he] would hold three or four counties south and west by moving forward twenty miles." He also expressed to Grant his growing frustrations with the uncooperative populous. Paine noted in the same correspondence that a local blacksmith refused to shoe his horse. He placed the blacksmith under arrest and threatened the man that if he did not shoe the horse in five minutes, he would be shot. Paine concluded, "I am compelled to be severe for nearly every man here is a rank secessionist." Fearing the telegraph lines would be severed by local Confederate sympathizers he issued an order "charging the citizens with the protection of the telegraph" and threatened "their freedom and their homes if the lines or operators were molested." That evening, Paine received news that Brigadier General Charles F. Smith would take over command the next day.[13]

Smith relieved Paine on the afternoon of September 8 and placed him in charge of Paducah's police force and maintaining discipline in the camps. Paine had known Smith from his days at West Point, when he was a cadet and Smith an instructor of infantry tactics. Their relationship was strained and steadily deteriorated as each day passed. A day after his arrival, Smith, Colonel Joseph D. Webster, an engineer with the First Illinois Light Artillery, and Paine toured the outskirts of the city to select sites for earthworks. Paine had begun construction of Fort Anderson, named for the Union commander at Fort Sumter, around the Marine Hospital on the Ohio River. Paine's plans included removing several buildings within two hundred yards of the fort. Smith, however, decided that a "board of survey" composed of officers would be assigned the task of selecting structures, including houses, to be torn down. The board's work was never completed. Those houses and other buildings were used by sharpshooters to fire on the fort during General Nathan B. Forrest's attack on March 25, 1864.[14]

On September 27, Paine was given command of the First Brigade of the District of Cairo, which included the Ninth Illinois and three other infantry regiments, a battery of artillery and a cavalry battalion. During the next several weeks, Paine sent detachments of his brigade on expeditions to surrounding communities. On November 6, Smith ordered Paine to march the First Brigade toward Milburn, near Columbus. Grant needed a diversion for his November 7 demonstration against the rebel outpost at Belmont, Missouri, opposite Columbus. Paine's troops marched from Paducah late that afternoon. The brigade camped for the night on Mayfield Creek about twelve miles from Paducah. The next morning, the lead regiments were within a few miles of Milburn when they heard the pounding of heavy artillery in the direction of Columbus. Paine pressed on to Milburn, before the booming faded and ceased. That evening he sent messengers to the Mississippi River seeking information on the battle and whether he should move on to Columbus. His messengers returned early the next morning with news that all the gunboats had gone back to Cairo with Grant's troops who were nearly trapped. By daylight of September 8, Paine's command was on the march back to Paducah. The footsore troops reached Paducah on the afternoon of November 9. Paine declared the expedition to be a success. Smith, however, thought differently.[15]

Two days after the brigade's return, Smith opened a court of inquiry, claiming Paine disobeyed orders and that his men destroyed property, robbed citizens and displayed a "most disgraceful character" as soldiers. Smith later praised the First Brigade for its orderly conduct and on November 16 sent Paine on another expedition to destroy a grist mill at Lovelaceville. Word of their ongoing dispute found its way up the chain of command as Grant, Adjutant General Lorenzo Thomas and Major General Henry Halleck, the newly appointed commander of the Department of Missouri, received a steady stream of reports from Smith and his staff officers.

General Charles F. Smith (National Archives).

Politicians from Paine's home state of Illinois and the northern press sided with Paine, which only widened the gulf between the two officers. Before the year concluded, Smith accused Paine of conspiring against him and scheming to oust him from command. On December 20, Smith issued Special Order No. 78, which relieved Paine of command and sent him to Cairo to await further orders. Grant favored Smith's decision and three days later assigned Paine a command at Bird's Point, Missouri. "There never was a more crestfallen man in the world than when [Paine] received the order to leave here and go to the Bird's Point," Smith wrote his wife on December 30. Paine boarded a steamer on Christmas Day for Cairo. Two weeks later, Lucian Anderson, a potential candidate for Congress to replace the expelled Burnette, assembled a group of Paducah citizens to have Smith replaced with Paine. The editor of the *Louisville Democrat* reported on January 8 that "no sooner was Paine superseded by another officer, than treason and traitors began to raise their heads and get bolder and bolder, until today secesh in Paducah is as proud and defiant in its tones as it is at Columbus."[16]

Paine assumed command at Bird's Point on New Year's Day of 1862. His orders specified that he form a brigade of all the military units stationed in southeast Missouri to protect the post and nearby rail line. One week after he took command, a Union cavalry battalion was ambushed by a band of guerrillas near Charleston, Missouri. On January 11, four soldiers were shot and killed while on picket duty at Bird's Point. After Grant was informed of the shootings, he ordered Paine to remove all citizens within six miles of the post and directed that "all citizens making their appearance within those limits are liable to be shot." He also ordered the detention of those found within the radius and "require[d] them to remain under pain of death and destruction of their property." Paine wrote Grant the next day that the number of those arrested might exceed one hundred and he questioned Grant on where to house them. "I shall find out who shot the pickets and when I do I shall shoot the guilty parties on very short notice," Paine vowed. Grant replied that if the guilty parties were captured that he would "order a court of commission" to investigate the shootings.[17]

By the third week of January, Paine had rounded up and imprisoned many Missourians he considered a threat to his post. He also received prisoners sent by Grant from Kentucky. Another problem for Paine was the number of slaves who sought refuge at Bird's Point, which overcrowded the camp and angered slave owners. When Grant was made aware of the situation, he ordered Paine to release the prisoners held without charges and return all slaves to their masters. Paine had reservations about delivering escaped slaves to their masters, but he complied with Grant's orders.[18]

As Grant prepared for his campaign up the Tennessee River, to capture Fort Henry; he reassigned Paine to command the Third Brigade of the Department of Missouri and stationed him at Cairo on February 1. His primary duties were to hold mutinous Union soldiers for trial and manage 12,400 Confederate prisoners forwarded from Fort Henry and Fort Donelson on the Cumberland River near Dover, Tennessee. Grant captured the two strong points between February 6 and 16. He was also charged with protecting the storehouses at Paducah and commanding the units in southeast Missouri. Completely overwhelmed, Paine wrote Halleck for help. He also contacted the governors of Illinois and Indiana to help relocate prisoners elsewhere. Halleck was not pleased with Paine seeking outside assistance without his consent, which reinforced his notion that Paine was more of a politician seeking aggrandizement than a military officer.[19]

On February 8, Paine received a report that five Union civilians had been murdered

Bird's Point, Missouri (*Frank Leslie's Famous Leaders and Battle Scenes of the Civil War*).

near Bloomfield, Missouri, by Rebel cavalry. Paine ordered the battalion commander who sent the report to "hang one of the Rebel cavalry for each Union man murdered and after this two for each." He concluded his correspondence by ordering his men to "continue to scout, capture and kill." A St. Louis newspaper printed Paine's decree. Halleck launched investigation and interviewed Paine, who claimed that he thought the Rebel troops were caught in the act. He said once he was made aware of the error, he immediately rescinded the order. Halleck published his disapproval of the order and reprimanded Paine. Halleck later issued General Order No. 48, which said officers leaking information to the press would be arrested and tried by a court-martial. The Republican press supported Paine. A correspondent from the *Cleveland Plain Dealer* wrote that "had this policy been pursued from the start Rebels would have been scarce in Missouri." Growing weary of Paine, Halleck sought to have him reassigned to another command.[20]

A member of Halleck's staff, Colonel George W. Cullum, disagreed and recommended that it would not be wise to "supersede Paine in command." Though he was a "politician and not always discreet," he was "energetic, full of zeal, has pluck and knows localities." Cullum suggested that Paine be assigned a "brigade in the field." Halleck did not agree and remarked that "Paine will not be permitted to command any depot" because of his continued violation of orders and his "throwing everything into confusion." Halleck, however, gave in to Cullum and transferred Paine to a field command under General John F. Pope.[21]

Paine reported to Pope outside Confederate-held New Madrid, Missouri, on March 4 and took command of the Fourth Division of the Army of the Mississippi. New Madrid had been under siege only a day prior to his arrival, but Pope was determined to occupy the fortified city. His first assignment was to repair the railroad and telegraph lines from Bird's Point to Sikeston, which he completed in less than a week. On March 10, a day before regular train service was restored, he was slightly wounded during a skirmish near Sikeston. Three days later, Paine led the Union left flank during the assault on Fort Bankhead at New Madrid but fell back under heavy fire. That night, the Confederates evacuated at New Madrid and crossed the Mississippi to Tennessee. On the morning of March 14, Paine and his men marched into the city. Pope's next target was nearby Island No. 10 in the Mississippi River.[22]

The high-water mark of Paine's military career came during the closing days of the Island No. 10 campaign. At daybreak on April 7, Paine's division embarked on four transports and rapidly traversed the Mississippi below New Madrid. Later that morning, his entire force made it across the swift and swollen river to Watson's Landing in Kentucky. Before him was the Rebel army in retreat, having evacuated Island No. 10 and its shore batteries hours earlier. Paine rapidly marched in pursuit south along a muddy wagon road toward Tiptonville, Tennessee, to cut off their escape. The men slogged through "marshes and quagmires" late into the night, capturing Rebel stragglers along the way. After midnight, Paine reached the rear guard of the Confederate army a few miles north of Tiptonville and attacked. The Rebels initially fled but formed a line further down the road. Paine organized his men into columns and pressed forward. The Confederate line broke and reformed once more. At 2:00 a.m., the enemy raised a flag of truce, and within a few hours the Rebel force surrendered unconditionally.[23]

Before dawn on April 8, Paine received a report that a ferry was transporting retreating soldiers across Reelfoot Lake. With his staff, eight soldiers and two cannons, Paine galloped off on the muddy road to the crossing; a regiment of infantry followed.

Before they reached the lake, two Rebel companies gave up without firing a shot. A single mounted soldier was left behind to guard them as Paine pressed on. When they reached the lake, he placed the guns overlooking the lake and awaited the infantry to secure the ferry landing. "We found two new six pounders, and loads of clothing, commissary stores and ammunition strewed all round and along the roads," wrote one of Paine's men. He continued, "Arms of all kinds were found under logs, behind fences and in every place to get them out of sight." Some of the men remarked that the "large mosquitos" were the worst enemies. The victory at Tiptonville was complete.[24]

At 8:00 a.m. on April 8, Paine arranged a formal surrender at Tiptonville. Roughly 2,500 men, led by Brigadier General William W. Mackall, were marched to an open field surrounded on three sides by soldiers of Paine's division. An order was barked to stack arms and Mackall, along with his staff and two other captured Confederate generals, walked in line to Paine; Mackall presented his sword in defeat. During the next few days, Paine's men scoured the nearby forests and farms to collect stragglers and military supplies left in haste. Overall, 4,400 Confederate soldiers were taken prisoner along with a large number of small arms and heavy and light artillery pieces. Paine's men presented him with the flag of the First Alabama Infantry Regiment. Pope acknowledged Paine's tenacity the next day in a letter to Halleck. He praised Paine for hounding the enemy so vigorously that they were "forced to surrender" without much of a fight. In his report submitted a month later, Pope stated that Paine "exhibited conspicuous gallantry and vigor" during the campaign. The *Chicago Tribune* declared "To God and Gen. Paine be the Glory!"[25]

General John F. Pope (National Archives).

Paine distinguished himself further during the siege of Corinth, Mississippi, where the Confederates fell back after Grant defeated them at the Battle of Shiloh, Tennessee, on April 6 and 7. From May 3 to May 22, Paine again commanded Pope's left wing. On the first day of the siege, Paine headed a reconnaissance toward Farmington, Mississippi, which brought on a sharp skirmish and a Confederate retreat. A witness noted that Paine's division "drove them in handsome style" and that his men "behaved splendidly." On May 9, his division was attacked by a much larger Rebel force. Outnumbered two to one, Paine held his ground for five hours before Pope ordered his withdrawal. At one point during the battle, he ordered a counterattack that drove the enemy back, but Confederate reinforcements arrived on the field and erased their gains. That evening, Pope reported to Halleck that the conduct

Surrender at Tiptonville, Tennessee (*Frank Leslie's Illustrated Newspaper*).

of Paine's troops was excellent and their "withdrawal was made by them very reluctantly."²⁶

Following the battle, as he had often done often during the war, Paine visited the wounded and sick men of his unit. During one of his visits he contracted typhoid fever, which left him near death. He was granted sick leave on May 23 and returned to Monmouth to recuperate. While at Monmouth he proudly displayed the captured flag of the First Alabama on a staff in front of the family home. On July 8, a surgeon at Monmouth examined Paine and found him "suffering from general debility and irritation of the bowels consequent upon an attack of bilious remittent fever of typhoid characteristics and that in consequence therefore ... unfit for duty." The high fevers caused a disorder in his large intestines that would plague him for the rest of his life. The illness is commonly known today as irritable bowel syndrome and is characterized by cramping, abdominal pain, bloating, constipation and diarrhea. The disorder can cause a great deal of discomfort and distress and at its worst can be disabling for extended periods of time. Other symptoms associated with the disease include bouts of depression and anxiety, which can heighten the physical characteristics of the ailment.²⁷

Paine reported to Major General William S. Rosecrans, Pope's replacement, at Tuscumbia, Alabama, on August 15, 1862. His health restricted his ability to participate in any extended military campaign. As a result, Paine's division was assigned to another general. His health worsened in September, and he returned to Monmouth. On October 6, he wrote Governor Yates requesting that he be ordered to Springfield to organize the militia if his health improved, but Yates politely declined the offer. By the middle of the month, Paine's strength improved enough for him to report for duty at Tuscumbia. He remained at Tuscumbia until November 24, when Rosecrans assigned him post duty at Gallatin, Tennessee. His primary responsibility was to guard the railroad line between Mitchellville and Nashville, the state capital. Prior to his departure from Tuscumbia, he made a speech that reflected his belief in total war. On September 27, he declared before his troops:

> Soldiers! This country is yours; these people have unwittingly planted everything we need in this beautiful valley, and it shall be dealt out to you with a lavish hand, and not stingily. If you want corn, these waving fields will supply your wants; take it. If you want fruit, vegetables, chickens, or potatoes, take them, they are yours. If the cows need milking, milk them yourselves, or make the milkmaids do it for you. Everything here in this rich and beautiful country is yours and are for your use—enjoy it; you deserve it all, for you are in arms, exposing yourself in defense of your country, against Rebels and traitors, who have no rights. They own no property but through the government. They are outlaws.

Several months before Grant chose to live off the land during his campaign to capture Vicksburg, Mississippi, and over a year before General William Tecumseh Sherman's March to the Sea, Paine advocated taking the war directly to the Southern people.[28]

General William S. Rosecrans (National Archives).

Paine stepped off the train at Gallatin on November 26 and entered into his duties as post commander. It was a position he neither wanted nor enthusiastically cared to take. Gallatin was strongly secessionist. A resident of the city proclaimed that its inhabitants were nearly all "strong Southern sympathizers" and that the "fighting men were almost without exception enlisted in the Confederate Army." With 2,000 infantrymen, no cavalry or artillery, Paine was responsible for thirty miles of railroad line, sixty miles of river and all the public roads in five counties. Nonetheless, he got busy developing plans to defend the railroad and telegraph lines in his assigned district. He also focused on improving the military hospitals in town and he established a camp for convalescing soldiers.[29]

Paine had begun to settle in by the New Year, and though guerrillas caused some minor difficulties, he managed to make significant strides in securing his district and

Gallatin, Tennessee (Tennessee State Library and Archives).

protecting local Unionists. A visitor to Gallatin from Ottawa, Illinois, wrote his local newspaper:

> This post is in the command of Gen. Paine, of Illinois, who may be set down, without further remark, as one of God's noblemen. Thoroughly acquainted with his duty, he reigns with mild resolution, which not only commands respect, but insures ready and willing obedience. Everything moves along smoothly and rightly, and we can lay down at night with conscious security, satisfied that no surprise can ever take us while his watchful eye is over us.

Unfortunately, the velvet glove would have to be removed to expose the iron hand as Paine's policies to fight guerrillas and tame rebellious populace proved to be ineffective.[30]

In February of 1863, as roving bands of guerrillas tore up rails and cut telegraph lines. Paine reported to Rosecrans that guerrillas dressed in federal overcoats were observed destroying tracks and burning government cattle pens fourteen miles from Gallatin. More upsetting to him was a report that a number of citizens aided in the destruction. Later that same month, a spy hired by Paine was taken from his home in Wilson County by guerrillas. Paine promptly arrested and imprisoned six physicians in the nearby village of Hartsville. He sent a messenger to the guerrillas warning that the doctors would be held hostage until the spy was returned. A few days later, the agent reappeared at Paine's headquarters at Gallatin.[31]

By early March, with his health not showing any real sign of improvement, Paine sought another assignment closer to home and family. The school commissioner, mayor and deputy revenue collector at Monmouth began a campaign to have Paine named provost marshal for the 4th Congressional District, which included the city. In a letter to Yates, they claimed "he would enforce the law with less opposition that any man that could be named in the district." Paine wrote his supporters on March 10 that he would gladly serve as the district's provost marshal. Unfortunately for Paine, the governor appointed someone else.[32]

As the weather began to warm, partisan activity increased dramatically. After the war, one of Paine's officers remarked that his regiment spent thirty-eight consecutive days "guarding forage trains, hunting bushwhackers, smugglers, etc." He also stated that the guerrillas "did not hesitate to murder if they had any personal grudge, or thought the victim had any money concealed and some of their deeds were barbarous to the extreme." In April, a scouting party reported that group of guerrillas kidnapped a Union man near Richland and murdered him after "literally hewing him to pieces." Another Union man was brutally killed in Wilson County; his body was found with his tongue removed. Outside Gallatin, an eighty-year-old man was dragged out of his home in the middle of the night and shot before his hysterically pleading wife. Continued acts of partisan savagery plagued Paine's command throughout the spring, summer and fall of 1863.[33]

In each instance, Paine responded with harsh resolve. Following the capture of the guerrillas who killed and mutilated the man from Wilson County, he ordered two of the perpetrators hanged and starved another in the town's jail. When the murderers of the octogenarian were identified, he told his troops "I don't want to see those men" and ordered they be hunted down. Days later they found one of the slayers and he "paid the price of his crimes in sight of the spot where the old wife had pleaded in vain for the life of her husband." Paine was particularly avenging toward slayers of Union soldiers. In July of 1863, Paine sent scouts to apprehend and punish a man who killed an officer on June 4. The scouts seized the man, executed him before his family and set his house aflame. In early November, Paine launched a "grand guerrilla hunt" from Gallatin. On the second day of the expedition, four cavalrymen were killed by guerrillas concealed along a roadside. In the pursuit that ensued, two bushwhackers were shot dead. The next day, Paine's men killed another dozen guerrillas and captured twenty more near Lebanon.[34]

Paine cracked down on Southern sympathizers who criticized the federal government, traded with the Confederacy or harbored guerrillas. He arrested business owners known to be shipping supplies south. He levied assessments and fees. He encouraged his troops to confiscate horses, livestock and feed from nearby plantations whose owners were unfriendly to the Union cause. Paine's justification was primarily based on his desire to make his command more self-sufficient and to reduce expenses to the army for supplying his men. He also advanced the idea that supplies not consumed by his men could be forwarded to troops at the front. He used the same tactics when he returned to Paducah in the summer of 1864.[35]

Paine's relationship with the citizens of his district was strained. An officer in his command observed that he "wasted no love on our erring brethren." He was described by a Gallatin man in the following way:

> He was a tall, slender man, of rather good appearance. Excessively vain and remarkably haughty, domineering, suspicious, quick tempered and irritable—a quality not lessened by his being a victim of dyspepsia—he was gracious to his flatterers but overbearing, grossly insulting, and bitterly vindictive toward those who deigned to hold aloof from or defy him. Cold, cruel, and heartless, he was deaf to cries of mercy when emanating from a supposed enemy, and equally callous to the privileges of age, sex, circumstance, or condition.

Paine's flinty reputation showed in a story that appeared in Northern newspapers in September of 1863. An Ohio soldier serving in Gallatin reported to his hometown paper a purported conversation between Paine and an elderly lady from a nearby plantation. The author of the article wrote that a lady of wealth had made an appearance before him seeking restitution for chickens confiscated by Union troops. He allegedly replied, "I'm sorry for you madam but I can't help it. The fact is, madam, we are determined to squelch out the Rebellion if it takes every chicken in Tennessee."[36]

Paine made numerous attempts to pacify the people by attending Sunday services at local churches and visiting the homes of prominent citizens. During those visits, he preached "the gospel of loyalty to such as could be gathered to hear him." In most instances, his calls for devotion to the Union fell on deaf ears. Paine banished citizens who refused to convert and remained persistently disloyal. He warned citizens at Lynchburg and Fayetteville that "if they staid inside the Federal lines they may think, feel and die secesh, but if they talked or acted treason, he would make them houseless, homeless and lifeless."[37]

Paine not only busied himself fighting insurgents and rooting out Confederate sympathizers, he also attempted to eradicate slavery within his district. In late May of 1863, he commenced a plan to hire out former slaves to farmers for $8.00 a month, have the federal government furnish them clothing and place plantation overseers under military authority. This was his response to plantation owners insisting that he return runaway slaves. Paine refused to send slaves back to bondage and instead devised a written contract whereby slaves were employed by plantation owners. This concept of paying wages to slaves in the occupied South proved to be an innovative approach but one that had many detractors. His superiors opposed Paine's plan. Major General Lovell H. Rousseau, commander of the District of Nashville, wrote Major General George H. Thomas, commander of the Department of the Cumberland, complaining that Paine had exceeded his authority and demanded that the plan be stopped. Thomas ordered Paine to void all contracts made between slaves and slave owners and to remove himself from the affairs of master and slave. Paine protested to Rousseau and Thomas but to no avail. Several months later, the adjutant general of the army, Lorenzo Thomas, was sent to Gallatin to investigate. Thomas found favor in Paine's plan, declared his actions "entirely proper" and pronounced the wage system a "wise one."[38]

In early November of 1863, Paine organized an infantry regiment of former slaves to replace white units that were reassigned a month earlier. The threat of guerrillas influenced his decision. The issuing of old muskets to African American men already residing in camp became an enlistment program with a white officer to command the unit. Those men later became part of one of the first black regiments from Tennessee, the 14th United States Colored Infantry. The arming of former slaves caused another major controversy in the community and further ruffled the feathers of higher ranking officers. Rousseau wrote Thomas that Paine encouraged his officers to impress slaves into military service and that the enlistments were illegal. The adjutant general returned to investigate and again Paine was found innocent of the charges.[39]

During his final months at Gallatin, Paine continued to pursue roving guerrilla bands in his district. In late January and early February of 1864, he led a battalion of cavalry and infantry up the Cumberland Valley. He was supported by a flotilla of gunboats and transports. Lead detachments of his command ventured beyond Gainesboro and as far south as Cookeville before turning back. The expedition was a success; Paine's force captured 102 prisoners, killed thirty-three of the enemy and wounded eight. His second in command, Colonel Henry K. McConnell of the Seventy-First Ohio Infantry Regiment, wrote in his after-action report that the partisan bands that had robbed and plundered the region for several months had been "completely broke up." After Paine's return to Gallatin, stories began to circulate among the town's residents that he had seized personal property for his own use during the expedition. Sixteen-year-old Alice Williamson of Gallatin wrote in her diary that furniture taken from the homes of Southern sympathizers was used to "furnish the contraband camp." These same accusations would be leveled against him at Paducah.[40]

In late April of 1864, Paine departed for Tullahoma to defend the roads and bridges between the Duck and Elk Rivers in south central Tennessee. He left behind at Gallatin a heartless reputation inflated by the local inhabitants. The number of rumored executions ordered by Paine during his twenty months in command ballooned. Witnesses claimed two at first, then "twenty or thirty" and then a total of 106 men. The body count more than doubled following the war. One story, which began to circulate twenty years after the war, had Paine ordering the execution of a thirteen-year-old boy. The tale was first published in a Nashville newspaper and later republished by papers in Illinois. Veterans under the command of General Paine condemned the story as false almost immediately. Brigadier General Daniel Dustin, who commanded the 105th Illinois Infantry Regiment at Gallatin, refuted the accusation and stated that members of his regiment found it "either to be supremely ridiculous or as a bitter falsehood." He warned the author of the story that "should anyone charge the General to his face with the commission of such an outrage the accuser would be in danger of just such a dislocation of the neck as fell to the lot of chickens in the hands of the 'yankee soldiers.'" Rebuking the majority of the town's residents, some unionist citizens circulated a petition requesting that Paine remain at Gallatin. Nonetheless, Williamson wrote in her diary after he departed, "I reckon we will have rest now for a while."[41]

Not long after his arrival at Tullahoma, he was ordered to clear insurgents in that section of Tennessee. In early June, Paine rounded up persons who harbored guerrillas and a month later embarked upon an expedition from Tullahoma to Fayetteville. Newspapers north and south reported that troops under Paine killed twenty-five bushwhackers during the expedition, nine of whom were executed on the public square in Lynchburg and several in Fayetteville. A fellow Union officer, Brigadier General Robert H. Milroy, said that Paine "had about 200 guerrillas shot since he has been stationed here" and that most were "quietly walked outside of the pickets and shot and no report is made of the matter and nothing said about it." Milroy declared he only witnessed the dead bodies of two guerrillas but that the stories associated with Paine had "struck terror into the people of secesh proclivities and they have all become intensely loyal." Another soldier wrote home that Paine's "measures are having a salutary effect on the citizens" and that town meetings were held that denounced the guerrillas and forbade them from coming around. On June 29, Paine was relieved of command and ordered to proceed to Memphis. He left Tullahoma the following week.[42]

Congressman Lucian Anderson (National Archives).

On June 18, Lucian Anderson, whom unionists elected to Congress from the First

District of Kentucky in 1863, and Rufus Williams, a Kentucky Court of Appeals judge met Lincoln to urge that assessments on Southern sympathizers be reintroduced in the Jackson Purchase and that Paine be assigned command in Western Kentucky. The president agreed with the two Mayfield men and on June 24 he directed Paine to transfer from the Department of the Cumberland to the Department of the Tennessee and report to Major General Cadwallader C. Washburn commanding the District of West Tennessee at Memphis. Paine met with Washburn on July 16. Washburn informed him that matters in Paducah were "all wrong" and that he needed a "firm hand" to make things right. Paine asked about the assessments that were referred to in the president's instruction, but Washburn offered no answer or advice. Before leaving Memphis, Washburn drafted an order creating the District of Western Kentucky, which included "all portions of Kentucky lying west of the Tennessee River" and the port of Cairo. The district was headquartered at Paducah. Paine was also given rank over Brigadier General Henry Prince at Columbus and Brigadier General Solomon Meredith at Cairo. Neither were enthused over Paine's appointment.[43]

Two

"This district is intensely disloyal"

Since Paine's departure on Christmas Day in 1861, Paducah had evolved into a busy military camp and supply depot for the Union army in the Western Theater. The population continued to resist the occupation in a subtle but determined manner. The women of the city shunned Union officers, neglected the sick and wounded soldiers in the hospitals and never wore the color blue in public. Preachers refused to pray for President Lincoln or for the United States during their Sunday sermons, and the hymn books in the local churches displayed none of the traditional patriotic songs. Men in the Fifteenth Kentucky Volunteer Cavalry, which consisted of recruits from the area, were considered scalawags and "not treated with the consideration to which their patriotism and eminent services entitled them." Paducah's business sector was also at odds with their occupiers as trade restrictions and corruption fueled illicit trade and a booming black market. The traffic in contraband to the Confederacy, uncontrollable since the early days of the war, had increased since March 25, when Major General Nathan Bedford Forrest's Cavalry raided the city. Some Union merchants claimed that the "Rebels are doing all the business and they are reaping all the advantages of trade."[1]

The two most influential tobacco and cotton brokers in the city, Bolinger, Casey & Company and Trimble, Duke & Company, bitterly fought each other over the markets and actively sought the favors of government officials supervising the port. Both had powerful ties in Washington and Frankfort. John T. Bolinger, a recent newcomer who relocated from Mayfield to Paducah in early 1863, was the county clerk of Graves County and a good friend of Congressman Anderson. Lawrence S. Trimble's unionism had waned since Burnett beat him in 1861. He ran against Anderson as a "peace democrat" in 1863 and lost again. These two rivals were suspected of shipping contraband to the South.[2]

Lawrence S. Trimble (National Archives).

Grant heard of their feud in April of 1863 when Colonel Henry Dougherty, the post commander at Paducah, was caught in a scandal with Bolinger and his business partners. Dougherty had replaced Colonel Silas Noble who was dismissed by Grant four months earlier for interfering with the civil authorities and overstepping his jurisdiction. On April 4, Grant intercepted a telegram that directly connected Dougherty to Bolinger's trading firm and their efforts to tamper with district elections. The message also implied that Grant supported the interests of Trimble and his associates and that Bolinger sought Grant's removal from the Department of the Tennessee. Grant denied he backed Trimble and ordered Dougherty transferred from Western Kentucky. Grant searched for an officer who "can be used neither by Bolinger, Casey & Co. or Trimble, Duke & Co." Colonel James S. Martin was assigned the post during the last week in April and remained in command until he too was relieved for permitting the surrender of slaves to their masters. After Grant was made aware of the accusations against Colonel Martin, he wrote to Halleck that "there are factions in West Kentucky who will make every effort to remove every officer they cannot control." Martin was replaced by Colonel Stephen G. Hicks in October of 1863. Hicks, a Georgia native who had settled in Illinois in 1832, served during the Mexican-American War and had been severely wounded at the Battle of Shiloh. Paine's immediate predecessor was the ninth post commander since the commencement of the war. Three of the last four commanders were reassigned or relieved for insubordination related to complaints brought forth by those in either the Bolinger or Trimble camps.[3]

In late spring of 1863, Grant began to remove troops garrisoned in West Tennessee and Western Kentucky to assist in the siege of Vicksburg. Vicksburg was the last major Confederate strong point on the Mississippi River. On May 31, he ordered all but a regiment of infantry and a company of cavalry to be sent from Paducah. Their departure greatly weakened the defenses of the city and the surrounding countryside. The result was a dramatic increase in guerrilla activity. Martial law was declared in July in the Jackson Purchase and pro–Union militia units, known as "Home Guards," were organized to keep order in the communities. At Mayfield, Colonel William W. Tice, formerly of the Forty-Second Kentucky Militia, attempted to organize a local unit in early March of 1864, but Confederate raids into the region prevented their enrollment into military service. In April of 1864, loyalists at Paducah petitioned the governor to return the Sixteenth Kentucky Cavalry, which had been organized at Fort Anderson a month earlier, to serve as Home Guards to protect the district against insurgents. The petitioners claimed that men of the Sixteenth were "well acquainted with the country and know the hiding places of the guerrillas." Governor Thomas E. Bramlette referred the request to Major General Stephen Burbridge, the Union commander in Kentucky, who informed the governor and the petitioners that the Sixteenth was no longer serving under his jurisdiction but that "adequate protection" would be sent. When none arrived, Unionists in the Jackson Purchase formed companies of Home Guards. On July 30, Captain M.A. Payne wrote the governor that "nearly 90" men had been organized at Paducah and that "five other companies" were being recruited in the region. He expected to have recruits for a full battalion within a few weeks.[4]

Thomas Jones Gregory, a former officer in the Twentieth Kentucky Volunteer Infantry and a deeply embittered Unionist, was elected as captain of Mayfield's Home Guard. Earlier in the war, he and his brother Frank were accused of being Yankee assassins and spies. In the fall of 1861, arrest warrants were issued by the grand jury of Graves

County for murder, and a bounty of $500 was placed upon their heads by Confederate supporters. Afterwards, about one-hundred armed secessionists rode over to the Gregory home eleven miles south of Mayfield near the hamlet of Dublin to lynch the brothers. The Gregorys were warned and barricaded themselves in the home. When the band arrived, they opened fire and the Gregorys shot back, reportedly killing three and wounding several others. As the vigilantes retreated, Thomas Jones and Frank fled in to the nearby woods. The secessionists returned and burned the house to the ground. Jones Gregory's brother Jasper was later killed in a skirmish with Rebels and his sister Mary murdered by guerrillas. His hatred of guerrillas became well-known in the Jackson Purchase. In August of 1864, the *Cairo News* reported that "Gregory's men were a terror to guerrillas" and followed a code to "take no prisoners and expect no quarter." Gregory set up his headquarters on the second floor of a commercial building owned by Bolinger and Anderson across from the Graves County Courthouse in Mayfield.[5]

Grant not only removed troops from the Purchase area, he also attempted to stop the rampant smuggling. In November of 1863, he ordered the railroad between Paducah to Union City and Hickman to Union City to be taken up and sent to Nashville to replace rails destroyed by Rebel cavalry in Tennessee and Mississippi. When Grant's order reached Paducah, outraged citizens sent letters and representatives to Frankfort and Washington to have the order overturned. On November 28, Grant received a dispatch from Bramlette stating that the railroad was built and owned by businessmen in Paducah and that its dismantling would be ruinous to the community. Grant responded the same day: "My experience satisfies me that the citizens of Paducah, almost to a man, are disloyal and entitled to no favors from the Government. The president of the road [Trimble], and no doubt nine-tenths of the Paducah stockholders are disloyal men." He did, however, suspend the order until the matter could be examined further by the War Department. In early December, Bramlette wrote Secretary of War Edwin Stanton that Grant had erred in his impression of Paducahans and that they were "perhaps somewhat Copperheadish but not disloyal." Congressman Anderson also wrote Stanton expressing his objections to the order and stressing the railroad's importance to the army and mail service in the region. Grant backed down, and in January of 1864 the military turned over the railroad to their owners.[6]

The controversy over African American men serving in the military came to a head several months before Paine arrived at Paducah. On December 10, 1863, Bramlette was notified that a regiment of free blacks would be recruited in Kentucky. He responded four days later declaring that if the army "came to recruit colored men for the benefit of Kentucky, we decline your

Governor Thomas E. Bramlette (National Archives).

services" and if they "came to recruit for the benefit of another State, we deny your right to do so and forbid it." Four weeks later, he warned that "no such recruiting will be tolerated here" and "summary justice will be inflicted upon any who attempt such unlawful purpose." The governor received reports of army officers impressing black men at Paducah in the second week of February. On February 18, both houses of the state legislature passed a resolution requesting the removal of all recruitment camps for black soldiers in Kentucky. Six days later, Congress passed an act to enroll all able-bodied black men between the ages of twenty and forty-five for military service. Bramlette, superseded by the federal government, issued a decree on March 15 to the people of Kentucky not to resist or commit acts of violence to prohibit the enrollment process. He later traveled to Washington to relay the anger of Kentucky slave owners over the allegedly unauthorized recruitment of black soldiers. A few weeks before Paine assumed command, Bramlette received a letter declaring that armed black men were forcibly taking slaves to impress into the army and that a "reign of terror" existed at Paducah.[7]

The most defining moment of the war for Paducah occurred when Forrest hit the city on March 25, attacking Fort Anderson, appropriating or destroying supplies and burning a steamboat. The events that day had a dramatic impact upon Paine's management of the district. Southern sympathizers reportedly assisted Forrest's men by furnishing food and pointing out Union-owned stores, shops and dwellings for looting. Paine later noted that "there were more persons in town who openly assisted Forrest in his attack in March than there were Union persons there, and a large, very large majority deeply sympathized with him and cordially wished him success." The first of Paine's objectives as district commander was to reimburse Union men for property lost during Forrest's raid. His plan for compensation included assessments upon the disloyal residents, which he believed Lincoln approved.[8]

When Paine's steamboat docked at Paducah, he did not fully comprehend the enormous task before him. He was unaware of the misfortunes of his predecessors or the influence and power of his adversaries. As at Bird's Point, Tuscumbia, Gallatin and Tullahoma, he entered Paducah prepared to safeguard the men under his command, protect the loyal citizens in his district and defend the nation against its enemies. He was prepared to use threats, intimidation and brute force to achieve his assigned goals. A fierce storm was gathering on the horizon.

Paine was warmly greeted by members of the local Union League of America at Paducah on July 19. The League represented the "true Union men of this section of the country" and was influential in Paine's appointment. The officers of the organization wrote General Washburn several days earlier to express their delight in Paine's appointment; they looked forward to his giving "traitors and secret Southern sympathizers their just dues." This resolute group of men had plans to stem the illicit trade to the South and protect their business interests in the region. Paine listened to their concerns as they walked him to the Continental Hotel where he was to spend his first night as district commander.[9]

Along the way, he heard distressing news that Colonel Henry W. Barry of the Eighth United States Colored Heavy Artillery Regiment, which was garrisoned at Fort Anderson, had been placed under arrest for disobeying orders. Colonel Stephen Hicks, the commander of the post, ordered Barry to return the wives and children of African American soldiers residing near the fort to their slave masters. Barry refused to comply on the grounds that their removal would destroy the morale of the soldiers and cause desertions.

Recognizing the significance of the dispute and to avoid further trouble between the officers, Paine decided to take command of the post immediately rather than wait until the next day. Within three hours of his arrival, he issued his first two orders as commander of the District of Western Kentucky. The first defined his military control over the district, and the second named the members of his staff. He called for Hicks and Barry in an effort to resolve the dispute between the two men. Hicks refused to budge and declared that he was following orders sent from Adjutant General Thomas. Paine telegraphed the adjutant general for clarification of the order. Barry remained under house confinement until a response was received.[10]

Paine's first official act as district commander was to arrest the captain of the steamboat *Masonic Gem* and confiscate its cargo. The *Masonic Gem* was unloading tobacco when Paine disembarked at Paducah. He was informed by a member of the Union League that the captain was not licensed to transport products to Paducah. The captain was confined for a few hours until a permit granted by General Washburn was presented to Paine.

Colonel Stephen G. Hicks (*William Newby: The Soldier's Return* by G. J. George).

The tobacco remained impounded for several weeks until a tobacco dealer arranged to pay the port fees. Early that evening, Paine met with Congressman Anderson, who was temporarily residing at the same hotel. The two discussed the intent of Lincoln's assessment order and what plans where needed for implementation. That evening, the two spoke at the Market House, the commercial center of the city, where an audience of local businessmen and citizens heard Paine outline his strategy to thwart smugglers. As the long day ended, Paine lay awake in bed listening to the sounds of gunfire in the direction of the Union pickets south of town. The next morning, Paine received reports that a popular partisan leader, known as "Colonel Outlaw," led attacks upon the outlying post during the middle of the night. He was Drew Outlaw.[11]

On July 20, Paine set up offices for his staff in the Continental Hotel and began his campaign to end the illicit trade with the South. He issued General Order No. 3, which declared that "no Rebel or disloyal person living in the District of Western Kentucky shall ship produce to market, or receive supplies by railroad or river" and that no shipments could leave Paducah without a permit from Paine's headquarters. The order also specified that no arms or ammunition could be sold in the district without a special permit. A list of those to be issued trade permits was to be composed and examined weekly. Several merchants soon lined up outside of Paine's headquarters to seek permission to operate their businesses. His response to all was blunt and direct.

> Gentlemen, it is a notorious fact that this district is intensely disloyal. It has caused more trouble to the Government than all your tobacco, cotton, banks and business is worth. The question is not how much money your men can make this year. 'Tis not how much tobacco, cotton, or hemp you can grow. The only question on trial here is "are your people of this district ready for Federal Salvation." If so well; if not, you must die. I have a plan to suggest, and I hope God will give me grace to sustain it. My plan will be the only plan of Federal salvation in this district. The first and great command-

ment is that all you disloyal, Rebellious people shall not circulate one dollar of capital in all the land. Not a dollar, no debt, or bill of exchange can be paid or made without my signature, and I pledge to you I will not approve any money transactions of a disloyal man. All his capital, all his money, every cent of it, shall be placed at the disposal of the Government. I will teach you that having encouraged this Rebellion, having comforted and aided your country's enemies, you must, aye, shall reap a traitor's reward.

When they protested that they had rights, he shouted, "Talk about your rights! Why you have no rights to talk about! A loyal citizen is the only one left with any rights at this time." Paine also reminded them that he was at Paducah in 1861 and that he advised then of a "better way, the only way to peace" but that his frequent appeals were ignored. It appeared evident to him that not much had changed, and now more than ever he was determined to make those who prospered during the war "feel the want of a nation's defense and support."[12]

Paine issued General Orders No. 4 and No. 5 the next day. The former limited the sale and trade of tobacco and cotton to only "known and tried loyal men," and the latter amended General Order No. 3 by granting the Port Surveyor's Office the authority to grant permits. The order also defined the permit application and inspection process and concluded with the proviso that violators were prohibited from conducting further business in the district and their goods were subject to seizure and confiscation. A ten-dollar port fee for every hogshead of tobacco and a special tax of twenty-five percent on all tobacco and cotton bought from "disloyal men or in which a disloyal men had an interest" was later collected by the Port Surveyor.[13]

Paine was slowly staunching the flow of contraband through Paducah. Having received no response from the adjutant general's office in regard to Colonel Barry's arrest, Paine wrote a letter to him, expressing his shock and dismay that the wives and children of dedicated combat solders were to be returned to their masters and he reiterated Barry's innocence. As the day came to an end, shots could be heard as guerrillas again fired upon the city's outposts.[14]

On the twenty-second, Paine appointed Major Henry Bartling as provost marshal of the District of West Kentucky. Bartling was a thirty-four-year-old from Champaign, Illinois. He was an officer in the Eighth Artillery and had commanded a company in the Second Illinois Volunteer Cavalry early in the war. During Forrest's attack on the city, he was severely wounded in the left arm while commanding a battery at Fort Anderson. The wound became a lifelong disability for Bartling. Before the war, he worked for the land department of the Illinois Central Railroad Company and owned a successful store in San Francisco during the gold rush. Bartling came highly

Major Henry Bartling (*United State Biographical Dictionary: Kansas Volume*).

recommended and was a "subject of congratulations with the citizens" of Paducah after his appointment. Paine assigned him the responsibility of managing the finances of the military district.[15]

Paine also assigned Thomas M. Redd, surveyor of customs at Paducah, to investigate the illegal trade from the port (Paducah was at the confluence of the Ohio and Tennessee rivers). Redd was a devoted Union man who had been the city's surveyor since February. His home was used by snipers during Forrest's attack to fire into Fort Anderson and was demolished by Colonel Hicks following the battle. Redd's first act was to close the clothing shop of E.B. Jones and Company. The proprietor, Edward B. Jones, attempted to ship pistols and ammunition. Paine ordered the weapons and the store stock seized, inventoried and assessed. Jones claimed he had been issued a special permit by Bartling to ship the pistols and ammunition. The claim was denied by Bartling, though clerks serving in his office recalled the permit being issued. Bartling later sold part of the property to pay for assessments levied on Jones.[16]

On Friday, the twenty-third, Paine issued General Order No. 6, which prohibited the collection of rent by landlords found not to be "unswerving, unconditional and undeviating Union persons." Tenants were to make payments to the post quartermaster after August 1. As Redd and Bartling expanded their investigations to locate parties involved in the transportation of contraband, Paine hired informants to spy on known Southern sympathizers. With the knowledge acquired from these sources, he systematically began to shut down the smugglers one by one. By the end of his first week in command, Paine had closed fifteen businesses and properties and placed them under the possession of the government.[17]

That Friday, while Paine was walking in the business district, he encountered Henry Emerson Etheridge, a former congressman from Tennessee and clerk of the United States House of Representatives. Like Trimble, Etheridge had been a Unionist but turned against the war when Lincoln issued the Emancipation Proclamation. Etheridge was in town for a series of anti-war speeches. The two met and a heated two-hour conversation ensued. Their dustup drew a crowd of passersby. Paine questioned Etheridge's loyalty and why he had not taken up arms against the Confederacy. Etheridge responded that he had "done more good for the country by keeping men out of the Rebel army and by inducing them to desert and perhaps had kept as many men out of the army as General Paine had ever captured." Paine angrily replied that he had "taken six or seven thousand at Island No. 10 and but for that God damned coward Halleck he would have captured a great many more at Corinth." Paine's disparaging comment about Halleck would be held against him in his court martial.[18]

Orders from Adjutant General Thomas not to return women and children of African American soldiers serving at Fort Anderson to their masters arrived on July 24. Paine released Colonel Barry later that day. Barry resumed recruiting former slaves and free blacks. The news was not taken well by Colonel Hicks who confronted Paine. The general had put Hicks in command of Fort Anderson. Paine relieved Hicks and replaced him with Barry.[19]

The businesses of suspected Rebel sympathizers continued to be closed, including the drug store of William A. Bell. Bartling told Paine that Bell was a "damned Rebel and copperhead" and involved in contraband. Redd said Bell "sympathized with the Rebellion." Another loyal citizen reported that Bell's wife had made clothing for the Confederate army. After Bartling's men secured his store, Bell approached Paine with letters of introduction along with notes of loyalty from prominent citizens. Paine handed back the letters after a brief glance and pronounced the authors Copperheads. He cursed Bell and advised him to sell his business. He decided to sell his business to the first purchaser he met on the street. Bell later was assessed $2,000 by Bartling for the sale of his store and for associating with known Rebels.[20]

Paine also detained former soldiers who served in the Confederate army. Marian G. Milam, a prominent druggist working in Paducah, was arrested and confined in the guardhouse on July 25 after he was found to have served with the Fifth Tennessee Volunteer Infantry Regiment from May of 1861 to July of 1862. Milam's uncle, Charles M. Kilgore, accused him of abusing Union sympathizers when he was in Weakley County, Tennessee. It was alleged that Milam initiated and participated in the tar and feathering of Unionists. Bartling judged Milam a Confederate spy and "a scoundrel of the deepest dye." Milam was held in prison for fifty-one days without any formal charges.

Emerson Etheridge (National Archives).

Another veteran of the Rebel army, John F. Davis, was arrested on July 27 by Bartling for the theft of a blank permit at district headquarters to sell his crop. Bartling also accused him of firing on the picket line earlier in the month. Davis was confined in the guardhouse for three weeks.[21]

Finding the Continental Hotel inappropriate for a military headquarters, Paine relocated his offices to the Commercial Bank building on the 25th. He chose the bank because of its location, and because the president of the bank, Lawrence M. Flournoy, was a suspected Southern sympathizer who was allegedly involved in the contraband trade. The bank had been visited by Forrest's men but was not robbed as other businesses were. Paine entered the building and told the bank's bookkeeper that "Flournoy was a damned Rebel" and a "cotton speculator making money off the war." His staff officers appropriated three rooms as military headquarters and allowed the bank's cashier and bookkeeper the remaining rooms. Paine set up his private residence at 420 Broadway, the home of Circuit Court Judge James Campbell, a "notorious sesesh." Campbell also was said to be a Rebel spy who sent messages across Union lines to enemy officers. That evening, Paine contemplated a plan to halt the bank transactions of disloyal men not residing in the district and imposing assessments on their stock holdings.[22]

Paine issued General order No. 7 on the morning of July 26. The decree prohibited all banks within the city from transferring or depositing funds except by special permit granted by district headquarters. When confronted by the bank representatives, Paine declared his purpose was to "tie up everything [and] that the banks were backed up by thirty pieces of silver and that he was backed up by bayonets." They protested that without the authority to transfer funds among other banks in the city, they would have to "give up the idea of doing business." Paine backed down and issued an addendum to the order which allowed the banks to conduct business with other city banks without permission from district headquarters. The responsibility of granting permits for money transfers outside of the district was assigned to Redd. The bank officers continued to press Paine to remove the remaining restrictions, but he made no further concessions.[23]

Guerrilla activity persisted in the region. In response to reports of shots being fired at boats traveling on the Tennessee River and Union men being harassed, Paine sent a detachment of 600 men to Haddix's Ferry below Aurora. The detachment led by Major John H. Peck and consisting of men from the 132nd Illinois Volunteer Infantry and the Eighth Artillery reached the landing by steamboat during the predawn hours of July 27. They tracked down a large band of guerrillas several miles inland where a skirmish occurred. Peck's men routed the guerrillas, killing five, wounding several and capturing seven. Many others were reported captured but escaped during the return march to the landing.[24]

Unable to make any serious impact on the partisan resistance in the outlying countryside, Paine decided to use the tactic he had employed successfully in Tennessee—brute intimidation. On the twenty-seventh, he ordered T.L. Jacobs, a Southern sympathizer and "horse thief" known to Paine, to deliver a proclamation to Rebel commanders at Dresden, Tennessee. Jacobs was issued a horse, given a military pass and ordered to inform all along the road to Dresden that "if another Union man is killed by bushwhackers or Rebels, five Rebel sympathizers will share the same fate for every Union man killed." The message also warned that guerrilla leader James Kesterson was to be executed before Jacobs' departure from Paducah. To ensure his return, Jacobs' father and two brothers were locked in the guardhouse. He came back the following week with the signatures of Rebel commanders on the reverse side of the proclamation.[25]

Nicknamed "Captain Kess," Kesterson was arguably the most notorious local guerrilla. He was a farmer who resided in Graves County. Kesterson favored the Southern cause but rather than join the Confederate army, he organized a gang of forty or fifty ruffians to terrorize and murder Union men. Before being wounded and captured near Clinton on July 9, Kesterson and his gang murdered about thirty men. Kesterson, also known as "Old Kess" though he was only twenty-five, was accused of gunning down a minister and shooting to death James B. Happy, a Mayfield business owner; both were unarmed, unresisting and outspoken Union men. Kesterson was recovering from his wounds at Columbus when Paine ordered him to Paducah on July 26. Paine had received a warning that if Kesterson was executed, "all the Union men, women and children would be shot in the district." Paine scoffed at the threat and had him imprisoned in the guardhouse. When interrogated, Kesterson admitted killing Happy on February 25, as well as the Reverend Owens and two other men. He said he shot Happy because he was a "damned Union man and would not keep quiet." Paine ordered his execution and advised Kesterson to "turn his whole attention to that being and if he has treasures laid up in heaven he had better draw for the full amount." The next morning, Kesterson was led by Colonel Barry and a squad from the Eighth Artillery and shot on the banks of the Ohio River below Fort Anderson.[26]

Paine also decided to clear secessionists from city and county government. The first to go was city councilman A.B. Kinkead. On the advice of Bartling and other "undoubted Union men" Paine arrested Kinkead on July 29. Kinkead submitted his resignation and was told to report to the provost marshal's office every day at 9:00 a.m. and 4:00 p.m. Paine remarked that if he didn't like the terms of his parole, he could be sent to Canada. Kinkead was escorted by a squad of soldiers to the city limits and told not to return until the next day. The next official to be removed from office was McCracken County Jailer, A.S. Jones. He was accused of mistreating Union men behind bars and of not obtaining a proper substitute for the draft. Paine released the prisoners, arrested Jones and sentenced him to a week in his jail. Gustavus A. Flournoy was removed as county judge, issued a pass outside the picket lines and told "not to return." Braxton Small, the clerk of the circuit court, was directed to resign and told that he would soon be sent with "many other citizens by way of New Orleans to Australia." Paine also ordered Mayor John G. Fisher to resign on August 4, but the city council refused to accept his resignation. The general reconsidered and withdrew the order two days later when several loyal citizens defended the mayor.[27]

On the evening of July 30, Paine sent orders to General Meredith at Cairo and General Prince at Columbus to shift troops from Columbus to Paducah. Prince was directed to have the 134th Illinois Volunteer Infantry Regiment ready for departure when he arrived at Columbus the next morning. At dawn on July 31, Paine left for Cairo where he met briefly with Meredith and his staff, boarded the steamship *Graham* and headed downriver to Columbus. He reached Columbus just before 10:00 a.m. where he ordered Prince to send a company of the Third Illinois Volunteer Cavalry to Milburn and Blandville to monitor county elections on August 1. The Third Illinois was then to be sent to Paducah to await further instructions. Paine embarked on the *Graham* with the 134th Illinois and steamed for Cairo. They reached Cairo at 4:00 p.m. and transferred to the steamer *Convoy* for the voyage to Paducah. Paine and the 134th Illinois reached Paducah on the morning of August 1.[28]

Upon Paine's arrival, he was informed that the telegraph lines had been severed between Columbus and Blandville. He confronted Wiley Dicus, the line repairman, who explained that he knew of fourteen guerrillas that were "in the habit of cutting the telegraph." Dicus named John Price and George Griffie as the most troublesome of the group. Price swore he would kill Dicus if he caught him reconnecting the cables. Griffie had stolen the horse of the telegraph repairer at Blandville and threatened to shoot him if he restored the line. Paine told Dicus that "a little wholesome shooting will be very beneficial to the telegraph as well as the service generally." Within a few days, Griffie was captured and imprisoned at Paducah and Price disappeared from the region. The line remained open between the two military posts during the rest of Paine's term in command.[29]

While Paine was en route from Columbus, Bartling initiated another series of fines and fees upon the allegedly disloyal citizens of Paducah. It began with a ten-cent permit fee for all items purchased in Paducah and taken beyond the picket lines. A five-dollar tax was placed on mules sold in the city, a 50-cent fee on all letters mailed by disloyal citizens and newspapers unfriendly to President Lincoln were charged an addition 50 cents a bundle. In addition, Paine increased the fines for drunkenness and disorderly conduct, taxed saloons ten to fifteen dollars a month and charged one dollar for every barrel of whiskey sold in Paducah. Prostitutes paid a fifty-dollar fee to ply their trade, and a certain Miss Hester Baldwin was levied at one hundred dollars. The funds collected were deposited in the provost marshal's relief fund for the widows and children of missing and dead Union soldiers.[30]

On his return from Columbus, John E. Woodward, the superintendent of trade at

Columbus, Kentucky (*Frank Leslie's Illustrated Newspaper*).

Paducah, approached Paine on behalf of the widow Ellen Birmingham. She had been denied permission by the bank cashier of Watts, Given and Company to withdraw funds from an account under her dead husband's name. Birmingham had deposited $1,000 of her own money into the account. The bank refused to release the funds on the grounds that the couple's infant son had legal title to a portion of her husband's estate and that a guardian must be appointed before she could access the account. Paine interviewed the woman and found her to be a "poor, honest, loyal person" who was barely surviving off the charity of others. He believed that the bank had retained the funds as a "pretext for using this woman's capital." Paine ordered the cashier, a suspected Southern sympathizer, to release her money to the city treasurer, W.F. Swift. The cashier refused, claiming that Paine had no authority to issue such an order. Swift returned with a squad of soldiers and told the cashier that the bank would be closed if he did not hand over the money. The cashier paid the money to Swift, who gave it to Birmingham.[31]

On the morning of August 2, Captain Gregory and his Home Guards captured guerrilla William Shelby Bryan in Dublin. Bryan was a Tennessee native who moved to Graves County in 1860 and was involved in a feud with Gregory dating to the beginning of the war. The two families had been close neighbors geographically but polar opposites politically. The Gregory family was fervently for the Union, while the Bryans supported the Confederate cause. The Bryans' eldest son, Jonathon Tate Bryan, was with the Twelfth Kentucky Cavalry Regiment at the time of William's capture. Bryan was tied up and brought to Mayfield where he was executed on the courthouse lawn by Gregory and his men.[32]

It was later claimed that Paine had him shot, though he had no direct authority over the Home Guard, nor is there any documentation that had he communicated with Gregory prior to Bryan's capture.[33]

Meanwhile, Adjutant General Thomas visited Paducah August 4 on an inspection tour of black regiments and camps along the Ohio and Mississippi Rivers. After he met with Paine and observed the condition of black troops at Fort Anderson and their family members in the nearby camp, he wrote Secretary of War Stanton that he found "everything progressing satisfactorily." He further recorded that Paine understood his views in regard to "colored women and children and will exercise a judicious policy with them." To the dismay and alarm of many of Paducah's white inhabitants, Paine commenced a policy that protected the African American community. One of his staff officers noted that he gave "audience to a poor black woman and listened with all possible attention to her complaint." He continued to encourage the recruitment of black soldiers, housed and fed their families and refused to return runaway slaves to disloyal owners. Paine also increased the visible presence of black soldiers in the city's defenses.[34]

Adjutant General Lorenzo Thomas (Library of Congress).

On August 6, Paine appointed Captain Roland H. Hall, provost marshal of the First Congressional District, as superintendent of rents and as disbursing agent for the United States government. Paine ordered Hall to form a committee to determine the loyalty of landlords; all persons who rented from disloyal landlords had to pay Hall. Hall chose for the committee Bartling, Redd, Albert Bradshaw, a former leader of the county's Whig Party; Dr. W. Henry Kidd, president of the Paducah's Union League; and businessmen J.E.D. Morgan, John Morgan and H.F. Lyon. The funds collected were to be paid to the "wives, widows and mothers of soldiers and to refugees" and the remaining funds given to the assistant quartermaster for disbursement to loyal men who had property destroyed during Battle of Paducah. Paine also informed Redd that all goods seized by the military authorities at Paducah for violations of the Treasury Department's trade restrictions were to be turned over to the surveyor of the port. Redd questioned whether he had the legal authority to accept seized goods and thus forwarded his concerns to the regional agent at Cincinnati. A week later, Redd was instructed by the Treasury Department to return all seized items to the military authorities and to have nothing further to do with it.[35]

Three

"Treason was no more"

In late July, Major General Stephen G. Burbridge, commander of the Military District of Kentucky, began to round up and detain leading Confederate sympathizers at Louisville. This was in response to a field order issued by General Sherman several weeks earlier to arrest Kentuckians who "encouraged or harbored guerrillas and robbers" and to prepare them for deportation outside of Union lines. Having read accounts of the arrests and deportations in Louisville newspapers, Paine made a list of persons to be apprehended. Over forty people were on the list, and they "were the men and women most prominent in assisting Forrest and Buford in their attacks upon Paducah and Rebels equally guilty residing in Columbus." Paine had threatened to send "damned Rebels" to Central or South America, but an article in the Lexington *National Unionist* from August 5 convinced him that Canada was a better destination. The article said that when secessionists "have to leave Kentucky they invariably choose to go to Canada." The next day Paine set in motion the banishment of the most outspoken Southern sympathizers in his district to Windsor, Ontario.[1]

On July 31, orders were sent to General Prince at Columbus to notify the people to be banished and tell them to make arrangements for their transportation to Cairo on August 8. The order stiplulated that those being expelled would be permitted to take only their "wearing apparel, jewelry, pictures, fine table ware and one medium sized box containing as they selected." All expenses for travel were to be paid by the deportees. Property left was to be inventoried and stored by the post quartermaster; homes and businesses were to be confiscated. Penciled at the bottom of Paine's order were the following names: William McKeene Hubbard, Burns M. Walker, James Pembroke Walker, William Cook, T.M. Horne (and family), Richard E. Cook, Edward S. Smedley, James A. Yantis, James Morton, W.R. Vance, George B. Moss, W.G. Malone (and daughters), J.W. Doughty, Joseph M. Moore and Charles McKinney & Company. All of them claimed they were true friends of the Union. But Moss, Horne and Moore sent a letter to Confederate President Jefferson Davis asking him to send the troops to occupy Columbus and Cairo. Not all on the list were subject to immediate banishment, as Yantis, Doughty, Smedley and others not named on the list were forwarded to Paducah for further "examination." Doughty was sentenced to be hanged for lynching a Union man and destroying government property. In all, about thirty persons were assembled at the city dock and herded on a steamer by a squad of African American soldiers led by Captain Phelps Paine, the son of General Paine.[2]

Back at Paducah, Paine followed a similar pattern whereby he alerted and informed those to be exiled on August 4 and to prepare for departure. Foremost on his list was

General Stephen B. Burbridge (*Harper's Weekly*).

Robert O. Woolfolk, a merchant in the city, who had an extensive record as being a radical Southern sympathizer. Before the war, Woolfolk had been an associate of Confederate General Lloyd Tilghman and constructed the general's home in Paducah. Tilghman occupied Woolfolk's home when he was recruiting soldiers in the city. After Tilghman's departure, following Grant's occupation of the city, Woolfolk moved his family into the house. His brother George served in the Confederate army. When Grant's troops arrived in the city in September of 1861, Woolfolk refused to lower his Confederate flag and replace it with the national flag. Men under the command of Brigadier General Lew Wallace eventually replaced the "traitorous flag" but only after a scuffle between General Smith's aide, who was ordered to remove the national flag after complaints from Woolfolk, and one of Wallace's unyielding officers. During Paine's brief tenure as post commander in early September of 1861, Woolfolk was overheard expressing his desire for Rebel victories and for Paine to be hanged. The night before he was to be expelled, Woolfolk sneaked away with his father-in-law, Robert Enders, on a boat traveling upriver to Evansville, Indiana, leaving behind his wife and six children. He would take a train to Detroit the next day.[3]

At 8 o'clock on the morning of August 8, Captain Harlow B. Norton and a squad of twelve soldiers from the Eighth Artillery marched to Woolfolk's home. When Paine was apprised of Woolfolk's escape, he verbally shouted to have him brought back "dead or alive." Woolfork's family, nonetheless, was directed to march to a waiting boat anchored on the river. One of Woolfolk's daughters, Kate Woolfolk Whitfield, wrote nearly fifty years later:

> The morning of the eighth broke clear and warm. Captain Norton with twelve negroes, some of them family servants, were our escorts. We marched down Broadway past headquarters to the river, my mother with six children and a colored nurse. Mrs. Joe Sam Hobbs [Clementine Hobbs], Mrs. Marence [E.A. Maurous], her sister Miss Kate Sanders [Catherine L. Saunders], relatives of the late Henry Jones, Mrs. Rollston [Mary Jane Rollston] and Mr. Robert Shanklin [Robert H. Shanklin], were, I believe, all who went at that time from Paducah.

The five others exiled along with the Woolfolks were prominent citizens whom Paine had been informed aided the Rebels during past raids upon the city—with maybe one exception. According to Whitfield, Kate Saunders was a harmless "old maid" who never received visitors, had meals delivered to her home and cared for over forty stray cats. Some of Paine's critics claimed after the war that he banished certain individuals so as to procure their elegant residences for his headquarters. All boarded the *Masonic Gem* that morning and sailed downriver for Cairo.[4]

The twelve exiles, along with Captain Norton and his guards, disembarked at Cairo and marched to the train depot. There, waiting in railcars at the station, was Captain Paine, his men and the twenty-one people banished from Columbus. After the Paducahans were transferred to the cars, the train departed for Chicago. Inside the coach, Paine's twelve men guarded one entrance and Norton's twelve men the other. The train made no stops along the way and reached Chicago that evening. The train station was full of onlookers as news of their arrival preceded them. The gawkers anxiously peered through the cabin windows, which led Whitfield to remark sarcastically, "just step this way, gentlemen, this way to see the caged animals." The train switched tracks at Chicago and proceeded on its trip to Detroit. The train halted at the end of the line late on the evening of August 9. The next morning, Captain Paine and his guard escorted the thirty-three exiles on a steamboat to Canada. The expatriates landed at Windsor at noon on August 10, where they were met onshore by British soldiers and Confederate prisoners who had escaped Northern penitentiaries. Their fellow Southerners walked them to the "Windsor," a "shabby old hotel" where many stayed until Paine's order was revoked on September 13, 1864.[5]

The reaction of the press to the banishment was one of either complete condemnation or high praise depending upon the political leanings of the publisher. A paper from Vincennes, Indiana, declared Paine a "disgrace to the national service" and that a "Payne [sic] Killer could be beneficially used on such subjects." The editor of the *Louisville Daily Journal* warned:

> He [General Paine] may have a troublesome set to deal with but a General fertile in expedients would find the means of thoroughly punishing them at home, instead of sending them abroad in the character of martyrs. Every one of them becomes a "victim" of military oppression among those they take refuge with. They add to the common howl which the Rebels and Rebel sympathizers abroad are eager to have sounded louder every day.

The paper's premonition proved accurate.[6]

In the meantime, General Paine closed the drugstore of S.P. Cope on August 8. He charged Cope with disloyalty and supporting anti-war Democrats. Cope had also been connected to a ring of quinine smugglers dating back over a year, which Paine was made aware of by Bartling. Cope confronted the general at his headquarters two weeks later. He denied all charges, but Paine replied that he had proof of his disloyalty and trading in contraband. Paine then asked Cope about black soldiers and emancipation. Cope, who in February of 1864 vehemently opposed the enlistment of his slave, refused to answer which only confirmed his disloyalty to Paine. Paine did, however, return the keys to his store, but he was not allowed to conduct business. Cope's residence was later used to house the offices of the assistant postmaster for the military district.[7]

In late July and early August, Paine received a steady stream of reports from his detectives and spies that traitors in Illinois were plotting to disrupt the upcoming elections. He wrote Governor Yates on August 8 that "there is a deep laid scheme within the State of Illinois and the adjoining states to resist the draft and carry the election by foul means" and they "act in concert with their brother Rebels South." His sources claimed that "arms, ammunition and means have been distributed among the disaffected in these states and the work is assuming rather formidable proportions ... the organization is under arms and but await[s] the word to rally around their leaders ready for action." He recommended to the governor that martial law be imposed, surveillance be conducted upon plotters and the "infernal secret institutions" be rooted out of the state. He further suggested that the Union League of Illinois be empowered to assist in subduing the traitors. "This is no unfounded cry of wolf but indisputable fact," he concluded. Whether Paine's informers were reliable is doubtful. Paine, like many others in the Midwest, had fallen prey to rumor and hysteria. Though Yates had received numerous reports for months regarding conspiracy and sedition, there never was a scheme to sabotage the election. The governor appreciated Paine's warning but did not act on it.[8]

Paine had another run in with the bank of Watts, Given and Company, when a cashier refused to allow funds to be withdrawn from a personal account. This time the bank denied C.O. Allard the permission to withdraw $8,000 to reopen and stock a flour mill that had ceased operations since the Confederate raids in the spring. Allard had made an agreement with Paine to supply the government with grain once the mill was operational. The cashier, G.F. Rabb, was directed by one of the bank owners not to pay because Allard's father, J.L. Allard, defaulted on a loan two years earlier and that an agreement was made by his father that his son would not withdraw the funds until the issue was settled. C.O. Allard was unaware of the agreement and sought Paine's assistance. Paine issued an order to have the money released, but Rabb replied he did not have authorization from his superiors to do so. Rabb stood his ground for eight days before Paine threatened to close the bank. A check was written to Woodward on August 16 and delivered to Allard to open and supply the mill.[9]

As Paine solidified his control over the city, he found the timing right to secure the surrounding countryside where guerrillas were still a major concern. The nucleus of the guerrilla movement in the Jackson Purchase was at Mayfield. So at 3:00 p.m. on August 9, Paine ordered over 1,500 infantry, cavalry and artillery to march south toward the town. Trailing behind the troops were refugees who had fled to Paducah when Forrest's army invaded the region in early spring. Included in their ranks was Congressman Anderson. Their hopes were to return to their businesses and homes under the protection of the Union army. Soon after their departure, the skies opened and a drenching rain soaked the soldiers and the followers. They hiked eight miles before setting up camp for the night. At dawn the next day, Paine appointed Colonel Barry as post commander and sent instructions to a detachment of the Third Illinois Cavalry Regiment at Wadesboro to meet him at Mayfield. He then galloped off with his staff where he met up with his troops later that afternoon.[10]

Paine and his men entered Mayfield late on the night of August 11 after a twenty-six-mile march that lasted almost two days. Willis Danforth, surgeon of the 134th Illinois Volunteer Infantry, found the "town literally deserted" when they arrived. Danforth later became Paine's chief medical officer. Paine and his staff set up headquarters at the Morris Hotel while his men camped on the court square and in surrounding buildings and warehouses. The occupation of Mayfield began the next morning as Paine ordered pickets out to cover the main roads into town and organized a command structure to manage the new post. Paine selected Colonel Waters W. McChesney, a twenty-seven-year-old native of Chicago who had a dubious military past. He was commissioned as colonel of the Tenth Regiment New York State Volunteers on May 15, 1861. The press later nicknamed the regiment "McChesney's Zouaves." At the Battle of Big Bethel, Virginia, on June 10, 1861, McChesney was reported to have "absented himself from the regiment nearly the whole time." A few days following the battle, McChesney returned to New York City, claiming ill health, and resigned on June 22. Private Charles Hunter of Company E wrote after his resignation that the "regiment to a man feel thoroughly ashamed at having his name given to them" and that he hoped the "name McChesney [would] never again be associated with the Tenth National Zouaves of New York." The regiment's historian recalled after the war that "he resigned his commission in consequence of the discovery that he did not possess the confidence of the officers of his regiment."[11]

Following his resignation, McChesney reappeared back in Chicago where he assisted as an officer in the preparation of infantry units. In the spring of 1864, the governor of Illinois called for a volunteer force of one hundred–day men to relieve the veteran soldiers from guard duty at forts in Kentucky, Tennessee, and Missouri. The 134th Illinois Volunteer Infantry Regiment was organized as one of those guard units at Camp Butler near the state capital at Springfield on May 31. McChesney exaggerated his qualifications to other officers and was elected colonel of the regiment. His popularity dissipated soon afterwards. By the end of June, rumors circulated through the ranks "concerning his bravery" and drunkenness while on duty. McChesney's health deteriorated so badly while he was stationed at Columbus that he seldom left his tent and made frequent trips back to Chicago to recuperate. Before being assigned post commander at Mayfield, he had only drilled the regiment twice and was criticized by his officers as being unable to manage a battalion drill. The enlisted men despised him. On one occasion, he was hanged in effigy in a tree near the parade field after he ordered a private to be strung up by his thumbs for being absent from roll call. The soldier had been washing his uniform. On another occasion, the colonel ordered his troops to halt and stack arms in ankle high mud, whereby a few men threw their knapsacks over ten feet in his general direction. The men constantly mumbled and groaned whenever he ventured out from his tent. The vast majority, if not all, of his officers and men had absolutely no confidence in his abilities to manage a military post.[12]

Paine selected the residence of John Eaker, a prominent Southern sympathizer and former Kentucky state senator, to serve as post headquarters. Eaker left Mayfield for Tennessee before Union troops entered the town, but Mrs. Eaker and her family still resided in the home. Paine ordered McChesney to set up his offices and informed Mrs. Eaker that she and her family had the "privilege of remaining in the house ten days" after which they were to report to Paducah where transportation would be furnished "to New Orleans and thence to Central America." He continued that, "all your lands and tobacco will go to the United States and this will be the end of John Eaker, his estate and family in the United States and you will not go alone madam, one hundred families from Graves County will go with you—these Rebels who cannot live under this Government must go out of it." Paine also levied a fine of $10,000 on Eaker to compensate the widow of James B. Happy who was brutally murdered by Rebel guerrillas across from the new post headquarters.[13]

Paine then returned his attention to McChesney and ordered that he sink a well near the courthouse, repair the railroad between Paducah and Mayfield and send cavalry detachments to instruct all Rebel farmers to deliver hay, corn, oats and cattle to the post's quartermaster for transport for Paducah. He insisted that McChesney operate his command "free of cost to the Government" and that "these Rebels must pay the cost of this war." He also declared that they must "pay five hundred dollars for

Colonel Waters W. McChesney (Library of Congress).

every widow they make or cause to be made, support and educate the orphan children of our soldiers and finally go to Central America, South America or the jungles of Africa to eat the apple of their discontent and die despised of men." As he exited the Eaker home, Paine told McChesney to build a fort around the court square and the courthouse. He demanded that the work be done as soon as possible.[14]

For the rest of the day, Paine moved forward with his program to secure the town and identify Rebel sympathizers. With the assistance of loyal Unionists who accompanied his army, he and McChesney created a list of disloyal citizens to be brought to headquarters and interrogated. Atop the list were William H. Miller, postmaster, D.M. Galloway, the county jailer, and local businessmen Amos Smith, William Hall, Charles McDonald, A.B. Carter and James A. McNutt. Paine authorized McChesney to seize the businesses and homes of the outspoken Southern sympathizers for military use and gave him free reign on where to house troops within the city. By the evening of August 12, Union troops had moved into every church, hotel and tobacco warehouse in Mayfield. They also took over the Graves County courthouse, the girls' seminary and the homes of identified secessionists.[15]

The following morning, a messenger arrived from Paducah with news of an attack made upon a Union garrison at Selma, twelve miles upstream from Smithland on the Cumberland River. The messenger reported that 200 Rebel cavalry were repulsed by sixty men of the Forty-Eighth Kentucky Volunteer Mounted Infantry but that there were over 1,000 men under the guerrilla Colonel Adam R. Johnson at Uniontown; the Rebels were disrupting river traffic along the Ohio and confiscating government property. Paine, fearing raids into his district, quickly gathered his staff and was en route to Paducah before noon. That same day McChesney removed Miller as postmaster and closed his grocery store. His men broke into Smith's store, appropriated and destroyed property and later occupied the building as a military post. McDonald's store was commandeered to serve as the office of McChesney's provost marshal. Property belonging to McNutt, Carter and Hall was confiscated, damaged or destroyed.[16]

Paine made it back to Paducah before nightfall passing the 136th Illinois Volunteer Infantry Regiment and a detachment of the Eighth Artillery, which were marching to Mayfield. More reports of guerrilla activity reached Paine's headquarters the next day as Colonel Johnson's Rebel force captured three steamers and a barge eight miles below Saline Landing. Along with the urgent reports from east of his district, Paine still had to deal with the ongoing problem of local businesses breaking trade restrictions. On August 13, T.J. Ashbrook, of Ashbrook, Ryan and Company, a wholesale grocer, sold a barrel of sulfur to J.P. Prince, of Prince and Dodd, a retail grocer. There was no witness to the sale but Redd had noticed a "considerable quantity of sulphur" on Ashbrook's store scale and on the pavement in front of his business. When Redd inquired who had the sulfur, the store's bookkeeper declared a transaction occurred earlier in the day between Ashbrook and Prince. Redd informed the bookkeeper that the sale of sulfur was in violation of trade regulations and that he was obligated to inform the military authorities. The army considered the yellow powder contraband; sulfur was used in medicines and in making gunpowder. The bookkeeper and later Ashbrook claimed ignorance of the regulation and offered to rescind the sale, but Redd replied the "deed was done" and they would have to "abide by the consequences." Redd informed Paine who immediately closed the stores of Ashbrook and Prince. Both men pled their innocence and eventually sought legal assistance from Congressman Anderson to reopen.[17]

At the same time, the Northern press continued to praise Paine's administration. A correspondent wrote the *Chicago Tribune* from Paducah that his policies had a "wonderful effect" and that "Union men were emboldened to speak their sentiments, treason was no more openly preached in [the] streets, and in truth Paducah is becoming quite a Union city." The article further maintained that "outrages upon Union men have ceased, and they are returning in peace and safety to their homes" and "guerrillas have pretty much left the vicinity of Graves and McCracken counties and order and quite is measurably restored." The writer concluded:

> We find that harsh measures are the best and will restore peace and the Union far quicker than the kid glove policy, which fights Rebels with rose leaves and would pay traitors instead of flogging them. The Union men all hope General Paine will be sustained, notwithstanding the Herculean efforts that are being made to remove him.[18]

Staunch Unionists approved of Paine's uncompromising approach to quelling the guerrillas. A nurse from Michigan working at the Marine Hospital wrote her sister in Lansing that Paine "evidently means to scour the country around here of guerrillas and all Union people are rejoiced." A resident of Paducah observed "we could see a difference in the feelings of the Union men, everybody, men, women and children who professed to be Union." A refugee from Calloway County testified that there had been a "radical change" since Paine's arrival and the "change was that there was no more shooting pickets around the place" and that "Union men who had been away from home three or four months and not permitted to go home to see their families went forty odd miles to visit their families." Bartling concurred and declared that it was "safe for a man to ride from here to the Tennessee line" where previously one "could not ride three miles with safety." One person remarked that "I heard no one complain of General Paine or his policy that claimed to be loyal."[19]

Paine's popularity and amongst the troops in his district reached its pinnacle in August of 1864. Soldiers garrisoned at Paducah before Paine took command said the post was in a "very dilapidated condition" and that military decisions were "imposed upon by the citizens." Many of the officers and men concluded

General Henry Prince (National Archives).

that decisions were made to appease affluent families and businessmen. To others, Paducah was vulnerable to attack and the lives of soldiers constantly under threat. Union officers who walked the streets alone reported being fired upon. A lieutenant colonel serving with the Eighth Artillery had been shot at numerous times. Law enforcement was regarded as ineffective, and the judicial system biased toward Southern sympathizers. In less than a month, Paine had a strict system of governance that protected the Unionist minority and gained the trust of the soldiers.[20]

While most citizens of Paducah hated Paine, he was considered by his associates to be a courteous and just administrator. Lieutenant Andrew Lucas Hunt, temporarily assigned to Paine's staff on August 6, wrote to his parents that he was "exceedingly pleasant and polite" and "pays as much attention to the negro soldier who is asking him for a house for his wife and children as he does to the congressman of the district." He shook hands with his staff every morning and when the guards on post saluted he would lift his hat and nod in recognition. Lieutenant Hunt said the General was "stern and strict in giving orders—just the man I would like to serve under." Paine regularly attended the Presbyterian Church where he listened to the sermons and "always bowed his head during the prayers." In the evening hours, Paine and his staff could be heard singing hymns from the balcony of the general's residence. He kept a small black and tan dog, which roamed the headquarters and was seemingly always underfoot. Paine was also fond of bird watching and made a pet of a squirrel that visited the residence from a nearby tree. Though he was later dehumanized by his detractors and political enemies, the soldiers and loyal citizens welcomed his presence in the city and respected his leadership.[21]

Paine, however, did have high-ranking enemies within his military district who sought to discredit his policies. General Prince at Columbus, still bitter about being superseded in rank by Paine the month prior, continued to speak negatively about his management of the district to anyone who would listen. Washburn, weary of the reports he received and the endless bickering amongst the two, removed Prince from command on August 14. Two days later, an agitated Prince wrote to Grant that Paine's "new policy propagates a new reign of terror by means of soldiers and hired assassins and unsettles every nook of society." He informed Grant of Kesterson's execution without a trial at Paducah, of "quiet and peaceable citizens" being banished to Canada and of Captain Gregory's "gang" being employed as executioners at Mayfield. He said he had not been a "participator in these acts" and "asked to be relieved—which has occurred from another authority." Grant did not respond to Prince. General Meredith at Cairo, though not as vocal as Prince, also communicated his discontent with Paine.[22]

After his return from Mayfield, Paine told his staff and others that he desired to resign. His health problems and growing opposition in Frankfort to making soldiers of slaves evidently prompted his decision. Paine set September 10, his forty-ninth birthday, as the day he wished to step down and return to his home in Monmouth. His secret was leaked to the press on August 14 and Unionist publications wanted him to stay. Democratic papers cheered the news of his departure.[23]

Meanwhile, news arrived of Rebel activity upriver. A small force of 200 men under Johnson crossed the Ohio and landed near Shawneetown, Illinois, on the night of August 13. The Rebels plundered farms and herded "200 fat cattle" and "sacked oats" to waiting barges, which they shipped to the Kentucky side of the river at Caseyville. Several Union transports that had grounded on a sand bar, eight miles below Shawneetown, were attacked the next day. The barges were boarded by Johnson's men and the government stores carried off. The steamers that towed the barges were later ransomed to their owners. In response, Paine received orders from Burbridge to lead 1,500 men to Uniontown on August 16 in an effort to encircle Johnson and his raiders. He immediately closed the Port of Paducah and pressed into service all boats tied to the docks and any boats traveling upriver. He gathered three regiments of infantry, the Thirty-Fourth New Jersey and the 132nd and 141st Illinois, a detachment of Cavalry and a battery of field guns from the Eighth Artillery. They embarked on the steamboats *Colossus, Fisher, General Lawrence* and *Arcola* for Uniontown on the morning of August 17. Before Paine departed, he ordered the return of the 136th Illinois and a battery of the Eighth Artillery from Mayfield to temporarily replace the regiments that left Paducah. He also informed Woodward to auction all seized tobacco deemed to be the property of Rebels.[24]

Illinois militia and a number of armed men sent Johnson's troops back across the river but "over one thousand guerrillas, armed with muskets, minie rifles, & ect.," supported by "intensely disloyal" inhabitants awaited on the Kentucky side. Johnson sent a message to the commander of the local militia that "if [they] would not resist, he would only take our Cannon and Government stores" and "if [they] resisted, he would plunder and destroy the town." Johnson's pickets repeatedly came down to the Kentucky shore to fire upon the town and only "solid shot from our cannon" drove them from the beaches.

"We cannot lay down at night without constant fear of our lives and property being destroyed," wrote a resident of Shawneetown to Governor Yates. As Paine's transports steamed up river, Johnson moved his men inland to avoid the firepower of the gunboats. The small flotilla passed Shawneetown and chugged on to Uniontown.[25]

The Union boats stopped down river from Uniontown before midnight on August 17. At 5:00 the next morning, Paine's men entered the town, but Johnson's command had been forewarned and departed the day before when troops under Brigadier General Alvin P. Hovey crossed the river from Indiana. Paine interrogated residents on the whereabouts of Johnson's force but received only claims of ignorance or tightlipped silence. Angered by their response, he ordered his men to confiscate the horses, cattle and other property of those who refused to cooperate. He also placed under arrest several prominent Southern sympathizers who had been identified by former slaves and returning Unionist refugees. At 2:00 p.m., Paine stationed 300 men at Uniontown and began the seven-mile march to Morganfield, the Union County Seat, where it was believed that Johnson had driven the cattle taken from Illinois. He reached Morganfield that evening at 6:00. He was notified that Hovey had moved south toward Madisonville in pursuit of Johnson earlier that day.[26]

Colonel Adam R. Johnson (*The Partisan Rangers of the Confederate States Army*, edited by William J. Davis).

Once at Morganfield, Paine set up a temporary headquarters to await further orders. Before nightfall, he sent a message to David C. James, a Union leader in the community, to meet with him the next morning. By daybreak, Paine decided to move his army southwest to Caseyville to cut off Johnson should he attempt to escape in that direction. During the meeting with James, Paine requested the names of all Union men between Morganfield and Caseyville. He gave Paine a list of about 12, but declared that "there were many others" whom he could not recall. When James asked what the list was for, Paine replied that it was his "objective was to take stock from all Southern sympathizers to pay for the stock captured by the Confederacy belonging to the United States." Paine then selected three slaves from nearby plantations to serve as guides to direct his infantry units on the three major roads to Caseyville. He informed his men that he did not "wish anything interrupted belonging to Union men."[27]

As the Union troops marched through the heart of Union County, they seized small arms, horses, cattle, buggies and carriages of those not recorded on James' list. They also destroyed property of outspoken Rebel supporters. One resident remarked afterwards that "farms were stripped of everything indiscriminately" and if owners were absent their "houses were sacked." Another recounted that Paine's men "broke into [his] house and piled up everything in the middle of the room and set fire to it." There were also numerous accounts of Yankee soldiers using abusive language and making threats. All along the route to Caseyville, slaves left their masters and followed the blueclad soldiers. Some of the male slaves were promised freedom and housing for their families by army recruiters if they came to Paducah and joined up. After a forced march of over twenty miles, the lead units of Paine's army began to arrive at Caseyville in a heavy rainstorm at about 7:00 p.m.[28]

Caseyville was a prosperous little village on the Ohio with a population of around 600. Early in the war, Forrest visited the place and wrote that his cavalry was welcomed with "smiles and cheers" and that the people "fed and greeted us kindly." Caseyville became a refuge for Rebel sympathizers and a center of guerrilla activity. Union steamboats that stopped were often robbed; passing boats were frequently fired on. Navy Commander Le Roy Fitch more than once threatened to destroy the place. In October of 1862, numerous citizens were found to be disloyal and arrested. Several months later, military authorities in the area levied assessments of over $35,000 to reimburse Union men for property taken by guerrillas. When Caseyville leaders refused to comply, they were arrested and sent to Paducah. A month before Paine's expedition, Lieutenant Colonel Samuel F. Johnson of the Fifty-Second Kentucky Infantry Regiment reported, while on patrol in Union County, that "it will take tremendous efforts to clear up this country" of Rebels. A citizen warned that Caseyville was a "great resort for guerrillas" and that they frequented the village "every three or four days" in the months prior to Paine's expedition. The soaked and footsore soldiers were not welcomed when they trudged through the village's muddy streets on the evening of August 19.[29]

Not long after entering the village, federal troops began to loot and ransack stores and warehouses on the main street and along the riverfront. The soldiers entered homes uninvited and demanded food and shelter from the storm. Peter Acker, a resident and business owner at Caseyville, recalled that he had between twenty-five and thirty men intrude upon his family dwelling the first night the village was occupied. The following morning, he caught several soldiers breaking into his store to find liquor. To appease the men and save his business from damage, Acker opened up and poured them drinks. Others came as word spread that whiskey was flowing. Soon, a number of intoxicated men were staggering in the streets. A neighbor of Acker's recalled that he "saw a great many drunk soldiers" loitering about and being obnoxious. Paine was informed by a staff member of the situation and immediately sent an officer and guards to close down Acker's establishment. A brief tussle occurred at the doorstep as one tipsy soldier refused to leave unless given another shot of liquor. When he refused to depart, the officer of the guard lifted him off the steps and threw him into the street. The officer then posted guards at the entrance and told Acker to lock the doors.[30]

An hour after the incident, Acker was arrested and charged for dispensing liquor to soldiers. A neighbor told Paine that Acker was an "obstinate malicious Rebel sympathizer"; a recently freed slave accused Acker of smuggling ammunition to guerrillas. Acker denied the accusations, but Paine ordered his store searched; troops found buckshot, pistol cartridges, a gun and more barrels of liquor. The ammunition and gun were confiscated and the liquor poured into the street. Acker appeared again before Paine who ordered that he be strung up by his thumbs and if not dead by evening he would be shot. Acker was brought to a large cedar tree at the center of the village and hoisted by his thumbs. However, the bed cords that were used to tie him kept slipping from his thumbs, so an officer tied the cords around his wrists and lifted him until he rested on his toes. Acker remained suspended for an hour until Paine had him untied and confined to his home.[31]

Before noon, Paine consulted with local Unionists and the colonel of the Union County Militia, G.L. Tombelle, to acquire the names of persons who were disloyal and aided the guerrillas so he could arrest them. Caseyville business owner David O. Conn topped the list. Paine had him arrested and sent men to confiscate anything of military use from his store. Conn's flour mill was broken into by thirty soldiers and twenty barrels and fifty sacks of flour were carried off. Another thirty men were sent to his general store where they broke down the door and took shoes and boots. Paine also seized the Curlew Mines, which Conn operated near Caseyville. Conn was brought to Paducah and imprisoned for a week before being released. Other Southern sympathizers that Paine targeted were John W. Hammock, Allen Omer, Caleb Tucker, Louis L. Talbott and Henry Parsons. All would have property seized and their homes and places of business ruined.[32]

Paine held a public meeting before his headquarters on the afternoon of the 20th to denounce the secessionist inhabitants for their misconduct. He accused them of encouraging guerrilla raids and aiding Johnson's men. He warned that "disloyal citizens and the Rebel sympathizers were to be made to pay for every Union man killed or wounded and for every dollar of property of a Union man burned, destroyed, stolen or carried off." He further declared that if another Union man was killed he would return with "fire and sword" and their "punishment should be terrible." He later asked the unconditional unionists to step to the right and those who were not to remain where they stood. Astonishingly, the entire crowd stepped to the right. When Paine asked how many of them supported the Emancipation Proclamation, several responded that they could not. He concluded the meeting by lecturing his listeners of their moral obligation to God and country.[33]

Throughout the day, confiscated cattle and horses were brought in and corralled at Commercial Point on the banks of the Tradewater River near the mill of John F. Alloway (Tradewater Mill). Colonel Peter Davidson of the 139th Illinois Infantry Regiment was placed in charge of the livestock. Paine told him to take only horses "serviceable for cavalry" and "fat cattle" to replace those stolen by Colonel Johnson's guerrillas. Davidson also acquired buggies and carriages to use as ambulances for the sick and wounded. As men arrived to reclaim their property, Davidson sent them to Paine's headquarters at Caseyville to settle their disputes. Paine met each of the men and simply asked if they were unconditional unionists. If they responded negatively, he denied them their property and loudly cursed them for being traitors. Those who established themselves as being loyal Union men had their property returned or were issued applications for government compensation.[34]

Late on the afternoon of the August 20, Paine's command herded the livestock and marched in two columns toward Smithland, one by way of Marion, and the other by Salem. Also traveling with the troops were over a dozen prisoners, including two Rebel spies who furnished "valuable information" to the Confederate forces in the region and partook in "destroying boats and capturing cattle." They were Richard Taylor and E.W.S. Matheny. Taylor was from Henderson, Kentucky, and had previously served as a private in the Tenth Kentucky Cavalry Regiment, Johnson's outfit. Matheny was from Smithland and had served with the Third Kentucky Mounted Infantry. Left behind at Caseyville was a detachment of 200 men to protect the loyal men in the village from Rebel retributions. From Smithland, Paine and his men pressed on to Paducah. On the outskirts of the city he met John Bolinger who informed him that guerrillas had threatened to burn his cotton and tobacco stored in warehouses at Hickman. Bolinger stated the situation needed immediate attention and requested permission to take the government steamer *Convoy* and remove the cotton and tobacco to safety. Paine had refused Bolinger's earlier requests to ship stocked merchandise from Hickman, but under the dire circumstances he granted permission. He stipulated that his son, Captain Phelps Paine, and an armed force accompany him to retrieve poll and county tax books held at Clinton, near Columbus, for the next month's scheduled assessments. Bolinger took the written permission and raced back to Paducah. The general reached the city at noon on August 21.[35]

Exhausted and ill from the expedition, Paine removed himself to his headquarters to write a final report of the expedition and to recuperate. Waiting for him on his desk were orders from Washington stressing that he was not under the command of General Burbridge and the Military District of Kentucky but with General Washburn and the Military District of West Tennessee, a confusion that Paine had tried to resolve prior to leaving for Uniontown.[36]

Paine wrote soon after the expedition that he had "seized sixty hogsheads of tobacco and shipped the same to Assistant Quarter Master at Evansville ... [and] also seized seventy four barrels of whiskey, one hundred and forty barrels of salt, two hundred and sixty bales of hay, belonging to the government, and seized and drove back here [Paducah] ninety head of cattle, one hundred forty seven horses and forty mules." He also confiscated ten buggies and carriages. The horses and mules were transferred to the military post's assistant quarter master and the customs surveyor received the whiskey, salt and cattle. The buggies and carriage were sent to the district provost marshal, Major Bartling, who sold them at auction with the proceeds added to the relief fund. The small arms were destroyed. An estimated 200 former slaves were also added to the muster rolls of the United States Colored Troops.[37]

Since Paine's departure from Mayfield on the morning of August 12, Colonel McChesney had taken little initiative to manage the troops under his command or build defenses about the city. The arrival of the 136th Illinois and a detachment of the Eighth Artillery the next day added to his problems as housing the existing troops was already a problem. Not having been issued tents, the men set up camp and slept anywhere they could find space. A soldier in the 134th Illinois wrote in his diary that his company slept on the brick pavement on the court square. A seemingly incurable illness that the colonel contracted at Columbus left him bedridden and incapable initiating construction plans for the fortifications. McChesney did follow Paine's advice and sent out scouting parties each day to scour the area for guerrillas. After receiving reports that citizens of Feliciana, in southern Graves County, had harbored and protected Rebels, McChesney sent a company of the Third Illinois Cavalry to burn the community to the ground. The company engaged a small Rebel force outside town on August 14, and after a minor skirmish the enemy escaped south to Tennessee with two wounded. Captain Robert H. Carnahan, the officer in charge of the detachment, chose not to torch Feliciana and left for Mayfield with a single prisoner late that afternoon.[38]

The arrival of Congressman Lucian Anderson in his hometown boosted the ardor of local Unionists, and on August 15 he organized a rally on the courthouse square. An Illinois soldier wrote in his diary that there was a "big crowd," which included, by the diarist's estimates, "many prominent guerrillas." Anderson and John Bolinger, who traveled with the congressman to Mayfield, made pro–Lincoln speeches in which they supported the emancipation of slaves in the "strongest terms." Bolinger began the rally by defining General Paine's policy. He declared that "one hundred Rebel families must be banished" from the United States and citizens of Graves County found not loyal to the Union cause "must pay $250,000." He also warned the audience that they must submit peaceably or necessary force would be applied. Bolinger also said that all able-bodied blacks must join the army to assist in the war effort. Anderson's presentation, less fiery, reiterated Bolinger's stand that people conform to Paine's control of the district and support the federal government.[39]

McChesney's health seemed to be on the mend on August 16 when he appointed Major John A. Wilson and Captain Samuel L. Andrews of the 134th Illinois to coordinate the construction of fortifications about the courthouse. Wilson was not well-liked by some troops in his regiment; he was considered a "very mean man" and one who "likes to show his authority." The first day, citizens were impressed to clean the streets in preparation of construction. The next day the doors and windows of the courthouse were boarded up with heavy oak planks punctured with loopholes for muskets and firing platforms were built. The laborers also commenced piling up earthworks at the north door entrance. After a few days of constructing fortifications, Private Thomas W.E. Belden, a trained civil engineer and graduate of Yale University, was detailed to lay out extensive earthworks about the courthouse. As the fortifications expanded, more laborers were required for the job and Wilson was given the task of locating men to do the work.[40]

The method he used to obtain laborers began with a list of names of men supplied by Unionist refugees who returned with Paine's army. A well-recognized Southern sympathizer was sent to notify the disloyal individuals to report to the post headquarters at Mayfield. The number of laborers was also supplemented by men who visited the town and could not provide proof of being a loyal citizen. Many of those who reported claimed to be Union men and sought exemption from work. All appeals for exemption were sent to Major Wilson who decided upon their loyalty and whether they were physically fit to work. In most instances, Wilson simply sought evidence they took the oath of allegiance or if a physician or surgeon found their condition too poor to perform hard labor. Captain Andrews would later recall that "many of the men ordered in to work were from old age and disease physically unfit to work." In cases where men were incapable of working, a substitute could be procured for a fee between $10 and $50, depending upon the individual's financial status. On a few occasions, influential men paid $300 to avoid work on the fortifications. Graves County Judge W.G. Blount was entrusted with furnishing substitutes and collecting fees. A week after he was assigned the position, he fell ill and Wilson took over those responsibilities. Andrews listed close to 1,000 names of those who worked on the fort before construction ceased on September 13.[41]

McChesney provided names of known Rebels in Graves County to Captain Gregory and ordered him to organize a band of cavalry to locate and confiscate all property that could be used by guerrillas. Gregory formed a group from the Home Guard and a few dozen members of the Third Illinois Cavalry to raid the farms and homes of the families on McChesney's list and any others found to be Southern sympathizers. His company primarily commandeered horses and mules, but they also carted away "hay, oats, hogs, apples, chickens, bacon, sweet potatoes, barley and grain." Within weeks, Gregory's band had stripped the county of most livestock and fodder. A resident of Mayfield remarked later that McChesney's troops had "ravaged the whole country, drove off and slaughtered nearly all the cattle and hogs within reach of town, both Union men and others, killing those unfit for beef for the hides [and] tore down nearly every log stable and house and barn in the town, burned rails for wood, destroyed the growing crop near town [and] cut down almost every shade tree in the village." McChesney's indifference toward military discipline led to other abuses as soldiers stole chickens from coops, bayoneted pigs in backyards and shot and slaughtered cows in pastures. An officer in the 134th Illinois wrote to his mother that "anything the men want they take" and that he was "very sorry to see so much confiscating going on." The troops became more brazen and uncontrollable each day they remained at Mayfield.[42]

As Gregory and his band raided the farms of Rebels, age-old vendettas among neighbors, which dated back before the war, resurfaced. The most extreme case was the murder of Eli Enoch. At dusk on August 17 a squad of men from the Home Guard rode to the farm of Robert Beasley, four and half miles east of Mayfield, where Beasley and Enoch were thrashing wheat in a field. The soldiers demanded that they and their horses be fed. When the men identified themselves to the soldiers, Enoch was told they had orders for his arrest. McChesney issued the order days earlier after Private Albert T. Riley of the Mayfield Home Guard accused Enoch of harboring guerrillas and being a Rebel spy. In truth, Riley had an "old grudge" to settle and purposely deceived McChesney to "procure Enoch's death." The Home Guards bound the hands of Enoch, put him on a horse and galloped toward Mayfield. Four hundred yards down the road the men stopped at Spence's Chapel, ordered Enoch to dismount at the adjacent cemetery and shot him. Two soldiers were sent back to Beasley's home to retrieve him and his father to bury Enoch who was still alive with two bullet holes in his chest when they arrived. He bled to death within the hour. When Beasley asked why they shot him, the soldiers replied they had orders to "kill all guerrillas." A few of the men apologized to Beasley and his father.[43]

On the morning of August 21, Privates John Hatfield and Aaron Abner from Company C of the Third Illinois Cavalry ventured about a mile beyond the Mayfield picket lines to a farm in search of buttermilk. They were ambushed by six guerrillas who killed Abner. But Hatfield ran to safety. When Hatfield returned and reported the incident, every available man in the Third Illinois went out in pursuit but failed to locate the perpetrators. Abner's body was found stripped and riddled with bullet holes. The corpse was brought to Mayfield and buried that afternoon. The men in his company vowed that his death would be avenged.[44]

Meanwhile, morale sagged among McChesney's troops. Their diaries and letters sent home described the deteriorating conditions and the constant fear of guerrillas while on picket duty or out on patrol. Lieutenant Hunt wrote to his mother on August 23 that "this is a miserable place to live in, we can't buy anything, no amusement [and] no water" and there is "nothing to do, nothing to read [and] can't sleep." The severe drought that ravaged the region necessitated water restrictions; the four wells on the courthouse square were dug deeper. But the water from the wells was muddy and the troops were eventually forbidden to use any water for washing. The number of men on sick call rose alarmingly from lack of clean water and proper diet. In the same letter to his mother, Hunt also expressed his fears of being in a hostile environment. He wrote "we are surrounded by Rebels" and that the picket was "fired upon four times last night." The following evening, Private Hawley V. Needham of the 134th Illinois Infantry jotted in his diary that "there was firing near the pickets" and horses stolen from the post's corral. The nightly guerrilla raids upon the city's outposts continued after dark. As morale sank further, McChesney remained reclusive. Hunt declared, "I have seen Colonel McChesney but once since I came here."[45]

Tensions were high when Gregory's scouts brought in a guerrilla named Walters, most likely Robert A. Walters, on August 24. The prisoner was caught about twenty miles south of the city. Soldiers in Gregory's Home Guard declared Walters a "notorious bushwhacker" and responsible for firing on Union picket lines. The following afternoon, Lieutenant Colonel John C. Bigelow, second in command at Mayfield, Lieutenant Hunt and Amos K. Tullis, the regimental chaplain of the 134th Illinois, interrogated the prisoner at the county jail for an hour and a half. Hunt found him to be "a most ignorant person" and very "surly and impudent." Walters confessed that he was at the Fort Pillow Massacre on April 12, 1864, and had joined Forrest's troops in shooting African American and white troops after they surrendered. He also confessed to shooting on the picket lines at Paducah two weeks earlier. He steadfastly denied being a guerrilla and pronounced himself to be a Confederate soldier. His neighbors and members of the Home Guard testified otherwise. The three interrogators reported to McChesney, who telegraphed Paine of their findings. Paine ordered Walters to be executed the next day. That evening, Lieutenant Hunt and Chaplain Tullis encouraged him to seek the Lord's forgiveness. Walters said his captors could do "what we wished with him" and "expect to be avenged."[46]

At eight o'clock the following morning, Lieutenant Colonel Bigelow marched the entire 134th Illinois beyond the picket lines to a field between a brick warehouse and the railroad tracks. Centered in the field was a six by three foot hole with a coffin placed next to it. The regiment formed up behind men working on the fortifications who were ordered out to watch Walters die. The cavalry was placed behind the 134th to prevent anyone from removing himself from the event. The prisoner was brought to the field by a dozen of Gregory's men. Lieutenant Hunt noted that Walters "walked with a firm step." The chaplain stepped up to Walters and said a brief prayer before one of Gregory's lieutenants tied his legs and blindfolded him. Before they could tie his hands, he reached up with both arms and cried for mercy. Two more men stepped up and tied his hands. Once they were secured, Colonel McChesney nodded to Lieutenant Charles E. Sinclair, who commanded the firing squad. Sinclair lined up Gregory's men fifteen paces from the target and ordered them to fire. At roughly 11:00 a.m., ten shots burrowed into the chest of Walters and he dropped immediately. The regiment's physician walked up, kneeled over the body and pronounced him dead. Colonel McChesney then ordered the men that worked on the fortification to step forward and view the body. McChesney warned, "men you have been brought out here to see a guerrilla shot—this shall be your fate if you are ever caught harboring guerrillas or bushwhackers or if any of you know of the approach or whereabouts of guerrillas and do not inform the Federal troops." Four of the workers were selected to place the body in the coffin and lower it in the grave. As they shoveled dirt on the wooden box, the other workers were led back to the courthouse and the soldiers returned to their duties.[47]

Meanwhile McChesney's health appeared to improve as he was seen more frequently outside of his headquarters and he was more attentive to his duties as post commander. He also became involved in city commerce. William Hall, a merchant and business partner of John Eaker, approached McChesney to ship tobacco worth between eight and ten thousand dollars to Paducah. McChesney was reluctant but after Hall's loyalty was determined, he allowed the shipment to proceed, with one condition: that he be given a hogshead of tobacco. Hall was not interested in the offer, but McChesney threatened to put him to work on the fortifications and have the tobacco distributed amongst the soldiers if he did not agree. Hall conceded and gave him the tobacco, which McChesney later sold at a poor price and told Hall that it was "nothing but a hogshead of root." McChesney retaliated when Hall approached him again and requested permission to ship five boxes of processed tobacco. McChesney demanded two of the boxes before he released the other three. Hall consented. During their conversation, McChesney noticed Hall toying with two silver half dollars, which he asked to see. Hall tossed him the coins; McChesney pocketed them and told his guest to leave.[48]

The extortion of property and money by McChesney did not end with Hall. Throughout his stay, he acquired items he found of interest. From the home of B.H. Clois he took a double barrel shotgun and a squirrel rifle. Mrs. Chapel Mayes had a clock taken and John Eaker a field surveyor's compass and chain. McChesney also collected fines and licensing fees, which he rarely documented or reported to the post adjutant or provost marshal. The fees for licenses included six dollars for every grocery store and barber shop, three dollars for medicines sold at drug stores and seven dollars for keeping dogs, plus an additional dollar per dog. The canine tax was abolished on September 1 when McChesney ordered all dogs within his command exterminated. He aimed to stop roaming dogs from barking and giving away the location of guards and pickets. The colonel also confiscated for his personal use groceries, coffee, cigars, drugs and other goods.[49]

At Paducah, Paine continued to receive orders from Burbridge though he was not assigned to the District of Kentucky. On August 22, Paine was ordered to grant a permit to Lawrence Flournoy to transport and sell goods from the city port. Flournoy was in New York City and the order was delivered by Samuel Hinton, a business associate and family friend. Paine suspended the execution of the order until he could tell Burbridge that Flournoy was a smuggler. Paine told Hinton that Flournoy was a "damned secessionist" and that he had "run off with the camp belles."[50]

Delegations from Union County had come before Paine a few days after his return to Paducah. They testified to the loyalty of family members and friends imprisoned at the post guardhouse. On August 23, seven prisoners were brought before Paine. He accused them of being members of the Sons of Liberty, a secret pro-southern organization in the midwest, but Paine had no proof. Unable to legally detain them further, he vowed, "I am going to send you damned sons of bitches home" and they were released. The Confederate spies Taylor and Matheny suffered the ultimate punishment.[51]

Earlier that day, Paine ordered Colonel Barry at Fort Anderson to execute both Taylor and Matheny. At 9:00 a.m., sixteen members of the Eighth Artillery, under the command of Captain Harlow B. Norton, marched the men under guard north of the fort along the banks of the Ohio River. Both were blindfolded and their hands fastened behind their backs. The soldiers were lined up before the prisoners and issued cartridges. Norton informed them that half were blanks and half were live rounds. Eight were directed to fire at Taylor and the others at Matheny. As they loaded their muskets, Chaplin Liston H. Pierce of the 132nd Illinois Infantry walked up to the prisoners and offered last rites. Both confessed their guilt but they were unprepared for death. Pierce provided what comfort he could and left the men alone with their heads bowed. Captain Norton then cried out, "Ready, Aim…. Fire." The shots echoed across the river to the Illinois side as the men fell lifelessly to the ground.[52]

Reports of another Confederate raid into the Purchase came to the attention of Paine a few days after the executions. Colonel James N. McArthur, who recently replaced General Prince as post commander at Columbus, wrote to Paine that a spy overheard a conversation between Generals Forrest and Abraham Buford, his subordinate, in which they discussed a combined assault into west Kentucky with the point of attack at Mayfield. Unlike his predecessors, Paine chose not to recall his troops to Paducah but to further

Fort Anderson at Paducah, Kentucky (Library of Congress).

reinforce Mayfield. He ordered the Thirty-Fourth New Jersey Infantry Regiment from Columbus and two companies of the Seventh Tennessee Cavalry Regiment from Moscow to assist in the defense of city. He boarded a train to Mayfield the next day to inspect the troops and examine the fortifications. Before his departure, he issued General Order No. 11, which required all boats that landed in the district to report to district headquarters prior to setting off. He also instructed all steamers within his district to charge half fares to any soldiers or their wives and families seeking transportation. While at Mayfield, he consulted McChesney and his staff on the conditions in and about the city. He was apprised that the fortifications at the courthouse were almost complete and that sniping at pickets had declined significantly since Gregory's men had captured three known guerrillas in recent days. Paine stayed at the Eaker house that evening where the general, the colonel and his staff told stories and sang songs late into the night.[53]

By morning, Paine was prepared to return to Paducah. He ordered McChesney to keep his troops near the courthouse so they could retire to the fortifications if attacked and to beef up patrols. Paine also recommended that McChesney assign Lieutenant Sinclair as the post's provost marshal to better document the taxes, fees and property received from Southern sympathizers. Paine left behind Lucien L. Lambert, acting assistant inspector general for the District of Western Kentucky, to perform a general inspection of all troops stationed at Mayfield. The inspection was completed later that morning when Lambert quickly passed and reviewed each of the companies and scribbled down any problems in his notebook. He remarked to one of the officers of the 134th Illinois, that he "never inspected a more tidy and neat regiment." He returned with his report to Paducah that afternoon.[54]

As night fell on August 29, shots were heard from near the picket line, and the entire post rushed to the fortifications. After an hour, the men were ordered to return to their lodgings in hotels, churches and warehouses. A few hours later, they were again called to the fort, but it was only a few Rebels firing at patrols a short distance from the city. At noon the next day, Captain Gregory's men brought in a prisoner captured the day before in a small skirmish, which involved sixteen guerrillas. The Home Guard killed one but the rest escaped into the night. The man they caught was Henry Bascom Hicks, known to many in town as "Bud," a seventeen-year-old schoolboy from Farmington in Graves County. He was interrogated by McChesney, Gregory and few of his staff. Hicks confessed that he was a guerrilla but had belonged to the band for only two weeks. It was also known that his older brother David was an officer in the Confederate army. McChesney without hesitation ordered Hicks to be shot at 3 o'clock. Hicks replied that "they had him in their own hands and they could dispose of him as they pleased—he was man enough to face the music." He was taken to the county jail to await his fate.[55]

At the appointed time, Hicks was removed from his cell and marched under guard to the edge of town where a shallow grave awaited him. Before the condemned teen were a group of off-duty soldiers, curious civilians and a line of eight men with carbines. One of Gregory's officers read aloud the charge and the sentence. He acknowledged the officer with a nod but calmly requested not to have his hands bound or to be blindfolded. His second plea was ignored and a man tied a handkerchief over his eyes. He asked the man not to tie it too tightly. Standing erect, Hicks awaited his fate. A short time after three o'clock the order was given to aim and fire. Shots rang out and he fell to the earth. The teen was dropped into the hole without a coffin and his hat placed over his face. A few minutes later, a man who worked on the fortifications was told to cover the body with dirt. No marker was to be placed at his grave. A soldier who witnessed the event wrote in his diary, that Hicks was "game to the last" and "his bearing was worthy of one who was to die in a better cause."[56]

During the waning days of August, Paine became involved in another dispute over the finances of a private citizen and a local bank. On August 30, May Kerr approached Colonel Barry claiming that the Norton Brothers Bank of Paducah owed her $150 in gold and refused to pay. Mrs. Kerr informed Barry that the bank would not pay in gold but in treasury notes, which were worth fifty dollars less than the gold. Barry, acting on behalf of Mrs. Kerr, visited the bank to retrieve the money. The cashier, John C. Steele, declared that Mrs. Kerr withdrew the money the previous fall and that the account was empty. Barry ordered the cashier to pay him immediately in gold or he would order the bank closed. Upset, Steele went to Paine's headquarters to protest but was turned away at the door. Paine knew the situation and chose not to hear Steele's complaint. Paine had been told earlier by his advisors that the absentee owner of the bank, William F. Norton, was an associate of Lawrence Trimble and was considered to be disloyal. Steele later accused Barry of using the gold as a payment for services rendered by Mrs. Kerr, whom he noted as a "woman of loose character." No evidence seems to indicate that Mrs. Kerr was a prostitute, outside of Steele's allegations.[57]

The month of August ended well for Paine and the Unionists of the Jackson Purchase. The District of Western Kentucky had a military force of over 4,500 men and several heavy artillery pieces to protect the region. Efforts to recruit men at Mayfield had been initiated by Captain Joseph F. Peck, a former officer of the Fifteenth Kentucky Cavalry, with limited success. The railroad between Paducah and Fulton had been repaired and the line from Union City to Columbus was close to completion. Unionists were able to travel safely throughout the district. At Mayfield, Union men claimed that the "guerrillas were going off" and that they would "rather have him [Paine] than any man that had ever been in command of this post." Even Union County, which did not fall under Paine's command, reported that there were "very few guerrillas in that country" and "very little property disturbed" since his expedition. A correspondent for the *Chicago Tribune* wrote on September 1, "it is now over thirty days since he [Paine] took command and matters in West Kentucky never presented so promising a face before." The "firm hand" that General Washburn expressed as being required when Paine was issued his orders on July 16 appeared to be working effectively.[58]

General Henry A. Tyler (*Confederate Veteran Magazine*).

September of 1864 began with increased cavalry patrols to ward off rebel invaders and pursue guerrillas. On the first of the month, a scouting party of forty-five men under Lieutenant Samuel T. Lucas surprised fifteen guerrillas near the Tennessee border. The guerrillas hastily retreated after a brief gunfight, which wounded two of Lucas' men. The Rebels left behind five rifles and eleven horses and mules that were brought back to Mayfield. The next day Paine sent out a circular requesting that all 100 day troops serving in his district remain for an additional fifteen days beyond their expiration time. He promised each man would receive a medal for his service, with extra pay. With less than three weeks before their service expired and repeated rumors of Forrest's intentions to raid West Kentucky, Paine was pressed to solicit the troops to stay longer. The troops at Cairo, Columbus and Paducah voted to remain the extra fifteen days, but those at Mayfield overwhelmingly voted down the request. Paine responded by sending a special messenger to Mayfield on September 4 to ask if the men would stay for additional seven days. Again, they voted no. Private Needham of the 134th Illinois scribbled in his diary that "someone is making money in the place and to stay here without water with a heavy sick list and more becoming so every day" was justification enough to reject Paine's final appeal to stay on.[59]

Colonel McChesney and Lieutenant Colonel Bigelow took the train to Paducah to convey the news to Paine. While en route, McChesney became gravely ill. His health, which had recently shown signs of getting better, now took a turn for the worse. After he delivered the results of the regiment's vote, McChesney's surgeon, Dr. Danforth, acquired a pass for him to report to Governor Yates in Springfield. Before leaving for Chicago, he telegraphed his orderly, Private James Fanning, to pack his belongings and send them to his residence in Chicago. Inside the large wooden crate, along with his clothing and personal papers, were numerous items stolen by McChesney. They included boxes of cigars and tobacco, books, a clock, gold watch, surveyor's equipment, a shotgun, a rifle with the name "Enoch" carved in the stock and other items taken from residents of Mayfield. Fanning nailed on the box lid, wrote the address on the crate and prepared it to be shipped by rail to Chicago. The crate remained at post headquarters until the next train left for Paducah. Lieutenant Edward D. Luxton, provost adjutant of the 134th Illinois, was placed in charge of delivering the crate. McChesney did not go to Springfield as ordered; instead, he returned directly to his parents' home in Chicago to recuperate from his illness.[60]

As Paine contemplated how to replace McChesney and the 134th Illinois at Mayfield, a coup to remove the general from command was set in motion at Frankfort. After receiving a number of reports and verbal complaints from Paine's political enemies, Governor Bramlette sent Lieutenant Colonel Jesse J. Craddock of the First Regiment Capital Guards on a clandestine mission to Paducah. Craddock returned a few days later and reported to Bramlette. On September 2, the governor wrote President Lincoln that the "citizens of Western Kentucky have for a long while been the subjects of insult, oppression and plunder by officers who have been placed to defend and protect them." He declared that the people of Kentucky were "not willing to sacrifice a single life or imperil the smallest right of free white men for the sake of a negro." With the presidential election a little more than a month away and his reelection far from certain, Lincoln consulted Grant on how to resolve Bramlette's grievances regarding Paine. Grant recalled numerous difficulties with Paine earlier in the war and after reading Craddock's report recommended his immediate removal from command. The next day, Grant telegraphed Halleck to remove Paine, claiming that "he is not fit to have a command where there is a solitary family within his reach favorable to the Government." On September 5, Halleck directed General Burbridge to relieve Paine. Burbridge telegraphed Paine the following evening ordering him to turn over command to General Meredith at Cairo. The dispatch was received at Paducah on September 7 but was not read by Paine until the morning of the eighth.[61]

Congressman Anderson was at Mayfield when the news of Paine's dismissal arrived. He was taken aback by the news, because the president told him a few weeks earlier in Washington that Paine would remain in command. He boarded the first train to Paducah, determined to save his general. Paine was ill and confined to his bed when Anderson met him on the morning of September 9. The general's condition left him physically incapable to mount a defense. Anderson took up his cause and telegraphed Stanton to revoke Grant's order immediately or the "Union men in this end of the State will all leave." He concluded the missive that if Paine is removed "all is lost." Anderson also sent telegrams and mailed letters to his political allies in Washington imploring them to beg Lincoln to reverse his decision. He encouraged his friend Green Adams, a former congressman from Kentucky and the auditor for the Treasury Department, to tell Lincoln to revoke the order. Adams hand delivered a dispatch to Lincoln from Anderson. His last appeal to Lincoln urged him to retain Paine in command at least until after the election in November. Neither the president nor the secretary of war responded to Anderson's pleas. His efforts having failed, Anderson wrote Adams that "I will write no more I am too damn mad."[62]

Two days before Paine was notified of his removal from command, he ordered the execution of a prisoner named Hess. He had been apprehended weeks earlier for guerrilla activities. On the morning of September 6, a squad of soldiers from the Eighth Artillery, led by Lieutenant Richard Schofield, dragged Hess to the banks of the Ohio River below Fort Anderson. His legs were tied together, his wrists bound and the prisoner was blindfolded. Scholfield's men lined up, leveled their muskets and shot Hess. Their aim was low and he fell wounded. Still conscious, Hess lifted himself on his elbows, pulled the blindfold from his eyes and begged for mercy. A private from 132nd Illinois Infantry, who witnessed the event, recalled that after "seeing the squad of negroes reloading their muskets [he] begged them for God's sake not to shoot him again but to take him to the hospital declaring that he was innocent." His desperate appeals were disregarded as Schofield ordered four members of his squad to step forward for the coup de grace. Hess was the last of the executions in Paducah under Paine.[63]

The executions at Mayfield continued until official word of Paine's removal reached the post on September 12. The same day that Hess was shot in Paducah, scouts of the Third Illinois Cavalry Regiment skirmished with over forty guerrillas near Boydsville. In a two and a half mile chase near the border of Tennessee, the Union soldiers shot and killed one and captured another. They returned with a prisoner named John Johnson to Mayfield early that afternoon. Upon arrival, Johnson was brought for interrogation before Colonel William H. Lawrence of the Third Illinois Cavalry, post commander since McChesney's departure. Johnson maintained he was a soldier in the Confederate army and was with General Forrest when he attacked Paducah. Captain Gregory, along with members of the community who claimed to know Johnson, declared that he might have been a Rebel soldier but was presently a guerrilla. With the evidence available, Lawrence concluded that the "proof was too positive" and sentenced him to be executed at 4:00 p.m. At the appointed time, Johnson was brought to the outskirts of town where a freshly dug grave awaited him. As Gregory's men prepared to complete their assigned task, a thunderstorm broke, and everybody scattered for cover. Gregory called for a postponement until the storm passed. Within a few hours the dark clouds dissipated, and Johnson was once again placed before the foot of his grave.[64]

Johnson moaned and murmured a prayer as his feet sank slowly in the mud. As Gregory's men blindfolded him and bound his wrists and ankles, he began screaming for mercy. Private Needham wrote in his diary that Johnson "broke out into the wildest lamentations, prayers and ejaculations [and] with his last breath denied being guilty." The firing squad of twelve men aimed at his chest and fired. He buckled and fell instantly to the ground. Needham reflected later that I "never wish to see another execution similar to this." The last of the executions at Mayfield was over, but the Union occupation of the town lasted for several more weeks.[65]

The next day a squad of Gregory's men shot two other guerrillas while out on a scouting mission. With the departure of Colonel McChesney, Gregory and his men became more emboldened. On September 10, Needham wrote in his diary that "Gregory's men shot two more guerrillas—four less than a week ago." Sergeant Hardie N. Revelle of the Thirty-Fourth New Jersey Infantry wrote his brother from Mayfield that "Gregory and [his] men have enlisted under the black flag [and] they ask no quarters and give none."[66]

Paine's health deteriorated further after he was removed from command. His surgeon, Dr. Robert F. Baker of the 132nd Illinois Infantry, found him incapable of performing his duties and recommended his discharge. His diagnosis was "dyspepsia or chronic gastritis of long standing which is now rapidly increasing in severity and accompanied with frequent and excruciating paroxysms of neuralgia of the stomach bowels and intestinal muscles resulting in nutritional anemia and general debility of the nervous system threatening complete destruction of health." Baker concluded that Paine's "degree of disability was total" and that he was not fit enough for even the veteran reserve corps. Two days later, Paine tendered his resignation to Adjutant General Thomas and enclosed the surgeon's recommendation. He requested that it be made effective on October 13, the date he wrote President Lincoln accepting his appointment as brigadier general three years earlier. He declared that "I have always served my country with the earnest desire to destroy its enemies." Thomas received his resignation but offered no reply.[67]

General Meredith arrived at Paducah from Cairo to assume command on the evening of September 11. With his departure, the War Department assigned Cairo to the District of Illinois, which was headquartered at Springfield and commanded by his cousin Brigadier General Halbert Eleazer Paine. Meredith visited the bedridden Paine, who informed him that the five regiments of one hundred–day troops from Illinois were to return home soon and that only two heavy artillery units and 400 men of Thirty-Fourth New Jersey would remain to defend the entire district. He also told Meredith that the lone cavalry detachment, the Third Illinois stationed at Mayfield, was ordered to Memphis the day before and would be en route the next morning. Unprepared for the departure of close to 5,000 men and the loss of all cavalry except for Captain Gregory's Home Guard, he telegraphed Halleck that night requesting reinforcements to be sent immediately. Before going to his quarters for the night, Meredith told his staff he would address the troops the next day and visit Mayfield in the next few days.[68]

On the morning of the twelfth, Paine issued General Order No. 15, which appointed Meredith commander of the district. He informed Meredith that he would depart Paducah the next day but would leave a few members of his staff to assist with the transition of command. Meredith quickly rescinded the order that prohibited banks from paying depositors, reopened some trade in the district, released the prisoners Paine had incarcerated and freed the exiles to come home. That evening, a large group of citizens led by W.H. Jones, a former McCracken county attorney, assembled in front of Meredith's headquarters and told the general that Paducah was a "loyal and law abiding community" and promised their "cordial cooperation in maintaining the supremacy of the Government." Meredith responded that he would not be influenced by any one group and had "no money making schemes to accomplish." He further said that "no man's blood should be attached to his rule [and] that if anyone under his command should suffer death, it would be by the act of a properly organized commission…." His remarks were loudly applauded, and one man said that "he was the right man in the right place."[69]

Meredith was a fifty-four-year-old North Carolina native who moved to Indiana before the war. He joined the army shortly after Fort Sumter, became colonel of the Nineteenth Indiana Infantry and fought at the Second Battle of Bull Run, where he was severely wounded. He recovered, was promoted to brigadier and commanded the storied "Iron Brigade" in the battles of Chancellorsville and Gettysburg. Wounded even more seriously at Gettysburg, he was judged physically unfit for field command and sent to the rear-area at Cairo. His command at Paducah would be just as troubled as Paine's administration had been.[70]

The official notice of Paine's removal from command reached Mayfield on September 12. The townsfolk and soldiers were also informed that Meredith would visit the following day. The new commander arrived late on the morning of the thirteenth and called for an assembly of the troops and the residents near the courthouse. He began his speech by declaring that all men who had worked on the fortifications were free to go home. The fortifications were to be leveled by the troops and the courthouse and courtsquare returned to their previous condition. All horses and mules confiscated from disloyal citizens were to be returned and buildings used for military purposes to be evacuated and restored to their owners. He next read the criminal charges made against Colonel McChesney and announced that he would be arrested and tried in a military court. But he disappointed the hundred days men, ordering them to remain on active duty for two or three weeks until reinforcements could be sent. A few men protested. Meredith shouted that they needed to be taught discipline and that he was going to "make soldiers of them." The meeting ended and the soldiers were dismissed. Meredith boarded the next train to Paducah.[71]

The men of the 134th Illinois were infuriated by Meredith's proclamation. Private Needham wrote in his diary that night:

> instead of carrying out Paine's policy of hunting Rebels he [Meredith] takes them in his loving embrace—going to have a love feast. I suppose he is going to feed in the same trough with the lousy grey backs and they will become Union men. Oh! Won't they? Sent them all home to bushwhack as much as they please. I hope they will catch someone, but us poor devils are due to be kept a while to make soldiers of us. Go home vets, won't we? Gregory's men are so mad they threaten to disband. Everyone jaws or curses or threatens or swears.[72]

Lieutenant Hunt wrote to his mother a day later that "we will have no more military executions for they must be against General Meredith's policy but a man who will sneak up on a picket and shoot him ought to be shot when he is caught." He wrote his brother three days later that "General Meredith is just the opposite to General Paine—he is a Copperhead" and "afraid of hurting a Rebel." Morale disintegrated, and the number of soldiers on sick call in the days following Meredith's visit rose to almost 200. A few officers wrote letters to the governor of Illinois and political friends to have them sent home. Lieutenant Hunt's father wrote Governor Yates, asking that his son and the rest of the regiment be "immediately sent home and muster'd out of the Service."[73]

Four

"A Reign of Terror"

On the afternoon of September 13, Brigadier General Speed S. Fry, Colonel John M. Brown and Lieutenant Colonel Craddock arrived at Paducah to launch an inquiry into Paine's administration. Fry and Brown were appointed by General Burbridge as a board of investigation. Fry was a native of Danville, attended Centre College and was a Mexican-American War veteran. He joined the Union army early in the war and helped establish Camp Dick Robinson, the first recruiting center for Union troops in Kentucky. He saw combat at the Battle of Mill Springs on January 19, 1862, and was said to have shot Confederate General Felix K. Zollicoffer. He was promoted to commander of the Eastern Division of Kentucky and established his headquarters at Camp Nelson, the largest training facility for African Americans in Kentucky. In the spring of 1864, he was assigned to recruit and train African American men from Kentucky to serve in the United States Army. Like most white Kentuckians, he opposed blacks serving in the military. While in command at Camp Nelson, he refused to feed and shelter the families of black recruits and turned them away in cold weather. Many died. Fry was at Camp Nelson when he received Burbridge's telegraph to serve on the board.[1]

Colonel Brown was temporarily stationed at the headquarters of the Military District of Kentucky in Lexington when Burbridge approached him to assist Fry. Brown was a native of Frankfort and a graduate of Yale; he practiced law in St. Louis and Louisville prior to the war. He was the son of Kentucky's first United States Senator, James Brown, and half-brother of Senator Benjamin Grazt Brown of Missouri. He served as an officer in the Tenth Kentucky Cavalry early in the war and took part in numerous skirmishes in Eastern Kentucky, East Tennessee and Western Virginia. In January of 1864, he was assigned to the Forty-Fifth Kentucky Infantry Regiment and three months later promoted to command the Fourth Brigade, First Division of the District of Kentucky. Brown led his brigade against General John Hunt Morgan's cavalry in May and June of 1864 and engaged the enemy at Mt. Sterling and Cynthiana.[2]

Lieutenant Colonel Craddock was second in command of the "Capital Guards" at Frankfort in September of 1864. Bramlette appointed him on January 26, 1864, after the legislature approved a resolution empowering the governor to raise a military force to defend the state. Craddock had served as an officer in the Second Kentucky Cavalry Regiment and had seen action at Shiloh, Perryville and Chickamauga. He also served as Bramlette's primary helper in the removal of Paine. Craddock was a native of Hart County, Kentucky, and like the governor, Fry and Brown, he was a conservative Union Democrat. The three men had a clear agenda: build a case for Paine's ouster.[3]

Fry brought the order to remove Colonel Barry as post commander and replaced him with Colonel Hicks. Barry had been accused of extortion, theft and abusive language unbecoming of an officer in a report sent to Governor Bramlette days earlier. The black soldiers under Barry's command mistrusted Hicks. They recalled Hicks' attempts to return refugee families of soldiers to slavery and his confining Barry. They also were aware of Fry's mistreatment of black refugees at Camp Nelson. A number of them denounced Fry as a "secesh" general and a traitor. Hicks, upon hearing the angry remarks, arrested some of them and put them in the guardhouse. That evening, Paine and his wife Charlotte, who came from Monmouth to help her ailing husband, boarded a steamboat for St. Louis.[4]

The board of investigation began to take oral testimonies at 11 a.m. on September 14. The first to be interviewed was Major Bartling, who was asked a series of questions that focused on the seizure of businesses, confiscation of private property, the loyalty of the citizens, taxes and fees Paine imposed and the financial management of the military district during the general's administration. Nineteen others were questioned by Brown and Fry that afternoon and the following day, including the assistant adjutant quartermaster, surveyor of the port, members of Paine's staff and local businessmen and government officials. Each interview addressed specific allegations made against Paine from reports forwarded to Frankfort. The most significant of those reports was from Brigadier General Jeremiah T. Boyle, who on September 8, wrote a letter on "behalf of an oppressed and injured people" of Western Kentucky to Burbridge. The letter listed a dozen charges against Paine, stemming from corruption to "cowardly acts of oppression and cruelty," and demanded he be put on "trial before a proper judicial tribunal."[5]

Boyle was a Union Democrat and friend of Bramlette. He also was the former commander of the District of Kentucky and his nephew, John Boyle, was adjutant general of Kentucky in 1863 and 1864. His opposition to emancipation and the enlistment of black soldiers led to his dismissal from the army on January 12, 1864. Afterwards, Boyle and his nephew established a law partnership and lucrative trading business in Louisville. His involvement with the investigation into Paine stemmed from a dispute over shipments of tobacco from Paducah to Louisville. Paine's trade restrictions initiated a bitter feud between the two men. The conflict worsened when Paine rejected Boyle's letters proclaiming the loyalty of his business partners and when he denied Boyle's requests to release the shipments. Boyle, incensed, wrote Burbridge, who ordered Paine to allow the shipments. Paine refused, informing Burbridge that he had indisputable proof that the men in question were disloyal. Boyle later claimed that Paine attempted to extort money from his nephew by placing a $100 fee for every hogshead of tobacco shipped from Paducah to Louisville. Boyle was determined to bring down Paine.[6]

Soon after the interrogations concluded, some of those interviewed claimed that responses that reflected positively on Paine were not recorded and demanded that they be added to the record. Their demands were disregarded. Two of Paine's staff officers recalled being threatened by Fry that if they did not supply satisfactory answers, they would be arrested and sent to the guardhouse. Craddock posted notifications all about the city requesting information on allegedly illegal activities conducted during Paine's command. They brought a tremendous response as people "rushed en masse" to file grievances and seek restitution. For several days, Fry and Brown collected written statements and evidence from over ninety residents and military personnel. Colonel Brown wrote his friend Daniel W. Lindsey, the adjutant general of Kentucky, that the "work to be done here looms bigger and bigger daily" and the massive collection of affidavits was

Left: General Speed S. Fry (Library of Congress). *Above*: Colonel John M. Brown (Kentucky Digital Library).

enough to "burn a wet mule." On September 15, Fry sent Captain Henry B. Grant, inspector general for the Military District of Kentucky, to Mayfield to conduct interviews and hire notaries to take written statements. He gathered over fifty affidavits from citizens of Mayfield and Graves County. Fry also sent an officer to Uniontown, Morganfield and Caseyville. Over two dozen complaints were filed from the communities in late September and early October. The Board also accumulated sworn testimonies from Hickman, Ballard, Calloway and Livingston Counties and from Louisville and Lexington. In all, over 200 affidavits and statements were presented to the board.[7]

The vast majority of affidavits sought compensation from the federal government for reputed financial losses during Paine's administration. Some of the claims filed for damages occurred prior to Paine's command and others were submitted to county courts before the arrival of the board in Paducah. The more notable claims were from business owners in Paducah and Caseyville. In most cases, the affiants claimed that horses, mules, hogs and chickens had been seized. Some affidavits had attached itemized lists that included razors, combs, clothes, hats, shoes, knives, pencils, pens, books, playing cards, a French harp (harmonica) and numerous perishables, such as grain, hay, oats, barley, corn, potatoes, apples, raisins and other foods. A number of men in Mayfield and Graves County sought reimbursement for exemption fees and payments made to substitutes for work on the courthouse fortifications. Slave owners in Union County wanted their runaway slaves returned or compensation for their loss of property. The applications for restitution exceeded over $150,000 or about $2 million today.[8]

Along with the hundreds of statements and affidavits, Fry requested all the financial records and papers kept by Major Bartling and Lieutenant Luxton, the post adjutant at Mayfield. Bartling initially balked at the request. He was not entirely sure of the integrity of the board and wrote Meredith asking that a "competent officer" be appointed in charge of the transfer of records and that he be provided a receipt of all contents. He also sent Meredith an iron safe, which included the soldier relief fund, provost marshal fund, loose checks and his own private savings. Luxton delivered the records in his possession to

Captain Grant along with a signed affidavit that said he forwarded all funds received to Major Bartling at Paducah and that Colonel McChesney "never kept an account of the moneys received by him or paid out while he was in command at Mayfield." Grant also confiscated McChesney's wooden crate and had it sent to Meredith at Paducah. On the recommendation of the board, Meredith ordered the arrest of McChesney on September 20.[9]

On September 15, a telegraph dispatch from a correspondent of the *St. Louis Republican* was sent from Paducah with charges of corruption, brutality and mass murder. It was intercepted by the telegrapher at Cairo and brought to Colonel Peter Davidson, the post commander. He "disapproved" of the content of the dispatch and stopped it. The correspondent sent it by steamboat to St. Louis and it got in the paper. The correspondent wrote that Paine was in command "fifty-six days and shot sixty-seven men" and that not one was "ever tried by a military commission or a court of any kind." He also claimed that Meredith released fifty-one men from the jail at Mayfield and the guard house at Paducah. The author praised General Meredith's assumption of command and wrote that the "bloody days of Robespierre have been blotted out" with the departure of Paine. Anti-Lincoln newspapers across the Northwest republished the article. The *Chicago Times* ran the story under the headline "A Reign of Terror: A Suppressed Dispatch" on September 19. The *Monmouth Review*, in Paine's hometown, duplicated the *Times* headline a few days later. On September 22, Kentucky newspapers reprinted the story, which caused a public outcry. The term "Reign of Terror" became synonymous with Paine's administration at Paducah.[10]

Paine was at St. Louis awaiting a boat home when he heard the news. While browsing a local newspaper, his wife noticed a "short paragraph" that announced the ongoing investigation at Paducah. This was the first he heard of it. He had received no official dispatches or orders since he was relieved of command on September 7. With his health still in decline and unable to do much about the accusations at St. Louis, he continued on his voyage home. On September 20, Paine wrote Major General John M. Schofield of the army of the Ohio, that his health had improved but that he wished to resign. He wrote that his "body is mostly worn out" and although his spirit to subdue the enemies of his country was as strong as ever, Paine physically could not fulfill his duties. Schofield did not reply. Ten days later, Paine wrote Lorenzo Thomas from Monmouth that his health was very poor and that he awaited orders from Schofield. He also reminded Thomas of the resignation request he sent on September 12 and hoped that he would accept it at once. His resignation was denied the same day he wrote Thomas, but Paine did not know it.[11]

Fry and Brown completed their investigation at Paducah on the morning of September 24. The last of the testimonies were from members of the 132nd Illinois Infantry who witnessed the four executions near Fort Anderson. The officers and soldiers of the Eighth Artillery, who performed the executions, were not interviewed. The board went upriver to Caseyville that afternoon where they took testimony. They remained in Union County two days before returning to Louisville to submit their findings to General Burbridge. More affidavits and complaints flowed in as the board compiled its final report.[12]

A day after his arrival in Louisville, Lieutenant Colonel Craddock visited the *Louisville Journal* to offer his side of the investigation. A scathing article probably written by Editor George D. Prentice followed on September 27. Prentice was a pro-slavery conservative Unionist. His hit piece boosted the campaign to discredit Paine. The article claimed that Paine left Paducah without orders and was "absent without authority." It charged that his staff officers took "French leaves" when the board of investigation began to interview witnesses and that official records documenting their alleged crimes disappeared with them. Paine's subordinates who remained at Paducah were named as conspirators in a complex scheme of embezzling money and property from loyal citizens. Colonel Barry, Major Bartling, Superintendent of Trade Woodward, Provost Marshal Hall, Bolinger and Congressman Anderson were all named as guilty parties in a vast ring of corruption.[13]

Prentice depicted the seizure of Paducah businesses and the fees levied on tobacco and cotton as part of a devious plan to monopolize trade to enrich Paine and his collaborators. He concluded that the banishment of prominent families to Canada was not because of disloyalty but simply for the confiscation of their property and homes. Prentice played up Paine's remarks made to Emerson Etheridge, in which he denounced General Halleck as a "damned scoundrel and a coward." The article said his son, Captain Phelps Paine, stole furniture and items for his room. The story said McChesney was a dictator who "ruled with an iron hand" and that the construction of fortifications served no purpose but to force loyal residents into hard labor and to destroy the town. The story also repeated the charges of mass executions; it claimed that forty-three graves of executed prisoners had been counted by Craddock and that Paine ordered McChesney to execute several men without trial at Mayfield. The story listed over two dozen counts of insubordination, corruption and other crimes supposedly committed by Paine.[14]

Other newspapers published accounts of the investigation. How a paper played the story depended on its political slant. The Democratic *Portsmouth*, Ohio, *Daily Times and Daily Milwaukee News* were typical. All three sided with the commissioners. The *Times* said, "the *Louisville Journal*, publishes an exposition of a malfeasance in office by General Payne [sic], at Paducah, implicating Hon. Lucian Anderson ... and others in various transactions. General Meredith, the successor of Payne, in Western Kentucky is having all the parties arrested." The Buckeye State paper claimed, "this is the end of the tyrant Payne [sic], and we confess we shall not be surprised of any rascality that he is not capable of being the principal or accomplice."[15]

The *Milwaukee News* luridly headlined its story "THE BLOODY DEMON E.A. PAINE." The story claimed that at three different places in the First District, Anderson and Bolinger spoke to "the people and told them, that, if they did not vote for Lincoln, they would not be allowed to trade, their property would be taken, and they would be reduced to beggary and a starving condition. Every possible effort was made to exasperate the people in order to have a pretext to seize their property." The paper charged that McChesney bossed "Mayfield with an iron hand," adding that "he nearly destroyed the beautiful town by cutting down the shade trees and erecting a fortification around the court house on the public square." The *News* poured it on: "On this work all citizens were required to labor, neither sickness nor age exempting a man from duty." Those refusing to toil were "assessed a fine of from $50 to $300." According to the *News*, "the fortification was a useless piece of work, as many of the hills surrounding the town commanded the square." Contrary to the story, no hills overlook the courthouse in Mayfield, which tops a rise.[16]

Before the article began to circulate across the country, the hundred day troops stationed at Columbus, Paducah and Mayfield were being recalled and sent back to Illinois to be mustered out of the service. The 134th Illinois departed Mayfield for Paducah on

Left: **Colonel Henry W. Barry** (National Archives). *Above:* **George D. Prentice** (*History of Kentucky* by William E. Connelly & E. M. Coulter).

September 18 after removing the fortifications around the courthouse. They remained at Paducah for four days before boarding a troop transport for Cairo. By the first week of October, the 132nd Illinois at Paducah and 136th and 141st Illinois at Columbus also left the state. The District of Western Kentucky was reduced to the 34th New Jersey Infantry Regiment, two cavalry detachments, one from the Third Illinois and one from the Seventh Tennessee, two heavy artillery regiments, the Fourth and Eighth Heavy Artillery regiments and one light artillery unit, Battery B of the Second Illinois Light Artillery. Union troops in the Jackson Purchase had been cut to fewer than 2,500, less than half of the strength Paine had. The post commanders at Mayfield and Columbus called for reinforcements. The assistant inspector general at Columbus urgently wrote that "it will be utterly impossible to maintain an effective picket line around this post and without a greater force the post will certainly ... be in a precarious situation in case of an attack." Meredith consolidated his troops at Paducah and Columbus.[17]

The departure of troops in the region did not go unnoticed by the guerrillas. On September 26, a guerrilla force of 160 men warned residents of Ballard and Hickman Counties that Mayfield would be attacked soon. A skirmish occurred that night three miles from Paducah. The few troops stationed in the city were drawn into line of battle and double pickets sent out. Jennie Fyfe, a volunteer nurse working at the Marine Hospital in Paducah, described the chaos to her sister in a letter on September 27. She wrote that the "Rebels are everyday expected" and the troops left to defend the city were too few and "not indeed in a very good condition to meet an attack from the enemy."[18]

To prevent the capture of Mayfield by guerrillas, Meredith ordered new fortifications constructed southwest of town and increased the number of cavalry patrols. The fortifications progressed rapidly with work details consisting of soldiers from the Third Illinois. Mayfield residents were not included in the construction. On October 5, Meredith

Soldiers of the 134th Illinois Infantry (Library of Congress).

received reports that a large number of guerrillas were in the vicinity of Columbus and that a portion of Forrest's army was en route to take the city. In response, Meredith directed that all federal troops traveling through Paducah and Columbus be stopped to defend against Rebel assaults. On the night of October 9, the pickets at Mayfield were fired on and the entire post called out and put on alert. Four days later, a spy galloped into Mayfield. He informed Colonel William H. Lawrence, the post commander, that Generals Forrest and Buford had addressed their troops at Corinth, Mississippi, declaring they were to march upon Paducah. Forrest announced that they were going to free the Jackson Purchase from the "hand of the oppressor" and enable the people to "vote right" in the presidential election, apparently meaning cast ballots for Democrat George B. McClellan, a Union General. Buford told his Kentucky regiments that he was determined to "drive the damned Yankees from Kentucky soil and to have the polls in [his] own hands on the 8th of November." The spy said that the Rebels had ten captured rifled cannons they planned to use during the invasion. Lawrence telegraphed Meredith at Paducah of the impending invasion and informed him that the fortifications at Mayfield were in no condition to withstand such artillery. Meredith ordered the immediate evacuation of Mayfield and alerted the post commander at Columbus.[19]

With the exception of a few federal agents, the post at Mayfield was abandoned on the evening of October 15. The troops marched into the night and reached Paducah at sunrise the next day. Meredith wired Burbridge at Lexington that reinforcements were desperately needed to defend the district. Burbridge responded that he had no men to spare but forwarded Meredith's request to General Halleck who replied, "there are no available troops to re-enforce Paducah." Halleck said the War Department did not deem the appointment of Meredith to be "judicious" and that the place required "a man of more military experience." Halleck found Meredith's calls for more troops to be an overreaction and notified Burbridge to pass his request to General Washburn at Memphis. Two days after Lawrence pulled out of Mayfield, sixteen Rebel soldiers entered the town to purchase supplies and question the inhabitants on Union troop movements. They received the information and supplies they sought and in a few hours departed.[20]

After receiving word that no reinforcements were forthcoming, Meredith called a meeting of Paducah citizens on the afternoon of October 18. Standing before the Market House, he disclosed Forrest's intentions of attacking the city and issued an appeal to organize a home defense force. He asserted that no private property would be removed from the city and that federal troops would only safeguard government property. He warned that "if they would do nothing towards protecting it, [then] he would not." Short speeches were given by Congressman Lucian Anderson and others. Over four hundred men heeded the General's call to arms and enrolled in the city's Home Guard. That night, members of the Union League held a torchlight procession through the streets in support of the reelection of Abraham Lincoln and the Unconditional Union ticket. Meredith and Anderson sent urgent letters to President Lincoln pleading that reinforcements be sent as soon as possible. Meredith wrote that Paducah was "threatened every day with an attack" and there was not a "sufficient force to make a proper defense of the country."[21]

With the withdrawal of Union forces at Mayfield, it seemed inevitable that guerrillas would return. On October 19, forty insurgents torched the unprotected Graves County courthouse, which they burned to the ground. News of the event reached Paducah that evening along with stories of "many depredations" committed upon Unionists. Meredith sent a cavalry detachment from the Third Illinois the following morning. They

General Solomon Meredith (National Archives).

remained at Mayfield until October 27 when they were recalled to Paducah under the threat of another invasion by Forrest. Two days later, a small band of guerrillas returned and shot Amos Smith, a local grocer, and a man named Cole for not willingly providing supplies to the raiders. Before they departed, they hanged seventy-year-old Peter Wortham, claiming he was a Union spy. They left his body strung from a tree not far from the ruins of the courthouse.[22]

As Mayfield reverted to days like those before Union occupation, Paducah prepared for the worse. Meredith issued a warning to the citizens that an attack was imminent, after hearing that thousands of Rebel troops were reported gathering along the Kentucky-Tennessee border. He advised local businessmen to move their stock across the river. A correspondent from Louisville wrote that during the last week in October "all the stores of the place have been emptied and the goods shipped to Vincennes [Indiana] or Cairo." Meredith issued an emergency order requiring that passing steamboats be used for the removal of federal troops and fleeing Unionists. All remaining able-bodied men were armed and kept at work on the fortifications about the city. On the last day of the month, a scouting party returned with five men captured at Boydsville. The stories told by the prisoners and scouts added to Meredith's uneasiness. Rebel forces under Forrest had taken unmanned Fort Heiman in Calloway County on the Tennessee River. There his horse-drawn artillery ambushed boats and snarled river traffic. After capturing three boats and burning one, Forrest soon shifted operations upriver where his artillerymen shelled and burned the big supply base at Johnsonville, Tennessee, on November 4. A number of gray coats, however, were sighted eight miles south of Mayfield, pushing north.[23]

With his health slowly returning, Paine was ordered to Louisville to meet General Schofield in regard to his next assignment. He arrived on October 15, but Schofield had moved his headquarters to Chattanooga. Paine was told by Schofield's staff to remain at Louisville. While in the city, he visited the *Journal* to confront Prentice. Before entering the publisher's office, he met a Union officer whom he asked to accompany him to see Prentice. After a brief introduction he told Prentice, "I don't know this gentleman but I see that he is a United States officer and I have brought him to be a witness of the conversation between us." Paine then pulled from his vest pocket another *Journal* article attacking him. He waved it at Prentice and demanded to know its anonymous source. The officer replied, "General Paine you need inquire no further, I authorized everything stated in that article and everything in it is true." Startled by the announcement, Paine asked the man's name; it was Craddock. An argument ensued between Paine and Craddock, which concluded with Paine's insistence that Craddock publish a declaration admitting he lied.[24]

Paine was ordered to Nashville later that day and departed on the morning of October 25. The orders stipulated he would receive further instructions at the depot in the city. No orders awaited him; frustrated, he wrote Schofield, now at Cedar Bluff, Alabama, with another request for instructions and explained that he was "well enough to go on duty." He received no immediate reply. Schofield had more pressing concerns; General John Bell Hood and the army of Tennessee had consolidated at Tuscumbia, Alabama, and were menacing middle Tennessee. General Forrest was marching north along the Tennessee River into Kentucky. Paine remained in limbo at Nashville for weeks as stories continued to swirl in the press denouncing his rule in western Kentucky.[25]

With Paine's reputation in ruins, the *Journal* targeted Congressman Anderson and Bolinger. An article likely written by Prentice, claimed both men were part of a complex scheme to embezzle thousands of dollars from businessmen in Paducah. The two allegedly encouraged Paine to close the businesses of competitors, impound their stock, fine them and require they pay Bolinger and Anderson to reopen their shops. He reported that they threatened citizens to vote for Lincoln or the entire region would be closed to trade, their property seized and all "reduced to beggary." Added to Bolinger's "crimes" was the assertion that he illegally used a government steamboat to transport private property for financial gain and was in cahoots with Paine to avoid paying permit fees. The *Journal* further accused Bolinger of being the "agent of a guerrilla band" and that Anderson was a "swindler" and "scoundrel."[26]

Anderson and Bolinger fought back. Anderson replied to Prentice's attacks on October 24 in the *Louisville Press*, a Unionist newspaper, and declared the charges preposterous and libelous. He held Prentice personally responsible for the defamation of his character and cited the *Journal* as the "slanderer of Union men and Federal officers, the defender of traitors and apologists for guerrillas." Two days, later the *Press* printed a letter from Bolinger, which said he too was falsely accused and offered a reward of $5,000 to anyone who could find proof in the allegations made in the *Journal*. No one took him up, but Prentice countered on the twenty-seventh, noting that Bolinger's letter had "guilt peeping out of every sentence of his letter like a rat from a hole." He scoffed at Anderson's call for a retraction and warned that he should best worry about the numerous other illegalities listed by the board of investigation.[27]

Meanwhile, Colonel McChesney had been under house arrest in Chicago since September 20. No formal charges accompanied the warrant for his arrest, but Chicago papers reported his confinement. His family and friends campaigned to seek his release. The *Chicago Tribune* published a letter from his father, Robert McChesney, which condemned his accusers. Influential friends of the colonel's family began to pressure local politicians and military authorities in the city to have him released. Weeks passed before General Burbridge sent for him for questioning but McChesney's health had declined so rapidly since his return to Chicago that his physician confined him to his bed.[28]

The regimental surgeon of the 134th Illinois who got the order for McChesney to return home was also placed under arrest in Chicago on September 24. Dr. Danforth was charged with stealing furniture from a residence he occupied in Paducah. Danforth denied the allegation, but General Meredith insisted that the property be returned before he would issue an order for his release. Danforth continued to profess innocence. He and McChesney remained in the custody until the "pleasure of the War Department" was to be made known.[29]

Meredith examined the contents of the wooden crate that McChesney left at Mayfield. Inside were the allegedly stolen items, the private effects of McChesney and a small tin box. Meredith ordered the box broken open. It contained personal correspondence and official documents. Meredith placed the articles of value and the tin box in the charge of a government detective sent by General Burbridge. The remaining items in the crate were to be forwarded to McChesney in Chicago by his former adjutant, Lieutenant Luxton. Unaware of the search and seizure of his property, McChesney wrote Meredith to return the crate so he could prepare his defense. Meredith replied on November 2 that the crate and its contents had been sent to Chicago with Luxton two weeks earlier. McChesney wrote Luxton on the location of the crate. Luxton responded on November 14 that when he sought to take possession of the crate but that it had been opened and many articles had been removed. The tin box could not be located, and Luxton's inquiries on its whereabouts could not be answered by Meredith or his staff. Luxton was given permission to collect McChesney's clothing, but his belt and sword were turned over to Meredith's assistant adjutant general as more evidence.[30]

Prior to receiving Luxton's response, McChesney received an unusual letter from a woman named L. Jansens of Paducah. She wrote that her brother found near Fort Anderson a metal box that contained his papers and asked if he wished to have them. McChesney answered in the affirmative and queried about the condition of the box and asked if she could provide more information on how it was found. Jansens returned the box with its broken lock four weeks later. She included a note that told of soldiers who knew of the box and visited her to view the documents. She declared they came to find clues to support charges against McChesney but found nothing and returned the box to her.[31]

In the meantime, McChesney's family and friends continued to press for his release. They approached Major General Joseph Hooker, who was recently placed in command of the Northern Department, which included Illinois, to use his influence. Hooker sent a letter to the assistant adjutant general in Washington, Edward D. Townsend, requesting that McChesney be "released from arrest and mustered out of the service." Lieutenant Colonel James Oakes, assistant acting provost marshal for Illinois, received so many applications for his release that he wrote Lorenzo Thomas at the War Department to request that charges be relayed to his office and that a decision be made on whether McChesney should remain under arrest. Too weak to write, McChesney dictated to his father a letter for Paine on December 15. He pleaded with the general to use his influence at the War Department to secure his freedom before his health deteriorated further. Unfortunately, Paine's public image had been so badly damaged in the press that he was shunned by even his closest allies in Washington.[32]

McChesney's letter was delivered to Paine at the Willard Hotel in Washington, where he had been lodging for the past few weeks. Since departing Nashville in late November, he sought an interview with the secretary of war and the president, but to no avail. Paine's resignation was accepted by Secretary of War Stanton on November 30 and published in the Washington newspapers. However, Stanton reversed his decision after Judge Advocate General Joseph Holt recommended further investigation into charges against Paine made by Smith and Fry. He suggested that Paine submit an explanation for each of the charges; there were ten that needed to be addressed. The first one accused him of using abusive language, harshly treating individuals, and making disrespectful remarks toward superior officers. The second charge focused on the arrests and confinement of citizens; the third, on the banishment of citizens to Canada; the fourth, on the unauthorized seizure and confiscation of private property; the fifth, on the restriction of trade and business with his military district; the sixth, on the authority to levy assessments and fees; the seventh, on the issuance of government transportation to private individuals; the eighth, on the forced removal of local and county officials; the ninth, on the execution of individuals without trial; and the tenth, on the misappropriation of property and extortion.[33]

Holt's report further advised Stanton to investigate other charges made by Fry and Brown against officers serving under Paine. He suggested charges be brought against Major Bartling, Colonels McChesney and Barry and Captain Hall for bribery, embezzlement and the misappropriation of seized property for personal use. Holt added that McChesney should be investigated for executing prisoners without trial and engaging in corrupt practices to impress citizens to construct fortifications at Mayfield. He concluded that the "violent denunciations" made by Fry and Brown against Paine were in "main hasty and ill considered" and that specific information essential to the investigation was neglected. The numerous affidavits and testimonies submitted to Fry and Brown, Holt surmised, came from "persons hostile to General Paine or from parties who are interested in applications for specific pecuniary or other relief" and that General Fry's commission had not presented an "impartial view of General Paine's conduct of affairs in Western Kentucky." In closing his report, he specified that Kentucky was under martial law when Paine was in command.[34]

Four days after Holt submitted his report, Congress began its second session. On the second day of the session, December 7, Senator Lazarus W. Powell of Kentucky introduced a resolution directing the secretary of war to transmit Fry and Brown's report and all evidence received by the commission on Paine's conduct at Paducah to the Senate. Powell, a leading Democrat who had turned down his party's nomination for president and vice president three months earlier, was a loud and frequent opponent of the administration's policies on emancipation and blacks serving in the military. It had become common knowledge among the political insiders in Washington that the War Department had possession of the board of investigation's report, and Powell sought to make it public. The resolution was brought forth as the last item of the day, and the Senate adjourned before it was opened for discussion and consideration.[35]

Judge Advocate General Joseph Holt (National Archives).

The next day, Powell called for the resolution to be considered. Senator Lyman Trumbull, a Republican from Illinois and an acquaintance of General Paine, called out Powell and asked what sort of report he was requesting and whether Paine had any knowledge of the commission that investigated his command. Powell responded that he did not know Paine or what was in the report; he had read of it in Kentucky newspapers and had spoken to members of the commission. He claimed they had proof that Paine "showed the most outrageous instances of cruelty

Senator Lazarus W. Powell (Library of Congress).

and barbarity that were ever inflicted in any Christian or civilized age." Trumbull defended his fellow Illinoisan by stating that Paine was a "gentleman of good reputation and standing" and that the only complaints he was made aware of were from Rebels and traitors who found his administration too harsh. Powell countered that he had "documents" in his possession that described Paine's brutal command while at Gallatin, Tennessee, but that he wished not to introduce them until all other evidence was presented to the Senate. Garrett Davis, Kentucky's junior senator, stood and declared that he had read Fry and Brown's final report and supported Powell's resolution. Trumbull moved that the resolution be referred to the Committee on Military Affairs since neither Powell nor Davis could demonstrate whether the commission had any official standing or was held with Paine's knowledge. The motion for a resolution was tabled and the Senate moved on to other business.[36]

The Senate readdressed Trumbull's motion to refer Powell's resolution to the Committee on Military Affairs on December 12. Powell made one final appeal for the immediate and direct transmittal of the report from the War Department to the Senate and clarified his stance, explaining that he had never seen the report but only read newspaper accounts of the commission's findings. Trumbull's motion was called for a vote and passed thirty to eight. Powell and Davis voted against the motion. The resolution was sent to the Committee of Military Affairs for review and consideration. After the vote, Trumbull was applauded by the Republican press for his stand against the "malevolent" Powell. George T. Allen, a federal medical inspector at Paducah, thanked Trumbull in a letter he wrote on December 19. Allen penned that loyal Kentuckians were grateful to him for his noble defense of Paine.[37]

Senator Lyman Trumbull (National Archives).

Paine spent three weeks preparing his response to the charges in Holt's final report along with other accusations made by the commission. He delivered a 37-page response to Secretary Stanton at the War Department on Christmas Eve. His explanation began with a brief introduction on the chaotic conditions at Paducah when he arrived on July 19, 1864. He described the broken-down military command structure he inherited, the conflict between Barry and Hicks and low morale amongst the troops. He addressed the nightly guerrilla attacks on the picket lines and the "unrelenting hostility of Rebel sympathizers" toward him and his officers. He justified his plans to collect assessments, find relief for the suffering wives and children of Union soldiers and halt illegal trade from

Western Kentucky. His introduction concluded with Paine questioning Burbridge's authority to order a military commission and how the commission functioned.[38]

Paine admitted that he had become "addicted to the use of profane language" but he denied abusing loyal citizens. He confessed that he had been "compelled to use expletives" when dealing with Southern sympathizers, yet he asserted it was the only thing they understood. He refuted accusations that he had spoken disrespectfully of superior officers, claiming his accusers were disloyal and hated him. Paine defended his decision to arrest and confine individuals who were convicted by the testimony of loyal Union men within the community. The men and women expatriated to Canada were among the most outspoken Southern sympathizers in the military district and their removal was necessary to prevent further resistance to Union occupation. He denied that he ordered unauthorized seizures or encouraged lawlessness. He maintained that no property of *loyal* families was seized or damaged, and he said he issued specific orders to his soldiers to respect the property of all Union men. The trade restrictions were needed to prevent the shipment of contraband, according to Paine, and the confiscation of goods was required to ensure that Southern sympathizers paid their fair share of assessments. The authority to levy assessments and fees was justified by President Lincoln's order to Paine and approved by Assistant Attorney General Townsend. Paine attached a copy of the order.[39]

The use of government transportation by Bolinger, Paine said, was to prevent the destruction of his property. Bolinger had informed him of an impending guerrilla raid, and Paine consented to the use of the steamboat to save the tobacco and cotton. He also pointed out that his superior, General Washburn, had repeatedly given similar permissions. His rationalization for the dismissal of city and county officials was simply that they were hostile to him and the federal government. General Jeremiah T. Boyle had removed disloyal offce holders when he was military commander in Kentucky. Paine vehemently denied that he extorted money or property from citizens. He professed that it was an outlandish falsehood generated by Dr. D.D. Thompson, a known Southern sympathizer who welcomed General Forrest to his home during the Confederate raid in March of 1864. In regard to the executions, Paine offered explanations for each of the four men shot by firing squad. All had admitted during interrogations that they murdered Union men or soldiers and that their "prompt summary punishment [was] absolutely necessary" to maintain order in the district. Word of Kesterson's execution, Paine declared, actually stopped further "pillage, robbery and murder" in the Jackson Purchase.[40]

Paine also addressed other accusations made by Fry and Brown, which Holt had not mentioned in his final report. He effectively demonstrated why it was vital to regulate the banking institutions in the city, halt disloyal and absentee landlords from collecting rents and the construction of fortifications at Mayfield. He oversaw the operations of the banks to prevent wealthy disloyal depositors from transferring funds prior to the enactment of the president's assessment program. The rent paid to absentee landlords by loyal citizens and government employees was diverted by Paine to the relief fund to assist with the growing number of widows and children of federal soldiers relocating to Paducah. The fortifications at Mayfield, he contended, were crucial in the fight against guerrillas that regularly raided the city and surrounding regions. He admitted that the courthouse was "not the most eligible [place] but the use of the well was absolutely indispensable" since it was the "only place [water] could be procured within a mile." Paine also responded to individual charges made by citizens who claimed financial losses or physical harm during his administration. Paine's explanation to Holt was comprehensive and concise. He was confident the charges would be dismissed and his resignation would be approved before the end of the year.[41]

The year 1865 seemed promising for Paine. He looked forward to returning to his law practice. His hopes were dashed when Governor Bramlette delivered a speech to both houses of the Kentucky legislature on January 6. Bramlette's message repeated the charges made by the board of investigation and the stories in the *Louisville Journal*. The governor presented to the legislature a copy of Fry and Brown's final report with recommendations and letters to and from President Lincoln, General Burbridge and Secretary of War Stanton. The documents accused Paine of abusing his power as commander at Paducah. Bramlette's letter to the president on September 2, 1864, not only condemned Paine but declared that Congressman Anderson was a willing and active partner in a "system of oppression and plunder" and shared in the "spoils iniquitously extorted from the citizens" of West Kentucky. The governor raised the stakes considerably by publicly accusing a member of Congress from his own state of coercion and extortion. The report and accompanying letters were made available to the press, which resulted in another series of damaging articles and editorials against Paine and Anderson.[42]

Bramlette's message was welcomed by Prentice, who, as state printer, got immediate access to the message and supplementary documents. The *Louisville Journal* published the governor's message and the letters. In an editorial introducing the article, Prentice praised Bramlette. He declared that "no public official ever discharged his duty with a heart more faithful to his country" and that the governor's message "breathes the spirit of fervent devotion to the Union." Prentice reflected on other points in the message and endorsed Bramlette's opposition to enlisting blacks in the army. He declared that the people of Kentucky "have ever opposed making the status of the negro an object of struggle in this trial to preserve our national life." Both Bramlette and Prentice admitted slavery was in its final days but they argued that granting equality to people of color, which abolitionists like Paine favored, had to be resisted at every turn.[43]

Meantime on the floor of the United States Senate, the Commission on Military Affairs submitted its first report on January 16. The report did not include the results of the committee's investigation into Powell's resolution. To encourage the committee to move forward with the investigation, Senator Powell submitted a resolution that requested President Lincoln to order the trial of Paine before a military tribunal, and, if found guilty, that he be punished to the full extent of the law. Two days later, Powell inquired about the committee's investigation on Paine's conduct at Paducah and whether its members had any intention to deliver their findings. Without waiting for a response, he asked that the committee be discharged from its duty to conduct the investigation and that his earlier resolution to direct the War Department to hand over Fry and Brown's report and all other evidence to the Senate be put to vote. What ensued was a lengthy debate.[44]

The chairman of the committee on military affairs, Henry Wilson of Massachusetts, replied to Powell. He said that a backlog of other responsibilities had prevented the committee from performing a proper investigation, but that the panel would submit a report in the next day or two. Powell demanded that the committee be removed from the process and that the resolution be moved forward that instant. He told his colleagues that he had in his hand Governor Bramlette's State of the Commonwealth message, which contained Fry and Brown's report. He read excerpts from the report that said Paine was guilty of visiting upon Western Kentucky "fifty-one days of terror and rapine" and that in all the "dark and bloody annals of tyrants and men who overthrow the rights of citizens" there has never been such a villain who had committed such acts of "barbarity, cruelty and plunder." What Powell did not have were the affidavits that doubly damned Paine.[45]

Senator Trumbull rose and calmly stated that he was surprised that the distinguished senator would express opinions before hearing all the evidence and would so boldly declare a man's guilt without even a trial. Trumbull notified Powell that he had met Paine and that the general had no objection to publicizing the board of investigation's report as long as he could answer the charges against him. He assured the Senate that Paine was not a "blood-thirsty and guilty man"; rather, "he has but done his duty" for his country. Powell replied that he was unsure whether Paine was culpable, but argued that the "report stamps him with the most damning guilt." He also insinuated that Paine fled Paducah before the commission arrived and that he concealed evidence. Trumbull said Paine had neither avoided the commission nor removed records from district headquarters. Trumbull pointed out that the commission "kept away" until Paine had departed Paducah and the "whole thing was an ex parte proceeding." He added that Powell displayed a baseless "perversity" and "determination to hold Paine guilty." Powell objected and claimed that the board "never kept away one minute in order to allow General Paine to be absent or to go away." He was however willing to concede and amend his resolution to incorporate Paine's answers if it were put to a vote.[46]

Senator John Conness, a California Republican, entered the fray by announcing he would not vote to order the resolution back from committee. He confessed that he was tired of Powell's ceaseless "tirade against Union officers" and his denouncements against the Government. Senator B. Gratz Brown of Missouri, an Unconditional Unionist, concurred with Conness. Democratic Senator Thomas A. Hendricks of Indiana backed Powell in that Paine "ought to be put on trial for the good of the public service [and] for the honor of the Army" but he thought the resolution should remain with the committee until it could be thoroughly investigated. Powell rose to his feet once again and denounced Paine as a coward and vowed that there was not an "honest man in all Kentucky who would dare vindicate this man." He attacked Conness, sarcastically dubbing him the "*censor morum* of the Senate." Powell did not care if Conness "should faint under the exhaustion" of hearing the myriad of crimes committed by General Paine. Conness fired back that he would "not disgust the Senate nor violate the properties of this place by engaging in a vulgar tirade with the Senator of Kentucky."[47]

As Powell and Conness went at one another, Trumbull was handed two letters, which he scanned quickly. After Conness finished his final riposte, Trumbull stood and announced that he had just received correspondence from Paducah that contradicted Powell's charges against Paine. He read from one letter:

> All the stories of his having killed so many innocent men is no more less than bosh; he had five guerrillas killed here, and only five. As to his ever receiving any money or being engaged in any swindling transactions is simply absurd, and is believed by no one here. If the man can be found who will swear that General Paine was ever engaged in swindling or embezzling while in command in this district the people would like to see him.

And from another:

> The usual policy against our officers is, if possible, to corrupt them by presents, dinners, and attentions; or, if this cannot be done to seize upon some act of indiscretion, mistake, oversight or shortcoming, and clamor them into disgrace. General Paine's case comes within the latter category.

He concluded that other papers were forthcoming and that he would make them available to the Committee on Military Affairs. Seeing that he was beaten, Powell withdrew his motion.[48]

The Committee on Military Affairs reported back to the Senate on January 23. The panel agreed that Paine's explanation should be included in the resolution along with Holt's final report and all papers related to the case. The amended resolution was agreed upon and passed by the Senate. Stanton received the resolution the next day and requested Holt's staff to copy and send all papers related to the case to him. Powell's resolution requesting the president to order Paine's court-martial was tabled until the Senate received a response from the secretary of war. Stanton sent a letter to the Senate on January 30 stating that Paine's court-martial had been ordered. Powell proudly proclaimed victory.[49]

Five

"Conduct to the prejudice of good order and military discipline"

Paine received the general court-martial order, titled Special Orders No. 51, at his hotel room in Washington on February 1, 1865. The court-martial was to begin on February 8 at Cairo, Illinois. The members assigned to the court were Major General David Hunter, Major General Samuel P. Heintzelman, Major General Silas Casey, Brigadier General Henry B. Carrington, Brigadier General William Harrow, Brigadier General John B. McIntosh and Colonel John Connell. Colonel William McKee Dunn was appointed as judge advocate of the court. Hunter was no stranger to controversial military tribunals. He had presided over the dubious court-marital of Major General Fitz John Porter two years earlier. Dunn was the assistant judge advocate general for the military departments of Ohio, Tennessee, Cumberland, Missouri, Arkansas, and Kansas and had recently arrived from Louisville. Judge Advocate General Holt was directed by Stanton to prepare charges against Paine. However, before Paine could leave Washington, he was summoned to testify before the House of Representatives, which was investigating Anderson.[1]

Lucian Anderson had serious problems of his own; Governor Bramlette's message ignited a fact-finding congressional probe into his activities during Paine's command at Paducah. Congressman Green Clay Smith of Kentucky introduced a resolution on January 18 to form a three-person committee to be appointed by Speaker of the House Schuler Colfax to look into the charges made by

General David Hunter, Member of the Court (National Archives).

Left: **General Samuel P. Heintzelman, Member of the Court.** *Right:* **General Silas Casey, Member of the Court** (National Archives).

Bramlette of "corruption, bribery and malfeasance" against Anderson, too. The resolution was amended to increase the number of committee members to five. The speaker selected Congressmen Glenni W. Scofield of Pennsylvania, James C. Allen of Illinois, John H. Hubbard of Connecticut, James S. Brown of Wisconsin and Smith on the 19th. Allen asked to be excused the next day and the speaker appointed John B. Steele of New York in his place. Five days later, Steele was replaced by William M. Stuart of Nevada, and James S. Rollins of Missouri supplanted Brown on the committee on February 1. The committee began to interview witnesses on February 6. Paine was the first to testify. He emphatically denied that he or Anderson were guilty of any criminal activity while he was in command at Paducah. He told the committee that he had "never received any money, property or valuables of any kind whatever for any official or non-official purpose" and that he "never seized, or ordered to be seized, any money or property of any kind for [his] own benefit or for the use of Mr. Anderson." He reassured the committee

General William Harrow, Member of the Court (Library of Congress).

Five. "Conduct to the prejudice of good order and military discipline"   81

Left: **General John B. McIntosh, Member of the Court.** *Right:* **Judge Advocate General William M. Dunn, Prosecutor (Library of Congress).**

that he knew of no unlawful or dishonorable acts to have been committed by Anderson. Paine departed Washington the next morning for Cairo.[2]

At midnight on February 8, General Hunter, Colonel Connell and Judge Advocate Dunn met at the St. Charles Hotel at Cairo to discuss the approaching trial. Cairo was recovering from a mass drunken riot caused by returning Union troops passing through the city a few days earlier. Citizens had been robbed of thousands of dollars and their property damaged or destroyed. At the time of their meeting, many businesses remained closed and the river trade temporarily diverted to other ports. The meeting was brief, and they simply agreed to gather the next morning at 10 a.m. The men awoke to grey skies and frigid temperatures in the low twenties. Overnight, General Hunter received a telegraph that relieved General Carrington from participating on the court. Generals Heintzelman, Casey and Harrow arrived by steamboat a few hours before the scheduled meeting. With the city of Cairo in a state of disorder, all agreed that moving the trial to Paducah would be in the best interest of the court and that it would be much easier for witnesses to testify at Paducah rather than at Cairo. Hunter telegraphed the War Department for permission to change venue and for further instructions.[3]

The court met at 10 a.m. on February 10, but since no orders had come from Washington regarding the change of venue, they quickly adjourned. Before the meeting concluded, Judge Advocate Dunn reported to the members of the court that he had not received formal charges against Paine nor a list of witnesses to subpoena. Hunter requested that Dunn telegraph Holt that the court had assembled and needed charges and a witness list before it could proceed. Dunn sent a telegram to Holt with Hunter's request later that day.[4]

The court reconvened on the morning of Monday, the 13th, but promptly adjourned as again as no word had come from Washington. A telegram from the judge advocate's office came that afternoon, which authorized the transfer of the trial to Paducah. Another

General Henry B. Carrington, Member of the Court (Library of Congress).

telegram followed that included the orders for the court and a list of charges against Paine. The members of the court assembled the next day, read the charges and arranged to meet in Paducah in two days. That evening, the court members, along with General Paine who had arrived at Cairo the day before, left on the steamboat *Champion* for Paducah.[5]

At 10 a.m. on February 16, the court opened for its first session at Paducah. All the members were present and the trial seemed set to begin, but Dunn informed the court that he would not be able to provide witnesses until the next day. A frustrated Hunter adjourned the court until the next morning. Paine received the news without much concern. He appeared confident and at ease when he left the courtroom, though frail and walking with a cane. A group of interested citizens stood outside where some greeted him when he passed by. Nurse Jennie Fyfe wrote her sister in Michigan that he had "many friends here among the Union people" and they welcomed his return to the city. The long-anticipated trial would have to wait another day.[6]

Conditions in the Jackson Purchase had become more dangerous since Paine left. A correspondent from the *Chicago Tribune* wrote from Paducah on February 7 that Western Kentucky had been "purposely left to the tender mercies of guerrillas" and only two county courts and four post offices were in operation west of the Tennessee River, which bounded the Purchase on the east. Meredith's command had been reduced by almost 1,500 men since Paine's departure. Emboldened by the troop reductions, roving bands of guerrillas looted farms and took whatever horses and livestock that could be found. A major skirmish on the road between Columbus and Clinton, which included about 150 guerrillas, occurred less than two weeks before the trial began. With the withdrawal of federal troops from Mayfield, the population of refugees swelled at Paducah as hundreds of citizens fled to the safety of the Union lines. Even more crossed the Ohio River into Illinois or Indiana. Many Purchase men dodged the draft. Most Paducah citizens still charged under Union occupation. It was reported that "four-fifths of the men drafted in some of the counties never report[ed]" for duty. The enlistment of black soldiers, nonetheless, remained steady.[7]

Locals were turning against Meredith. So were some of his officers and men. Colonel McArthur at Columbus and Colonel Barry at Fort Anderson refused to follow Meredith's orders. Meredith charged McArthur with "disobedience of orders" in January and Barry with "conduct to the prejudice of good order and military discipline" in February. On January 25, he placed McArthur under arrest and assigned Colonel Hicks to assume his command at Columbus. On February 6, Barry reportedly remarked in public that "General Meredith is the damnedest liar out of hell" and allegedly repeated the same thing two days later. Men in the ranks, particularly in black regiments, mumbled slurs whenever he was in their presence. The Union League and Unionist businessmen at Paducah were were anti–Meredith. Newspapers disapproved of Meredith's "lenient conduct toward secessionists and those whose sympathies were with the Rebellion." An army physician at Paducah remarked that he did not "know a Rebel who does not shout for Col. Hicks and Gen'l Meredith." The day when deliberations began in Paine's trial, Special Order No. 79 was issued from the War Department, which relieved Meredith of command of the District of Western Kentucky. But he was reinstated on February 27.[8]

After Meredith was fired, a correspondent from the *Cincinnati Commercial* wrote:

> It is noticeable that those who are loudest in their complaints of General Meredith's administration of affairs in Western Kentucky and most energetic in vociferating on his removal fail to bring other than

the most general accusations against him. There are no specifications. Even the small knot of radicals in Paducah who clamor about the General do not condescend to indulge in particulars and leave us wondering what on earth all the bother is about. The general who administered military law in Western Kentucky before General Meredith was removed because he exercised too much severity toward secessionists and the General now goes overboard because he indulges an excess of mercy. We presume it would be impossible to place in command of that district any man who would be acceptable to the extremists on both sides....[9]

The much-anticipated trial began behind closed doors on Friday, February 17. General Hunter, acting as president of the court, called the trial to order promptly at 10 a.m. He asked Paine if he objected to any of the members; Paine replied that he did not. The judges of the court and prosecutor Dunn were then sworn in, and Charles Carpenter was appointed reporter of the court by Dunn. Hunter next called for the charges to be read to the accused. Paine stood as he heard each of two charges and twenty-seven specifications made against him.[10]

The first charge was "violation of the Fifth Article of War" in that he used "contemptuous and disrespectful words" against Governor Bramlette at Caseyville on August 20, 1864. The second charge was for "conduct to the prejudice of good order and military discipline" and included twenty-six specifications. The first specification said he cursed Halleck at Paducah on July 31, 1864. The remaining twenty-five stemmed from complaints made by citizens against Paine for alleged criminal acts. He stood accused of coercing bankers to pay depositors; closing stores owned by disloyal merchants; allowing the use of government transportation for non-military purposes; illegally confining men without due process of law; and unlawfully seizing horses and other property of loyal citizens. Nineteen of the specifications were connected to property seizures at Paducah and Union County, three focused on arrests, two on banking and one on government transportation. He unhesitantly pleaded not guilty to all charges.[11]

Paine's enemies claimed Holt deliberately left out the most serious charges: the banishment of citizens to Canada, the removal of local and county officials, the execution of prisoners without trial and restricting trade and levying assessments. The judge advocate general dismissed those charges because Kentucky was under martial law when Paine was in Paducah.

Holt determined that Paine acted within the scope of authority granted to him by President Lincoln. In his final report to Secretary of War Stanton on December 1, 1864, he declared that Paine could be "properly criticized and reviewed only in connection with the action of the President in investing him with extraordinary authority." Lincoln's Proclamation 113 exempted Paine from charges that prevented "aid and comfort furnished by disaffected and disloyal citizens" to insurgents and the suppression of those that "disturbed the public peace" or "made flagrant civil war [by] destroying property and life in various parts of the State." To support his conclusion, Holt cited Stephen Vincent Benet's definition of martial law in *A Treatise of Military Law and the Practice of Courts-Martial (1864)* and General Halleck's interpretation of military law in his book *International Law; or, Rules Regulating the Intercourse of States in Peace and War (1861)*. Section I of the *Instructions for the Government of Armies of the United States in the Field, General Order No. 100*, also known as the Lieber Code of April 24, 1863, likewise defined martial law in hostile territory. These three publications were considered to be the legal basis for martial law during to the Civil War.[12]

After Paine was read the charges, Judge Advocate Dunn delivered his opening remarks. William McKee Dunn was a fifty-year-old southern Indiana native who had been a lawyer for close to thirty years. He served in the Indiana House of Representatives in 1848 and 1849, was a delegate to the Indiana constitutional convention in 1851 and 1852 and was elected to Congress in 1858 and 1860. When the war started, he served briefly as a volunteer aide-de-camp major to General George McClellan. He was a conservative Republican, but not an Abolitionist. After his reelection campaign failed in 1862, Dunn became judge advocate of volunteers for the Department of Missouri. On June 22, 1864, he was appointed lieutenant colonel and assistant judge advocate general of the army. Dunn was a stout and balding man with long sideburns. He had piercing grey eyes, which appeared squinty. He seemed stern and unwelcoming.[13]

Dunn called his first witness, V.S. Gillespie. Gillespie was a store clerk who said he heard Paine and Emerson Etheridge arguing on the street in July. Dunn began by asking Gillespie what he had heard. He informed the court that Paine called General Halleck a "God damned coward" and demanded that Etheridge discontinue his anti-government preaching within the city. Paine, serving as his own defense attorney, asked Gillespie whether either party during the argument spoke angrily. He responded that both appeared "very calm under the circumstances." Paine followed up with a question on his loyalty, asking him where he lived prior to the war. Gillespie replied that he was a resident of Mississippi but a "firm supporter of the United States Government." Paine had no further questions of the witness but requested that be made available for questioning later. The court complied with the defense's request.[14]

The next witness called to the stand was John Sinnott, a mule trader from Cincinnati who said he overheard the tiff between Paine and Etheridge. Sinnott stated that he believed Paine had said Halleck was a "damned coward." Paine asked him to repeat the exact words he heard. Sinnott was unable to do so. Paine questioned whether the argument was provoked and if Etheridge was ordered to leave Paducah. Sinnott remarked that Paine was not provoked but that Etheridge was expected to leave the city.[15]

James R. Alexander, a physician from Paducah, followed Sinnott. Dr. Alexander told the court that he was walking down Broadway when he saw Paine and Etheridge in an animated discussion and heard Paine say that Halleck was a "damned coward and a damned rascal." He added that Etheridge did not taunt Paine into making such derogatory remarks. Paine asked whether Alexander had taken the oath of allegiance to the federal government. He answered in the affirmative, declaring he took the oath as a "matter of form" when General Charles F. Smith was in command of the post in the fall of 1861. Paine asked what he meant by "matter of form." Alexander told the court he had "always been loyal" and "everybody knew the position [he] occupied." He also reminded those in the courtroom that he fled the city after he received a written notice from radical secessionists a day before General Grant arrived at Paducah. To corroborate his story, he declared that the notice was submitted and published in the *Louisville Journal* a few days after he crossed the river into Illinois. Dunn redirected and asked if he remained loyal since taking the oath. He replied, "I expect I have—I put a substitute in last September—I was not drafted, I think I have, I believe I have according to my ideas." The perturbed Dr. Alexander was then dismissed by the court.[16]

After Dr. Alexander stepped down, Robert O. Woolfolk was called to the stand. Woolfolk and Paine detested each other. The prosecution began by asking him how long he had known Paine. Woolfolk stated that he met Paine when he first came to the city in September of 1861; he admitted that there had been a certain animosity between them since. Dunn asked what remarks Paine had made regarding General Halleck. Woolfolk replied that he overheard Paine denounce General Halleck as "a damned coward" who had "played into the hands of the Rebels." Dunn concluded his examination by inquiring whether he had taken the oath of allegiance and served in the Confederate army. Woolfolk indifferently declared he had done so "a half dozen times since this war commenced." He also said that he had taken the oath when he applied for permits to leave the city and when he served as a member of the grand jury. He swore to the court that he had never served in the Rebel army.[17]

Paine rose from his chair and started his cross examination. He immediately went on the offensive, questioning Woolfolk's loyalty and his activities earlier in the war. With evidence received from his Unionist friends in the city, Paine asked a series of questions regarding Woolfolk's pro–Southern leanings and ties to the Rebel forces. He asked Woolfolk if he had purchased horses, clothing and medicine in Paducah and sent them to Columbus in 1861 and 1862 when it was under Confederate occupation. Woolfolk answered that he had not. Paine queried whether he had carried correspondence to officers in the Rebel army. Woolfolk responded he had never done so. Paine retorted, "Were you not arrested for taking letters through Union lines which had not been approved and endorsed?" Woolfolk leaned forward and said, "I was not." He then paused, looked about the courtroom and recalled that he had been detained once for being outside Union lines. He acknowledged being apprehended by a Union cavalry patrol near the Tennessee border but that it was a misunderstanding and he was quickly released. While he reflected on the incident, he changed his earlier answer and admitted to have sent letters to his brother who was in the Confederate army. Paine challenged him further and asked if he had not said on several occasions that he was a Rebel and that he would never submit to the Union cause. Woolfolk replied, "I have [always] said that I was a sympathizer with the South" and that "I preferred seeing this government as it was." His response caught Paine by surprise, as he expected Woolfolk not to crack so easily.[18]

Not letting Woolfolk off the hook, Paine questioned why he objected to having a United States flag displayed at his home when federal troops entered Paducah in September of 1861. Woolfolk remarked that he had no objection to the American flag but that he should not be forced to have one placed at his residence. "Did you keep Rebel flags in your house and exhibit them?" Woolfolk answered, "I might say I did and did not." He explained that his daughter was given a very small hand-sewn Rebel flag from a relative but never publicly displayed it. Paine also accused Woolfolk of making life-threating remarks against him. A week before the trial began, Woolfolk was heard to have said that "General Paine ought to be hung" and if he returned to Paducah he would shoot him. Woolfolk initially rejected the allegation, but after Paine indicated that two Union officers had sworn otherwise he answered, "I said it, sir." The last subject Paine addressed was Woolfolk's departure from the city the night before he and his family were to be sent Canada. Paine claimed that he violated a "parole of honor" not to leave Paducah without permission. Woolfolk denied such a pledge existed and that he had never been given parole. He said he left after he received word that he was to be held as a hostage. He told the court that "I had no idea of leaving ten minutes before I did." Paine concluded his cross examination with "have you ever rejoiced at the success of the so called Confederates?"

Unapologetically, Woolfolk responded, "I have sometimes, sir." Paine's most vocal antagonist had shown his true colors, and his creditability as an impartial witness was placed in serious doubt.[19]

Five. "Conduct to the prejudice of good order and military discipline"

Before the court adjourned, Gillespie was recalled to the stand. Paine asked if he could be more specific regarding his conversation with Etheridge. Gillespie could not recall the precise words. Because they spoke for two hours, he found it impossible to remember all that was said. The court recessed at 3:00 p.m. and agreed to reconvene at 10:00 the next morning. The eventful first day of the trial ended with a confident Paine exiting the courtroom.[20]

The second day of the trial began as scheduled. The prosecution called W.P. Caldwell as its first witness. Caldwell was a dry goods merchant from Paducah who observed the argument between Etheridge and Paine. He testified that Paine called General Halleck a "god damned coward" and that both men had made disparaging remarks toward each other. Paine asked whether Etheridge taunted him by proclaiming that the "Rebel army was better than ours and had better officers." Caldwell did not recall that being said but it appeared to him that Paine's pejorative words regarding Halleck were purely "incidental" and not encouraged by Etheridge. Paine questioned Caldwell's loyalty and whether he had sought advice from outside the court, to which Caldwell responded that he was loyal citizen and that his testimony had not been swayed by others. Having no other witnesses present to describe the events of July 22, Dunn move on to the charge of coercion.[21]

The charge focused on the circumstances whereby Paine ordered the Watts, Given and Company Bank to pay to Ellen Birmingham and C.O. Allard. Dunn called G.F. Rabb, the bank cashier, to explain. Rabb informed the court that the widow Birmingham had sought to withdraw funds from her departed husband's account several times but was denied on grounds that a guardian must be appointed to represent the couple's infant son prior to emptying the account. In the case of Allard, Rabb said that an earlier agreement between Allard's father and one of the bank's owners prohibited the son from withdrawing money from the account. Paine interceded in both instances, according to Rabb, and issued orders to have the funds released or the bank would not be permitted to conduct business. As with earlier witnesses, Paine had been given intelligence on Rabb and the owners of the bank. He began his questioning by asking if Watts, Given and Company had engaged in any contraband trade during the war. Rabb stated he did not believe so. If that was the case, Paine inquired, why had the bank provided gold to a known Southern sympathizer to take through the Union lines? Rabb did not know. Paine asked if owners of the bank were loyal men. Rabb claimed he believed they were. Was he a loyal man? Rabb said he had "taken the oath of allegiance to support the government and furnished a substitute to the Federal army." Paine asked if any of the bank's owners had sons in the Confederate army. Rabb confirmed that Watts had one son that served early in the war. Paine asked again if the bank's owners were "unqualifiedly loyal to the United States government." Rabb believed Given supported the federal government, but Watts strongly favored the South. He also informed the court that Watts had not returned to Paducah since Union forces occupied the city. Rabb provided the court with orders written by Paine, the bank's day ledger and copies of withdrawal receipts.[22]

The city's treasurer, John E. Woodward, was summoned to define his role in the dispute. He told the court that Mrs. Birmingham approached him; she was impoverished and begged him for help. She feared the involvement of attorneys would leave her with nothing, and she desperately needed money to support her child. Woodward agreed to speak to Paine on her behalf. The next day he met with Paine, who issued the order for the bank to release the funds to Woodward. He said he gave the entire sum to Birmingham.

Allard approached Woodward in early August of 1864 with a request to be introduced to General Paine. The two met, whereby Allard explained to Paine that the bank withheld money from his account based upon an unsettled debt between Given and his father. Allard claimed that Given attempted to pay his father in Confederate currency for shipping a large amount of flour to New Orleans early in the war but that his father refused to accept the money. Allard's father then declined to pay Given the profits from a shipment of cotton in which they shared an interest. In retaliation, Given notified Rabb not to conduct business with either the father or son until there was a settlement. Paine agreed with Allard and issued an order to pay him from his account. Allard delivered the order but Rabb would not comply. Paine next sent Woodward with a squad of soldiers to enforce the order. The court adjourned before the witness completed his testimony.[23]

The court next met on Monday, February 20. Woodward was called back to the stand to further clarify his part in the controversy. He reiterated his role as a go-between and relayed Paine's desire to right wrongs inflicted by the bank upon the two disadvantaged parties. During cross examination, Paine asked if any of the firm's members were loyal to the Union. Woodward responded, "they were considered by everybody as Southern sympathizers" and that Given had a son in the Rebel army. He also stated that both Given and Rabb had conveyed a certain amount of pleasure when notified of early Confederate victories. Paine thanked him and he left the courtroom.[24]

John A. Bracken, a mill owner from Lovelaceville, came before the court to address the accusation that Paine had coerced him. He claimed that Paine threatened to destroy his mill and other property if he failed to pay the attorney of Leonidas H. Edrington, also of Lovelaceville, legal fees incurred from a lawsuit, which dated to the spring of 1862. Bracken said that on November 17, 1861, troops under the command of General Paine seized and closed his mill and ordered Edrington to take care of the property until it could be ascertained whether Bracken had manufactured flour for the Rebel forces at Columbus. He was detained by the Union army for forty days at Paducah before being acquitted and released. While in Edrington's charge, over $1,000 in damages allegedly occurred to the mill. He immediately sought restitution from Edrington and filed a lawsuit in the Ballard County Circuit Court.[25]

Edrington hired Philip D. Yeiser, the commonwealth attorney for the First Judicial District, as his legal counsel. Yeiser's trial preparation included seeking a deposition from Paine, who was then stationed at Gallatin. The lawsuit was dismissed in March of 1863 at the insistence of Bracken, who at the time was incarcerated for an undisclosed act of disloyalty. Bracken had made an arrangement with Colonel Dougherty, post commander at Paducah, that he would terminate the lawsuit for his release. Yeiser was made aware of Bracken's decision and billed Edrington $250 for his services. Edrington refused to pay the fee, declaring he was forced into guardianship over the property. When Paine took command of the District of Western Kentucky, Edrington appealed to him to assist in compensating Yeiser. Paine sent for Bracken and confronted him about the lawsuit. Paine admitted he was the party liable, not Edrington, and requested he pay Yeiser. Bracken refused; Paine threatened to burn down his mill if he did not pay Yeiser. Bracken capitulated. He was ordered to see Yeiser, deliver the money and return with a note of payment. Yeiser reduced the fee to $200 and accompanied him to Paine's headquarters with Edrington's original promissory note and signed receipt of payment.[26]

Bracken testified that he was coerced to compensate a person with whom he had no financial agreement. During cross examination, Paine asked if he manufactured and

Five. "Conduct to the prejudice of good order and military discipline"   89

sold flour to the Rebel army at Columbus, to which he replied, "never sir, not a pound." Paine repeated the question in a sterner tone and Bracken answered, "not that I know of ... never to my knowledge." Were you loyal at that time? Paine inquired. Bracken remarked he had been but that he remained a "silent man" and that his "business and situation" required him to "keep still." He was asked if he was aware of who seized and dismantled his mill. He was led to believe it was Paine. At this point, Paine reminded the court of the order issued by General Charles F. Smith to him on November 16, 1861. It read,

> You will proceed with two regiments of your brigade leaving a sufficient guard for each camp with a section of artillery and a company of cavalry to Lovelaceville to night by easy marches and take possession of the grist mill run by John Bracken for the use of the Rebel forces without burning or destroying the mill. You will render it useless. Bring back all the flour or grain in the mill. You will arrest and bring back all of the persons named in the paper presented by you today, as aides and abettors of the Rebellion.

Paine challenged Bracken's loyalty by referring to the number of times he was arrested for supplying feed to Confederate cavalry and his failure to report guerrilla activities. He pleaded innocent to all of Paine's allegations. Yeiser, Edrington and Bracken's lawyer, James B. Husbands, were questioned before the court later that day and the next. Paine's energies were spent on proving Bracken's disloyalty and arguing that the suit brought against Edrington was unjust and malicious.[27]

Illegal seizures and business closures was the next charge the court took up. On February 21, J. Scott Ford testified that Captain Phelps Paine, the son of General Paine, confiscated tools, furniture, bedding, mosquito netting, blinds, clothing, groceries and other items from a stable he owned in Paducah. Ford was told that General Paine had issued the order to remove his property. During questioning, he confessed that he did not witness Captain Paine take the items, did not know the exact date the items were taken and did not have an inventory of the property removed from the stable. He was made aware of the missing articles when a friend noticed his blinds and mosquito netting on the windows of the army telegraph office, which was inhabited by Captain Paine. Ford was sent to the provost marshal who promised that he would get back all which he declared as being his property. The day that Captain Paine was reassigned, Ford received all the articles he claimed from the office except the bedding. He sought to be reimbursed $280 for the missing bedding plus a "great many small things" he could not recollect had been taken. The defense inquired how he arrived at the value of the articles; he said that "it was that much and more too" but could offer no definitive cost for the items. Unable to justify what was taken and what was later returned, the court ended his pretexts and called for the next witness.[28]

The next two witnesses addressed the closure and sale of William A. Bell's drugstore. R.M. Humble, a physician from Mayfield, described his understanding of events and the role he played in the purchase of the business. He and his partner, T.H. Mayes also of Mayfield, bought out the stock in Bell's store shortly after Paine ordered him to cease conducting business in the city. Humble met with Paine prior to the sale to seek his consent for the transaction. Paine referred him to the provost marshal and the port surveyor for permission. Bartling and Redd approved the sale with the stipulation that $2,000 of the $5,000 sale price be delivered to Bartling as an assessment fee for being a disloyal citizen and Southern sympathizer. Bell was paid $5,000 by Humble and Mayes, $1,000 up front and the rest to be paid later. Bell, however, refused to pay the assessment. When

Mayes sought a trade permit from the provost marshal's office, his request was rejected on the grounds that the assessment had not been paid. Unable to do business, Humble and Mayes sold their interests to Paducah businessman Jacob Weil for $4,000. The agreement included a provision that Bell would not receive the $4,000 until he paid the $2,000 assessment. Bell eventually capitulated and paid Major Bartling.[29]

William Bell added his version of the story when he testified later the same day. Bell declared that during their first encounter, Paine had verbally abused him and falsely accused him of being a "Rebel and copperhead." Paine advised him to sell his business and remove himself from the city. After he left Paine's headquarters, Bell approached Humble and offered to sell him the stock in his business. He informed the court that the sale of his business was done under duress and not of his own free will. Bell admitted that he had not initially paid the assessment and that he only did so to obtain half of the $4,000 from Weil. A member of the court inquired whether General Paine ordered the store closed and who instructed him to pay the assessment. Bell responded that no orders were issued by Paine to close his store or pay the assessment. He further remarked that he had not left the city after being advised to do so, and that the $2,000 assessment fee had since been returned to him.[30]

Late in the afternoon, William L. Mayes, a relative of T.H. Mayes, was called to testify in regard to an act of coercion committed by Captain Roland H. Hall with allegedly the acknowledgment and backing of Paine. Mayes stated that Hall threatened him with bodily harm if he did not pay $150 for a horse reputedly stolen by his son-in-law. Hall wrote a letter to Mayes that if he did not compensate him for the loss that he would pay him a "visit long to be remembered." Paine arrested Mayes after Hall placed charges against him for harboring guerrillas. Paine, according to Mayes, was given the opportunity to either return the horse or pay the $150 to have the charges dropped. Mayes denied he knew anything about the stolen horse but acknowledged that he did have a son-in-law who served in the Confederate army and had been at his residence when the theft occurred. Paine then ordered Mayes to locate his son-in-law and the horse and deliver them to district headquarters. During cross-examination, Paine questioned Mayes if he had seen the stolen horse, if his son-in-law took the horse and if he ever rode the horse. He answered no to all. Paine announced to the court that he knew of eyewitnesses who would testify to the contrary. After he ended his cross-examination, Paine requested that the court hold Mayes in custody for committing perjury and that he be confined until his witnesses could testify. The judge advocate informed the court "that a Court-Martial has no power to put a witness in arrest for perjury." Paine's application was overruled.[31]

The prosecution called D.Y. Craig, a farmer from McCracken County, to shed more light on Mayes' involvement with Hall's missing horse. Craig lived within a mile of Mayes' home and knew both Mayes and his son-in-law. He attested that he had overheard Mayes admit to Paine at Union headquarters that he could not control the actions of his son-in-law or other armed men who entered his premises. He recalled seeing Hall's letter noting the amount to be paid by Mayes though he observed no money exchange hands. Craig also stated that he saw Mayes' son-in-law at the gate of Mayes' home a few days after the conversation at Paine's office but was unable to discern whether the horse was Hall's. He further established that Mayes' son-in-law had served in the Confederate army and was considered a guerrilla by those in his community.[32]

The next progression of witnesses testified on Paine's expedition to Union County and the charges of illegal seizures, destruction of private property and the mistreatment

Five. "Conduct to the prejudice of good order and military discipline" 91

of civilians. W.P. Tucker, a farmer from Union County, was called to explain the statements he had given in his affidavit of September 24, 1864, regarding horses, cattle and buggies confiscated by troops under the command of General Paine. Dunn asked Tucker about the property seized from his neighbors, but he reversed his earlier statements by claiming he had no personal knowledge of any property being seized or damaged by troops under Paine's command. He commented that Paine had visited his residence and that a few of the general's staff dined in his kitchen. The officers treated him and his family "very well." The defense found no reason to ask further questions and relieved Tucker.[33]

John William Hammock, who resided four miles from Caseyville on the road to Morgenfield, said that soldiers from Paine's command took all his horses and cattle, ransacked his home and burned his furniture. Dunn asked if he saw who committed those acts. Hammock replied that he had not but believed them to be Paine's men. Paine interceded and queried how he knew the men were from his command. Hammock stated he was told so by others when he returned. Paine questioned his loyalty to the Union cause. Hammock responded that he was in favor of the federal government yet his "sympathies [had] been with the South to some extent" and that he had been arrested several times for supporting the Confederacy. Paine asked whether guerrillas had ever visited his residence. Hammock recalled only twice during the war when they stepped foot on his property but never entered his home. Paine continued and asked if he ever rejoiced at the capture of federal troops. Overall he had not, Hammock replied, but "there has been times that I have done so." Members of the court re-examined the witness if he knew who gave the order to destroy his property or if he had furnished supplies to the guerrillas. Hammock indicated he had not known who gave the order and that he had not willingly supplied Rebel troops, though he admitted Colonel Johnson's pickets had taken provisions from his farm. He also noted the cattle taken by Union troops were later returned.[34]

Another farmer from Union County, Allen Omer, followed Hammock. He filed an affidavit in late September of 1864 and testified before the court that he had property seized by Union soldiers under the command of General Paine. He charged that on August 19, 1864, men in blue uniforms took furniture from his home, cattle and horses from his fields and removed saddles, bridles and rope from his stable. The confiscated cattle were afterwards returned. When asked by Dunn who commanded the troops, the total number of men and if he ever met Paine, Omer declared he knew neither the officer in charge, or the number of troops; nor could he identify Paine in the courtroom. It was during cross examination that Paine introduced himself to Omer. As with the previous witnesses, Paine focused on Omer's loyalty. Paine asked if he had relatives in the Rebel army. Omer responded that he had a "great many" in the Confederate army, including a nephew and four cousins. Paine then inquired whether he had fed guerrillas at his residence just prior to the seizure of property by Union troops. Omer replied he had but it was done involuntarily. Pained closed by asking why he had not reported this to military authorities. Omer said that there were no federal officers nearby at the time to inform. Omer was read his testimony, and the court adjourned for the day.[35]

More witnesses from Union County came forth to testify on February 23. W.S. Buckner, a resident of Caseyville and who was mentioned in W.P. Tucker's affidavit, stated that horses and other personal items were taken from him and that he observed Union troops remove property from neighboring farms. He also had never met Paine before the trial and was unsure who commanded the troops that raided the farms. Buckner admitted to the court that he opposed blacks serving in the military and "may have in some instances" rejoiced in the success of Confederate forces. He later applied to the government to be compensated for the seized property, but his uncertainty on the number of horses taken, three or four, was a cause of concern with military officials.[36]

Three members of the Pierson family, James T. Pierson Jr., William Wright Pierson and Will S. Pierson, appeared to explain their experiences with the federal forces at Caseyville. James reported that he was aware that Paine was in Caseyville and that he saw "a good many cattle and horses coming into town." He did not, however, know where they came from or whose property they were. Will S., James' uncle, claimed that three of his horses and one mule were taken from his stable when he was away on business. Three of his male slaves also departed with the Union soldiers and were brought to Caseyville. He went to town and approached Paine to have his property returned. Paine issued an order that allowed Will S. to retrieve his horses. The mule was retained for government use and slaves enlisted into military service. During cross-examination, the defense questioned whether Paine had returned seized cattle and horses to loyal citizens. He answered that Paine, to the best of his knowledge, complied with all requests for the return of property. His son William, a merchant at Caseyville, testified that he was not at home at the time and thus could not contribute any further information.[37]

Thomas H. Welch, a physician from Union County, William Gregg and Caleb Tucker, farmers who resided near Caseyville, were called by the court to address charges defined in W.P. Tucker's affidavit against Paine. Tucker declared that he, Gregg and Welch were loyal Union men who suffered financially from illegal seizures by Paine's soldiers. Welch had horses, livestock, a buggy, harnesses, bridles and saddles seized, Gregg had a fine stallion and a few cattle taken and Tucker a half dozen horses and tack. When Paine was apprised of Welch's situation he ordered one of his staff officers to accompany the doctor to locate and recover his property. The men were able to find most of Welch's possessions at a temporarily constructed stockyard near the town. Paine assisted Gregg with a written order addressed to the regimental commander to return the stallion and cattle. The cattle were recovered, but a misunderstanding among regimental commanders prevented the return of the stallion. Tucker never reported the loss of property to the military authorities or applied for compensation. His loyalty was deemed to have been dubious by Paine and the court. Both Welch and Gregg expressed that Paine made every feasible effort to remedy the errors committed by his troops.[38]

An accusation made against Paine for seizing horses, false imprisonment and verbal abuse next received the court's attention. The complaint was described in a petition to General Burbridge from Catherine R. Greathouse of Uniontown on September 6, 1864, and in an affidavit submitted by her son, William Greathouse, on September 26, 1864. Mrs. Greathouse wrote in her petition that Paine's soldiers took four horses after threatening the life of her son. William was detained initially for furnishing a horse to a guerrilla officer and later for informing Johnson of the arrival of federal troops at Uniontown. The prosecution called Mrs. Greathouse to testify first. She was an animated fifty-eight-year-old, whose husband was a prominent attorney in the city. She acknowledged that Union soldiers took her husband's horses but admitted that she "didn't see General Paine but it was his command that passed [by] that day." She pointed out that it had to be Paine's men who arrested her son. Paine questioned the witness whether she had told an acquaintance to notify the guerrillas at Morganfield of Union troops at Uniontown. With a slightly raised tone she said, "No sir, I did not. I will tell you what I said. I was standing and looking at the boats as they landed and there was some gentleman riding by the place and I said in mercy sake can't you let Johnson know so that he can make his escape." Stunned by the response, he asked if she were a Southern sympathizer. Unabashed she replied, "Well, I reckon I am." He implored further whether she ever rejoiced at the success of the Confederate army. She answered, "I have done that very thing." With her sentiments clearly exposed, Paine ended his cross-examination.[39]

Her son William, who appeared older than his seventeen years-of-age, recounted how one of Paine's officers pointed a pistol at his head and intended to shoot him if he did not deliver the horses he demanded. He also addressed his arrest as a Rebel informer and his detention with other prisoners who were to be executed. He denied he was an informer and explained that Johnson's men were aware of federal troops at Uniontown before he traveled to Morganfield. He defended his mother by saying she did not send him to warn Colonel Johnson. Paine asked if the witness spoke to Johnson or his men. He replied he had never met Johnson but had spoken to friends he believed served with him. The court recessed for the day before Paine finished his examination. He resumed on the 24th by directly asking if William told "Johnson's men that the Yankees were coming?" He responded that he had not and that it was Johnson's men who reported the arrival of Union troops to him. Paine followed up with asking why he had not informed Union officers of Johnson's men at Uniontown. William stuttered, "I thought they knew the guerrillas was there ... that is what I thought they came for.... I did not report.... I did not know I ought to report.... I would not report on either side." After a few more questions, Pained dismissed the witness.[40]

W.P. Tucker's affidavit came into play again as Henry Parsons was called by the prosecution. Parsons, a farmer from Union County, had been identified by Tucker as having cattle, oxen and other property seized by Paine's soldiers. He testified that he "did not see any property whatsoever taken at all nor in possession of the Federal forces." Two horses, a yoke of oxen, a buggy and a wagon had gone missing, but he had no proof that Union soldiers took them. Dunn established that federal troops under the command of Paine were in the vicinity of Parsons' farm and that all but the oxen were found at Paducah. Parsons said that all his property had been returned and that he was later compensated by the government for the oxen. When asked if he knew of property having been seized from his neighbors, he swore, "only from hearsay." Paine asked a single question of Parsons—had he authorized the confiscation of his property? Parsons remarked, "No sir, I don't know anything about it."[41]

W.P. Tucker was recalled by Dunn to clarify the inconsistences listed in his affidavit. Tucker explained that he saw the horses of Buckner, Parsons and Caleb Tucker in the possession of Colonel Davidson on the road near his farm. He was uncertain whether General Paine was his immediate commander or if he was aware of the horses in Davidson's possession. He also corroborated that not one of those named in his affidavit, except Parsons, had applied to Paine for the return of seized property. Paine asked Tucker about the conditions that existed prior to and following his expedition into Union County. He acknowledged that bands of guerrillas freely roamed about the county, conscripted men and "lived off the people" since the war commenced. He expressed that a "great many Southern rights men" resided in Union County who assisted guerrillas with provisions and horses. These same men were "very much dissatisfied at the manner in which [Paine] acted while in the county." Did unconditional Union men grumble about the course he took? Paine asked. Tucker replied, as a "general thing they did not." However, some complained "very much that [they] were Union men" who had been mistreated and robbed of their property. Paine ended his questioning at that point and Tucker stepped down.[42]

The charge of false imprisonment and the abusive treatment of those in custody was brought to the forefront by James Dickey Moss. Moss sent a complaint to General Meredith on September 12, 1864, in which he said he was arrested without due process, "insulted and abused," and "wantonly robbed without authority of law." While in custody he wrote that he was gravely ill and "suffered greatly" at the hands of the guards. Prior to his arrest on August 11, he was the owner of a butcher shop in the city. His incarceration was due to his involvement in the capture of a runaway slave near Paducah in January of 1862. Moss and an accomplice abducted a black man within Union lines and forcibly removed him to Paris, Tennessee, which was then under Confederate control. He was compensated by the slave's owner for his capture and return. The slave escaped for the second time and reached Paducah in early August of 1864. The man told Major Bartling of his kidnapping and the beatings he received from his master for running away. Bartling sent for Moss, who fully acknowledged his role in the abduction. Bartling placed him under arrest and reported the offense to Paine with the recommendation that Moss pay a $1,000 fine, $300 of which would be given to the former slave for his suffering and $700 to the relief fund. Paine agreed with the punishment. Moss informed Bartling that he could not raise the money. Bartling said that he would remain in the guardhouse until the fine was paid. Within twenty-four hours Moss raised $600 and wrote a bond for the remaining $400 and he was released from prison. Two weeks later, he made the final payment.[43]

As he stood before the court, Moss gave a watered-down version of his complaint to Meredith. He confessed to have never met Paine nor had he known if the general ordered him to be confined. His earlier protests were not mentioned. He never brought up the allegedly harsh treatment at the guardhouse or verbal threats from Major Bartling. When asked by the prosecution under what authority had he kidnapped the escaped slave, he replied, "I cannot say positively it was anybody's authority." Moss stated that he approached the quartermaster at Paducah about returning the slave but that the officer in charge was unconcerned and overtaxed to get involved in the matter. He denied that he brought the kidnapped man into Confederate-controlled territory. Moss could not recall the date and was uncertain if Union forces had command of the region. Paine had no further questions.[44]

A late arrival from Union County was introduced before the court concluded for the day. Louis L. Talbot, a merchant and farmer from Commercial Point, near Caseyville, was called to explain the affidavit he filed, which claimed Paine visited his home "cursed and abused" him and took two slaves, two horses and five head of cattle. Dunn asked if he had ever met General Paine and who confiscated his property. Contrary to his earlier sworn statement, Talbot denied having met Paine and said that the cattle and horses were removed from his farm by Union soldiers he understood to be under Paine's command. Talbot also never filed an application to have the property returned nor to receive compensation for his losses. Paine had no questions for the witness, and the court adjourned.[45]

When the trial resumed the next morning, Dunn read Special Order No. 73, which granted the change of venue from Cairo to Paducah. The order was dated February 14 but was not telegraphed to Paducah until the 24th. The prosecution then called on T.H. Mayes to explain his part in the sale of William A. Bell's drugstore. Mayes, a farmer from Graves County, restated that he purchased Bell's drug store for $3,000 and was later told by Paine to pay Bell's $2,000 assessment fine if he wished to buy and trade goods in the city. Paine asked Mayes if he recalled their conversation regarding assessments, reminding Mayes that he never directed him to pay the fee and that a portion of Dr. Bell's assessment would be refunded. Mayes responded that his "recollection was very poor" and he could not remember the "particulars" of the conversation.[46]

The use of government transportation for private purposes by Paine was the next charge examined by the court. Captain Lewis T. Bradley of the steamboat *Convoy* was called to testify for the prosecution. Dunn asked the captain if he shipped cotton and tobacco for Bolinger and who ordered the shipment to be made. He inquired whether soldiers were employed to load the cargo. Bradley said his boat transported freight from Hickman to Cairo for Bolinger under orders from the "commander of the District of West Kentucky" and that soldiers had loaded the merchandise. Bradley produced and handed the order he received to Dunn who read its content to the court. The order, written on August 21, 1864, by Colonel McArthur at Columbus, instructed the district Quarter Master at Columbus to retrieve "seventy five bales of cotton and twenty five hogsheads [of] tobacco" and deliver them to Paducah. Once there, they would be stored and "subject to the orders of the General Commanding the District of West Kentucky." The shipment however was unloaded at Cairo, according to Bradley, by an order telegraphed by Paine to Bolinger from Paducah. Paine had only a few questions for the witness. He simply asked what route the Captain took and whether the boat kept on her regular schedule. Bradley replied the trip was from Paducah to Columbus and remained on schedule despite being sidetracked to Hickman. On September 19, 1864, the Captain also gave a deposition, which stated it was the "only instance" that General Paine gave such an order and had "since [that time] done the same thing under similar orders" by other Union commanders.[47]

Dunn called on Bolinger to explain his actions during that trip to Hickman. He admitted that the *Convoy* had transported him from Paducah to Hickman to collect cotton and tobacco stored in warehouses nearby the port. He also understood fully that the boat and its crew were employed by the government. Bolinger offered a detailed explanation about why Paine issued the order. Two weeks before, Bolinger had been denied a permit by Paine on the grounds he lacked evidence that the merchandise was purchased from loyal citizens. Prior to Paine's expedition to Union County, Bolinger received the certificates of loyalty from his business partner Judge Joseph M. Bigger in Hickman, but Paine was away from headquarters preparing his men for departure.[48]

The steamer paddled down the river on its scheduled route stopping at Cairo and Columbus. As the *Convoy* refueled at Cairo, Bolinger telegraphed Paine's headquarters to request that the cotton and tobacco be unloaded at Cairo to reduce the cost in shipping to Paducah. He was unable to obtain a response before going to Hickman. At Columbus, a squad of Union soldiers boarded the *Convoy* under orders from Colonel McArthur to protect the boat and government property. When the *Convoy* reached Hickman, the soldiers were placed to guard the wharf and warehouse during the transfer of freight. Bigger met the boat and directed the transference of the cotton and tobacco onto the *Convoy*. Being short of dockworkers, Bigger approached some the soldiers not on guard duty to assist with loading the cargo. Bolinger testified that Bigger did not pay the soldiers but "treated" the men for their services. Eighty-four bales of cotton and twenty-seven hogshead of tobacco were reported by Bigger to have been removed from Hickman. The soldiers disembarked at Columbus on the return voyage. While the boat was docked at

Cairo, Bolinger received a telegram from Paine's headquarters to unload the cargo there instead of Paducah.[49]

During cross examination, Bolinger repeated that Paine's original order was only to land at Hickman and remove the threatened cotton and tobacco. He also clarified that Paine neither ordered Union soldiers to accompany Bolinger to Hickman nor to load the cargo. Bolinger attested that he had paid all charges and fees associated with the transport of the freight and that the *Convoy* had carried private freight and passengers before his voyage to Hickman. He further conveyed that while en route to Hickman, Captain Bradley told him that "they wanted all the freight and passengers they could get in order to keep up the expenses of the boat." Bolinger had since that trip to Hickman, "gave the *Convoy* a great deal of freight" to ship. Under re-examination, he reaffirmed that the boat had not lost significant time in consequence of the trip to Hickman.[50]

Dunn called on Captain Toussaint C. Buntin, the assistant quartermaster of the District of West Kentucky at Columbus, to verify that the *Convoy* was under the employment of the federal government. Buntin stated to the court that the steamer was indeed owned and operated by the United States government. He could not recall if his office received direct compensation from Bolinger for the transportation of the freight or if the boat's earnings were reported to him. However, Buntin acknowledged that his office had received money for the private shipment of freight and that the funds had been documented in the quartermaster's account ledger.[51]

As more witnesses were made available, charges previously deliberated were readdressed by the court. The prosecution returned its attention to the charges of false imprisonment and mistreatment. Dunn called Marian G. Milam, a druggist from Paducah, to speak of his ordeal as a prisoner. Milam explained that he was arrested by the "personal order" of General Paine on July 25, 1864, without formal charges and jailed for fifty-one days. In a previous a previous testimony given to the board of investigation on September 15, 1864, Milam testified that he was subjected to the "roughest kind" of treatment, not given a sufficient amount of food, offered no medical treatment for a painful ailment and was "compelled to do work of the filthiest and most revolting kind." He told the court a similar story about the conditions he endured while imprisoned and that he had never been informed of the offenses he committed nor had he been tried in a court. Paine asked the witnesses if he had ever been refused medical attention or had been denied medicine by him personally. Milam responded that he had "never saw General Paine" when he was imprisoned and that he was permitted to leave the prison under guard at least once to seek medical attention and purchase medicine. Paine pointed out to the court that Milam had volunteered and served in the Confederate army earlier in the war and surrendered to federal troops when health issues prevented him from further service. The witness replied that when the war broke out he resided in Weakley County, Tennessee, and "if a man was living where I was, he could hardly keep out of it [the Confederate Army]." He presented the court an oath of allegiance certificate he received in the summer of 1862 and stated he had remained loyal since that time. Paine asked if he had taken an oath of allegiance to the United States government since his arrival in Paducah. Milam responded that he had not. After a brief re-cross examination, Milam exited the courtroom.[52]

The prosecution reverted to the charge of illegal seizures as Mary Crutchfield, who had rented a room in the home of J. Scott Ford, testified that property had been taken from the residence by Union soldiers in August of 1864. She recalled a door mat, bed clothes and some curtains and blinds were taken from the home and a few barrels from the nearby stables. She was unsure where the items were destined or whose command the soldiers were under. E.R. Jett, a trader from McCracken County, informed the court that two mules had been confiscated from the farm of J.C. Brooks of Ballard County by a Union cavalry detachment in the summer of 1864 but was uncertain of the date or who directed the men. A traveler who accompanied Jett, Frederick T. Whitworth, also attested that mules had been removed from Brooks' farm by Union soldiers but was unaware who authorized the seizure. Paine briefly cross examined the last three witnesses on the loyalty of John Bracken, whom Jett and Whitworth declared was not a loyal citizen, and the court adjourned for the day.[53]

The court reconvened on Monday, the twenty-seventh. The morning session began with the questioning of Captain Phelps Paine. Dunn inquired about the property removed from Ford's residence at Paducah. Paine stated that his father had not ordered him to take the property from the home but that the provost marshal, Major Bartling, had provided his headquarters with furniture, bedding, curtains and other items. He declared that he had no knowledge of where the furnishings had come from. He also told the court that when he was relieved from duty, General Meredith took possession of the headquarters and its contents. General Paine saw no need to cross examine his son.[54]

The prosecution next called Peter Davidson, former commander of the 139th Illinois Infantry Regiment, to describe the conduct of Paine's troops in Union County. Davidson arrived from Peoria, Illinois, the day before. He informed the court that he was ordered by Paine to "seize the property of Rebels ... all cattle, all serviceable horses and mules." When Dunn asked how he determined the loyalty of citizens, Davidson replied that he could not recall if Paine issued specific instructions. Dunn then questioned Davidson on petitions made by loyal citizens to reclaim property. The prosecutor named over a dozen claimants and listed the items that were reportedly taken. Davidson responded to each of the claims, but his recollection of names and singular events were fuzzy. After being asked about the appropriation of potatoes and an overcoat, he stated that "we took a considerable amount of property on that trip but the names of parties [and property] I cannot remember now." He admitted that a "good many" cattle, horses and mules were taken and that confiscated buggies were used as ambulances for the sick.[55]

During his cross examination, Paine queried why he was ordered to seize "serviceable horses and mules and particularly fat cattle." Davidson answered that the horses and mules were for the cavalry and the cattle a "matter of reprisal" to "punish Rebels and Rebel sympathizers for harboring guerrillas." Paine inquired why "fat cattle could be found in that part of Kentucky." Davidson recalled that it was here where the government cattle were stolen and brought ashore by Colonel Johnson's Rebel force and that the well-fed cattle were likely the animals taken. Paine asked who oversaw the property seized by federal troops and how the property was managed. Davidson acknowledged that he was in charge and detailed other officers in his regiment to "determine the right of property if there was any claimant who claimed to be a Union man and he was to [judge] upon it." Those officers, in turn, reported to him and he either returned the property or denied the request. He noted that a "considerable amount of property was turned over to parties who claimed to be Union men." In regard to the loyalty of Union countians, Davidson asserted that "they were almost all Rebel sympathizers" and "made it unsafe for Union people to live in their midst." He concluded by denying that any property was intentionally confiscated from loyal citizens.[56]

J.C. Brooks, a farmer from Ballard County, was brought before the court to clarify statements made by Jett and Whitworth two days before. Brooks had testified in an affidavit on September 19, 1864, that troops under the command of Paine "came to his house took two mules, one horse and ransacked his house taking off bed clothes and wearing apparel—in fact nearly everything they could lay their hands on." Brooks remarked that indeed property had been seized from his farm by Union troops, including mules, his and his son's clothes and a number of blankets from his slaves. He did not know the name of the officer in charge nor whose command he served under. When asked if he made an application to General Paine to have property restored, Brooks replied he had not. Brooks later visited Paine at his Paducah headquarters the following month and reported the incident. There Paine informed him that soldiers on that expedition had already been arrested and punished for their actions. Paine reminded Brooks in his cross examination that he specifically said that "if the soldiers did not stop taking goods from citizens that I would shoot some of them [and] if they behaved like guerrillas that I would punish them as I did guerrillas." Brooks commented that he had no recollection of that conversation.[57]

After Brooks retired, Dunn informed the court that "he had no other witnesses in attendance today, that he had found much difficulty in procuring the attendance of witnesses on account of the temporary absence of some [of them] from their homes and the removal of others from their late residences." He notified the court that he might have more witnesses in attendance the next day or in the upcoming days. The court suggested that in order to save time "the accused might enter upon his defense and then the witnesses for the prosecution might be examined as they arrive." Paine consented to this arrangement and entered upon his defense.[58]

Six

"Witnesses of known disloyalty"

Paine began his defense by submitting as evidence all orders he received from June 18 to August 16. The orders dealt with his transfer from the Department of the Cumberland to the Department of the Tennessee and included a telegram that directed him to advance 1,500 men to Uniontown.[1]

The first witness for the defense was Colonel Henry W. Barry. Paine asked Barry to explain military conditions at Paducah prior to his arrival. Barry said the post had been seriously neglected and the morale of the troops was very poor. Guerrillas ruled the countryside beyond and the pickets were attacked nightly. The police force was ineffectual, and army officers had been fired upon within the city. Barry also conveyed that his efforts to recruit black soldiers were undermined by the policies of past commanders who were swayed by local politicians and prominent city leaders. Before he could further testify, the trial adjourned for the day.[2]

Colonel Barry was recalled to the stand the next morning, where he continued to describe the mismanagement and chaos that General Paine inherited. He also spoke of the complete turnaround that occurred within days of Paine's assumption of command. "Peace and harmony reigned here [Paducah] and it was safe for us to go to the state line without being molested," he informed the court. He added that the number of black recruits at Paducah rose by over 1,300 men during Paine's brief time as post commander.[3]

Paine next called the colonel of Union County's militia, G.L. Tombelle. A lawyer from Morganfield, he said the county had been "entirely in possession of the guerrillas for a long time and it had gone to that extent that they eventually blockaded the Ohio River." General Paine's expedition immediately removed that threat. Tombelle recalled "a great deal of property was taken from the Rebels and a few Union men," but Paine's men "didn't know friends from foes," which led to confusion. He also explained that when Union men came to reclaim their property, Paine returned it. "I never saw him [Paine] in a single instance refuse to deliver up the property," Tombelle swore. Paine questioned the witness on the loyalty of the men who had testified earlier against him. He asked about Hammock, Omer, Gregg, Tucker, Talbot and Parsons, all of whom Tombelle was acquainted with. All but Gregg were well known Southern sympathizers according to the witness. The judge advocate followed by asking about the current conditions in Union County. He responded that it was "extremely dangerous for a Union man to travel through the country" and he "dare[d] not go outside the pickets."[4]

After Tombelle stepped down, the prosecution recalled Bartling. Dunn questioned the major about the incarceration of James D. Moss. Bartling gave a detailed account of Moss' involvement in the kidnapping of an escaped slave that led to his arrest. Moss and another man had hired the African American to cut wood. Once the man was outside the picket lines, he was handcuffed at gunpoint and forcibly removed to Tennessee. He escaped for the second time two and half years later and returned to Paducah, where he told Bartling about his abduction. He admitted to Bartling "that it was all true and that it was the dirtiest piece of business he was ever engaged in [and] that he felt truly sorry for it." Bartling disclosed that he alone arrested Moss and that it was his idea to detain him until a fine of $1,000 was paid. Paine was consulted and agreed with the punishment. Dunn next inquired about William Bell's claim that he was coerced to pay the provost marshal $2,000. Bartling stated that General Paine told him that Bell had "made an application to sell out his stock of goods and that as he was an exceedingly disloyal man." Paine granted Bell permission to sell his business provided he contribute $2,000 to the relief fund. Bell paid him on August 5, 1864, and it was documented in his accounts ledger. Dunn concluded his examination by questioning Bartling about the property removed from J. Scott Ford's home. The witness responded that he received an order from Captain Paine to furnish his office headquarters with bedding, mosquito bars and netting. Bartling requested Ford to provide the items. He agreed "provided they were returned to him when General Paine got through with them." Bartling gave back the borrowed property after Paine was removed from command. Ford notified him that "everything was returned but one counterpane."[5]

Paine approached the witness and began a long series of questions. Bartling was first asked about the relief fund and who it was intended to aid. The fund was for the "relief of the wives and widows of soldiers with their children," replied Bartling. Paine asked if any assessments were made on Southern sympathizers or former Rebels to reimburse Union citizens for their losses during the war. Bartling acknowledged that a committee was appointed by General Paine to levy assessments and that Bell was one of the few who was assessed. When asked about the loyalty of Woolfolk, Alexander, Rabb, Caldwell and Milam, Bartling said they were all Southern sympathizers and that their testimony must be considered suspect. He also expounded on the state of affairs at Paducah before and after Paine's arrival. He spoke of "deplorable conditions" and said that Union men dared not venture outside of the picket lines without a military escort. But when Paine instituted his new policy "Union men were happy and jubilant and the Rebels exceedingly discouraged."[6]

Dunn reexamined the witness. He asked who ordered the imprisonment of Milam. Bartling replied that Paine issued the order. Paine then asked if the fine imposed upon Moss was a form of military punishment and if Ford was a Rebel sympathizer. He agreed that the penalty was punishment but expressed that Ford was a loyal man. Dunn asked if Bell was regarded in the community as loyal citizen; Bartling said "not entirely."[7]

Elijah Rudolph, a farmer from McCracken County, was called by the defense to describe the character of William Mayes. The witness, a neighbor of Mayes, testified that his reputation was "bad" and that he could not be trusted under oath. The judge advocate inquired how long he had known Mayes and how close he lived to Mayes. Rudolph stated he had known Mayes for ten years and that he lived about two miles from his farm. Dunn foresaw no need for further questions and Rudolph was dismissed.[8]

The defense next brought before the court the Reverend William M. Starks, a farmer and merchant from Calloway County. Starks explained that he, James B. Happy and the Reverend W.W. Bigger of Graves County had been appointed to serve on the assessment committee by General Andrew Jackson Smith in late 1863. General Smith was in command at Columbus from August of 1863 to January of 1864. On November 4, he received General Order No. 4 from General Grant, which stipulated that "for every dollars' worth of property taken from [Union] citizens, or destroyed by raiders, an assessment will be made upon secessionists of the neighborhood and collected by the nearest military forces." Smith directed the three men to procure tax and assessors books from each county and create a list of those to be assessed. However, before a list could be finalized, Smith was reassigned and departed Columbus. A completed list was turned over to Colonel Hicks at Paducah, after which he issued an order to notify the parties named and command them to pay. Hicks' order was suspended by General Grant after he was informed that the Kentucky legislature had passed a law forbidding "military assessments for past injuries." Starks

General Andrew Jackson Smith (Library of Congress).

provided Paine the list after he assumed command at Paducah in July of 1864. Paine directed the two remaining committee members (Happy had been murdered by Kesterson five months earlier) and Thomas M. Redd to modify the list and execute Smith's original orders. The amounts were to be set by the committee and approved by Paine. The amount to be assessed was formulated by the committee. Paine used that formula when he fined Dr. Bell. To Starks' knowledge, there were no other assessments collected since the "guerrillas were so thick they could not get out" to serve the notices.[9]

As with other witnesses for the defense, Paine requested Starks to reflect on the conditions of Paducah before he arrived and what followed after he left. He told of terror beyond the picket lines. Starks cited the murder of "old man Happy" in front of his family at Mayfield; he had been shot at numerous times. He also mentioned the flight of many Union families to Illinois. Post-Paine, Starks said that he would not travel anywhere outside the pickets without the accompaniment of "no less than two hundred" soldiers. It was 3:00 p.m. when Starks finished, and the court adjourned for the day.[10]

The trial resumed on the morning of March 1. To dispute the testimony of William Mayes, Paine called D.Y. Craig, J.H. Hines, J.W. Caldwell, Roland H. Hall and Robert Glover. Craig was another Mayes neighbor. He asked if Mayes could be trusted to tell the truth under oath and if he was an unconditional Union man. Craig said he could not and that he was uncertain if he was loyal. Hines was the justice of the peace in McCracken County and neighbor of Mayes. He said Mayes was a "notorious liar in common conversations" and "would not believe him under oath." Caldwell knew Mayes and agreed he could not be trusted under oath. Hall had known Mayes for over ten years and agreed that Mayes was untrustworthy and that his testimony was untrue. Hall accused Mayes' son-in-law, a soldier in the Confederate army, of stealing his horse during Forrest's raid. Hall admitted that he wrote Mayes, demanding the horse or compensation. He charged Mayes with harboring guerrillas, and Paine had him arrested. Mayes paid Hall for the stolen horse, and the charges were dropped. Hall indicated if Mayes brought him the horse he would refund the money. Glover testified that he saw Mayes' son-in-law, whom he had known for a few years, with Hall's horse. He believed the horse thief was a guerrilla.[11]

P.H. Hall, a resident of Weakley County, Tennessee, and a former major in the Union army, was called to describe the impact of Paine's policies in northwest Tennessee. Hall explained that Paine's execution of Kesterson and the theat to execute other captured guerrillas if Union men were murdered greatly subdued the guerrillas. "They never interfered with any Union man while General Paine was in command," he said. The judge advocate asked Hall how frequently he visited the district before and during Paine's administration. He replied that he visited Paducah frequently for months prior to Paine's arrival and only once during.[12]

More witnesses for the prosecution began to arrive later that day. Ila M. Davis, a physician from Union County, said Paine's soldiers took horses, cattle, saddles, bridles, medicines and a case of surgeon's pocket instruments. The cattle and all but one horse wandered back to Davis' pasture. The drugs and medical equipment remained missing. Paine questioned why Davis had not applied for compensation. The witness said he understood from the statements of others that no property was being given back. He was asked if he knew of Union men being refused their property, and Davis responded he did not. When inquired if there had been any noticeable changes after Paine's expedition, he stated that there were very few incidents with guerrillas and that the "expedition made a difference."[13]

Thomas L. Sturgeon testified about property removed from the flour mill of David O. Conn where he was an employee. He said that black troops broke into the mill and took ten barrels of flour, poured them into sacks and carted them off. He heard from others later that the same soldiers returned and seized another ten barrels. Dunn asked if Paine was present. He was not, admitted Sturgeon; he claimed the general was at a hotel not more than 400 yards away. Sturgeon was unsure who was in command of the troops or if Paine issued an order to remove the flour. "There didn't seem to be any one in command of them," Paine followed with a number of questions about guerrilla intrusions into the county. Sturgeon affirmed that they frequented Caseyville, attacked government boats on the river and were rumored to have stolen cattle. Paine also asked if whiskey dealers in the town supplied his soldiers with "intoxicating liquors thereby making them insubordinate." Sturgeon replied that he believed so.[14]

Paine recalled John E. Woodward to testify on the loyalty of Dr. Bell. The witness declared that Bell was "as a great many others—a sympathizer with the Rebellion," but that he had never seen him commit any acts of disloyalty. Woodward was aware that Bell did associate at times with those who were disloyal.[15]

John S. Greathouse, husband of Catherine Greathouse, came before the court to tell how his property was confiscated and released to him. Greathouse stated that he was not present at Uniontown when his four horses had been taken and thus had no clue who took them. He said his wife told him it was Paine's men. He said Paine appointed an officer to help him locate his horses. The officer accompanied Greathouse to the stables and corrals where three of the horses were found. The fourth horse was never recovered. Greathouse concluded by stressing that Paine "unhesitatingly gave me every assistance by orders and sending men to get my horses."[16]

The defense put Richard Branham, a trader from Caseyville, on the stand to further corroborate the conditions in Union County before and after Paine's expedition. Branham claimed that "we were very much annoyed by guerrillas for two years previous to General Paine's visit" and they were "very frequently in our county and town [and] there was very few weeks that they were not in town." Since Paine's expedition, Branham said that there was "very little property disturbed by guerrillas" and that "all the guerrillas seemed to have left the country." Branham implied the threat of Paine's return even caused prominent Southern sympathizers to ask the guerrillas to keep out of the county. The day ended with his testimony.[17]

When the court reconvened the prosecution questioned Bettie Barbour Hughes and her son Joshua Hughes to offer the court a broader perspective on the seizure of property by soldiers under Paine's command. The Hughes' family farm was three miles from Morganfield on the road to Caseyville. Hughes was the widow of Willis G. Hughes, a former state legislator, Union County judge and Whig Party leader. Prior to his death in 1863, Hughes was a leading Unionist. The Hughes' farm was visited by a squad of the Thirty-Fourth New Jersey under Lieutenant Colonel Timothy Moore. The men seized four horses, a yoke of oxen and three cows. They also left with three slaves, saddles, ammunition and a flute. Hughes acknowledged that she did not approach General Paine about the seizures. She filed a written application to be compensated, but received no reply. Her son, who was visiting Union County from Henderson during Paine's expedition, corroborated his mother's testimony.[18]

Acker testified for the prosecution. A Bavarian by birth, he told the court that when he observed a handful of soldiers attempting to break into his business that morning, he warned the men to stay out and sought an officer to guard his store. He said the officer demanded a drink. Acker was hesitant, but the officer told him that if he did not comply, the soldiers would loot the store. He served the officer and other soldiers. After a few men became intoxicated, a higher-ranking officer arrived and ordered Acker to close his store. The storekeeper was arrested and charged with distributing alcohol to enlisted men. A slave told Paine that Acker had provided ammunition to the guerrillas. Paine ordered a search of his home which turned up 400 pounds of shot, a gun, gun locks and pistol cartridges. As punishment for concealing armaments at his home and selling liquor to soldiers, Paine had Acker strung up by the wrists in the center of town.[19]

Under cross-examination, Paine asked Acker if he was an unconditional Union man. Acker replied, "I don't know" but "I have been for my government ever since I have been living here." He swore he "let politics alone entirely [and] never let politics be talked about in [his] storehouse." He denied any collaboration with guerrillas, selling liquor to soldiers or knowing of stolen government cattle. Dunn redirected questions, hoping to magnify the pain and humiliation suffered by Acker and Paine's disregard of repeated requests that Union men be brought forward to prove Acker's innocence. The witness stepped down, and the prosecution called another witness to the events of August 20 at Caseyville.[20]

Phillip Snow, a carpenter from Caseyville who resided a block away from Acker, recalled seeing a great number of intoxicated soldiers roaming the streets, a few of whom pounded on his door demanding food. Snow asked one of the men where he got the liquor, and the soldier pointed to Acker's store. Snow said he saw Acker hung from the wrists for less than twenty minutes. Acker led the court to believe that he was tortured for over an hour. Snow alleged that "guerrillas all considered Acker a Rebel" and obtained ammunition from him. He said he never observed the transactions but heard reports from those who had. Snow and the Union men in town found Acker to be a "strong Rebel sympathizer" and his business frequented by guerrillas seeking whiskey and weapons.[21]

Dunn called upon Joseph Gerrish, a storekeeper from Caseyville, to give his version of General Paine's expedition into Union County. Gerrish said Union soldiers plundered his grocery store on the night of August 18 and took "almost everything." He valued his loss as over $700. Paine asked if he could identify which men looted his store and who was their commanding officer. Gerrish replied that there likely was not an officer present that he was uncertain if Paine knew of the crimes committed by his men. Garrish applied to Paine for reimbursement, and the general promised to restore the stolen property and compensate him for the damage in his store. An attempt was made to locate the pilfered property, and an officer was appointed to assist Garrish. The officer blamed black soldiers, but Garrish believed it was a squad of white soldiers. He had still not been compensated at the time he testified at the court-martial. Garrish was asked if Acker was a Unionist, and he responded that he was not. But the witness doubted that Acker would willingly furnish whiskey or ammunition to guerrillas.[22]

The judge advocate conceded that the only witness cited in the twenty-first specification of the second charge, W.H. Kibbey of Morganfield, could not be located to testify. The specification declared that Paine's troops violently abused the Kibbey family and seized "five horses, three saddles, several blankets, bridles and halters and two guns" on August 19. The prosecution again rested its case but reminded the court that other witnesses had been summoned and had yet to arrive in the city.[23]

The accused called grocer Samuel M. Purcell to describe the character of Dr. Bell. He testified that Bell was not at all loyal, but belonged to the "opposite party" and "never acted with the [Unconditional] Union Party." Dunn had no questions for the witness.[24]

Thomas M. Redd, the surveyor of customs at Paducah, appeared to offer his opinion on the loyalty of Bell, Alexander, Woolfolk, Rabb, Caldwell and Ford. He said he had sound evidence that Bell, Woolfolk, Rabb and Ford were Southern sympathizers and that Alexander and Caldwell had been Union men but changed their views when the army made soldiers of slaves. The court adjourned before he completed his testimony. The following day, March 3, Dunn queried Redd whether the men could be trusted under oath. Redd believed that Alexander and Caldwell could be, but that Bell, Woolfolk, Rabb and Ford most likely would lie. Under reexamination, Paine questioned Redd if Alexander and Caldwell were "strictly loyal men." He answered that the two were not outright Rebels but they strongly opposed emancipation and blacks serving in the army. Redd would not specifically comment on their loyalty.[25]

Another late arrival from Union County, James T. Pierson, entered the courtroom to address the charge of disrespectful remarks made by Paine against Bramlette while he was in Caseyville on August 20. Pierson was a farmer and Union Democratic member of the Kentucky state legislature. He said General Paine referred to the governor as a "traitor or Rebel or something to that effect" but could not "recollect exactly the words he spoke." When asked when and where he heard those remarks, Pierson said at Paducah on the last day of August. His response contradicted the place and time recorded on the official charge. He said that several others overheard the statements made by Paine, including Tombelle who was still in the courtroom. Dunn concluded his questioning.[26]

Paine approached Pierson and asked if he felt a "great injustice was done [to] Governor Bramlette" if such words were spoken. Dunn objected to the question on the grounds that it was irrelevant. Paine countered by stating the defense wished to "ascertain the animus of the witness" and that the accused had the "right to search out the witness' mind if there is not some promptings." Pierson's bias, according to Paine, "might be used as testimony against a Federal officer who had enrolled Negro troops." Paine sought to prove a motive for a false accusation. The court was cleared as the judges discussed the legality of Dunn's objection. When they returned, the court overruled the objection and ordered the witness to answer. Pierson responded that a "great injustice had been done to Governor Bramlette" to be accused of disloyalty. Paine asked if he opposed the enlistment of black soldiers. He said he initially was against the idea but had come to believe that the government had the right to enlist black soldiers. Pierson felt that loyal slave owners should be compensated for their loss of property. Had Governor Bramlette opposed the enlistment of black soldiers after the United States Congress passed a law authorizing its existence? queried Paine. Dunn again objected, claiming that "Governor Bramlette's views on the question of the enlistment of negroes had nothing to do with [the] case." Paine explained to the court that he sought to prove that the governor had "prevented the enlistment of [black] troops directly or indirectly in the State of Kentucky" after a direct order was issued by the army. Had the governor done so, in the opinion of Paine, he gave aid and comfort to the enemy. Thus, if a statement were made that the governor was a "traitor" or "Rebel," then Paine's remarks were factual and not slanderous. Dunn contested that "whether the Governor of Kentucky at the time these words were used was a traitor or a Rebel is not a question for the consideration of the court."[27]

The court again retired to consider Dunn's objection. When the judges returned, they overruled Dunn's objection. The court was of the opinion "that it is proper for the accused to produce testimony to show mitigating circumstances in the case." Pierson conceded that Bramlette opposed the enlistment of blacks since it would be "demoralizing to the balance of the slaves in the State." When asked if he was an unconditional Union man, he said that he preferred to be considered a "Union man without any conditions at all." The court wanted a complete account of the events that led Paine to make those statements. Pierson said that he was part of a small delegation from Union County that went to Paducah to seek the release of a man arrested at Caseyville. General Paine met the delegation and announced that the "great mass of the people of Kentucky were Rebels and traitors" and that "Governor Bramlette and George D. Prentice were at the head of the whole concern."[28]

Tombelle was recalled to the stand by the prosecution and Dunn asked if he remembered such a discussion between the delegation and General Paine. Tombelle had no recollection of the conversation in which Paine allegedly spoke negatively of Governor Bramlette. The defense questioned whether Pierson was an Unconditional Union man. The witness responded that he did not "regard him as an Unconditional Union man by any means" and that Pierson had been critical of the Lincoln administration on the issue of emancipation. Tombelle said that Pierson "was very much opposed to Negro enlistments or anything of the kind." Paine then recalled Richard Branham who stated that he did not consider Pierson to be "a true Union man" and that he never cooperated with "the true Union men of Union County." Branham said Pierson won by a very narrow margin and that many disloyal citizens voted for him. Four other witnesses testified that Pierson was not an Unconditional Union man.[29]

Acting Ensign William W. Phillips told the court about conditions of the Paducah port before and during General Paine's command. Phillips found the situation to be "rather deplorable" and that any "man who professed to be a Union man had a feeling as if he had no one to protect him." After Paine took over, Phillips added, "Union men, women and children appeared to be animated and said there were hopes of living again." The court concluded for the day following Phillips' testimony.[30]

Day fourteen of the trial began with the recall of Henry Bartling by the defense. He was asked how his department handled seized property from Union County, specifically in regard to carriages and buggies. He claimed that as provost marshal, he received numerous confiscated items from Southern sympathizers and Rebels. He recalled that Paine delivered about a dozen carriages and buggies after the Union County expedition, of which one or two were given back to their owners and the rest turned over to the United States Treasury Department to be sold at auction. Dunn had no further questions for the witness.[31]

The former officer of the guardhouse at Fort Anderson, Second Lieutenant William P. Cunningham of the Eighth Artillery, was called by the defense to describe the treatment that Marian G. Milam received when he was behind bars. He explained that Milam "often had permission to leave the guardhouse." Twice a week, on Thursday and Saturday, Milam was escorted to town by guards to be shaved and to purchase medicine. Cunningham reported that during his incarceration Milam had a minor case of diarrhea and a sore on his hand. The judge advocate asked how many times Milam was permitted to procure medicine. The witness could not remember the exact number but remarked that "he [Milam] went out whenever he wanted to." He frequently was allowed access to the office of the company commander and was treated very kindly by the officers.[32]

Paine called on Thomas Atherton to testify about the loyalty of John Bracken and his activities early in the war. Atherton lived across the street from Bracken's mill at Lovelaceville when Paine's troops arrived in November of 1861. He declared that Bracken was not an Unconditional Union man and that he permitted corn meal to be sent from his mill to Rebel forces at Columbus. Atherton recalled that he saw men loading flour sacks onto a large wagon drawn by four horses in October or November of 1861. He inquired where the flour was to be sent and was told the destination was Columbus. One of the men warned him that if he told Union authorities, "we will get after you." He said the men and the wagon left on the road toward Columbus.[33]

P.H. Hall was recalled to the witness stand to testify on the loyalty of W.P. Caldwell. Hall had been acquainted with Caldwell for almost fifteen years. Paine asked if Caldwell had supported an armistice with the rebelling states. A member of the court objected to the question, and the courtroom was cleared for deliberation. After a brief discussion, the court reconvened and the objection was overruled. Hall continued by stating that Caldwell was in "favor of suspending hostilities for sixty to ninety days" and supported a negotiated peace with the Confederacy. He said Caldwell supported Union Major General George B. McClellan, the Democrat for president, over Lincoln and concluded his testimony by proclaiming "if is not out of order I will say I believe Mr. Caldwell today is a loyal man."[34]

To further determine the loyalty of Dr. Milam, Paine questioned his uncle, Charles M. Kilgore from Weakley County, Tennessee. When asked how Milam treated Union citizens early in the war, he responded, "very bad." He also insisted that Milam was not an unconditional Union man but an outright Rebel. The judge advocate asked how he knew that Milam mistreated Unionists. Kilgore stated he had not seen the acts first hand but received the information from well-respected Union men in his community. Kilgore's son, who was seriously ill in Carbondale, Illinois, and could not travel to Paducah, told his father to inform the court that if it were not for Milam's bad health, he would be serving in the Confederate army. The son believed Milam to be "a big a Rebel as he ever was and came here [Paducah] only to be protected so as to make money." With Kilgore's remarks, Paine announced his defense closed, and Dunn said he had no further witnesses to call.[35]

Paine slowly lifted himself from his chair, leaned upon his cane and began his summation. He asked the court to find him not guilty on the first charge of slandering Governor Bramlette. He declared the judge advocate had not proved the exact language alleged to have been said and that "words to that effect" does not apply in a military court. He reminded the court that James T. Pierson, a witness for the prosecution, was the only person to testify that such a statement was made. Tombelle, who was present during the supposed conversation, gave a different account. Several of Pierson's neighbors testified that he was not an unconditional Union man, though he claimed to be before the court. Paine asserted that Pierson had not told the truth and that the "negro question had soured his mind toward the Government."[36]

On the second charge, first specification—disrespectful language toward Major General Halleck—Paine claimed that any negative statements were taken out of context and misunderstood. Paine admitted that when Etheridge said Halleck was over Paine, he may have hastily said, "I did not care a damn." He said it was "not out of disrespect to General Halleck but to show Mr. Etheridge that he need not quote absent officers to govern." Paine also focused on the bias of some of the key witnesses. W.P. Caldwell was a friend of Etheridge. Other witnesses who overheard the confrontation, particularly James Alexander and Robert Woolfolk, were provenly disloyal.[37]

Paine discounted the second and third specifications of the second charge—coercing the bank of Watts, Given and Company to pay Birmingham and Allard—and said the president had declared martial law in Kentucky. He cited that martial law as defined by the British Duke of Wellington who told the House of Lords on April 1, 1851, that "martial law is neither more nor less than the will of the General who commands the army." Paine explained that local and county courts were not in operation and Birmingham required an immediate solution to her economic straits. So desperate was Mrs. Birmingham, he noted, that the bank cashier initially gave her twenty dollars to feed her infant child. Paine stated it was his moral obligation to assist the woman and her child. He said that in the case of C.O. Allard, it was proven that the father refused to pay a debt owed to one of the bank's owners and that the son's account was used as an instrument to induce repayment. Paine repeated that the funds were needed to reconstruct Allard's mill to supply the growing number of federal troops and government workers in his military district.[38]

The charge made by John A. Bracken that Paine overstepped his authority by ordering him to pay L.H. Edrington's attorney, P.D. Yeiser, was dubious since no proof existed that Edrington damaged or destroyed Bracken's property. All the character witnesses who testified established that Edrington had always been a loyal citizen while Bracken a Southern sympathizer. Paine informed the court that he had followed General Smith's

November 16, 1861, order to seize and disable Bracken's Mill and that he alone was responsible for any damages afterwards. Paine encouraged Bracken to sue him and to leave Edrington alone.[39]

He next addressed the specifications related to William L. Mayes and William A. Bell. Paine again challenged the loyalty of the two men; Mayes had let his son-in-law, a soldier in the Confederate army, visit his residence. His neighbors testified seeing the son-in-law at his house and one witness reported seeing his son-in-law on the stolen horse. He pointed out that several witnesses swore that Bell was not an unconditional Union man and could not be trusted under oath. He reminded the court that Bell admitted that he neither ordered the closure of his store nor the seizure of his property.[40]

Paine refuted specification nine, which faulted him for allowing private freight to be transported on a government boat. Paine said that he ordered the boat to Hickman to retrieve the cotton before it was captured or destroyed by enemy forces. He remarked that his intentions were to help Bolinger, a Union man, who had lost over $30,000 earlier in the war. Paine reminded the court that Captain Toussaint C. Buntin, the assistant quartermaster of the District of West Kentucky, had testified that Bolinger paid for shipping the tobacco and cotton.[41]

Paine further argued that the dozen other specifications were unsubstantiated and lacked any credible evidence. He said that only in the case of Peter Acker had he specifically ordered the seizure of personal property and explained that he did so to punish Acker for "letting men have whiskey." The order to "seize [the] fat cattle, mules and horses" of disloyal citizens was issued by Paine to Colonel Peter Davidson and disseminated down the ranks at Uniontown. He stressed that he issued no order to confiscate personal property other than livestock and that "no man or officer has ever testified to it."[42]

In concluding his summation, Paine addressed the *Louisville Journal*'s attacks on him:

> If the court will allow, I would like to state that I requested a court should be appointed by the Secretary of War to give me an opportunity of vindicating myself from charges which were preferred

General Henry W. Halleck (National Archives).

of malfeasance on murder that had been made in the newspapers. I regret that such charges have not been put against me as would have enabled me to have made a more general defense and now whatever maybe the decision of the court, I assure you that I shall be perfectly satisfied with it if I suffer for an offense against the rules and regulations of the Army of the United States.

Afterwards, Paine returned to his seat and awaited the Judge Advocate General Dunn's summation.[43]

Dunn offered the prosecution's rebuttal. He first submitted the court transcripts and indexes to the testimony given under each specification by each witness. He called attention to Section 1 of General Orders, War Department, 1863, No. 100 on martial law and President Lincoln's Proclamation 113, which declared martial law in Kentucky. He read the final sentence of the proclamation aloud to the members of the court.

> The martial law herein proclaimed and the things in that respect herein ordered, will not be deemed or taken to interfere with the holdings of lawful elections or with the proceedings of the constitutional legislature of Kentucky, or with the administration of justice in the courts of law existing therein between citizens of the United States in suits or proceedings which do not affect the military operations or the constituted authorities of the government of the United States.

He also read from Judge Advocate General Joseph Holt's opinion of the evidence submitted to the court: "The experience of the war has shown that little weight is to be attached to the unsupported evidence of witnesses of known disloyalty when it jeopardizes the lives or liberty of loyal men."[44]

He cited the testimonies related to Paine's alleged slander of General Halleck. Dunn argued that the defense had not disputed the loyalty of witnesses Sinnott and Gillespie. Thus, the statements by them must be considered truthful and creditable. As to the charge that Paine wrongfully compelled the bank of Watts, Given and Company to pay Ellen Birmingham, Dunn said the money could not be drawn from the bank except by an administrative order from the husband's estate. As defined by common law in Kentucky, the earnings of a married woman belong to her husband and Paine's intervention, though done with the best of intentions, was illegal. Dunn also said Paine had no right to pressure the bank to pay C.O. Allard. Only civil courts had legal jurisdiction to decide issues of private property between citizens. Dunn addressed no other charges and ended his rebuttal. After a long day, which lasted into the early evening hours, the court adjourned.[45]

The trial reconvened on Monday, March 6, at 10:00 o'clock. Hunter announced that a verdict had been decided and Paine was directed to stand to hear the ruling. On charge one, specification one, the court found him not guilty of using "contemptuous and disrespectful words" against Bramlette. On the second charge, first specification, of "publically denouncing his superior officer," General Halleck, Paine was found guilty. Hunter read on. Second charge, second specification, not guilty; third specification, not guilty. Paine was found not guilty on the remaining twenty-two specifications of the second charge.[46]

Paine stood silent as Hunter read the sentence. On the guilty charge of denouncing General Halleck, Paine was to be "reprimanded by the President of the United States." After the court's decree, Hunter noted for the official record that:

> After a long and patient investigation of all the charges and specifications against General Paine the court deem it their duty to state that they can find nothing [improper with] his integrity as a man or his honor or ability as a soldier. On the contrary they find his whole administration marked by vigilance, ability and earnest and intelligent zeal for the best interests of the Government. There is multiplied testimony in the facts of the record to show that from a [confused] and chaotic state of affairs

that on the account of General Paine everything was soon brought into a complete state of order and safety and the lives and property of Union men much [more] secure through the whole district of Western Kentucky and for a considerable distance into Tennessee. He only appears to have been a terror to [the roving] Rebels, thieves and cut throats, but not a union man, woman or child say of him a word of evil.

Paine was released to await further orders and he quietly left the courtroom. The court adjourned until the next day to review the conviction and further discuss their findings.[47]

The next day at 11:00 a.m. the members of the court convened for the last time. They met briefly and agreed to the following addendum to be sent along with Paine's sentence to Judge Advocate General Holt in Washington.

> In regard to the fact that the improper remarks made by General Paine with regard to General Halleck and for which the court has found him guilty of conduct to the [profession] of good order and military discipline, much in the heat of a warm and exciting argument and elicited by a tantalizing remark of his opponent Emerson Etheridge, who was at that time stumping the country for the purpose of embarrassing the Government in its policies, and knowing that he has since regretted his remarks, we the undersigned recommend that the sentence be remitted.

All the members signed the document.[48]

Before the verdict was in, the *Louisville Journal* charged whitewash and cited a letter the paper received "from a gallant officer at Paducah, who is very familiar with General Paine's case." The communique claimed that Holt's list of charges was minus "those two very ugly ones": that the general personally ordered the execution of a soldier and a civilian without trial and that on "his own authority [he] ... levied sums, from $1,000 to $10,000, upon men and women in Paducah and its vicinity." The judge advocate also left out other charges "that could easily be proved" and left in only those that could easily be refuted, according to the letter. The author also wrote that "the important witnesses for the prosecution are away—why he knows not, and that a very strong outside pressure is brought to bear." In addition, the letter writer vowed that Paine's friends were boasting that he "would be reinstated in thirty days and that his enemies will have need to look to themselves." *The Journal* concluded that if the correspondent was truthful, Paine's "trial, so called, is a cheat, an imposition, a humbug." The spin that the trial was a fraud had begun.[49]

As Paine returned to his hotel on the evening of the seventh, Dr. James R. Alexander confronted him before his old headquarters at the Commercial Bank on Broadway. Alexander shouted to him from across the street, but Paine ignored him. The agitated Alexander rushed at the general. As he neared Paine, he pulled a handgun from his overcoat, pointed the weapon and yelled that Paine had insulted and dishonored his father-in-law, Judge James Campbell. Paine backpedaled and attempted to calm the enraged man. Unable to do so, Paine demanded a fair fight. Alexander obliged and dropped the pistol and lunged toward Paine. He lifted his cane to defend himself, but Alexander knocked him in the street and fell atop him. They struggled for several minutes until guards from the nearby provost marshal's office pulled them apart.[50]

As Alexander was taken into custody, a jeering crowd gathered. Captain Edward L. Chapman, the district provost marshal of the Department of the Cumberland, was struck in the face by a relative of Alexander's. Chapman grabbed his assailant and punched back. The crowd grew larger and more vocal; armed soldiers arrived to assist the guards. Meredith and his staff galloped up and demanded to know what started the melee. He assured the mob that Alexander would be released on bond. The other offenders, he promised, would go before a committee of officers the next day. Judge Campbell, who was present, pledged to pay the bond for Alexander. Tensions eased, and Meredith ordered the crowd to disband and everybody went home.[51]

Later that night, the stable of Major Henry W. Davis, medical director of the District of Western Kentucky, went up in flames. Alexander's relative, who had struck Captain Chapman, was as an orderly of Dr. Davis and believed to have been sleeping in the barn. Most fortunately for the man, he had fled the city, but four horses were burned alive.[52]

On the morning of March 8, Paine penned a letter to Adjutant General Thomas. He declared that the trial was over and asked that his resignation be accepted at once. He ended his letter, "I have served almost four years, am nearly fifty years old and desire to retire from the service more than anything else." Paine then packed his luggage and departed on a steamboat to Evansville. At Evansville, he boarded a train to Illinois Town (presently East St. Louis), where he took another steamer up the Mississippi River to East Burlington for the final leg of the trip by train to his home at Monmouth. He would never return to Paducah.[53]

News of the verdict was first published by the *War Eagle* in Cairo on the afternoon of March 8. The *Chicago Tribune* ran excerpts from the *War Eagle* article the next day. Other newspapers picked up on the story, and by the end of the month it had been printed in every major paper in the North. On March 10, the *Louisville Journal* blasted Holt, questioning why the charges of murder and coercion were omitted from the court's pre-trial instructions:

> Among the charges thus forwarded there was one that General Paine, upon his own responsibility, had ordered and enforced the execution of two men, a citizen and a soldier, without trial or examination, and another that he had, without even the shadow of authority levied heavy pecuniary contributions upon such men and women in Paducah as he chose to select for his purpose, and compelled them to pay as the only means of escaping a far severer punishment—probably death.

The paper blamed Holt's omission in part to his "pretty strong tendency to radicalism" and his unwillingness to prosecute a guilty man.[54]

The verdict and recommendations of the court reached Holt in Washington a few days. The report reached Lincoln's desk on March 28. Holt concurred with the decision and recommended the "sentence may be remitted without detriment to the interests of the service." On the same day in Monmouth, Paine again wrote a letter to General Thomas pressing for his resignation to be accepted and for official notice of the acceptance be sent to him immediately. Thomas approved Paine's resignation on April 5, 1865. His military service had finally come to an end, but the fight to clear his name had just begun.[55]

Seven

"Unity of the Spirit"

Though the trial had ended, the war in the Jackson Purchase raged on. Near Columbus, a group of farmers was robbed of over $1,800 by bushwhackers whose "faces and hands [were] blackened like negroes." A correspondent from Paducah wrote that guerrillas had become so daring that they attacked wagons that supplied wood to the city garrison. A company of the Columbus-based Fourth Colored Heavy Artillery was ambushed at Moscow, leaving one man wounded. Hickman had been "visited by both Rebels and guerrillas, her citizens abused and robbed, and three business houses burned." There appeared to be no end to the chaos.[1]

On the evening of March 22, startling news reached Paducah that Captain Gregory had been killed while attempting to capture the notorious guerrilla leader, Captain McDougal. Gregory had mustered out of the Home Guard on February 12. But General Meredith persuaded him to lead cavalry patrols. At dawn on the 22nd, Gregory and a detachment of twenty-two men mounted their horses and galloped south. About thirty miles from Paducah, he received a report that McDougal and around fifty or sixty of his men were at the house of Thomas Hayden just south of Fancy Farm. He ordered five of his men to remain with the horses and the rest to surround the house. Gregory smashed the front door open with the butt of his Spencer carbine. After he crossed the threshold he turned his rifle on the surprised McDougal and shot him dead. Gregory's men rushed into the house and a gun battle ensued. Gregory was struck by a bullet and collapsed to the floor. Six guerrillas died and twenty were wounded. The rest escaped on foot into the nearby woods. Union Corporal John T. Ramsey was also slain; he and Gregory were put in a wagon and brought back to Paducah where they were buried. The Rebel dead were left where they were shot and buried by Hayden and his neighbors the next day.[2]

Two weeks after Captain Gregory's death, a song commemorating his military service, titled "Gregory's Avengers," was published in the Paducah *Federal Union*.

Oh hero, of heroes!
Brave veteran of fame.
On our States bright Escutcheon
There is no prouder name,
When threatened—invaded
By an insolent foe,
The strong arm of Gregory
Death terror and woe

Chorus,
Then draw, draw the gleaming steel,
For Gregory is the word,

And till we avenge him,
We'll never—never—sheathe the sword.

When death tempest revealed,
In carnage and woe,
In front we would see him
Dealing death to the foe,
When contest was fiercest
His dark plume was seen,
And his death was a victory
As his proud life had been.

(Chorus)

Like a proud wounded eagles,
Our grief we'll not speak,
But our ire is the fiercest,
When a tear's on the cheek,
No more to battle,
He'll lead us again,
Our hearts torn with anguish
That Gregory is slain.

(Chorus)

The fair and the gallant
His memory will bless,
And cursed be the coward
Who honors him less,
With might we'll avenge him
While life blood shall flow,
Three cheers for our country
And death to the foe.

(Chorus)

Now [Lieutenant M.L.] Smith is our leader
The gallant and true,
And we'll show the cowards
What brave hearts can do,
The foe and the invader
We'll hurl from their den,
And say to them proudly,
We are Gregory's men.

(Chorus)[3]

Grave of Captain Thomas Jones Gregory (photograph by Berry Craig).

News of the Confederacy's demise came as the dogwoods began to bud and blossom. After the fall of Petersburg and Richmond, General Meredith issued a special order to the citizens of Paducah on April 5. It called on the city to "unite in celebration of these splendid results by a general illumination of their residences and places of business" that evening. As nightfall approached, storm clouds blew in from the west while Meredith gave a "strong and patriotic address to the citizens of Paducah." The violent storm drove off the spectators and left streets muddy and deserted. The Unionist newspaper in Paducah claimed the illumination was a success, declaring "many houses were lit up with much taste." A visiting correspondent from Cairo declared that Meredith's speech was "heartedly responded to" and "Paducah was in a blaze of light." Whether the radiance of the celebration was as brilliant as the one after the Confederate victory at Manassas in July of 1861 was not mentioned in contemporary letters or diaries, but for many in Paducah and the Jackson Purchase, the Union victories were not a cause for celebration.[4]

The surrender of Confederate forces under General Robert E. Lee on April 9 brought forth more celebrations among local Unionists, yet there was a conspicuous undertone of bereavement. On April 14, Meredith issued a proclamation that invited all citizens to "illuminate their public and private buildings." The celebration, however, was not mentioned in the local or regional newspapers. A few Secesh clung on the hope that Forrest would turn back the tide and return, but their numbers dwindled as more battle-weary soldiers passed through Union lines to surrender.[5]

After President Lincoln's assassination, Meredith issued General Order No. 12, which ordered "appropriate funeral honors ... be paid by the troops at each post" in the Military District of West Kentucky and that obsequies be held at Paducah on April 19 at noon. He also asked that business be suspended for the day and that "crepe should be hung over every door and the churches should be draped." He called on Paducah's most prominent political and religious leaders to participate. Rufus King Williams, judge of the Kentucky Court of Appeals, Joseph F. Brown, pastor of the Christian Church, John M. Herrington, reverend of the Baptist Church, J.T. Hendricks, minister of the Presbyterian Church and Edward C. Slater, pastor of the Methodist Church, were invited to speak. Slater, considered by local Unionist to be a Southern sympathizer, reluctantly agreed and was to preach a funeral sermon. Thousands gathered on the streets around the military district headquarters. However, as the procession prepared to depart, another rainstorm struck and the funeral was hastily postponed.[6]

A second attempt was made on Monday, April 24. Again, thousands turned out at Meredith's headquarters. It was a somber yet spectacular moment in the history of the city. At noon, the cannons at Fort Anderson boomed a twenty-one-gun salute, which opened the funeral ceremony. The procession was led by General Meredith and his staff mounted on the best steeds from local stables. A horse-drawn hearse with a decorated empty casket was directly behind them. The officers and soldiers from the Seventh Tennessee Cavalry, Second Illinois Artillery, Forty-Ninth Illinois Infantry and the Forty-Fourth Wisconsin Infantry marched behind the hearse. The men were in full dress uniform, brass buttons polished and shiny. The officers and non-commissioned officers wore crimson sashes, bleached white gloves and rested their swords upon their shoulders. The enlisted men trooped with bayonets fixed to the slow beat of a drum. The national and regimental colors of each unit fluttered at the forefront of the procession. After the military contingent, members of the Paducah Union League, the clergy and community leaders followed in small groups. The spectators walked in mass behind the dignitaries. Some of the women were garbed in black mourning dresses. The procession moved quietly down from Poplar Street (7th Street) to Court Street (Kentucky Avenue) to Main Street (Market Street) then backtracked southwest on Broadway to "grounds in front of Mr. Given's residence." There, the fallen president and the "illustrious dead" of the war were eulogized and honored.[7]

The Reverend Edward C. Slater (Broadway United Methodist Church).

Beneath clear skies, the Reverend Brown gave the opening prayer. It was a heartfelt and simple supplication that expressed the tragic loss the nation had suffered and the need for God's assistance in such troubling times. Brief addresses by Judge Williams and the Reverend Harrington followed. The Reverend Slater next delivered a sermon that expounded the "Unity of the Spirit" and the "loyalty of citizenship." He proclaimed that Lincoln was "a model for his countrymen in his moral sensibilities." Slater cited Lincoln's emancipation proclamation and called it the "crowning glory of his presidential life." Forty-five years later, a witness in the crowd recalled that "he spoke for the South, for the North, for the nation, and accepted for the country the emancipation proclamation."[8]

The closing prayer was delivered by the Reverend Hendricks, but before the services concluded, the audience called out Colonel Hicks to make a speech. Hicks had served with Lincoln in the Illinois State Legislature during the early 1840s. A bit surprised, Hicks gave an off-the-cuff address in which he praised Lincoln's "purity, incorruptibility and great talents." He also expressed his "willingness to forgive all Rebels" and apologized for his initial opposition to emancipation. The funeral service concluded with Hicks' remarks.[9]

One week later, Grant ordered Meredith to be removed at Paducah. He was replaced on May 2 by his second in command, Colonel Caleb H. Carlton of the Eighty-Ninth Ohio Infantry Regiment. Meredith's withdrawal was instigated by Indiana Republican Congressman George W. Julian and a few citizens of Paducah. Meredith had lost to Julian in the 1862 Congressional election, and the general had planned to campaign against him again. A few weeks prior, Julian and Congressman Anderson met with Secretary of War Stanton and encouraged him to relieve Meredith. Julian, a staunch abolitionist, charged that Meredith was sympathetic to traitors, failed to protect Union men and was a detriment to the Republican Party's efforts in Western Kentucky. Stanton agreed and set in motion the removal of Meredith. But Anderson changed his mind, and on April 25, added his signature to a letter to Stanton, which declared Meredith was desperately needed at Paducah for "military protection" and to "carry the next [State] Legislature." Meredith was not convinced and wrote Anderson demanding answers. Anderson replied that he was misled by Julian and would "like no [further] part in the matter."[10]

On May 16, over 2,500 people congregated at the market square in Paducah to hear speeches from "prominent Union men" in support of General Meredith. They condemned the men who led to his removal as "unworthy of belief" and the "worst enemies of the Union." They also unanimously passed resolutions that denounced his antagonists, expressed their gratitude to the general and encouraged President Andrew Johnson to "reinstate and continue him in command until he shall have finished his noble work." The resolutions were sent to Johnson the following day. Similar meetings at Mayfield and Woodville on May 20 echoed the opinions expressed at Paducah and presented similar resolutions. The ministers of the five major churches in Paducah also wrote the president requesting the "restoration of Brigadier General Meredith to his command." Their efforts were unsuccessful and Meredith left Paducah on May 22.[11]

The conclusion of the war brought new problems that required immediate action. Returning Confederate soldiers stirred up old fears among the Unionists. On May 10, the Reverend William M. Starks, who had served on Paine's assessment committee and whose life had been frequently threatened, wrote Governor Bramlette of the desperate need to raise and organize a regiment of militia to offset the power of the ex-soldiers. Starks said "a number of Rebel soldiers and guerrillas are coming in and taking the amnesty oath [and] still there are a sufficient number left to keep the country in a very disturbed state." He also mentioned that a convention to nominate a candidate for

Congress and candidates for the state legislature had to be adjourned because "condition of the country being such that no preliminary meetings had been held thro[ough out] the Dist[rict] to select delegates." He declared "men here are desirous of going to work to organize Co[mpanie]s and Reg[iment]s" and need only the "assurance of being sustained" by the government. Starks' request was denied.[12]

No sooner did the war end than most of the Unionists were voted out of office. Congressman Anderson chose not to run for a second term. The *Federal Union* reported that the elections of August 7, 1865, passed off "very quietly" since the mayor had ordered all the saloons closed. The turnout was "very light" but that the "Unionists have carried the city," according to the editor. Yet outside the city's limits, "men of notorious Rebel proclivities have been allowed to vote without even a challenge from the judges." In every county in the Jackson Purchase, outside McCracken, the Unionists were overwhelmingly defeated. The successful candidate for Graves County sheriff was a rebel veteran. Paine and Anderson's nemesis, Democrat Lawrence Trimble, was elected to Congress with a comfortable margin of victory.[13]

The demilitarization of the Jackson Purchase began in the summer of 1865 as the troops were transferred from the District of Western Kentucky or mustered out of the service. The Forty-Fourth Wisconsin Infantry and Forty-Ninth Illinois Infantry mustered out and departed Paducah in late August and early September. The Seventh Tennessee Cavalry mustered out at Columbus on August 9. The Fourth Artillery departed Columbus in June and mustered out on February 25, 1866. The Eighth Artillery, which was not in the Lincoln Memorial Procession, mustered out at Fort Anderson on February 10, 1866. The African American troops had served their country with honor but would be treated as second class citizens. A Paducah man wrote in his diary, "about two weeks since the last troop of Negroes left here, leaving us for the first time in over four years to revel in visions of peace. The town begins to assume somewhat of its old looks and habits." By the end of the month, the withdrawal of Union troops from the Purchase was almost complete.[14]

On April 7, 1866, a branch of the federal Freedmen's Bureau was established at Paducah. The program was created to help slaves in their transition to freedom. Congress passed the Bureau bill over President Andrew Johnson's veto. Two days later, the Democrats of Paducah met at the McCracken County Courthouse to discuss Johnson's veto of the Freedmen's Bureau Bill and the Civil Rights Act. The meeting was chaired by Judge Gustavus A. Flournoy, whom Paine removed for disloyalty. Secessionist Circuit Judge James Campbell was elected to

President Andrew Johnson (Library of Congress).

head a committee to draft resolutions. Eight resolutions were agreed upon. One declared that "the policy of the President of the United States, Andrew Johnson, as recently evinced by his vetoes of the Freedmen's Bureau bill, and the still more outrageous bill known as the Civil Rights bill, meets our hearty and unequivocal approbation, and by them Andrew Johnson has endeared himself to all good and true men." They also resolved that "the right of every state to manage its own internal and domestic affairs" was one of "great fundamental principles" written in the Constitution and would be the platform of the region's Democratic Party. The "states rights cry," which white Southerners raised in defense of slavery, was reborn in the Purchase.[15]

The Freedmen's Bureau closed operations in the Jackson Purchase in July 1868. The efforts of the bureau were met by most whites with contempt and violence. County superintendents and teachers hired by the bureau were threatened and assaulted and their homes and school buildings vandalized. The local courts turned a blind eye to the abuses committed by former slave owners and employers of African Americans. The Ku Klux Klan and other violent and clandestine organizations determined to stem African American equality gained popularity and acceptance in every community in the Purchase. The beating and lynching of black men was not uncommon, and the last lynching occurred over fifty years later at Paducah in 1916. The Purchase became part of the white supremacist, Jim Crow South.[16]

Quintus Q. Quigley, a close friend of Woolfolk and Trimble, wrote in his diary after viewing an independence parade in 1876:

> The most disagreeable part of the whole pageant was the sight of negroes and white men occupying carriages in the procession, which is one of the results of the defeat of the Confederacy and the effect of forces exerted by the conqueror over the conquered. As conquerors they had the right to make conditions such as they saw proper but they had no right to accept the surrender of the states, admit it back into the Union and then use Federal power and arms to thrust upon the states unauthorized laws and customs as a measure of humiliation and disgrace. Yet they could but argue it for they could not resist. I felt, however, that I was willing to rejoice in a Union preserved even at such costs and sacrifice, convinced that in a few years the states of the South will rise up and assert and occupy the position they formerly did as controlling states in the Union in shaping legislation and making and toning society and public sentiment. And that soon the Negro would drop into his proper place.

His racism was typical of the denialism and victimization that fueled the "lost cause" myth of the South for generations. Jennie Fyfe wrote her sister that "I often find myself wishing a little more of the Rebellious spirit could have been taken out of the contemptible Rebels." Paine's vision of "Federal salvation" and African American equality would not become a reality until the civil rights movements of the 1950s and 1960s.[17]

Meanwhile, lawsuits related to Paine's

Quintus Q. Quigley (*Lawyers and Lawmakers of Kentucky*, 1916).

command at Paducah clogged county, state and federal courts for decades. Soon after the war, John E. Woodward, the former superintendent of trade at Paducah, was sued by Samuel Fels for having sold him tobacco that the plaintiff charged was fraudulently seized by Paine. The Kentucky Court of Appeals decided for Fels in January of 1866, though Woodward could not afford to pay. The high court also ruled on two other cases that involved Woodward in January of 1867: *Woodward vs. H. & S.C. Hook* and *Woodword vs. McDonald & Roberts*. Woodward was sued by both firms for the port fees assessed on tobacco shipments. Woodward's defense was that Paine had taken his ledgers when he departed, thus there was no proof of receiving payment. In both cases the court found in Woodward's favor. The case of *Edrington vs. Bracken* finally came to a conclusion in June of 1867. The Court of Appeals ruled that Bracken was responsible for paying the legal fees of Edrington's attorney. The next year, the court heard *Rau & Ricke vs. Boyle & Boyle*. Rau and Ricke claimed Paine illegally confiscated their tobacco shipment at Paducah and that Boyle & Boyle, who were to secure permits, were in part responsible for their losses. The court found that the agreement between the two had not stipulated Boyle & Boyle. Numerous cases in lower courts were settled with less publicity.[18]

Also, for over half a century, Congress entertained claims against the federal government for damages during Paine's command. Woodward sought compensation for his losses. In February of 1873, Woodward was denied reimbursement by the Senate Judiciary Committee. Unable to settle his judgment in full with Fels, the committee recommended that his claim not be paid. He was denied a second time five years later, when his petition was "discharged from further consideration." In November of 1877, the Allard & Crozier Mill Company, owned by J.L. Allard and William Crozier, submitted a claim for the cost of 200 barrels of flour that Paine confiscated September 6, 1861. Crozier and Allard were considered disloyal and thus the flour was appropriated by Union troops. Sixteen years later, the Committee on War Claims found that both men were loyal and remunerated them. The heirs of Solomon Blue of Union County submitted a claim in August of 1890 to the Committee on War Claims. They wanted compensation for ninety head of cattle taken by soldiers under Paine in August of 1864. Blue's loyalty was confirmed and his heirs received $6,050 for the cattle. Fifty-five other petitions from residents of Paducah were submitted to the Committee on War Claims but went nowhere.[19]

Perhaps the most interesting case involved a claim filed by the government of Graves County against the United States government in 1908. The county sought $14,000 "for use of and damage to their courthouse by the military forces of the United States during the late Civil War." The county argued that the conversion of the courthouse into a fort had "rendered it unfit for occupancy for courthouse purposes." County officials also wanted to be compensated for the "reasonable rental value" during the occupancy of the building by federal troops. The court of claims found that Graves County was "loyal to the Government of the United States throughout the late Civil War" and awarded the county government $1,500. The court recommended to Congress that the county receive the funds on March 17, 1914. The destruction of the courthouse by guerrillas after the departure of Union forces in October of 1864 was never mentioned in the claim.[20]

Eight

"Served the Union Army and did his duty"

After Paine's return to Monmouth, he slowly began to revive his neglected law practice. When news of General Lee's surrender arrived, he joined the city in celebration. He welcomed the news with excitement and great relief. Lincoln's assassination, however, deeply saddened Paine. At an April 17 public meeting to mourn the death of the president, Paine presented three resolutions to be delivered to Lincoln's family on the behalf of the citizens. They recognized Lincoln's heroic efforts to "put down this wicked and atrocious Rebellion," proclaimed him the "savior of this Republic" and expressed the "hearty sympathy" of Monmouth. The resolutions were adopted, sent to the grieving family and published by the local press. However, the man who had appointed Paine brigadier general, assigned him command of the District of Western Kentucky and relieved him was now unable to remit the sentence as recommended by the court and the judge advocate general.[1]

After Lincoln's death, Paine began an active campaign to clear his name. He wrote the office of the secretary of war on May 15 requesting a copy of the court's findings and sentence. He did not receive a reply. On October 10, he wrote Judge Advocate General Holt asking that he be "furnished with a copy of the whole trial taken from the records of the court." Again, he was denied a response. The road to redemption was not going to be easy.[2]

On January 27, 1866, Democratic State Representative Thomas H. Corbett of Ballard County proposed a resolution in the Kentucky House to appoint a three-man committee to reinvestigate Paine's command at Paducah. Corbett had been a strong Secessionist and his resolution gave the committee the authority to "send for persons and papers" and to report what steps were necessary to "bring this commissioned bandit to a punishment commensurate with his crimes." The resolution was referred to the Committee on Military Affairs. The following day, newspapers in Louisville printed the resolution, which reignited the old stories of Paine's alleged crimes and multiple executions. Nothing came of the resolution.[3]

In February of 1866, the *Frankfort Yeoman* claimed that Judge Advocate General Holt had tilted the court in Paine's favor. The paper charged that his directions to the court were designed to "insure an acquittal" and the "facts as would have condemned him [Paine] to be shot" deliberately omitted. The article also claimed Holt ordered the court to "administer such an oath to witnesses as to confine their answers" and that "no questions which would criminate the accused or throw any light upon the subject under investigation" were asked by the prosecution. The *Yeoman* hammered Holt's action as "one of the saddest results of the war" and concluded:

> If Payne [Paine] can be reached and be placed under the hangman's hands, it may render a signal service to the thousands in the Southern States, who are languishing under just such a tyranny at this present time as he exercised over the district of Paducah two years ago. It will be the handwriting on the wall which shall notify their oppressor that the vengeance of an outraged people though it cometh slowly, cometh as surely as death, and as inexorable as the grave.

Other papers in the South reprinted the story.[4]

On June 16, Congressman Trimble gave a speech in the house. Titled "The Constitution and the Union," his remarks criticized the Republican Party's Reconstruction policy. He said his constituents opposed making African Americans equal with whites, rejected the Freedmen's Bureau and denied the federal government's power to reconstruct the South. Midway through his presentation, he described his arrest and imprisonment before the election of 1863 and denounced the "incarnate fiend Paine."[5]

During the spring session of the circuit court at Paducah in 1867, two murder indictments were filed against Paine. The indictments alleged that Paine had two guerrillas shot without trial. The heretofore rabidly secessionist *Paducah Herald* republished the unsubstantiated 1864 accusations from the *Louisville Journal* and demanded a conviction. The editor of the *Herald* declared that Paine had "murdered in cold blood sixty-three persons—nearly all citizens who violated no laws" in just sixty days. He anticipated that Paine would receive his "just deserts" and that there was "no torture ever invented by the old Spanish inquisition which would be a tithe of what the blood-thirsty devil deserves." The *Peoria Democrat* spread the story and claimed, "sixty-three souls [were] brutally robbed of mortality by Lincoln's night prowling hyena, [the] bloody handed Paine." The image of Paine as the devil was growing.[6]

At about the same time, an anti–Paine article circulated in Tennessee papers. Supposedly while Paine was in Tullahoma, he and group of officers had gathered for a drink at a local tavern to celebrate a Union victory. A "plain old countryman from the vicinity" entered and was invited to take a drink with the officers. After a few swills, they asked him to make a toast. He purportedly raised his glass and said:

> There is a land of pure delight.
> Where Saints immortal reign;
> A heaven for both black and white,
> And a hell for General Paine.

Paine supposedly had to be restrained from striking the man. Since Paine was a teetotaler, the story was almost certainly false. More disparaging yarns about Paine being outwitted and publically embarrassed by wily Southerners were to be spun for decades to come.[7]

On February 15, 1867, Paine's name was brought up on the floor of the United States Senate. Thomas A. Hendricks, a Democrat from Indiana, claimed that an officer in Paducah had a "man arrested in the night and shot at sunrise." He meant Paine. Senator Trumbull again came to Paine's defense and asked Hendricks how he knew that. Hendricks quickly withdrew his charge. He did, however, ask why Trumbull voted against Powell's resolution to have the board of investigation's report delivered to the Senate. A lively debate ensued between the two men. Trumbull accused Hendricks of a renewed assault upon an officer "who served the Union Army and did his duty." He also reminded the senator that Paine had been court-martialed and acquitted of all but a minor charge.

Hendricks pleaded ignorance about the trial and outcome and quickly sought to end the discussion. Before he could do so, Senator Garrett Davis of Kentucky interceded and said that Colonel John Mason Brown, a member on the commission that investigated Paine, told him all the charges were true and could have been proven had the commission been given the opportunity to testify before a court. The Senate adjourned for the day before Trumbull could reply and the dustup ended. [8]

Nonetheless, Fry and Brown's report and Bramlette's letter to Lincoln had resurfaced in late July of 1867, when the election of Trimble was contested by his Republican opponent George G. Symes. Symes disputed the election on the grounds that Trimble was disloyal during and after the war, had prevented Union men from voting through intimidation and participated in election fraud. During the Congressional investigation, Anderson, Bolinger and Paine were cited. To discredit them, Trimble's supporters released the board's report and the governor's letter to the press. Democratic newspapers smeared Paine. Trimble kept his seat and Paine's character sullied further.[9]

Undaunted, Paine fought on to preserve his reputation and to get his sentence remitted. On February 14, 1869, he wrote the secretary of war for a copy of the recommendations of the court. Whether those recommendations were ever sent to Paine is not documented. Paine evidently stopped writing, and he faded from public scrutiny. Unfortunately for Paine, the torment reemerged after the publication of *Collins' Historical Sketches of Kentucky* in 1874. The author, Richard H. Collins, paraphrased the *Journal*'s 1864 criticism of Paine and added opinions of his own. On July 19, 1864, according to Collins, Paine began "fifty-one days' reign of violence, terror, rapine, extortion, oppression bribery, and military murder." He characterized Paine's trial a farce and claimed the court omitted the "most startling, terrible, and easily proved outrages." He said Paine's sentence was "shamefully inadequate." Numerous historians would cite Collins' book in writing about Paine.

Just before the publication of Collins' book, Paine's law practice and investments had yielded him considerable wealth but the panic of 1873 cost him most of his fortune. After 1878, he and his wife moved from Monmouth and resided with their daughter Maria and her husband James B. McConnell in St. Paul, Minnesota. By 1880, the general and his spouse had relocated to Jersey City, New Jersey, where their stepdaughter Elizabeth and her husband Richard E. Davis resided. While there, Paine was an attorney for a firm that speculated in gold and silver mines in the northwest United States. On December 16, 1882, he died at his home on Tuers Avenue at age sixty-seven. He was buried at a cemetery a block away from his residence two days later. His wife, Charlotte, soon returned to St. Paul to live with her daughter Maria. Several years later, General Paine's remains were reinterred at the family plot at Oakland Cemetery in St. Paul. A simple government headstone was placed over his grave in 1892. His epitaph reads, "Brig. Gen'l E.A. Paine U.S. Vols."[11]

Following his death, some of Paine's fellow West Pointers praised his "active and vigorous" leadership during military campaigns and his unyielding "determination to punish the enemy." During the annual reunion of the Association of the Graduates of the United States Military Academy, a member wrote:

> He was a strict disciplinarian, but so kind at heart, and so brave in action, that he was beloved by his soldiers, and always commanded their confidence. He visited hospitals daily, looked after the various wants of all his men, and was untiring in his efforts to have their needs supplied in the best manner possible.

It was also noted that in "private life he was universally admired for his liberality, warmth of heart and kindness to the poor." Though many of his contemporaries opposed his politics, they did not question his devotion to the men he commanded nor the military and public service he provided his country.[12]

After his death, more Kentucky histories were published that disparaged Paine: Nathaniel Southgate Shaler's *Kentucky: A Pioneer Commonwealth* (1885) and Zachariah Frederick Smith's *School History of Kentucky* (1889). Smith's book became a standard text in classrooms throughout the state. Other school texts including Emma M. Connelly's *Story of Kentucky* (1890), *A History of Kentucky* by Elizabeth Shelby Kinkead (1896), and *A Young People's History of Kentucky for Schools and General Reading* by Ed Porter Thompson, a Confederate veteran (1897) were unkind to Paine. State histories such E. Polk Johnson's 1912 *A History of Kentucky and Kentuckians* and William Elsey Connelley and Ellis Merton Coulter's *The History of Kentucky* in 1922 revitalized Paine's reputation as a monster. Other histories followed a similar pattern with *Military History of Kentucky* from the Federal Writers' Project of the Work Projects Administration (1939), *The Civil War in Kentucky* by Lowell H. Harrison (1975), and *A Brittle Sword: The Kentucky Militia, 1776-1912* by Richard G. Stone (1977). They, too, propagated the "reign of terror" story.[13]

Recent historians have traveled the same heavily-worn path. The *Kentucky Encyclopedia* published in 1992 and Lowell Hayes Harrison and James C. Klotter's *A New History of Kentucky* in 1997 were hard on Paine. In the past decade, *On Jordan's Banks: Emancipation and Its Aftermath in the Ohio River Valley* by Darrel E. Bigham, *Savage Conflict: The Decisive Role of Guerrillas in the American Civil War* by Daniel E. Sutherland, and *The Civil War in the Jackson Purchase, 1861-1862* by Dan Lee all followed the same Paine storyline. Most recently, John Philip Cashon's *Paducah and the Civil War*, published in 2016, continued Collins' Paine-as-villain theme. From the 1920s onward, local authors hammered home the "reign of terror" notion. Fred G. Neuman's *Story of Paducah* and D. Trabue Davis' *Story of Mayfield through a Century* offered essentially condensed versions of Collins'. And though the later works of John E.L. Robertson's *Paducah 1830–1980* and *Paducah: Frontier to the Atomic Age* offered a more balanced account of Paine, his image remains largely tainted and unchanged.[14]

Mayfield historian Lon Carter Barton scorched Paine in "The Reign of Terror in Graves County," his 1948 article in the *Register of the Kentucky Historical Society*. Barton wrote that Paine's "dictatorial rule" was the "most terrifying single period in the history of Graves County." Barton, a former state legislator and teacher, was a member of the Sons of Confederate Veterans; his mother was an influential member of the Mayfield chapter of the United Daughters of the Confederacy. In an interview in 1990, he remarked that he had "enough ancestors in the Confederate Army to probably outfit a company." He even claimed the dubious Tullahoma toast was made by a Confederate soldier captured near Mayfield.[15]

Paine's image had evolved into a caricature of evil. He was portrayed as a fiend who cruelly subjugated a "righteous" population and executed "innocent" men. By the turn of the twentieth century, the surviving people he banished were celebrated as living martyrs. The children of Robert O. Woolfolk retold their version of events for over fifty years. His daughter Kate's account appeared in the *Paducah News-Democrat* in February of 1903. She directed her recollections to the "younger generations who have grown up since the old days of 61-65." She praised her father's escape the night before and her mother's "courageous" actions before "drunken" soldiers and "vengeful" black guards who were former family servants. She boasted that her mother had sown several thousand dollars into her dress the night before they departed; when the captain of the steamer asked her for her ticket, she responded that the "government is defraying the expenses of this trip." The expenses were paid by the officer of the guard. In her conclusion, she wrote that "when he (Paine) was in Kentucky he made memories, which can never die of his cruelty and injustice."[16]

Paine and the banished families were in the national spotlight again in July of 1907. The story reemerged when Memphis socialite, Mary Latham, stated at the annual convention of the United Daughters of the Confederacy (U.D.C.) in Birmingham, Alabama, that she was one of the women exiled to Canada. She was the wife of Thomas J. Latham, a federal judge, wealthy land developer and president of the Memphis Water Company. Mary Latham was a well-known philanthropist in Memphis and a prominent member of Tennessee's U.D.C. She was a founder and first president of Memphis' Sarah Law Chapter of the U.D.C., former president of the Tennessee Division of the U.D.C., a major contributor to the Nathan Bedford Forrest Monument at Memphis and an elected state agent for the Jefferson Davis Monument Association. A U.D.C. chapter was named in her honor. On the third night of the convention, she denounced Paine and told of her banishment to Canada. Her words were published in *Confederate Veteran* magazine. She compared Paine to Nero and said he exceeded the Roman emperor in "heartless cruelty." Latham said she witnessed a woman who came to Paine and upon bended knee begged him not to execute her son, but that black soldiers shot the boy that evening. She described her banishment and the women whom she defined as the "best connected and wealthiest in the city and a number of her most beautiful and accomplished young ladies." She said that when the women landed on Canadian soil, John Hunt Morgan and his men accompanied them to their hotel where they "sung Dixie war songs till a late hour." Morgan was never in Canada. She also implied that it was through her efforts that the "most obnoxious and cruel tyrant" Paine was removed from command at Paducah. Latham later retold the story at almost every public engagement when given the opportunity.[17]

Mary Latham (*Confederate Veteran Magazine*).

The surviving exiles and many people who resided in Paducah during the war knew Latham's recollections were untrue, but they kept silent. During the annual reunion of the Forrest Cavalry Corps in Memphis on October 17, 1906, she pushed her way on stage to be seen next to the keynote speaker Colonel D.C. Kelley. Henry A. Tyler, commander of the corps and reunion organizer, shoved Mrs. Latham aside and informed her that she was not to be part of the program. Tyler, who was from Hickman, knew Latham to be a fraud and wished not to have the ceremony tarnished by her presence. The two bickered on stage, and the dispute that followed became known as the Tyler-Latham Controversy.[18]

The dispute reached its climax in the summer of 1907 after Tyler publicly charged Latham and her husband of disloyalty to the South during the war. He stated that "she had been known to ride in Union parades" and that her husband "secured permits from the Union ranks and peddled whiskey." Her claims of having been banished to Canada, according to Tyler, were false. A committee of seven veterans was appointed to investigate his charges. Tyler proposed that if she had intentionally made false statements, she should be "expelled from the Sarah Law Chapter" of the U.D.C. and the "charter be confiscated." Judge Latham opened a campaign against Tyler, seeking to discredit him and revoke his Cross of Honor. Mary Latham encouraged several chapters of the U.D.C. to have him "strongly censored." A duel was narrowly averted between an associate of Tyler, Colonel W.A. Collier, and Judge Latham. A former mayor of Memphis had to intercede to settle their differences.[19]

On July 23, Tyler arrived at Paducah to locate the surviving members of Paine's banishment order and other citizens of the city who may have knowledge of Mary Latham's activities during the war. Within a few days, he collected several affidavits and the addresses of those who had relocated elsewhere. He released his findings to the Paducah newspapers on July 26. The *Paducah Daily Register* and the *Paducah Evening Sun* printed letters from the five remaining survivors of the group from Columbus and Paducah. Kate Woolfolk Whitfield referred to her article from 1903. It had a list of a dozen names from Paducah that did not include Latham. Kate's oldest sister Mary, known by the family as Nannie, was a nun in a convent in St. Martinsville, Louisiana. She wrote that she could not remember any other names than those mentioned by her sister. Kate's other sister Roberta, known as Bertie, recalled meeting Latham at a hotel in Cairo, and that she requested Captain Paine to allow her to accompany them to Canada. The request was apparently denied. Both Josephine Horne Overall of Columbus and Sarah L. Malone Breyard of Union City were positive that Latham had not traveled with the group. Joseph L. Rollston of Paducah wrote that "no such woman as Mrs. T.J. Latham was with them" in Canada.[20]

To further substantiate the charges against Mrs. Latham, Tyler also submitted affidavits from several well-known citizens of Paducah who were present or witnessed the banished families. Judge Lorenzo Dow Husbands, Quintus Q. Quigley, Thomas J. Atkins, J.R. Puryear, Fannie E. Rowland and Martha Grungy Terrell all confirmed the statements made by the five survivors. Though Tyler's evidence seemed solid, the Lathams carried considerable clout with those on the investigation committee. Prior to Tyler's visit to Paducah, a majority of the committee members found Tyler "had been misled by statements of others and that the charges were abundantly disproved." Tyler refused to appear before the committee on the grounds that the "members were chosen so that his evidence would stand no chance and that under the rules of evidence, as drawn by it, the Lathams were required to prove nothing." Both would later claim victory as Tyler was not censored and Latham returned to her leadership duties in the U.D.C. She never again spoke publically of her days in Paducah.[21]

As the Civil War generation faded away, the story of Paine's "reign of terror" was reborn. In the 1930s, the U.D.C. and the S.C.V. in Mayfield began to collect stories from the few surviving witnesses. Robert Fleming Wright, a teenager at the time Colonel McChesney commanded the city, told the commander of the local chapter of the S.C.V. of his experiences in 1932. He recalled working upon the breastworks that surrounded the courthouse and the three executions by Captain Gregory's men. He remembered the execution of "Bud" Hicks. Eighteen years later, Hicks was reinterred at Maplewood Cemetery in Mayfield with full military honors and with some 5,000 in attendance. Inscribed upon his tombstone:

> To the memory of Henry Bascomb Hicks who was shot by order of the federal tyrant A.E. Payne on the streets of Mayfield, Ky. August 21st, 1864. He was 18 years old, he was not a soldier but a schoolboy, yet when ordered to his death he refused to be blindfolded. He said, 'I can look you in the eye.' To this type of young Southern manhood we pay all due honor and reverence.

As was common with many of the post-war stories related to Paine, his name was misspelled and dates were incorrect. The commander of the S.C.V. would commonly refer to Paine as the "scourge of Mayfield."[22]

During the Second World War, other anti–Paine myths surfaced locally. One was about a mock salute to Paine given by a young guerrilla named Sam Hughes. The other was about two young lovers, Susan Russell and Alex Montgomery, who were reunited in Canada during the expulsion. Hughes was captured with two other men at Uniontown and was to be executed at Paducah. As the story goes, while on the Paducah-bound steamboat *Samuel B. Orr*, his guards asked if he would have a drink with them. He answered, "I don't drink with Yankees." But after a bit more encouragement he agreed, only if he were allowed to offer a toast. The guards agreed, and Hughes raised his glass and said, "Here's to Jeff Davis, may his cause last for eternity." He took a sip and continued, "Here's to Paine, may his soul rot in hell." Paine supposedly was told of Hughes' "tribute." As Hughes and his fellows stood before the general to receive their punishment, Paine exempted Hughes from death by firing squad. When Hughes asked Paine with he spared him, the General reportedly replied, "I heard about the toast you gave for me, Hughes, while you were on the boat. You're right, my soul will rot in hell but I never thought any man was brave enough to say it publicly! For that you can go free whether you wish or not!" Hughes was sent back to Union County with the corpses of his accomplices, or so the tale ended.[23]

The yarn about Susan Russell begins when she refused to "step off the walk" for Union soldiers to pass. Russell, "a bright and pretty young lady," was ordered by Paine to be taken from her family "under the guard of Negro soldiers" and escorted to Chicago. From there she was then transported to Canada. Unknown to Russell, her fiancé Alex Montgomery, a soldier in Morgan's cavalry, was captured a few months earlier and imprisoned at Camp Douglas in Chicago. He escaped to Canada about the same time of her deportation. While walking the streets of Montreal, a haggard young man came up and begged for food. She asked, "Who are you?" and he responded, "I'm Alex Montgomery, Miss. With Morgan's cavalry. I gotta go back." She cried, "Alex!" He recognized her, and they embraced. The two lovers met in exile because of the cruelty of General Paine, according to that whopper of a story.[24]

Both stories are fiction. There is no record of a Samuel Hughes being captured at Uniontown, or Union County, and taken to Paducah. The *Samuel Orr* was burned by its Confederate crew in 1862, to prevent it seizure by Union gunboats. There is also no record of a Sarah Russell having been expelled to Canada. Neither is there any documentation of any exiles going to Montreal.[25]

Thus, the myth of Paine's "reign of terror" persists in the Purchase. Propagated by the

Grave of Henry Bascomb Hicks (photograph by Berry Craig).

United Daughters of the Confederacy and the Sons of Confederate Veterans in the early twentieth century and perpetuated by some high school teachers, the myth has become deeply embedded in local history and folklore. In recent decades, the introduction of the internet has amplified the myth. The William Clark Market Museum House at Paducah has a website that not only repeats Collins' dubious history, but also implicates Paine as the impetus of General Grant's General Order No. 11, which called for the expulsion of all Jews in his military district. The Graves County government website states that troops under Paine's command so "heavily damaged" the courthouse that the county was left no other recourse but to file a lawsuit against the federal government for compensation. Civil War blogsites pillory Paine.[26]

Epilogue

In 1865, Congress acquitted Lucian Anderson of "charges of bribery, corruption and malfeasance in office." A select committee reported that they examined all witnesses "pro and con" and in "none of the testimony is there anything about said charges which would in the slightest degree sustain said charges." To the contrary, they said, the "evidence entirely exonerates Anderson from all wrong." The report was voted on and was accepted along party lines. Anderson returned to his law practice in Mayfield and in 1882 established the Bank of Mayfield. He died on October 18, 1898, at age seventy-four. He is interred in the family cemetery not far where his home stood.[1]

John Bolinger did not immediately return to Mayfield, but remained in Paducah to expand his business. He resigned as Graves County clerk in August of 1865. By the early 1870s, Bolinger was back to Mayfield and sold real estate. Later in the same decade, he became involved with the Greenback Party and organized Greenback Clubs in the Jackson Purchase. In 1882, his business failed and left him more than $30,000 in debt. His creditors hounded him for the remainder of his life. In his twilight years, he sold buggies and carts in Mayfield. In the summer of 1892, he campaigned and lost as a third-party candidate for Congress. He died at Mayfield on January 19, 1895, at age 70, and is buried in the Maplewood Cemetery.[2]

After being mustered out of the army, Henry Bartling was appointed special Indian commissioner to the Chippewas in Minnesota and later the Delawares in Kansas. In 1869, he moved to Topeka where he was employed with the land department of the Atchinson, Topeka & Santa Fe Railroad. Bartling was elected mayor of Topeka in 1873 and reelected in 1874. In 1875, he relocated to California to supervise construction of the narrow-gauge rail line between San Francisco and Santa Cruz. He returned briefly to Topeka and inaugurated construction of the Topeka & Southwestern Railway before permanently settling in San Francisco. He was an active member of the Grand Army of the Republic in California and was one of the founding directors of the Los Angeles Panorama Company, which purchased, sold, leased and exhibited panoramic paintings. Bartling also served as the secretary of San Francisco's New City Hall Commission and the Associated Charities Commission. He died on November 27, 1889, at the age of fifty-nine.[3]

Henry Barry mustered out on May 11, 1866. Soon afterwards he attended the school of law at Columbian College (presently George Washington University) where he graduated in 1867. Later that year, he moved to Columbus, Mississippi, and became a member of the state's constitutional convention. He was elected to the state Senate in 1868 and after Mississippi's readmission to the Union in 1870, was elected as a Republican to

Congress. Barry was reelected to two more terms before he died from a stroke on June 7, 1875, at age of thirty-five. He was buried at Oak Hill Cemetery in Washington.[4]

Dr. Willis Danforth returned to his medical practice in Chicago following the war. In 1869, he was elected professor of surgery and surgical anatomy at Hahnemann Medical College, a position he held until 1876. He was later elected president of the Chicago Academy of Medicine and was the associate editor of the *United States Medical and Surgical Journal*. He also served as vice president of Chicago Homeopathic Medical Society and the surgeon-in-chief at Scammon Hospital. Mary Todd Lincoln was a patient of his in 1873 and 1874. He would testify at her sanity hearing in May of 1875, where he and six other physicians found the former first lady mentally unsound. She was sent to a private mental hospital for about a year. In 1879, Danforth was elected president of the Illinois State Homeopathic Society and two years later, after he relocated to Milwaukee, he became the president of the Wisconsin Homeopathic Society. In April of 1891, he fell and fractured his hip. After two unsuccessful surgeries, he died of blood poisoning on June 5, 1891, at age sixty-five.[5]

On April 19, 1865, Waters W. McChesney died of the illness that had afflicted him in Mayfield. The officers of the 134th Illinois met the next day and unanimously adopted a resolution that expressed their deepest sympathy and condolences to the bereaved family. The meeting and resolution were published in the *Chicago Tribune* on April 22. His remains were interred in the family plot at Oakwood Cemetery in Troy, New York.[6]

Speed Smith Fry mustered out of the Union army in August 24, 1865. He was the supervisor of internal revenue in Kentucky from 1869 to 1872. He lost his hearing, which may have been the result of a severe case of influenza that he contracted during the war. In 1883, he campaigned for lieutenant governor on the Republican ticket and lost, but four years later was elected to the state legislature from Boyle County. His party selected him to run for speaker of the house but he lost to the Democratic candidate. Fry was a trustee member and superintendent of the Soldier's Home near Louisville at the time of his death on September 1, 1892 at age seventy-five. His body was buried in Bellevue Cemetery in Danville, the Boyle County seat.[7]

John Mason Brown left the service in December of 1864 and resumed his law practice in Lexington. He relocated to Louisville in 1873 and opened a law firm, which eventually became one of the most prosperous and influential practices in the state. His interest in history led him to publish several pamphlets and books on Kentucky pioneers and early politics in the state. He was one of the ten founders of the Filson Club Historical Society in 1884. In the years prior to his death, Brown was influential in securing a system of public parks for Louisville. He died on January 29, 1890, at age sixty-two after a prolonged bout of pneumonia. He was buried at Cave Hill Cemetery in Louisville.[8]

Solomon Meredith returned to his home in Indiana after the war but only briefly. He was appointed assessor of internal revenue for his congressional district in 1866 but the following year accepted a position as surveyor general of the Montana Territory, which he held until 1869. Afterwards, he farmed and raised prized livestock at his farm near Cambridge City, Indiana. In 1870, he helped organize the Cambridge City District Agricultural Society and became its first president. Meredith died on October 2, 1875, at the age of sixty-five. He was buried at Riverside Cemetery in Cambridge City.[9]

In 1868, George Dennison Prentice was bought out by Walter N. Haldeman, owner of the *Louisville Courier*, which had been the state's leading Confederate paper. The new paper was the *Louisville Courier-Journal*. Though Haldeman and Prentice had been bitter rivals, Haldeman allowed him to stay on as a subeditor. While traveling in a winter storm to visit his son south of Louisville, he contracted influenza, and the pneumonia that followed led to his death on January 22, 1870, at age sixty-seven. He was buried in Cave Hill Cemetery.[10]

Lawrence Strother Trimble served three consecutive terms in Congress. By the end of the 1870s, his political career had come to an end in Kentucky and he was in financial trouble. He escaped his creditors and departed Paducah in 1879. He moved to Albuquerque, New Mexico, and practiced law until 1889. He regained his fortune and became one of the most prosperous attorneys in the southwest. He was the lone Democrat to attend the New Mexico state constitutional convention in 1889 and 1890. He died on August 9, 1905, and his remains were interred at Fairview Cemetery in Albuquerque. Trimble was seventy-eight.[11]

Timeline

September 10, 1815—Paine was born at Parkman, Geauga County, Ohio.

June 23, 1834—Lucien Anderson is born.

July 1, 1835—Paine arrives at the United States Military Academy at West Point.

July 1, 1839—Paine graduates from the United State Military Academy at West Point. He ranked 24th out of 32 in his class.

July 8, 1840—Paine is commissioned a Second Lieutenant in the 1st Regiment of Infantry stationed in Florida.

August 24, 1840—Paine submits resignation from United States Army stating his father's health was in decline.

1842–1845—Paine served as a deputy U.S. Marshal for the State of Ohio.

1842–1845—Paine served as a Lt. Colonel in the Ohio State Militia.

1843–1848—Paine practiced law at Painesville, Ohio.

1845–1848—Paine served as a Brigadier General in the Ohio State Militia.

1848–1861—Paine practiced law at Monmouth, Illinois.

1852–1853—Paine served in the Illinois State Legislature.

March 5, 1858—Paine is elected the first president of the Monmouth Temperance League.

October 1858—Paine canvasses Illinois in support of Abraham Lincoln for United States Senate.

April 23, 1861—Paine is elected colonel of the 9th Illinois.

April 25, 1861—Paine is mustered into service.

April 30, 1861—The 9th Illinois was ordered to Cairo, Illinois.

June 11–12, 1861—McChesney resigns from the Tenth New York Infantry after the Battle of Big Bethel where he "absented" himself from the battlefield.

June 22, 1861—McChesney resigns commission and returns to Chicago.

August 26, 1861—The U.S. Treasury Department closes the port of Paducah to commercial traffic.

September 1, 1861—McChesney is honorably discharged from the Army.

September 3, 1861—President Lincoln appoints Paine as Brigadier General.

September 5, 1861—Paine leaves Cairo with General Ulysses S. Grant's forces for Paducah, Kentucky.

September 6, 1861—Paine reaches Paducah with the Ninth Illinois. Grant leaves Paducah and places the post in Paine's command.

September 7, 1861—General John C. Fremont sends Colonel Joseph D. Webster to Paducah to direct construction of fortifications. Paine suggests that houses near the fort be condemned and torn down to prevent enemy troops from using them during an attack.

November 6–10, 1861—Paine commands expedition to Milburn, Kentucky. He comes within 11 miles of Columbus before turning back for Paducah. His troops marched 62 miles in three days.

November 16, 1861—Paine was ordered by General Charles F. Smith to proceed to Lovelaceville with two regiments and take possession of John Bracken's mill.

November 17, 1861—Paine orders J.A. Bracken's mill at Lovelaceville, Kentucky, to be closed and that Lee Edrington be placed in charge of the mill.

December 20, 1861—Smith relieves Paine of command at Paducah and transfers him to Cairo for further orders.

December 23, 1861—Paine ordered to Bird's Point, Missouri.

January 1, 1862—Paine arrives at Bird's Point and assumes command.

February 1, 1862—Grant orders Paine to take command at Cairo and Mound City, Illinois.

February 8, 1862—Paine issues order to "'hang one of the rebel cavalry for each Union man murdered…"

February 26, 1862—Paine gets reprimanded for orders to hang rebels.

March 12, 1862—Paine assigned command of the 1st Division of the Army of the Mississippi under General John Pope.

March 12, 1862—Paine is reported wounded at Sikestown, Missouri.

March 14, 1862—Paine involved at the skirmish near New Madrid, Missouri.

April 7, 1862—Paine captures Confederate troops at Tiptonville, Tennessee.

May 3–22, 1862—Paine took part in the siege of Corinth, Mississippi, and engaged in a skirmish at Farmington, Mississippi.

May 27, 1862—Paine had a severe attack of typhoid fever which caused "chronic irritability of the bowels, loss of appetite, pain in the left side and nervous prostration."

June 3, 1862—Paine is given a 20 day leave to recover from illness.

June 23, 1862—Paine is given a 20-day extension to July 13.

August 15, 1862—Paine assumes command of the 1st Division of the Army of the Mississippi at Tuscumbia, Alabama.

November 22, 1862—Paine is placed in charge at Gallatin, Tennessee, by General William Rosecrans.

December 8, 1862—Paine ordered to guard railroad from Mitchellsville, Tennessee, to Nashville.

May 1863—Paine initiates a plan to pay slaves wages and that overseers be subject to military authority.

August 1863—Paducah placed under martial law.

August 1863—Citizens of Mayfield, Kentucky, form a company of guards to protect the city from guerrillas.

November 2, 1863—Lucien Anderson and John Bolinger were captured and taken hostage by Confederate Colonel W.W. Faulkner.

November 4, 1863–600 rebel cavalry robbed every store in Mayfield, broke up the railroad and destroyed the rolling stock.

November 9, 1863—Paine launches a "grand guerrilla hunt" at Gallatin.

November 12, 1863—Grant orders the rail lines from Paducah to Union City, Tennessee, be taken up and moved to Nashville.

November 28, 1863—Grant writes Governor Thomas E. Bramlette that the citizens of Paducah are almost all disloyal and deserve no favors from the government.

December 5, 1863—Grant suspends order to take up tracks at Paducah.

December 14, 1863—Grant reports that Columbus, Paducah and Hickman have become havens for disreputable persons.

December 26, 1863—Congressman Anderson requests authorization from the War Department to raise a regiment of black troops in the First District. Authorization was granted.

January 13, 1864—Skirmish near Mayfield.

January 18, 1864—Bramlette writes General Jeremiah Boyle that recruiting black soldiers will not be tolerated in Kentucky.

January 25, 1864—Lucien Anderson introduces legislation that required the federal government to compensate loyal slave owners after state legislature enacted the emancipation act. The resolution failed.

January 30, 1864—Paine adopts a policy of hiring slaves to their owners.

February 18, 1864—Both houses of the Kentucky legislature support a resolution protesting the enlistment of blacks into the military and request the President remove all such enlistment camps in the state.

February 24, 1864—The U.S. Congress passed an act directing all able bodied black men between 25 and 45 to enroll into the national forces.

February 22, 1864—Mayfield invaded by guerrillas. J.B. Happy is murdered.

March 10, 1864—Guerrilla raids occur at Clinton and Mayfield.

March 22, 1864—Guerrilla raid at Fancy Farm, Kentucky. Catholic Chapel burned to the ground.

March 23, 1864—Guerrillas capture train and kill a black man near Mayfield.

March 25, 1864—Confederate troops under the command of General Nathan Bedford Forrest enter Paducah and a battle ensues.

April 2, 1864—After Forrest's raid to Paducah the War Department orders the ports closed to trade and halts all trains in the region.

April 28, 1864—Colonel Harry W. Barry arrives at Paducah to recruit a colored regiment.

May 12, 1864—Guerrillas overrun a picket guard at Mayfield and take ten prisoners.

May 23, 1864—A railroad bridge was burned and water tank destroyed by guerrillas not far from Mayfield.

May 25, 1864—Anderson is elected as an alternate delegate by the Unconditional Unionist Party to attend the Baltimore Union Convention.

June 1864—Three Union citizens were shot by guerrillas near Paducah.

June 18, 1864—Lincoln writes Secretary of War Edwin Stanton that Lucien Anderson and Judge Rufus Williams urge that suspended assessments be placed into operation and Paine be placed in command at Paducah.

June 24, 1864—General William T. Sherman sends orders from near Kenesaw Mountain, Georgia, to transfer Paine to the Department of the Tennessee and that Paine report to General Cadwallader C. Washburn at Columbus, Kentucky.

June 25, 1864—Special orders no. 90 from General Sherman relieves Paine of command in the Department of the Cumberland and assigns him duty to the Department of the Tennessee.

June 29, 1864—Special field orders no. 177 from General George H. Thomas relieves Paine from command in the Department of the Cumberland and orders Paine to report to General Washburn at Columbus.

June 29, 1864—Joseph Holt appointed chief of the Bureau of Military Justice.

June 29, 1864—Paine en route to Columbus to await orders from Washburn.

July 2, 1864—Congress passes an act that grants only shipping permits to loyal persons.

July 5, 1864—Lincoln suspends writ of habeas corpus in Kentucky, better known as Proclamation No. 113.

July 10, 1864—Skirmish occurred at Clinton. Jim Kesterson wounded and captured.

July 12, 1864—Skirmish occurs within fifteen miles of Columbus. Rebel officer captured.

July 16, 1864—Captain Barry arrested for not returning women and children of black soldiers to their owners.

July 16, 1864—General Stephen G. Burbridge issues General Order No. 59 stating that southern sympathizers within five miles of a guerrilla attack would be arrested and deported beyond the Union lines, their property seized and captured guerrillas executed.

July 17, 1864—Captain Thomas Jones Gregory and a party of home guards were ambushed near Paducah. Nine men were killed and several wounded.

July 19, 1864—Paine arrives at Paducah and sets up his offices at the Continental Hotel.

July 20, 1864—Paine and Congressman Anderson make speeches before the Market House at Paducah.

July 20, 1864–Paine orders Colonel Barry's released and countermands order compelling colored persons to be returned to slave owners beyond Union lines.

July 20, 1864—Guerrillas attack the picket line at Paducah.

July 20, 1864—Paine issues General Order No. 3 that disloyal persons living in the district shall not be allowed to ship supplies. Permits are to be issued through military headquarters for all outgoing shipments. No arms or ammunition is to be sold in the district.

July 21, 1864—Paine issues General Order No. 4 that allows only loyal men to buy or sell cotton and tobacco.

July 21, 1864—Paine revises General Order No. 3 with General Order No. 5. The order specifies who will issue permits and who may seek applications to do business at Paducah.

July 22, 1864—Paine appoints Major Henry Bartling as Provost Marshal of the District of West Kentucky.

July 23, 1864—Paine gets into a two-hour verbal argument with Emerson Etheridge and was alleged to have said General Henry Halleck was a "god damned coward."

July 23, 1864—Paine issues General Order No. 6 prohibiting the collection of rent by those that are not unconditional Union men.

July 25, 1864—Paine takes over part the Commercial Bank as his headquarters.

July 26, 1864—Paine issues General Order No. 7 prohibiting all banks within the city limits from paying money, making transfers of deposit without a permit from district headquarters.

July 27, 1864—Skirmish at Haddix's Ferry, Kentucky, on the Tennessee River.

July 27, 1864—Paine issues an order to T.L. Jacobs to go to Dresden to inform the people that if another Union man was killed, that five rebel sympathizers would share the same fate. Jacobs' father and two brothers were held as hostages. Ten days later Jacobs returned with the signatures of rebel commanders on the reverse side of the proclamation.

July 27, 1864—Paine modifies General Order No. 7 after complaints from the banks and that drawing deposits from other banks would not require approval.

July 27, 1864—Kesterson is executed below Fort Anderson along the bank of the Ohio River.

July 28, 1864—Paine issues General Order No. 8 which declares that all confiscated property from rebel sympathizers will be turned over to the Quartermaster's Department.

July 30, 1864—July returns from the District of Western Kentucky—6,441 aggregate, 28 heavy artillery and 7 field artillery.

August 1, 1864—W.F. Swift was appointed Military Superintendent of Trade at Paducah by Paine.

August 1, 1864—Paine visits Cairo and Columbus by steamship.

August 2, 1864–134th Illinois Infantry arrive at Paducah.

August 2, 1864—Troops under Captain Gregory execute a man named William Shelby Bryan at the courthouse in Mayfield.

August 4, 1864—Adjutant General Lorenzo Thomas visits Paducah and reports "everything is progressing satisfactorily."

August 6, 1864—Paine appoints Captain R.H. Hall Superintendent of Rents and Disbursing Agent, Special order no. 15.

August 8, 1864—Disloyal citizens from Columbus and Paducah arrive in Cairo en route to Canada.

August 11, 1864—Paine and Colonel W.W. McChesney arrive at Mayfield with 1500 men.

August 11, 1864—Paine orders McChesney to occupy Mayfield sink a well, prepare fortifications and repair the railroad.

August 11, 1864—Twelve miles above Smithland, Kentucky, rebel cavalry attacks a garrison of Union troops. Paine is ordered to send reinforcements. 1,000 guerrillas under Colonel Adam R. Johnson reported at Uniontown.

August 12, 1864—Third Illinois Cavalry arrive at Mayfield.

August 13, 1864—The 136th Illinois Infantry and some of the Eighth United States Colored Heavy Artillery arrive at Mayfield.

August 13, 1864—Colonel Johnson's guerrillas capture three steamers eight miles above Saline, Illinois.

August 14, 1864—A Union cavalry force from Mayfield was involved in a skirmish near Feliciana, Kentucky.

August 15, 1864—The 136th Illinois and Eighth Colored Heavy Artillery depart Mayfield for Paducah. Congressman Anderson and Bolinger make political speeches at Mayfield which advocate Lincoln's policies and emancipation.

August 16, 1864—Paine receives an order from General Burbridge to move 1,500 men to Uniontown, Kentucky, at once.

August 16, 1864—McChesney orders the fortification of the Graves County Courthouse.

August 16-17, 1864—Eli Enoch was executed by Captain Gregory's men near his home in Graves County, Kentucky.

August 18-19, 1864—Troops under Paine's command enter Union County, Kentucky.

August 18, 1864—Troops under Paine arrived that evening at Caseyville, Kentucky.

August 19, 1864—Skirmish near Hickman, Kentucky.

August 20, 1864—Troops under Paine's leave Caseyville.

August 21, 1864—Pickets fired upon by guerrillas at Mayfield killing one Union soldier.

August 21, 1864—Paine returns to Paducah from expedition to Union County.

August 22, 1864—Union scouting party was fired upon and a member of the Third Illinois Cavalry killed.

August 23, 1864—One Union soldier was killed by guerrillas near Mayfield.

August 23, 1864—Richard W. Taylor and A.W.S. Matheny were executed below Fort Anderson along the banks of the Ohio River.

August 23, 1864—Paine releases the prisoners taken at Union County.

August 24, 1864—Union pickets fired upon by guerrillas and horses stolen near Mayfield.

August 25, 1864—Paine issues General Order No. 11 which declares that soldiers' wives and family members will be given half fares on steamship transportation and that all boats must report to district headquarters.

August 26, 1864—Robert A. Walters was executed at Mayfield

August 28, 1864—Charles E. Sinclair was appointed Provost Marshal at Mayfield by McChesney.

August 30, 1864—Union scout engages 16 guerrillas near Mayfield.

August 30, 1864—Harry "Bud" Hicks was executed at Mayfield.

August 31, 1864—Returns from the District of Western Kentucky—4550 aggregate, 7 heavy artillery, no field artillery.

September 3, 1864—Bramlette writes Lincoln of citizens being insulted, oppressed and plundered in Western Kentucky.

September 4, 1864—Grant writes Halleck that Paine must be removed.

September 4, 1864—McChesney leaves Mayfield claiming a serious illness.

September 5, 1864—Halleck writes Burbridge to relieve Paine.

September 6, 1864—Burbridge telegraphs Paine that he is relieved of command and to report to General John M. Schofield commanding the Department of the Ohio for further orders.

September 6, 1864—A prisoner named Hess is executed below Fort Anderson along the banks of the Ohio River.

September 7, 1864—Paine receives General Burbridge's order being relieved of command.

September 7, 1864—Skirmish near Boydsville, Kentucky. Union troops killed one and captured one.

September 8, 1864—General J.T. Boyle writes Burbridge that Paine has oppressed the people of his district. He listed over a dozen allegations of misconduct and demands his removal and court-martial.

September 9, 1864—Congressman Anderson writes Secretary Stanton to revoke Grant's order to remove Paine.

September 9, 1864—Bramlette appoints Speed S. Fry and Colonel James Mason Brown to a board of investigation into Paine's activities at Paducah.

September 10, 1864—Anderson writes Lincoln to retain Paine as post commander at Paducah and that ten days prior Lincoln had reported supporting Paine's policies. Anderson also remarks that Paine has a severe illness "and cannot possibly recover" and "his removal will destroy all our prospects for success."

September 10, 1864—Paine's surgeon "finds him incapable of performing" his duties because of a long-standing case of chronic gastritis.

September 11, 1864—Third Illinois Cavalry ordered to proceed to Memphis. Unionists at Mayfield sign a petition to have them remain.

Timeline

September 11, 1864—General Solomon Meredith leaves Cairo to take command at Paducah. He arrives that evening.

September 12, 1864—Paine issues General Order No. 15 appointing Meredith in command of the district.

September 12, 1864—Third Illinois Cavalry departs Mayfield for Paducah.

September 12, 1864—Meredith opens limited trade and permits supplies to cross the Ohio River.

September 12, 1864—Paine departs Paducah for St. Louis.

September 12, 1864—Paine tenders his resignation claiming several attacks of 'neuralgia' and requests it take effect on October 13, 1864.

September 13, 1864—Meredith visits Mayfield.

September 14, 1864—Board of Inquiry begin taking oral testimonies.

September 15, 1864—General Fry arrives at Paducah to launch investigation. He immediately arrests and places in jail a number of black soldiers for denouncing him as a secesh general.

September 16, 1864—Major Bartling sends General Meredith his office's book and papers, along with a safe that contained the relief funds.

September 17, 1864—General McChesney is placed under arrest in Chicago.

September 17-19, 1864—The 134th Illinois Infantry left Mayfield for Paducah.

September 20, 1864—Paine writes to General Schofield stating his "body is mostly worn out" and that he wishes to resign.

September 23, 1864—General Fry submits his report to Bramlette on the conduct of Paine's administration.

September 23, 1864—Third Illinois Cavalry returns to Mayfield from Paducah.

September 23, 1864—Items seized by Paine sold at auction by order of Meredith.

September 24, 1864—Meredith orders the arrest of Surgeon Willis Danforth.

September 24, 1864–134th Illinois Infantry arrives at Chicago to muster out.

September 30, 1864—Paine writes General Lorenzo Thomas from Monmouth that his health is very poor and that he is awaiting orders from General Schofield.

September 30, 1864—Paine's resignation is denied by the Adjutant General's Office.

September 30, 1864—Returns of the District of Western Kentucky—3,519 infantry, no artillery.

October 3, 1864—Meredith ordered a fortification built southwest of Mayfield.

October 13, 1864—Meredith orders the withdrawal of troops from Mayfield.

October 15, 1864—Paine reports to Louisville to await orders.

October 16, 1864—Meredith orders Mayfield abandoned and the post evacuated based on reports of a raid by General Forrest. Meredith and Lucien Anderson issue appeals at Paducah to organize a home defense. 400 enrolled and organized into companies.

October 18, 1864—McChesney writes Burbridge that he is too sick to travel to Lexington and asks that the investigation into his command be moved to Chicago.

October 19, 1864—Forty rebels burned the courthouse at Mayfield.

October 20, 1864—Meredith orders troops back to Mayfield.

October 25, 1864—Paine reports to Nashville to await orders. He declares that he is well enough to perform his duties.

October 26, 1864—Union cavalry withdraws from Mayfield. Businessmen at Paducah are advised to pack their stock aboard steamers. All businesses in the city are closed.

October 27, 1864—Meredith warns people in Paducah of an eminent attack. People begin fleeing to Illinois.

October 29, 1864—Guerrillas enter Mayfield and kill Amos Smith and man named Cole. They also hanged a 70 year old man named Wartham for providing information on rebel movements.

November 6, 1864—A detachment of the 3rd Illinois was ordered back to Mayfield.

November 14, 1864—A band of 200 rebels rob stores at Hickman.

November 23, 1864—Grant submits a list of officers to be mustered out of service—Paine was on the list.

November 28, 1864—Charges are filed against Major Bartling for unbecoming military conduct, embezzlement and illegal imprisonment.

November 30, 1864—Paine's resignation was accepted but the Secretary of War annulled the action.

December 1, 1864—Judge Advocate General Joseph Holt sends Secretary of War E.M. Stanton final report on the case against Paine.

December 7, 1864—Senate requests that the War Department transmit all records of the investigation into Paine to the Senate.

December 24, 1864—Secretary of War Stanton receives Paine's explanations on conduct.

December 28, 1864—Paine writes General Lorenzo that he expects his resignation to be accepted on January 1, 1865.

January 4, 1865—Governor Bramlette addresses the Kentucky Legislature in regard to allegations against Paine. He includes the board of investigation's report to support the allegations.

January 10, 1865—General Fry's report is published as part of Governor Bramlette's message.

January 14, 1865—Guerrillas under Parson Garland enter Mayfield broke open stores and robbed individuals.

January 16, 1865—A Senate resolution passed that Paine be arraigned and tried for his conduct at Paducah and if found guilty should be punished.

January 18, 1865—A debate occurs in the Senate over whether Paine's investigation should be requested and whether it should be made public.

January 23, 1865—The United Senate passes a resolution that the Secretary of War send the report and evidence taken by the military commission against Paine.

January 25, 1865—Secretary of War requests a copy of the proceedings against Paine.

January 27, 1865—Kentucky House of Representatives resolves to form a committee of three to investigate the administration of Paine at Paducah.

January 28, 1865—Secretary of War reports to the Senate that the President will furnish the commission's report.

January 30, 1865—Secretary of War orders charges against Paine for a court-martial to be held in Cairo on February 8, 1865.

January 31, 1865—Skirmish occurs outside of Columbus near Clinton.

February 1, 1865—Special order no. 51 of the War Department, Adjutant General's Office, appoints a court-martial to meet at Cairo, Illinois, for the trial of Paine.

February 6, 1865—Paine testifies before a U.S. House of Representatives looking into charges of bribery and corruption made against Congressman Anderson. Paine states under oath that he never seized any money or property for his own benefit or others.

February 7, 1865—Skirmish occurs near Clinton.

February 8, 1865—Three members of the court met at midnight at Cairo and agreed to meet at 10 a.m. the next day.

February 9, 1865—Paine arrives that evening at Cairo.

February 9, 1865—Court met at 10 a.m. at Cairo. Colonel William McKee Dunn telegraphs the War Department that the court had no charges, instructions or list of witnesses and that Paine was not present. Dunn also states that court wishes to meet in Paducah and seeks authorization to do so.

February 10, 1865—Court met at 10 a.m. at Cairo. Dunn informs court that he has no charges against Paine or a list of witnesses.

February 13, 1865—Telegraph from War Department authorizes court to transfer to Paducah.

February 14, 1865—Court received the charges against Paine and ordered the transfer to Paducah.

February 14, 1865—Paine and members of the court leave Cairo on the steamer *Champion* for Paducah.

February 15, 1865—Paine arrived in Paducah for the trial.

February 16, 1865—Court met in Paducah. The judge advocate informed the court that he was unable to provide witnesses.

February 17, 1865—Court proceeded with the trial. Paine had no objection to the court members.

February 17, 1865—The following witnesses testified at Paine's trial: John Sinnott, James R. Alexander, R.O. Woolfolk, and V.S. Gillespie.

February 17, 1865—Special order no. 79 from the Department of the Cumberland, relieves Meredith of command.

February 18, 1865—The following witnesses testified at Paine's trial: W.P. Caldwell, G.F. Rabb, and J.E. Woodward.

February 20, 1865—The following witnesses testified at Paine's trial: J.E. Woodward, J.A. Bracken and P.D. Yeiser.

February 21, 1865—The following witnesses testified at Paine's trial: J.B. Husbands, Leonidas H. Edrington, J. Scott Ford, R.M. Humble, William Bell and W.L. Mayes.

February 22, 1865—The following witnesses testified at Paine's trial: W.L. Mayes, D.Y. Craig, W.P. Tucker, J.W. Hammack and Alan Omer.

February 23, 1865—The following witnesses testified at Paine's trial: W.S. Buckner, James T. Pierson, Will S. Pierson, W.W. Pierson, Thomas H. Welch, William Gregg, Caleb Tucker, Catherine Greathouse and Robert William Greathouse.

February 24, 1865—The following witnesses testified at Paine's trial: Robert William Greathouse, Henry Parsons, W.P. Tucker, James Dickey Moss and L.L. Talbot.

February 25, 1865—Paine's mother arrives in Paducah.

February 25, 1865—The following witnesses testified at Paine's trial: T.H. Mayes, Lewis T. Bradley, J.T. Bolinger, Toussaint C. Buntin, M.G. Milam, Mary Crutchfield, E.R. Jett and Frederick T. Whitworth.

February 27, 1865—The following witnesses testified at Paine's trial: Phelps Paine, Peter Davidson, J.C. Brooks and Harry W. Barry.

February 27, 1865—Meredith reinstated as commander at Paducah.

February 28, 1865—The following witnesses testified at Paine's trial: Harry W. Barry, G.L. Tombelle, Henry Bartling, Elijah Rudolph and W.M. Starks.

March 1, 1865—The following witnesses testified at Paine's trial: D.Y. Craig, J.H. Hines, J.W. Caldwell, Roland H. Hall, Robert Glover, P.H. Hall, Ila M. Davis, Thomas L. Sturgeon, J.E. Woodward, John S. Greathouse and R. Branham.

March 2, 1865—The following witnesses testified at Paine's trial: Betty Barber Hughes, Joshua D. Hughes, Peter Acker, Phillip Snow, Joseph Gerrish, S.M. Purcelle and Thomas M. Redd.

March 2, 1865—P.D. Yeiser, J.P. Prince, C.M. Thompson and John Mason Brown testify before Congress in the case against Lucien Anderson. Yeiser, Prince and Thompson stated that Anderson did not receive any money in relation to the closure and reopening of the stores at Paducah. Brown stated he was only acting as the court reporter and knew nothing of the matter.

March 3, 1865—The following witnesses testified at Paine's trial: Thomas M. Redd, James T. Pierson, G.L. Tombelle, R. Branham, G.W. Price, Francis H. Shouse, H.B. Eaty, H. Munchhoff, James Kerney and William H. Philips.

March 3, 1865—Congressman Anderson was acquitted of charges against him in the Senate.

March 4, 1865—The following witnesses testified at Paine's trial: Henry Bartling, W.P. Cunningham, Thomas Atherton, P.H. Hall, Charles M. Kilgore and closing remarks from Paine and the judge advocate.

March 6, 1865—The court read their decision and Paine was found guilty on the first charge, second specification. Court sentenced Paine to be reprimanded by the President Lincoln.

March 7, 1865—Paine assaulted by Dr. James R. Alexander.

March 8, 1865—Paine wrote to General Thomas that his resignation be accepted at once.

March 22, 1865—Captain Gregory was killed by guerrillas about thirty miles from Paducah.

March 28, 1865—Report of court-martial sent to President Lincoln.

March 28, 1865—Paine again presses General Thomas for his resignation to be accepted.

April 1865—General Court-Martial Orders, No. 567 of the War Department reports on the charges and sentence against Paine.

April 5, 1865—Paine's resignation accepted.

April 19, 1865—McChesney dies in Chicago.

April 25, 1865—Anderson asks Stanton to relieve Meredith in command until the end of the upcoming elections.

May 1, 1865—Grant orders Meredith to be relieved of command at Paducah and he is relieved the next day.

May 15, 1865—Paine requests the Secretary of War for a copy of the court's findings.

October 10, 1865—Paine requests the Judge Advocate General to send him a copy of the court's findings.

1866–1878—Paine returns to his law practice at Monmouth.

February 14, 1869—Paine requests the Secretary of War to furnish him a copy of the recommendations of the court.

April 20, 1880—Paine is working as an attorney for gold and silver speculators in New Jersey.

December 16, 1882—Paine dies at Jersey City, New Jersey.

February 15, 1903—Letter sent to a Paducah paper by Kate W. Whitfield, one of Woolfolk's daughters, which recalled the events of the banishment to Canada.

July 19, 1907—Tyler-Latham Controversy begins after Mrs. Mary Latham claimed to have been banished to Canada.

March 13, 1914—City of Mayfield files a claim for damaged caused on the courthouse during McChesney's command.

March 17, 1914—The Federal Government awarded Graves County $1,500 for damages to the courthouse by Union troops during Civil War.

Appendix I
Charges and Specifications Preferred Against Brigadier General E.A. Paine, United State Volunteers

Charge I. Violation of Fifth Article of War.
Specification. In this that Brigadier General E.A. Paine, United States Volunteers, did use contemptuous and disrespectful words against Hon. Thomas E. Bramlette, the Governor and Chief Magistrate of the State of Kentucky, in which state he said Paine was then quartered, by openly and publically denouncing him the said Bramlette as a "rebel" and averring that all his supporters were "rebels," or in words to that effect.

This at or near Caseyville, in Union County, Kentucky, on or about the 20th day of August 1864.

Witnesses: Hon. Willis W. Gardner, Hon. J.T. Pierson and W.S. Pierson

Charge II. Conduct to the prejudice of good order and military discipline.
Specification 1st. In this that Brigadier General E.A. Paine, United States Volunteers, did publically speak of and denounce his superior officer, Major General H.W. Halleck as a "God damned coward" and as a "damned rascal," or in words to that effect.

That at or near Paducah, Kentucky, in or about the last of July 1864.

Witnesses: V.S. Gillespie, William P. Caldwell, John Sinnott, Dr. James Alexander, R.O. Woolfolk

Specification 2nd. In this that Brigadier General E.A. Paine, United States Volunteers, did wrongfully and arbitrarily order and compel Watts, Given and Company, bankers to pay to Mrs. Birmingham, widow of Thomas Birmingham, citizen, the sum of nine hundred and eighty dollars ($980) on deposit in their bank to the credit of the said Thomas Birmingham, although the sais Mrs. Birmingham was not entitled by law, as the personal representative of her said husband, or otherwise, to be paid the same, and although the said Watts, Given and Company refused and protested against the payment of the same until the said Mrs. Birmingham should be qualified as administrator of her husband.

This at Paducah, Kentucky, on or about the 18th day of August 1864.

Witnesses: G.F. Rabb, Cashier, J.E. Woodward, Mrs. Birmingham

Specification 3rd. In this that Brigadier General E.A. Paine, United States Volunteers, did wrongfully and arbitrarily order and compel Watts, Given and Company, bankers to pay to C.O. Allard, citizen, the sum of eight thousand dollars ($8000) on deposit to this credit with said bankers, this against the consent and protest of said Watts, Given and Company, who had or honestly claimed to have a valid offset or defense in law to the payment of said sum arising out of their private business transactions with said Allard.

This at Paducah, Kentucky, at or about the 8th day of August 1864.
Witnesses: G.F. Rabb, D.A. Given and J.E. Woodward

Specification 4th. In this that Brigadier General E.A. Paine, United States Volunteers, did wrongfully and arbitrarily order and compel John A. Bracken, citizen, to pay one Yeiser, attorney at law, a promissory note for two hundred and fifty dollars ($250) in no way due or payable from him to said Yeiser or claimed by said Yeiser to be so due or payable, but which had been given and was still due to said Yeiser by and from one Edington for the amount of said Yeiser's charges as attorney for said Edington by said Bracken to recover damages for a trespass alleged to have been done him by said Edington while acting under directions of said Brigadier General Paine, but which suit had been withdrawn and discontinued by said Bracken long before he was ordered and compelled to pay said sum by Paine.
This at or near Paducah, in or about July 1864.
Witnesses: John A. Bracken, P.D. Yeiser, L.H. Edington

Specification 5th. In this that Brigadier General E.A. Paine, United States Volunteers, did wrongfully arrest James Moss, citizen, and keep him in arrest till he paid to the Provost Marshal the sum of one thousand dollars ($1000) illegally required by said Paine to be paid by him on the ground that he had wrongfully returned a negro to his master, whereas the said negro was not legally entitled to the protection of the military authorities of the United States, and the said Moss was not legally punishable by said authorities for his action in the case.
This at Paducah, Kentucky, in or about August 1864.
Witnesses: James D. Moss, Major H. Bartling, 8th U.S. Colored Heavy Artillery

Specification 6th. In this that Captain R.H. Hall, Provost Marshal of the 1st Congressional District of Kentucky had peremptorily and with threats ordered W.L. Mayes, citizen, to pay to him the said Hall the sum of one hundred and fifty dollars ($150) for a horse of the said Hall alleged by him to have been seized or stolen by a son-in-law of said Mayes thereupon proceeded to the headquarters of Brigadier General E.A. Paine, United States Volunteers at Paducah, Kentucky, and applied to him to be protected against payment of said sum so wrongfully demanded by said Hall—he the said Paine did refuse to give him such protection and did order and require him to pay the said sum before he left town; and in that, furthermore, when the said Mayes, having paid the said sum to said Hall in consequence of his threats and of the said Paine, afterwards applied to said Paine for reimbursement of redress, he the said Paine refused to grant him any relief whatever.
This at Paducah, Kentucky, in or about July 1864.
Witnesses: William L. Mayes, Thomas A. Duke

Specification 7th. In this that Brigadier General E.A. Paine, United States Volunteers, did wrongfully and arbitrarily order and cause the store of W.A. Bell, citizen and merchant, to be closed and his trade and business to be wholly suspended, and when subsequently he the said Paine permitted said Bell to sell out his stocks, which said Bell then did, though at a considerable loss, he did wrongfully require and exact of him to pay the Provost Marshal the sum of two thousand dollars ($2000) out of the purchase money received by him for said stock. All which was ordered and done by the said Paine on the ground of the alleged disloyalty of Bell, whereas the said Bell was a loyal and law-abiding citizen and had a short time previously as the said Paine was informed and knew, taken and subscribed a formal and comprehensive oath of allegiance to the United States, and had thereupon been invested with the full privilege and benefit of trading at Paducah, Kentucky, by the Post Commander.
This at Paducah, Kentucky, in or about August 1864.
Witnesses: W.A. Bell, Major H. Bartling, M. Weil, R.M. Humble

Specification 8th. In this that Brigadier General E.A. Paine, United States Volunteers, did wrongfully issue an order authorizing the taking from the house of J.S. Ford, citizen, certain property belonging to the said Ford, to wit, 2 quilts, 2 counterpanes, 2 mosquito bars and 2 window blinds and the delivery of the same to his son Captain Phelps Paine, Assistant Adjutant General on his staff, for the said Captain Paine's private use, which said property was so delivered and take pursuant to such order and authority, and was never restored in any part to its owner.

This at Paducah, Kentucky, in or about the month of July 1864.

Witnesses: J. Scott Ford, Private Empson Brownfield, 111th Illinois Volunteer Infantry, Major H. Bartling

Specification 9th. In this that Brigadier General E.A. Paine, United States Volunteers, did wrongfully, and in violation of paragraph 1017 of the Revised Army Regulations, grant to John F. Bolinger, citizen, the use of a Government transportation for his private purpose—to wit the use of the steamer "Convoy," a vessel then in the employment of the United States, for the transportation of about eighty four bales of cotton and twenty seven hogsheads of tobacco belonging to said Bolinger, or to him jointly with other citizens, from Hickman, Kentucky, to Cairo, Illinois, where the said cargo was discharged; and did furthermore grant to said Bolinger the use of labor and services of about seventy five soldiers of the Army of the United States as a guard or escort of said cargo, and to load the same, which said soldiers were actually employed by said Bolinger as such guard and escort and to load said cargo for him.

This at Paducah, Kentucky, and other places above mentioned on or about the 1st of August 1864.

Witnesses: L.T. Bradley, J.F. Bolinger, J.M. Bigger, W.F. Norton

Specification 10th. In this that Brigadier General E.A. Paine, United States Volunteers, did, on or about July 25th, 1864, wrongfully and arbitrarily arrest and place in close confinement in the guardhouse, M.G. Milam, citizen, and keep him so confined for a period of fifty-one days thereafter, thereby subjecting him, while in ill health, to severe treatment and suffering, and this without bringing him to trial for any offense or preferring and charges or accusations whatever against him.

This at Paducah, Kentucky, at or about the date and period above mentioned.
Witnesses: M.G. Milam

Specification 11th. In this that Brigadier General E.A. Paine, United States Volunteers, did wrongfully and arbitrarily arrest Peter Acker, citizen, and cause him to be tied up by the hands for about three quarters of an hour, during a portion of which time he, the said Paine stood by and vehemently cursed and abused him the said Acker.

This at or near Caseyville in Union County, Kentucky, on or about August 19th, 1864.
Witnesses: Peter Acker, W.W. Gardner, James T. Pierson

Specification 12th. In this that Brigadier General E.A. Paine, United States Volunteers, did wrongfully authorize and cause a detachment of the troops under his command to proceed to the house and premises of J.C. Brooks, citizen, and to take from said premises a horse and two mules belonging to said Brooks, and to ransack his house and take therefrom a quantity of bed clothes, wearing apparel, and other articles belonging to him or his family, and that he the said Paine has never restored any part of said property to said Brooks, or compensated him in any manner for the same.

This at or near Paducah, Kentucky, in or about July 1864.
Witnesses: J.C. Brooks & family, Privates Jett & Whitsworth, Kentucky State Guard

Specification 13th. In this that Brigadier General E.A. Paine, United States Volunteers, did wrongfully and violently order and cause to be broken open and entered, by troops under his command, the grocery store of Joseph Gerrish, citizen, and did cause to be destroyed, or carried away therefrom, nearly the entire stocks in trade of said Garrish, being of the value of about six hundred and seventy five dollars ($675) and has never restored the same in any part to him the said Gerrish or compensated him therefor.

This at Caseyville, in Union County, Kentucky, on or about August 19th, 1864.
Witness: Joseph Gerrish

Specification 14th. In this that Brigadier General E.A. Paine, United States Volunteers, did wrongfully authorize and cause the grocery store of Peter Acker, citizen, to be entered by troops under his command, and a large quantity of groceries and other goods, belonging to said Acker and amounting in value to about seventeen hundred and twenty four dollars ($1724) to be taken therefrom or destroyed, none of which goods have been restored to said Acker by said Paine, nor has compensation ever been made by him therefor.

This at or near Caseyville, in Union County, Kentucky, on or about August 19th, 1864.
Witness: Peter Acker

Specification 15th. In this that Brigadier General E.A. Paine, United States Volunteers, did wrongfully authorize and cause the troops under his command to take from the premises of one Greathouse, a loyal citizen, five horses belonging to him, and break open the storehouses of said Greathouse and commit waste therein, and that said Greathouse any property so taken from him, or in any way compensated from thereof.

This at or near Uniontown in Union County, Kentucky, on or about August 20th, 1864.
Witnesses: Mrs. Catherine R. Greathouse, William Greathouse

Specification 16th. In this that Brigadier General E.A. Paine, United States Volunteers, did wrongfully order and cause to be taken, by troops under his command, from the premises of L.L. Talbott, citizen, certain property of said Talbott, to wit, two negroes, two horses, and several head of cattle, he the said Paine at the same time cursing and abusing him the said Talbott, and said Paine has never restored said property to said Talbott or compensated him for the loss of the same.

This at or near Morganfield in Union County, Kentucky, on or about August 19th, 1864.
Witness: L.L. Talbott

Specification 17th. In this that Brigadier General E.A. Paine, United States Volunteers, did wrongfully authorize or suffer the troops under his command upon an expedition into Union County, Kentucky, to seize and take from Mrs. Fisher, a resident of said county, two horses belonging to her or her family, and has never restored the same or compensated her therefore, the said Mrs. Fisher being a loyal woman and having a husband and son in the Army of the United States.

This near Morganfield, in said Union County, on or about August 19th, 1864.
Witnesses: W.P. Tucker, Mrs. Fisher

Specification 18th. In this that Brigadier General E.A. Paine, United States Volunteers, did wrongfully authorize or suffer the troops under his command, upon an expedition into Union County, Kentucky, to seize and take from the premises of F.H. Shouse, citizen, two horses belonging to him, and has never restored the same to said Shouse, being a loyal man and having served as a Government assessor, and been, on account of his loyalty, driven by guerrillas from this place of residence, from which he was then absent.

This near Morganfield in said Union County, on or about August 19th, 1864.
Witness: W.P. Tucker

Specification 19th. In this that Brigadier General E.A. Paine, United States Volunteers, did wrongfully authorize or suffer the troops under his command, upon an expedition into Union County, Kentucky, to seize and take from the store of D.O. Conn, citizen, certain property belonging to him of about the value of nine hundred dollars ($900) and consisting principally of about twenty pairs of men's boots and one hundred and fifty pairs of women's shoes, and further to break into and enter the mill of him the said Conn, and take therefrom certain property belonging to him, viz. about two hundred and fifty dollars ($250) worth of flour consisting of twenty barrels and fifty sacks of flour, none of which property has ever been restored to said Conn by said Paine, nor has any compensation been made by him therefor.

This at or near Caseyville, in said Union County, on or about August 20th, 1864.
Witnesses: D.O. Conn, Thomas L. Sturgeon

Specification 20th. In this that Brigadier General E.A. Paine, United States Volunteers, did wrongfully authorize or suffer the troops under his command, upon an expedition into Union County, Kentucky, to seize and take from the premises of John W. Hammack, citizen, several head of cattle belonging to him, and to break into his house and set fire to and destroy his furniture and household goods, and that none of the property of said Hammack so taken or destroyed has been restored to him, nor has compensation been made to him therefor by said Paine.

This at or near Caseyville, in said Union County, on or about August 19th, 1864.
Witness: John W. Hammack

Specification 21st. In this that Brigadier General E.A. Paine, United States Volunteers, did wrongfully authorize or suffer the troops under his command, upon an expedition into Union County, Kentucky, to enter the house of W.H. Kibbey, citizen, where they conducted themselves violently and abused said Kibbey's family, and to seize and take from his premises, certain [amount] of his property, to wit, five horses, three saddles, several blankets, bridles and halters and two guns, none which articles of property have ever been restored by the said Paine, nor has he compensated said Kibbey therefore.

This near Morganfield in the said county, on or about August 19th, 1864.
Witness: W.H. Kibbey

Specification 22nd. In this that Brigadier General E.A. Paine, United States Volunteers, did wrongfully authorize or suffer the troops under his command, upon an expedition into Union County, Kentucky, to seize and take from Ila M. Davis, citizen, certain property belonging to him, to wit, three mares, two colts, five head of cattle, one pair of physician's saddle bags, about thirty vials of medicine, one case of surgeon's pocket instruments and a saddle and bridle, which said articles the said Paine has never restored to said Davis or in any manner compensated him for the same.

This at or near Caseyville in said Union County, Kentucky, on or about August 20th, 1864.
Witness: Ila M. Davis

Specification 23rd. In this that Brigadier General E.A. Paine, United States Volunteers, did wrongfully authorize or suffer the troops under his command, upon an expedition into Union County, Kentucky, to seize and take from Mrs. Bettie B. Hughes, widow, a resident of said county, the following property belonging to her on her family, to wit, five horses, five yoke of oxen, three cows, two saddles (one a child's saddle), a gun, a flute and two negroes, none of which said property has been restored to said Hughes by said Paine, nor has compensation ever been made by him therefor.

This at or near Morganfield in said county, on or about August 19th, 1864.
Witness: B.B. Hughes

Specification 24th. In this that Brigadier General E.A. Paine, United States Volunteers, did wrongfully authorize or suffer the troops under his command, upon an expedition into Union County, Kentucky, to seize and take from Allen Omer, citizen, the following property belonging to him, to wit, three horses, five head of cattle, five bridles, one man's saddle, three side saddles, and twenty dollars worth of furniture and rope, and that the said Paine has never restored any of said property to said Omer or in any way compensated him therefor.

This at or near Caseyville in said Union County, on or about August 19th, 1864.
Witness: Allen Omer

Specification 25th. In this that Brigadier General E.A. Paine, United States Volunteers, did wrongfully authorize or suffer the troops under his command to enter the house of J.S. Ford, citizen, in his absence, and to seize and take from there a large quantity of furniture and household goods belonging to him and his family amounting in value to the sum of two hundred and seventy eight dollars ($278) and that said Paine has never restored any said property to said Ford, or in any way compensate him therefor.

This at Paducah, Kentucky, in or about August 1864.
Witnesses: J.S. Ford, Miss Mary Crutchfield

Specification 26th. In this that Brigadier General E.A. Paine, United States Volunteers, did wrongfully authorize or suffer the troops under his command, upon an expedition into Union County, Kentucky, to seize and take horses, cattle, and other property from the following citizens of said county, to wit, W.S. Buckner, W.S. Pierson, Dr. Thomas Welch, William Gregg, Caleb Tucker, and Henry Parsons, and that the said Paine has never restored the property so taken from said parties or any of them, or compensated any of them therefor.

This at or near Caseyville in said Union County, on or about August 19th, 1864.

Witnesses: W.P. Tucker, W.S. Buckner, J.T. Pierson Jr., W.W. Pierson, Thomas Welch, William Gregg, Caleb Tucker, Henry Parsons

Appendix II
The Men Who Worked on the Fortifications at Mayfield, August 17 to September 13, 1864

Researcher's Note:

On the night of August 11, 1864, 1,500 Union infantry, cavalry and artillery entered and occupied the town of Mayfield, Kentucky. The troops had departed Paducah two days earlier and marched the twenty-six miles under the command of Brigadier General Eleazer A. Paine. Mayfield had been the center of the partisan movement in the Jackson Purchase and the nucleus of guerrilla activities in the region since the conflict between the States began. Paine, who was the commander of the District of Western Kentucky and headquartered at Paducah since July 19, 1864, ordered the 134th and 136th Illinois Infantry Regiments along with a company of the Third Illinois Cavalry Regiment and a detachment of the 8th United States Colored Heavy Artillery to secure the town and stabilize the region.

On the morning of August 12, Paine selected the residence of John Eaker, a prominent Southern sympathizer and former Kentucky state legislator, to serve as post headquarters. He next ordered that a well be sunk near the Graves County Courthouse, the railroad between Paducah and Mayfield be repaired and that a stockade be built around the court square. Paine then authorized Colonel Waters W. McChesney, regimental commander of 134th Illinois Infantry, to seize the businesses and homes of outspoken Southern sympathizers for military use and to house troops within the city. By the evening of 12th, Union troops had moved into every church, hotel and tobacco warehouse in Mayfield. They also took over the county courthouse, the girl's seminary and the homes of the known secessionists. Paine returned to Paducah the following afternoon leaving McChesney as post commander. During the next few days, McChesney removed local and county officials with pro-secessionist leanings, rounded up citizens who provided aid to the rebels and confiscated the property of Southern sympathizers. He sent out pickets and scouting parties daily to root out and capture roaming bands of guerrillas.

On August 15, United States Congressman Lucian Anderson of Mayfield organized a rally on the courthouse square to advocate President Abraham Lincoln's management of the war and emancipation of slaves. Another local Unionist, John Bolinger, warned the audience that they best submit peaceably or necessary force would be applied until they obeyed. He declared that one hundred rebel families would be banished and the citizens of county found not loyal to the Union would pay $250,000. The next day, McChesney appointed Major John A. Wilson and Captain Samuel L. Andrews of the 134th Illinois to coordinate the construction of fortifications about the courthouse.

The first day citizens were employed to clean the streets in preparation of construction. On the second day, the doors and windows of the courthouse were planked up with heavy oak scathing, the walls punctured with loopholes for muskets and staging built for the men to shoot from. The laborers also commenced on piling up earthworks at the north door entrance. After a few days of constructing fortifications Private Thomas W.E. Belden, a trained civil engineer and graduate of Yale University, was detailed to lay out extensive earthworks about the courthouse. As the fortifications expanded more laborers were required and Wilson was given the task of locating men to do the work.

The method used to obtain laborers began with a list of names of men supplied by Unionist refugees that returned from Paducah with Paine's army. A well-recognized Southern sympathizer was sent to notify the disloyal individuals to report to the post headquarters at Mayfield. The number of laborers was also supplemented by men who visited the town and could not provide proof of being a loyal citizen. Many of those which reported claimed to be Union men and sought exemption from work. All appeals for exemption were sent to Major Wilson who decided upon their loyalty status and whether they were physically fit to work. In most instances Wilson simply sought evidence that they took the oath of allegiance or if a physician or surgeon found their condition too poor to conduct hard labor. Captain Andrews later recalled that many of the men ordered to work were physically unfit due to old age and disease. In cases where men were incapable of performing hard labor a substitute could be procured for a fee between $10 and $50 depending upon their financial status. On a few occasions, men of influence paid up to $300 to escape working on the fortifications. Graves County Judge W.G. Blount was initially entrusted with furnishing substitutes and collecting fees. A week after Judge Blount was assigned the position, he fell ill and Major Wilson took over those responsibilities. Captain Andrews would list close one thousand names of those that worked on the fort before construction ceased on September 13.

Suffering from a serious illness, Colonel McChesney boarded the train for Paducah on September 4 and would not return. General Paine was removed from command the following day by order of General Henry W. Halleck. The official notice of Paine's removal reached Mayfield on September 12. Brigadier General Solomon Meredith replaced Paine and traveled to Mayfield on the 13th. On his arrival, he assembled the workers and remaining troops at Mayfield and declared that all men that had worked on the fortifications were to be relieved of their duties and to return to their homes and farms. The fortifications were then to be leveled by the troops and the grounds brought back to their original state. All horses and mules confiscated from disloyal citizens were to be returned and buildings used for military purposes to be evacuated and restored to their rightful owners. The 134th Illinois departed Mayfield on September 18 leaving a few cavalry companies to scout the nearby countryside for Confederate advances into the region or track down bushwhackers. The cavalry abandoned the town on October 15 after reports of Confederate troop movements in West Tennessee. Four days later, a band of guerrillas invaded Mayfield and burned the Graves County Courthouse the ground.

Colonel McChesney was placed under arrest at his home in Chicago and ordered to stand trial for bribery, embezzlement and the misappropriation of seized property for personal use. He died of the illness he contracted in Kentucky before a court be convened. Paine was brought before a military tribunal in late February of 1865. The charges consisted of twenty-seven specifications stemming from coercion, illegal arrests and confinement, unlawful property seizures, misappropriation of private property, banking improprieties and derogatory denouncements made against high ranking officers and government officials. He was acquitted of all charges except that of insulting a superior officer.

The list of workers was preserved by Captain Andrews and submitted as evidence in the court-martial of General Paine. The records from Paine's trial were retained by the Judge Advocates General's Office of the United States Army. Those records were relocated to the National Archives and presently housed at the National Archives Records Administration under the Records of the Judge Advocates General's Office (Army), Entry 15, Court-Martial Case Files, 1809–1894, File no. MM-1609, Boxes 1032–1033.

The list of names below is the transcription of that list. A cross reference of the surnames indexed in the Graves County, Kentucky, Census of 1860 by Pat Record in 1979 was conducted in 2013 to locate the possible identities of those that worked on the fortifications. The information mentioned in brackets is likely matches to the names in the 1860 Federal census and the ages of the men that worked on the fortifications. The letter "x" signifies that the surname was not found in the census or very common names such as Jones, Smith, etc., which were so numerous that it was impossible to identify the names in the index to the work list. It is important to note that both the census and the work list were written phonetically and in many instances improperly spelled.

August 17, 1864

1. W.O. Melvin [20]
2. L. Melvin [Levi Melvin—14]
3. J.S. Melvin [James or John—25 or 23]
4. E.B. Carter [46]
5. James C. Carter [22]
6. A.P. Carter x
7. A.J. Carter [14]
8. William Dick x
9. John Myers [22]
10. J.H. Patterson [J.R. Patterson—43]
11. D.B. Turner [41]

August 18, 1864

12. J.M. Yarborough [46]
13. W.A. Yarborough [37]
14. Hugh Hendley [35]
15. J.D. Beasley [52]
16. J.H. Grigg [42]
17. H. Overby x
18. A. Humphries [67]
19. B.F. Johnson [33]
20. Wm. Cochrain [58]
21. J.W. Ryan [34]
22. Samuel Yandle [43]
23. Daniel Justice [39]
24. Aaron Hendon [62]
25. John Wilkins [45]
26. A.H. Sheridan [33]
27. J.F. Hudspeth [20]
28. J.S. Hudspeth [17]
29. E.M. Ligon [E.M. Ligon—57]
30. J.W. White [35]
31. J.C. Leach [43]
32. J.W. Watts [50]
33. B.S. Crofford [B.S. Crawford—37]
34. Thomas West x
35. John Harpole [John W. Harpool—52]
36. J.D. Crouch [33]
37. J.I. Simmons [34]
38. William Davis [37]
39. Dave Orr [67]
40. Thomas Collins [55]
41. James A. Boyd x
42. Frank Metcalf x

August 19, 1864

43. Frank Mayes [28]
44. W.G. McNeely [54]
45. W.C. Pullen [51]
46. J.A. Pullen [47]
47. M.P. McNeely [25]
48. Nathan Moore [64 or 21]
49. D.M. Galloway [45]
50. J.J. Watson [Jasper J. Watson—23]
51. W.B. Jones
52. J.S. Potter x
53. I.J. Hall [30]
54. L.S. Galloway [41]
55. J.C. Galloway [19]
56. F.G. Sassuin [R.G. Sisson—50]
57. Henry Wiel x
58. R.A. Mayes [26]

August 20, 1864

59. R. Rowland [Reuben Roland—31]
60. George Glenn x
61. John Powers x
62. George Washington x
63. Alfred Hawson [32]
64. H.C. Stubblefield [19]
65. J. Hargrove [49]
66. W.A. Moore [William Moore—28]
67. M. Hargrove [24]
68. T.S. Smith
69. G.W. Hargrove [29]
70. D. Bean [34]
71. Cary Minton x
72. R. Skinner x
73. J.B. Brissie [J.B. Bressin—42]
74. A.R. Boone [34]
75. Abraham (colored)
76. J.C. Henry (colored)
77. G.B. Cope x
78. J.W. Trovise x
79. G.M. Elliot [George M. Elliott—37]
80. W.B. Dunbar [30]
81. J. Turnbull [Jefferson Turnbull—50]
82. I. Gardner [50]
83. Wm. Galloway [27]
84. C.H. Greer [44]
85. J.B. Abernathy
86. B. Abernathy
87. E. Dolan
88. P. Reynolds [Prior Reynolds—47]
89. M.L. Cochran [Leander Cochran—30]
90. R.B. Watson x
91. J. Wiel [Jacob Weil—32]
92. S. Scott
93. Jeff Alexander [25]
94. B.F. Cloys

August 22, 1864

95. James Gillum [23]
96. J.B. Williams [37]
97. T.A. McMichael x
98. W.D. Dunbar [30]
99. T.W. Sayer [F.W. Sayre—30]
100. James Austin [28]
101. P. Krindrich
102. H.W. Cochran [53]

103. Geo. Rollins
104. Y.M. Ogborn [Thomas M. Ogburn—35]
105. Wm. C. Robbins [54]
106. T.B. Cochran [36]
107. J.A. McNutt [43]
108. J.S. Thomas [37]
109. A.G. McFadden [45]
110. W.C. Nowell
111. John Adair [68]
112. G.W. Skinner x
113. J.T. Blyth [41]
114. Rufus Williams [Rufus K. Williams—49]
115. H. Conley x
116. A. Nance (colored)
117. Dawson (colored)
118. Robert Branch x
119. J.G. Moore x
120. A. Cook [27]
121. T.C. Bayliss [Samuel Bales—36]
122. J.W. Thomson [60]
123. L.J. Alexander [37]
124. R.M. Yates x
125. P.S. Gentry x
126. J.R. Moore x
127. J.M. Stuart x
128. W.H. Slaughter [45]
129. Z. Walker x
130. S.T. Elliot [28]
131. A. Parks [39]
132. J. Prestwood x
133. T.J. Cutsinger [47]
134. E.J. Miller x
135. R.B. McFadden x
136. W.H. Miller [29]
137. Sam Hayes [46]
138. C.B. Mills x
139. T. Hendren [25]
140. H.J. Beadles x
141. W.S. Stephens [42]
142. J.C. Leech [43]
143. W.M. Maxey [64]
144. J.W. Thomas [John Thomas—31]
145. Ja. Thomas [James Thomas—24]
146. M. Riley [37]
147. Jeff Copeland [Jefferson Copeland—40]
148. J.H. Cashon x
149. A.H. Wiley [53]
150. A.T. Stone x
151. H. Holt [N.H. Holt—22]
152. Thomas Conard x
153. Charles Dallam [19]
154. D.D. Nicks x
155. Perry Bragg [17]
156. J.T. Caraway x
157. J. Caraway x
158. D. Wilson [57]
159. J.C. Cochran [James O. Cochran—26]
160. E.S. Hart [57]
161. J. Boyd x
162. Jack (colored)
163. Jerry (colored)
164. Henry (colored)
165. B. Hurst x
166. Turstead x
167. Barton x
168. Dave Campbell [38]
169. J.J. Thurmond [J.H. Thermon—45]
170. J.P. Adair [31]
171. J.W. Millet x
172. J.C. Elliot [34]
173. Robert Carrico [J.R. Carrico—32]
174. B.J. Pencall x
175. J. Hester (colored)
176. J.D. Hawlin x
177. John Wrather x
178. W.H. Clark [W.S. Clark —60]
179. Wm. Mayfield [34]
180. F.E. Long x
181. A. Gallaway x
182. J.A. Mays [John Mays—20]
183. D.N. Bradley [23]
184. Moses Anderson (colored)
185. S. Anderson [16]
186. J.W. Higgins [John Higgins—31]
187. Titus Holmes x
188. H.T. Pomerville x
189. John (colored)
190. Thomas Hudspeth [15]
191. P. Wright [Preston Wright—48]
192. Matt Morrow x
193. J.D. Richil x
194. D.C. Harris x
195. J.M. Brook ×
196. William Cochran [58]
197. N.J. Brooks x
198. E.S. Browning [E.L. Browning—28]
199. M.B. Todd x
200. John Field x

August 23, 1864

201. J.W. Scott [45]
202. E. Nance [E.L. Nance—29]
203. John Dawson [57]
204. P.T. Parkerson [P.F. Purguson—30]
205. T.S. Clark x
206. H.C. Prayer x
207. Eugene Mays [18]
208. J.T. Galloway [23]
209. J.B. Walls [32]
210. John Baldwin [John Boldin—36]
211. C.C. Wade [35]
212. I. Hamlet [Isaac H Jamlet—21]
213. J.M. Wilson [49]
214. J.M. Donnell [John Donnal—32]
215. T.S. McCandley [T.S. McCandless—34]
216. W.H. Stamper x
217. J.W. Scoggins [34]
218. T.J. Acles x
219. J.A. Sellers [Jesse Sellars—44]
220. J.T. Aylesbury x
221. B.F. Patterson [Benjamin Patterson—24]
222. L. Johnson x
223. B. Ryan x
224. J.C. Hester [32]
225. A.G. Ezell x
226. J.W. Marine [J.W. Merean—50]
227. T.B. Phelps [29]
228. J.F. Glass [James Glass—25]
229. G.D. Stephens [C.D. Stevens—49]
230. R.J. Wright [54]

231. G.W. Hunt [George W. Hunt—24]
232. J.T. Lockridge [James T. Lochridge—28]
233. D.M. Freeman x
234. W.W. Tice x
235. C.M. Stone x
236. C.W.B. Burkett x
237. S.T. Buckingham [31 or 62]
238. J.J. Hughes x
239. M. Hargroves [Finis M. Hargroves—24]
240. J.M.V. Cochran x
241. Thomas Maxey [19]
242. D.T. Stevens x
243. Mac (colored)
244. J. Wiggins [J.A. Wiggins—27]
245. W.C. Hamlet [31]
246. J.H. Thurmond [45]
247. J.W. Fowler x
248. Wm. Caldwell [37]
249. W.B. Crook [W.A. Crook—27]
250. John Milbourn [43]
251. Thomas Stock [T.C. Stark—38]
252. John Rhodes [54]
253. J. Henrich [J. Hendrick—28]
254. J.H. Permater x

August 24, 1864

255. J.C. Pryor [43]
256. Jas. Harrison [49]
257. J.H. Clark [J.M. Clark—27]
258. F.M. Jones
259. Wm. Ellison [25]
260. W. Bennet [32]
261. John Overby [18]
262. Sam Grant [27 or 59]
263. J.E. Grant [James Grant—33]
264. J.H. Grant [36]
265. W.R. Grant [William Grant—42]
266. C.W. Wilson x
267. John Nance [J.W. Nance—34]
268. John Mobery [31]
269. Wm. Doyle x
270. H.J. Dill [J. Dill—25]
271. W.C. Gilbert [Webster Gilbert—37]
272. J.M. Grant [27]
273. J.M. Grant [repeated]
274. J.D. Fendren [James D. Fendure—19]
275. J. Wilford [58]
276. William Wilford [16]
277. C.D. Grant [Charles D. Grant—28]
278. J.J. Cope [T.J. Cope—33]
279. J.W. Harpole [52]
280. S.P. Cope [39]
281. Al See [Alpea Sea—64]
282. Jno. S. Crawford x
283. R.H. McGowan [44]
284. Wm. Edwards x
285. Hamon Rule x
286. David East x
287. Jas. Anderson [J.T. Anderson—42]
288. Madison Wright x
289. J.H. Pate [John Pate—16]
290. J.R. McGowan [39]
291. C.W.J. Carter [Charles Carter—35]
292. J.W.S. Gosset x
293. L.F. Stafford [39]
294. J.D. Brackenridge [42]
295. Z. Johnson [56]
296. J.A. Osmond x
297. J.R. Byron [31]
298. Rich New x
299. H.H. Hadzins
300. John Fisk [38]
301. J. Boyd x
302. Ed Wimberly
303. H. Wimberly [Henry Wimberly—17]
304. J. Smith
305. R. Waggoner [Richard Wagoner—41]
306. J.J. Crouch [John J. Cronch—39]
307. Geo. R. Waggoner [21]
308. J.S. Adams [54]
309. W.H. Watson [William Watson—54]
310. T.C. Wilson x
311. Jas. Wilson [Jim Wilson—25]
312. Jas. Elliott [37]
313. Jo. Potts x
314. Jo. Elliot [31]
315. Jas. Hathcote [James Hathcock—42]
316. I. Thompson x
317. O. Whitt x
318. W.W. Maxey [64]
319. A.J. Clark x
320. W.J. Clark x
321. H. Wyatt [Henry Wyatt—46]
322. R. Wyatt [Rolley Wyatt—12]
323. A. Adams [Abram Adams—50]
324. R. McGill x
325. Dave McGill x
326. Jas. McGill x
327. J.R. Mills [James Mills—29]
328. B. Miller [Ben Miller—33]
329. J.M. Farmer [James M. Farmer—31]
330. Jas. Biggs [62]
331. S.L. Toon [47]
332. J.S. Scaggs [John Skaggs—34]
333. Thomas Glisson x
334. Wm. A. Krell x
335. J.M. Mills [James Mills—29]
336. Jno. Sullivan [27]
337. S.W. Darrington [50]
338. C. Richardson [64]
339. W.W.A. Miller [30]
340. J.S. Thompson x
341. J.W. Crouch [33]
342. Jno. Smith
343. M. Copeland [Mark Copeland—54]
344. Jno. Miller [56]
345. Jas. Miller [James K. Miller—15]
346. Chas. Crouch [17]
347. B.G. Smith
348. Wm. Thompson [41]
349. Jo. Grant x
350. B. Ray [Barton Ray—38]

351. A.J. Copeland [Andrew J. Copeland—34]
352. J.M. Rule x
353. R.S. Ballard x
354. S. Biggs x
355. R.J. Carrico [H.J. Caricco—35]
356. C. Carrico [Columbus Carrico—20]
357. William Jones
358. J.F. Edwards x
359. Jasper McCallain x
360. William Cope [40]
361. J. Summerville [James Summerville—20]
362. J.J. Head [Jeremiah Head—40]
363. W.H. Maxey [William Maxey—22]
364. W.P. McCullan [W.A. McCuen—36]
365. L.E. Wilson x
366. Levi Dick x
367. J.H. Wilson [27]
368. J. Elliot [39]
369. B.F. Foster [B.J. Foster—38]
370. W.S. Nance [40]
371. J. Richardson [James Richarson—25]
372. W.C. Linn [H.C. Lynn—26]
373. Z. McGarey x
374. Geo. P. Pertle [George Pirtle—25]
375. W.T. Reddick x
376. W. Jackson [W.H. Jackson—35]
377. T. Holt [J. Holt—64]
378. E.S. Weldon [21]
379. J.H. Jenkins [J.L. Jenkins—44]
380. Jas. Dennison x
381. J.H. McGary x
382. J.J. Holbrook [John Halbrook—74]
383. Jo. McGary x
384. S.L. Scarbrough x
385. D. Dennison x
386. F.M. Brown [M. Brown—29]
387. Wm. Dennison x
388. J.L. Holcomb x
389. Jack Tharp x
390. A.M. Moitt [A.M. Myatt—30]
391. T.B. Eaker [29]
392. J. Baterman [Jerry Bateman—53]
393. L.J. Alexander [37]
394. E. Tucker [Eliza Tucker—39]
395. H. Tucker [Harvey Tucker—35]
396. M.W. Jones [23]
397. J.B. Knight [John Knight—19]
398. J.E. Wilkerson [J.S. Wilkerson—48]
399. J.F. McElrath [35]
400. L.B. Copeland [Levi B. Copeland—29]
401. W.A. Crook [23]
402. Jno. Cope [J.H. Cope—30]
403. Washington Cope [Washington D. Cope—44]
404. David Carter x
405. W. Alexander [William Alexander—32]
406. J.D. Alexander x
407. Wm. Gilbert [William Gilbert—44]
408. P. Gilbert [Peter Gilbert—47]
409. J.L. Batts x
410. J. Ashbrook [John Ashbrook—53 or 19]
411. J.R. Scarbrough x
412. G.W. Ryan [George R. Ryan—31]
413. W.D. Oliver [29]
414. Wm. Copeland [26]
415. J.D. Brockway [Joseph D. Brockman—22]

August 25, 1864

416. T. Grant [Thomas Grant—40]
417. A.G. McGowan x
418. Jas. Anderson [J.T. Anderson—42]
419. J.H. Sheridan [John Sheridan—56]
420. J.G. Maxey [James Maxey—15]
421. W.C. Conoly [W.C. Conley—29]
422. Chas. Gilbert [C. Gilbert—51]
423. J.T. Sullivan [J.F. Sullivan—30]
424. M. Sullivan [22]
425. D.D. Buchanan x
426. H.P. Doughty [Henry Dowdy—46]
427. Jo. Daughty [Joseph S. Dowdy—19]
428. J.M. Dowty [James W. Dowdy—15]
429. Dave Sellers [David Sellars—29]
430. W.P. Jones
431. G.A. Dowty [George Allen Dowdy—18]
432. Jno. Sanderson [20]
433. W.T. Wyman [W. Wyman—31]
434. J.G. Gibson x
435. Bill Bracy x
436. Alex Bracy x
437. Wm. Bradly [William Bradley—30]
438. Sam Patterson [Saml. Patterson—31]
438a H.C. Holand x
439. I. Copeland [Isaac Copeland—47]
440. Jas. Landman [Thomas J. Landeman—54]
441. R. Sheppard [Robert Shepherd+34]
442. P.R. Bryan x
443. W.G. Holifield x
444. Galvin Nance x
445. R.G. Wright [Robert Wright—19]
446. R.T. Nance [54]
447. A. Dowdy [Allen Dowdey—54]
448. R. Sanderson [Robert Sanderson—48]
449. Jacob Perkins [34]
450. Sam Woods x
451. D.J. Perbles [David D. Peebels—33]

The Men Who Worked on the Fortifications

452. Jno. Dowdy [John W. Dowdy—16]
453. W.J. Wright [52]
454. W.R. Jordan [William Jordan—39]
455. J.M. Sellers [John M. Sellers—30]
456. J.B. Sanderson [Jacob Sanderson—29]
457. R.C. Patterson [A.C. Patterson—24]
458. T.W. Galladay x
459. W. Garnett x
460. J. Rogers [57]
461. H. Gregory [Hardin Gregory—52]
462. W. Dodson [William Dodson—50]
463. W.M. Williams [W. Williams—34]
464. No name listed
465. G.W. Boswell [G.H. Boswell—39]
466. Jas. Johnson x
467. Jno. Gregor [Jones Gregory—50 or 39]
468. A.A. Boswell [49]
469. H. Bryant x
470. T. Howard (Collin's negro)
471. C.S. Paine x
472. W.H. Watson [William Watson—54]
473. A.G. Kesterson [G. Kesterson—30]
474. E.F. Alexander [30]
475. A.A. Wrather x
476. W.A. Wrather x
477. T.T. Noel x
478. D.T. Liggone [D.T. Ligon—34]
479. H.T. Bridgeforth x
480. R.W. Bridgeforth [32]
481. C.J. Whitmore [C.J. Whittimore—38]
482. J.A. Hutchenson [J.A. Hutchison—32]
483. R.M.P. Fields [R.N.P. Fields—42]
484. J.H. Neale [J.H. Neal—36]
485. J.T. Wright [23]
486. N.A. Morgan x
487. H. Shelden [Hartwell Shelton—39]
488. W.J. Rhodes [W.T. Rhodes—29]
489. E.R. Shelden [Elisha Shelton—17]
490. J.J. Wingo [57]
491. R.W. Stevison x
492. J. Turner x
493. J.K. Lewis x
494. J.C. Carman x
495. G.W. Martin [31]
496. S.P. Bostic [S.E. Bostic—39]
497. J.I. Glass [James Glass—29]
498. H.L. Lewis x
499. H.A. Bogard x
500. D. West [Darius West—50]
501. J. West [John West—68 or 15]
502. Jas. Lester [James Lester—35]
503. N.B. Cothorne [Napoleon Cothran—24]
504. W.P. Davis [37]
505. R. Turnbole [R.L. Turnbow—30]
506. W.R. Reddick x

August 26, 1864 [dates not listed again until September 1, 1864]

507. Wm. Lester [William Lester—19]
508. Jas. Jolly x
509. J.R. McGowan [39]
510. Robt. Wright [19]
511. George (colored)
512. Charlett (colored)
513. W. Holifield x
514. T. Holifield x
515. A. Holifield x
516. J. & S. Bush (colored)
517. Christopher (colored)
518. Bird (colored)
519. Major (colored)
520. Beri (colored)
521. John (colored)
522. C.H. Johnson x
523. Henry Gardner x
524. G. Hobbs x
525. H.M. Boswell
526. S.A. Miller x
527. N. Thomas x
528. W. Rogers [William Rodgers—39]
529. J.J. Bidwell x
530. A.T. Jones
531. Dan (colored) and Jo. Miller
532. L.H. (colored)
533. H.T. Rogers x
534. A.C. Wilkins x
535. R. Lawrence [Rhodan Lawrence—28]
536. A.F. Morris [A.S. Morris—33]
537. George (colored)
538. Graveson x
539. J.W. Chambers x
540. J.J. Guthra [Joel J. Guthrie—38]
541. Bill (colored)—T. Benson x
542. A.J. Carey [29]
543. J.T. Carey [31]
544. J.M. Rogers x
545. R.E. Mason x
546. G. Washing x
547. John Lester [11—son of James?]
548. J.N. Lester [James Lester—35?]
549. W.C. Chambers x
550. A.J. Watts x
551. R. Williams x
552. Ellis (colored)—J. Shelton
553. Thom. Bird [20]
554. Jas. Bird [15]
555. M. Honicut [Martin Honeycutt—46]
556. G.W. Flood [George Flood—15]
557. A.J. Woodson [A.T. Woodson—39]
558. W.M. Sullivan x
559. Jon Fisk [38]
560. Wm. Grey x
561. Jas. Kelson x
562. J.M. Finney x
563. J.R. Finney [Joseph Finny—25]

Appendix II

564. W.A. Finney [William Finny—32]
565. Jas. Turner [James M. Turner—26]
566. J.B. Turner x
567. R.T. Anderson x
568. G.W. Slaughter x
569. J.J. Finney [27]
570. J.L. Richardson [James Richardson—25]
571. W.R. Slaughter x
572. Henry Magee [George H. Magee—34]
573. J.H. Swift x
574. S. Slaughter x
575. Marion x
576. B.S. Enoch [Benjamin Enoch—36]
577. B.T. Jean x
578. C. Jones
579. R.P. Toon [Richard Toon—27]
580. W.D. Virgin [44]
581. J.D. Virgin [33]
582. J.C. Elliot [34]
583. R.B. Wright x
584. A. Wheeler [Allen Wheeler—34]
585. T.H. Gibson [Thomas H. Gibson—42]
586. W.R. Wilson x
587. G. Rowland x
588. H. Ryan x
589. C. Percell x
590. Geo. Hayden x
591. B.P. Hayden x
592. R. Hayden x
593. T.C. Mills x
594. R.H. Austin x
595. E.S. Chenault x
596. T.W. Puckett x
597. N.O. Niel x
598. D. Asherbrook [David Ashbrook—17]
599. T. Hayden x
600. J.A. Hayden x
601. J.M. Hayden x
602. Jno. Hayden x
603. R.T. Puckett x
604. N.A. Rowland x
605. I.W. Rowland x
606. T.E. Rowland x
607. G.W. Staton x
608. J. Staton x
609. T.M. David x
610. J.M. Reilly [James Riley—12]
611. J.T. Reilly [J.T. Riley—43]
612. E. Cave x
613. W.W. Parrott x
614. S. Bradford [Spencer Bradford—38]
615. W.A. Finney x
616. J. Seay [J.T. Seay—49]
617. T. Edwards x
618. James Wade [J.F. Wade—21]
619. J.A. Lamb [J.A. Lamm—54]
620. J.B. Stevenson [31]
621. J.M. Mahan [James Mahan—28]
622. R.K. Bennet x
623. W.A. Mahan [William Mahan—25]
624. J.M. Lamb [James Lamm—29]
625. W.C. Lamb [William Lamm—27]
626. G.F. Orr [58]
627. F.M. Orr [19]
628. G.W. Lamb [George Lamm—34]
629. R. Barringer [James Barrager—16]
630. W.E. Abbot [William Abbott—19]
631. R.M. Clayton [39]
632. J.H. Lamb [Joseph Lamm—26]
633. L.M. Barringer [L.M. Barrager—41]
634. M.S. Chenault x
635. Jno. Chapman [58]
636. H. Chapman [36]
637. Jno. Alcock [John Allcock—30]
638. T. Alcock [Thomas Allcock—39]
639. M.T. Cobbs [54]
640. S. Cargill [Samuel P. Cargill—37]
641. J.M. Armstead [James Armistead—30]
642. R.A. Lewis [32]
643. P.B. Adams [55]
644. J. Eddens [Joseph D. Edens—42]
645. F.M. Cargill [28]
646. J. Powers x
647. B.G. Tilber [B.G. Tilla—32]
648. J.M. McReynolds [Joseph McReynolds—29]
649. J.H. Pryor [John H. Pryor—30]
650. D.F. Cargill [Daniel F. Cargill—31]
651. J.P. Powell [54]
652. W. Powell [27]
653. J.B. Coleman x
654. R.J. Hughes x
655. M. Jones

[Number jumps from 655 to 666 on the list]

666. W.S. Killonger x
667. W. Sellers [55]
668. Z.B. Thomas [39]
669. T. Barriger [T.W. Barrager—36]
670. A. Carney [47]
671. W. Doughty [William Daudy—36]
672. W. Rogers [William Rodgers—39]
673. C. Farthing [Coleman Farthing—46]
674. E.W. Hughes [47]
675. G.W. Tucker x
676. B.F. Cargill [36]
677. J.P. Hansen [James P. Hanson—27]
678. M.A. Rogers x
679. R.B. Stubblefield [32]
680. H.M. Short [50]
681. W.B. Miller [W.P. Miller—50]
682. J.T. Childress x
683. J. Head [Jefferson Head—54]
684. A. Head [Andrew J. Head—20]
685. J.J. Head [Jeremiah Head—40]
686. J.W. West [John W. West—33]

687. F. Sayer [F.W. Sayre—30]
688. R. Boyd [Robert C. Boyd—34]
689. N. Ligon x
690. A. Hammond x
691. J. Croley [James Croley—56]
692. B. Croley [Burrel Croly—26]
693. J. Croley Jr. [James Croley—17]
694. B. Washburn [Benjamin Washburn—25]
695. J.C. Williams [30]
696. Griggs [J.L. Grigg—42]
697. R. Parrett [Rodean Parrott—54]
698. J.H. Jones
699. D. Sullivan [J.D. Sullivan—32]
700. Ed. Eaker x
701. B.T. Monroe x
702. W. Huddlestone [W.C. Huddlestone—41]
703. R. Glissen x
704. A. Guine [39]
705. W.M. Prickett x
706. P. Prickett x
707. F. Williams [F.E. Williams—36]
708. J.M. Farmer [James M. Farmer—31]
709. G. Frey [61 or 17]
710. Wm. Tucker x
711. J. Austin x
712. Jno. O'Connor x
713. Jim O'Connor x
714. W. Wilson [William Wilson—17]
715. J. Indaman [Jesse C. Inman—37]
716. H. Thomas x
717. L. Simmons x
718. Ban (colored)
719. Lew (colored)
720. Henry (colored)
721. W.B. Hodges [M.B. Hodges—45]
722. J. McReynolds [Joseph McReynolds—29]

September 1, 1864

723. R.T. Chandler [R. Chandler—34]
724. W. Frey x
725. H. Prayer x
726. E. Rambo x
727. J. Welmoth [Jackson F. Wilmoth—31]
728. H. Reed [H.S. Reed—25]
729. C.W. Sullivan [G.W. Sullivan—39]
730. J. Forbes [John Forbus—21]
731. G. Clapp [George Clapp—21]
732. J. Bossick [John Bostick—17]
733. J. Floyd x
734. W. Orton [W.T. Orten—25]
735. W.D. Morgan x
736. F.M. Morgan [32]
737. J. Jackson x
738. J.G. Vaughn [James Vaughn—22]
739. N. Pister x
740. H. Weeks [Henry Weeks—46]
741. C. Jackson [Christopher Jackson—14]
742. Ed Vaughn [E. Vaughn—43]
743. B. Burnham [Robert Burnham—15]
744. H. Wambly x
745. J.A. Bennett [Joseph Bennett—50]
746. A. Stevens [A.B. Stephens—43]
747. N.G. Holifield [N. Holifield—39]
748. J. Morgan [J. Morgain—27]
749. M.R. Bell x
750. Nat Wyatt x
751. J. Shainner x
752. W.T. Shainer x
753. J. Adams x
754. J. Stevens x
755. W. Peoples [Hugh W. Peebles—31]
756. A. Clapt [William Clapp—26]
757. W. Norris x
758. H. Norris x
759. J. Andris x
760. F.M. Morgan [32]
761. F. Rudd x
762. J.D. Smith
763. J.P. Norris x
764. W. Fuller [William Fuller—32]
765. J.W. Griffith [31]
766. C.C. Fuller [C.H. Fuller—19]
767. J. Rudd x
768. J. Gardner x
769. R.E. Harper [39]
770. T. Lindman [Thomas J. Landeman—54]
771. A. Fuller x
772. W. Rhea [William A. Ray—15]
773. H. Prince x
774. N. Watson x
775. J. Wilmot [Jackson F. Wilmoth—31]
776. E. Rambear x
777. W. Pembley [Wesley Plumblee—26]
778. J. Key x
779. F.B. Hasbrook [Freeman Halbrook—30]
780. S.C. Chapman [Samuel C. Chapman—30]
781. N. Edwards [Newt Edwards—63]
782. H. Casey x
783. W. Rheay [William Rhew—19]
784. Wm. Daffin x
785. J. Greer x
786. J. Edwards [Joseph Edwards—21]
787. N.J. Smith
788. A. Mason [A.H. Mason—28]
789. D. Daughty x
790. Wm. Mathews x
791. T. Reed [T.J. Reed—25]

Appendix II

September 2, 1864
[no further dates listed]

792. J. Sanderson [John Sanderson—20]
793. Illegible
794. W. Perkins [William Perkins—20]
795. J. Perkins [Jacob Perkins—34]
796. G. Dill x
797. A.A. Bearn [J.A. Burin—30]
798. P. Burgys x
799. J. Ray x
800. H. Ray x
801. G. Pritchard x
802. J. Riley x
803. J.B. Riley x
804. A. Shelton x
805. P. Paine [Press Payne—34]
806. M. Majors x
807. J. Washborn [James Washburn—49]
808. W. Scaggs [William Skaggs—20]
809. W. Parker [William H. Parker—18]
810. H. Cresson [L.K. Creason—39]
811. J. McElraith [J.F. McElrath—35]
812. J. Jones x
813. M. Chester x
814. C.D. Jones
815. W.J. Denison x
816. W. West x
817. B. Jones x
818. Wm. Chester x
819. D. Mathews x
820. F.B. McElrath x
821. D. Crouch x
822. H. Woods [Hiram Woods—20]
823. J. Boyd—john ~ [54]
824. J. Fleming [John Fleming—31]
825. T. Freeman [Thomas Freeman—19]
826. Wm. Pryor [20]
827. L. Burgess x
828. J. Foster [J.W. Foster—27]
829. J. Carney [Josiah Carney—54]
830. A.W. Brown [Alexander Brown—19]
831. D. Griffith x
832. J.M. Coleman x
833. J. Nicholson [James Nicholson—29]
834. D. Perkins [34]
835. J. Alcock [J.O. Allcock—49]
836. D. Alcock [D.O. Allcock—46]
837. A. Carney [47]
838. T. Faulkner x
839. W.T. Hackney [40]
840. A. Goins [Alfred Goins—36]
841. W. Wilkinson [William M. Wilkinson—47]
842. M. Stoddard x
843. J.H. House x
844. H. Shrode x
845. A. Gorde x
846. J. Payne x
847. T. Griffith x
848. N. Gill x
849. J. Hamilton [J.A. Hambleton—39]
850. Bob (colored)
851. P. Maxbery x
852. T. Pease x
853. B. Pease x
854. L. Fuller x
855. J. Low [J.R. Lowe—27]
856. J. Michael x
857. D. Freeman x
858. D. Ward [Dempsey Ward—20]
859. J.B. Ragsdale x
860. R.E. Pruit [Rew Pruitt—37]
861. J. Tarroin [J.H. Tarone—31]
862. E. Desmond x
863. W. Page [Wesley Page—49]
864. B. Peacock x
865. D.L. Robertson x
866. D.R. Robertson x
867. W.T. Tarroine x
868. C. Sullivan [G.W. Sullivan—39]
869. R. Dixon x
870. R. Pryor [Richard Pryor—41]
871. T. Gow x
872. J. Thomas [James Thomas—24]
873. J. Jackson x
874. W. Tucker [Warren Tucker—42]
875. W. Jackson [W.H. Jackson—35]
876. J. Jackson x
877. W. Watson [32]
878. F. Tucker [F.M. Tucker—29]
879. R. Prayer x
880. E. Jackson [Elias Jackson—39]
881. A. Gibson [A.C. Gibson—33]
882. J. Coleman x
883. J.P. McNeal [J.B. McNeil—38]
884. T. McNeal [Thomas A. McNeil—21]
885. H. Drew [Hosea Drew—24]
886. J.M. Farmer [James M. Farmer—31]
887. J. Cooley [J. Colly—34]
888. W.E. Hester [William Hester—23]
889. D. Smith
890. J. Lowe [John Lowe—47]
891. Jas. Sims x
892. W. Linn x
893. J. Hook x
894. R. Parrott [Rodean Parrott—54]
895. R. Mahan [W.R. Mahan—27]
896. M. Lowe [Mourning Lowe—53]
897. J. Hind x
898. T. Goins [Thomas Goins—28]
899. W. Morgan [William Morgain—39]
900. B. Ransom [Barrett Ramsom—20]
901. Jno. Prickett x
902. R. Nance [R.T. Nance—54]

903. J. Carey [J.T. Carey—31]
904. J. Alcock [J.N. Allcock—38]
905. T. Otery [Ottey]
906. F. Dunn [F.M. Dunn—29]
907. B. Dunn [David Done—28]
908. W.W. Ross x
909. C. Kessee [Charles Keesee—54]
910. A. Gore [31]
911. M. Mitcham [W.M. Mitchum—30]
912. T. Martin x
913. W. Hall [Willis Hall—49]
914. W. Oliphant [W.H. Oufill—38]
915. H. Wilds ×
916. T. Hall [Thomas Hall—34]
917. J. Peck [J.M. Peck—55]
918. F. Blain [Ephraim Blain—57]
919. J.T. Prickie x
920. M. Austin x
921. C. Akerson x
922. B. Bennett x
923. W. Mayers [W.J. Muyer—23]
924. T. Atherson x
925. B. Atherson x
926. M. Wright ×
927. W. Prest x
928. M. Samples x
929. J. Storels x
930. W. Byassee x
931. A. Stratton x
932. W. Morgan [William Morgain—39]
933. J. Hobbs [J.W. Hobbs—47]
934. J.J. Yasser x
935. J. Belcher x
936. J.S. Belcher x
937. C. Hatherton x
938. J. Henry x
939. W. Morgan [William Morgain—39]
940. J. Morgan [J. Morgain—27]]
941. B. Belcher x
942. Wm. McNabb x
943. Z. Willington x
944. J. Beers x
945. B. Burrah x
946. A. Pascall [A.R. Paschal—40]
947. J. Pascall x
948. H. Shrode x
949. C. Grant [C.W. Grant—45]
950. P. Grant x
951. W. Troutman x
952. P. Snider [Peter Snider—45]
953. J. Houser x
954. J. Snyder [Joseph Snider—16]
955. N. Miller [Nicholas Miller—36]
956. S. Wallis [S.C. Wallis—31]
957. S. Roser [Stephen Roser—18]
958. Geo. Kisling [George Kesling—42]
959. J. Yates [J.W. Yates—32]
960. J. Frost x
961. J. Seismer [John Seymore—32]
962. G. Strop x
963. W. Stawl x
964. A. Stawl x
965. A. Stensement?
966. W. Gow x
967. F. Allen [Frances Allen—39]
968. J. Jones x
969. H. Jones
970. R. Wilkinson [Robert A. Wilkerson—22]
971. J.E. Jones
972. Z. Taylor (colored—Wilkinson)
973. W. Carson [W.W. Carson—54]
974. W. Hall [Willis Hall—49]
975. T. Bradshaw [W.T. Bradshaw—33]
976. H.D. Magee [Henry D. McGee—20]
977. J. Wilkinson [J.M. Wilkinson—31]
978. R. Humphrey x
979. P. Curd [P.A. Curd—44]
980. G. Ford x
981. W. Prince [W.B. Prince—35]
982. W. Wilkinson Jr. [William M. Wilkinson—47]
983. W. Wilkinson Sr. [William Wilkinson—16]
984. Wm. Enoch [William Enoch—22]
985. R. Colton x
986. Sam Mason x
987. Jno. Mason [27]
988. Sam'l Mason [67]
989. J. Mack x
990. W. Shelton [William Shelton—57]

[count reverts back to 981]

981. J. Shelton [J.J. Shelton—54]
982. H. Shelton [Hartwell Shelton—39]
983. F. Martin x
984. J. Martin x
985. R. Crooks [R.F. Crooks—47]
986. W. Carter [Welk Carter—30]
987. A. Homes x
988. J. Paydon [John Patton—44]
989. Jno. Page [24]
990. Jas. Davis x
991. R. Linn [Reubin Lynn—36]
992. A.A. Flint [37]
993. N.L. Robertson x
994. T. Burough x
995. A. Crow x
996. H. Black x

Chapter Notes

Chapter One

1. Eleazer A. Paine to Lorenzo Thomas, 22 September 1861, Microfilm Publication M1064, *Letters Received by the Commission Branch of the Adjutants General's Office, 1863–1879*, CB File #P-40-CB-1864, National Archives Record Administration, Washington, DC. Paine formally notifies Thomas that he has accepted President Lincoln's appointment as Brigadier General dated 3 September 1861 and received by Paine on 5 September 1861; U.S. War Department. *The War of the Rebellion: A Compilation of the Official Records of the Union and Confederate Armies* (Washington, D.C.: Government Printing Office, 1880–1901), ser. I, vol. 4, 197 (hereafter cited as *OR*); John Y. Simon, ed., *The Papers of Ulysses S. Grant*, 31 vols. (Carbondale: Southern Illinois University Press, 1967), vol. 2, 196–197 (hereafter cited as *Grant Papers*); *Weekly Patriot and Union* (Harrisburg, PA), September 26, 1861. The article cited from a correspondent at Cairo names the gunboats as the USS *Tyler* and USS *Conestoga* and the steamships *G. W. Graham* and the *W. H. B.* The third vessel was not named.

2. Harriet Taylor Upton, *History of the Western Reserve*, 3 vols. (Chicago: Lewis Publishing Co., 1910), 925–926; "Person Sheet: Gen. Eleazer Arthur Paine," last modified May 28, 2001, http://stevepayne.home.mindspring.com/ps03/ps03_407.htm; "Person Sheet: Hendrick Ellsworth Paine," last modified June 6, 1999, http://stevepayne.home.mindspring.com/ps03/ps03_398.htm; "Person Sheet: Eleazer Paine," last modified December 14, 1999, http://stevepayne.home.mindspring.com/ps03/ps03_459.htm; United States Military Academy. *Register of the Officers and Cadets of the U.S. Military Academy* (West Point, NY: United States Military Academy Printing Office, June, 1839),[3]-24; George W. Cullum, *Biographical Register of the Officers and Graduates of the U.S. Military Academy at West Point, N.Y. from Its Establishment in 1802 to 1890* (Boston: Houghton, Mifflin and Co., 1891), 15–16; James Grant Wilson, *Biographical Sketches of Illinois Officers Engaged in the War Against the Rebellion of 1861* (Chicago: James Barnet, 1862), 17–18; Ezra J. Warner, *Generals in Blue: Lives of the Union Commanders* (Baton Rouge: Louisiana State University Press, 1964), 355–356; Jonathon A. Noyas, *"My Will is Absolute Law": A Biography of Union General Robert H. Milroy* (Jefferson, NC: McFarland, 2006), 144.

3. United States Military Academy. *14th Annual Reunion of the Association of the Graduates of the United States Military Academy at West Point, New York, June 12, 1883* (East Saginaw, MI: Courier Printing Co., 1883),73–75; Oliver Seymour Phelps, *The Phelps Family of America* (Pittsfield, MA: Eagle Publishing Co., 1899), vol. 1, 532, vol. 2, 892; *Chicago Tribune*, September 12, 1861; E.A. Paine, *Military Instructions: Designed for the Militia and Volunteers with Particular Directions to Commissioned Officers, Respecting their Duties at the Officer Musters* (Painesville, OH: Office of the *Northern Ohio Freeman*, 1843); William Urban, "The Temperance Movement in Monmouth, 1857–1859," *Western Illinois Regional Studies* 13, no. 2 (1990): 32–45. The Monmouth Atlas, the local newspaper, lists numerous marriages he performed from December of 1853 to August of 1857.

4. Eleazer A. Paine to Abraham Lincoln, 9 December 1854. Abraham Lincoln Papers, Manuscripts Division, Library of Congress; Edwin Erle Sparks, ed. *Collections of the Illinois State Historical Library: Lincoln Series* (Springfield, IL: Illinois State Historical Library, 1908), vol. 1, 531.

5. Monmouth College during the War of the Rebellion (Monmouth, IL: Monmouth College Oracle, 1911), 11; E.A. Paine to Sanford Bell, 15 April 1861, Yates Family Papers, Abraham Lincoln Presidential Library; Wilson, *Biographical Sketches of Illinois Officers*; Marion Morris, *A History of the Ninth Regiment Illinois Volunteer Infantry* (Monmouth, IL: John S. Clark, 1864), 7–14; Thomas J. McCormick, ed. *Memoirs of Gustave Koerner, 1809–1896* (Cedar Rapids, IA: Torch Press, 1909), 122–123; Eleazer A. Paine to Abraham Lincoln, 24 May 1861, Lincoln Papers.

6. *Daily Illinois State Journal* (Springfield, IL), June 18, 1861; *Daily Illinois State Journal* (Springfield, IL), June 5, 1861; Morris, *A History of the Ninth Regiment Illinois*, 7–14.

7. J.H. Battle, W.H. Perrin and G.C. Kniffen, *Kentucky: A History of the State*, 1st ed. (Louisville: F.A. Battey Publishing Co., 1885), pt. II, 81; *Miscellaneous Documents of the House of Representatives for the Second Session of the Fortieth Congress, 1867–1868* (Washington, D.C.: Government Printing Office, 1868), vol. 1, doc. no. 14, *Symes vs. Trimble*; J.E. Woodward Testimony, *Records of the Judge Advocate General's Office (Army)*, Entry 15, Court-Martial Case Files, 1809–1894, RG153, file no. MM1609, boxes 1032–1033, National Archives and Records Administration, Washington, DC. (hereafter cited as *Records*). J.E. Woodward testified before Paine's Court-Martial declaring that "very few did not illuminate" their houses.

8. *OR*, ser. I, vol. 4, 197; *Weekly Patriot and Union* (Harrisburg, PA), September 26, 1861. En route one of the troop transports suffered mechanical problems and was led to shore, where it was emptied of soldiers and supplies and transferred to the other ships. The break down caused a postponement of Grant's plans for a pre-dawn landing.

9. *Weekly Patriot and Union* (Harrisburg, PA), September 26, 1861; *The Crisis* (Columbus, OH), September 19, 1861.

10. Berry Craig, *Kentucky Confed-*

erates: Secession, Civil War, and the Jackson Purchase (Lexington: University Press of Kentucky, 2014), 136–138.
  11. *OR*, ser. I, vol. 4, 198.
  12. *OR*, ser. I, vol. 4, 198; *Daily Louisville Democrat*, January 8, 1862; *Reports of Committees of the Senate of the United States for the First Session of the Forty-fourth Congress, 1875–1876*, 3 vols. (Washington, D.C.: Government Printing Office, 1876), vol. 2, report No. 397; *Evansville Daily Journal*, September 18, 1861. Following the war, Thomas M. Redd sought compensation for a frame residence that was destroyed after General Nathan Bedford Forrest attacked Fort Anderson on March 25, 1864. Paine testified on behalf of Redd and described the events that led to the construction of the fort.
  13. *OR*, ser. I, vol. 3, 475; *Grant Papers*, vol. 2, 203–204; William R. Plum, *The Military Telegraph during the Civil War in the United States* (Chicago: Jansen, McClurg & Co., 1882), vol. 1, 331.
  14. *Morning Louisville Democrat*, September 13, 1861; United States Military Academy. *Register of the Officers and Cadets* [3]; *Grant Papers*, vol. 2, 205–206. See research note; *Reports of the Committees of the Senate of the United States for the Second Session of the Forty-first Congress, 1869–1870* (Washington, D.C.: Government Printing Office, 1870), vol. 2, report No. 69; *Reports of Committees of the Senate of the United States for the First Session of the Forty-fourth Congress, 1875–1876* (Washington, D.C.: Government Printing Office, 1876), vol. 2, report No. 397.
  15. Cullum, *Biographical Register of the Officers and Graduates of the U.S. Military Academy at West Point*, 15–16; Morris, *History of the Ninth Regiment Illinois*, 15–16; *OR*, ser. I, vol. 3, 301–303; Janet B. Hewitt, ed. *Supplement to the Official Records of the Union and Confederate Armies*, 100 vols. (Wilmington, NC: Broadfoot Publishing Co., 1994–2001), pt. II, vol. 8, 568.
  16. *OR*, ser. I, vol. 3, 303–304; Morris, *History of the Ninth Regiment*, 16; C.F. Smith to E.A. Paine, 16 November 1861, *Records*; Allen H. Mesch, *Teacher of Civil War Generals: Major General Charles Ferguson Smith, Soldier and West Point Commandant* (Jefferson, NC: McFarland, 2015), 179–185. The court transcripts from Paine's court-martial on February 28, 1865 include a copy of the order issued by Smith to Paine to close down a grist mill operated by John Bracken of Lovelaceville; *Grant papers*, vol. 4, 189–190. A research note reports that Smith's appointment confirmation was stalled in the United States Congress after political pressure was brought upon by supporters of Paine and General Lew Wallace. The Chicago press accused Smith of being a Southern sympathizer after he refused to allow the removal of a Confederate flag from the home of Robert Owen Woolfolk. Smith wrote to Lorenzo Thomas that he had "long known that a base conspiracy was on foot in this place" and that Paine was one of the "chief conspirators to oust me from the command"; *Grant papers*, Vol. 3, 331–332. See research note; *Reports of the Committees of the House of Representatives made during the Second Session Thirty-eighth Congress, 1864–1865* (Washington, D.C.: Government Printing Office, 1865), report no. 29, 1. Paine testified on behalf of Congressman Lucien Anderson before a Select Committee on charges of corruption, bribery and malfeasance in office. Paine claims he left Paducah on December 25, 1861; *Grant Papers*, vol. 4, 190; *Daily Louisville Democrat*, January 8, 1862.
  17. Kurt H. Hackemer, ed. *To Rescue My Native Land: The Civil War Letters of William T. Shepherd, First Illinois Light Artillery* (Knoxville: University Press of Tennessee, 2005), 123–124. William Shepherd wrote to his father on January 2, 1862 that the general orders read before his regiment on New Year's Day; *OR*, ser. I, vol. 8, 47–48; *Grant Papers*, vol. 4, 459; *OR*, ser. II, vol. 1, 255; *Grant Papers*, vol. 4, 40. See research note; *OR*, ser. I, vol. 8, 495.
  18. *OR*, ser. II, vol. 1, 803; *OR*, ser. II, vol. 3, 211.
  19. *OR*, ser. I, vol. 7, 577–578; *OR*, Ser. II, vol. 3, 241; *OR*, ser. I, vol. 7, 604; *OR*, ser. II, vol. 3, 278.
  20. *OR*, ser. I, vol. 8, 569–569; *OR*, ser. II, vol. 1, 267–268; *Weekly Wisconsin Patriot* (Madison, WI), March 1, 1862. The quote was from the correspondent of the *Cleveland Paine Dealer* writing from Cairo.
  21. *OR*, ser. I, vol. 7, 944; *Grant Papers*, vol. 4, 450. See research note.
  22. Stewart Sifakis, *Who Was Who in the Civil War* (New York: Facts on File Pub., 1988), 485; John H. Eicher and David J. Eicher, *Civil War High Commands* (Stanford, CA: Stanford University Press, 2001), 413; *Wisconsin Daily Patriot* (Madison, WI), March 14, 1862 [Report was sent from a correspondent at Cairo]; Peter Cozzens, "Roadblock on the Mississippi," *Civil War Times Illustrated* 41, no. 1 (March 2002): 429–59; *Weekly Wisconsin Patriot* (Madison, WI), March 22, 1862 [Dispatch was sent from New Madrid by a correspondent of the *Chicago Times* a day after the siege ended]; Larry J. Daniel and Lynn N. Bock, *Island No. 10: Struggle for the Mississippi Valley* (Tuscaloosa: University of Alabama Press, 1996), 44, 61–62.
  23. *OR*, ser. I, vol. 8, 109–110; *Public Ledger* (Philadelphia, PA), April 15, 1862; John Quincy Adams Campbell, *The Union Must Stand: The Civil War Diary of John Quincy Adams Campbell, Fifth Iowa Volunteer Infantry* (Knoxville: University Press of Tennessee, 2000), 35–36.
  24. *Ottawa Free Trader* (Ottawa, IL), May 3, 1862.
  25. Daniel and Bock, *Island No. 10*, 139; *Daily Missouri Republican* (Saint Louis, MO), April 11, 1862; *OR*, ser. I, vol. 8, 109–110; *Public Ledger* (Philadelphia, PA), April 15, 1862; Campbell, *The Union Must Stand*, 35–36; *Omaha World Herald*, March 5, 2007; *OR*, ser. I, vol. 8, 78–79; *Chicago Tribune*, April 12, 1862. The surrendered flag of the First Alabama Infantry Regiment was passed down by Paine to his son Phelps, when after his death was given to the Grand Army of the Republic in Omaha. The G.A.R. donated the flag to the Kansas Historical Society which returned the flag to Alabama in 2007.
  26. *Rebellion Record: A Diary of American Events*, 12 vols. (New York: Arno Press, 1977), vol. 5, doc. 4, 4–6.
  27. *14th Annual Reunion of the Association of the Graduates of the United States Military Academy*, 75; *Monmouth Atlas* (Monmouth, IL), June 13, 1862; E.A. Paine to William S. Rosecrans, 8 July 1862, *Letters Received by the Commission Branch of the Adjutants General's Office*. The letter included a certificate from John A. Young a surgeon from Monmouth dated the same day. A note dated April 7, 1884 stated that Paine was granted 20 day sick leave on May 23, 1862, another was granted on June 2, 1862 and was extended to July 13, 1862 and extended further by the adjutant general's office; "Irritable Bowel Syndrome," United States Department of Health and Human Resources, National Digestive Diseases Information Clearinghouse, accessed December 16, 2011, http://www.digestive.niddk.nih.gov/ddiseases/pub/ibs.
  28. *OR*, ser. I, vol. 52, pt. 1, 271; *OR*, ser. I, vol. 17, pt. 2, 193; *OR*, ser. I, vol. 52, pt. 1, 304; E.A. Paine to Richard Yates, 6 October 1862, Yates Family Papers; *Macon Daily Telegraph* (Macon, GA), October 14, 1862.
  29. *OR*, ser. I, vol. 52, pt. 1, 305–306; *Southern Bivouac*, 6 vols. (Wilmington, NC: Broadfoot Publishing Co., 1992), vol. 4, 665; *OR*, ser. I, vol. 23, pt. 1, 262–263; Walter D. Durham, *Rebellion Revisited: A History of Sumner County, Tennessee from 1861 to 1870* (Nashville, TN: Parthenon Press, 1982), 132. Durham's chapter titled

"Bluecoats and General Paine" offers a well-researched description of Paine's twenty months at Gallatin.

30. *Ottawa Free Trader* (Ottawa, IL), January 17, 1863.

31. *OR*, ser. I, vol. 23. pt. 2, 33. Military Order of the Loyal Legion of the United States. *War Papers: Being Papers Read Before the Commandery of the District of Columbia, Military Order of the Loyal Legion of the United States*, 4 vols. (Wilmington, NC: Broadfoot Publishing Co., 1993), vol. 3, 241–62. The author, Henry Romeyn, was a recipient of the Congressional Medal of Honor for his service during the Indian Wars.

32. William H. Pierce to Richard Yates, 5 March 1863, Yates Family Papers.

33. *War Papers: Being Papers Read Before the Commandery of the District of Columbia*, vol. 3, 241–62; *OR*, ser. I, vol. 52, pt. 1, 355; S.F. Fleharty, *Our Regiment: A History of the 102d Illinois Infantry Volunteers* (Chicago: Brewster & Hanscom, 1865), 32.

34. Fleharty, *Our Regiment*, 33–42; *War Papers: Being Papers Read Before the Commandery of the District of Columbia*, vol. 3, 241–62; Arthur H. DeRosier, Jr., ed., *Through the South with a Union Soldier* (Johnson City, TN: East Tennessee State University Research Advisory Council, 1969), 70–71; Durham, *Rebellion Revisited*, 164.

35. Durham, *Rebellion Revisited*, 166.

36. *War Papers: Being Papers Read Before the Commandery of the District of Columbia*, vol. 3, 244; *Southern Bivouac*, vol. 4, 665–66; *Milwaukee Daily Sentinel*, September 11, 1863. The story was authored by a soldier in the Seventy-Ninth Ohio Infantry Regiment and originally reported in the *Dayton Journal*. After the war, some veterans of the unit declared they were turkeys rather than chickens.

37. *War Papers: Being Papers Read Before the Commandery of the District of Columbia*, vol. 3, 245; Leroy P. Graf and Ralph W. Haskins, ed., *The Papers of Andrew Johnson*, 16 vols. (Knoxville: University Press of Tennessee, 1983), vol. 6, 234–37; *Chattanooga Daily Gazette*, June 24, 1864.

38. Ira Berlin, ed., *Wartime Genesis of Free Labor: The Upper South* (New York: Cambridge University Press, 1993), 426–35; *OR*, ser. I, vol. 32, pt. 2, 103; *Daily Illinois State Journal* (Springfield, IL), June 5, 1863; *Milwaukee Daily Sentinel*, June 10, 1863. The article includes an extract of a letter from Paine to General Rosecrans dated June 1, 1863.

39. *OR*, ser. I, vol. 30, pt. 4, 255–56; Military Order of the Loyal Legion of the United States, *Personal Narratives of Events in the War of the Rebellion, Being Papers Read Before the Rhode Island Soldiers and Sailors Historical Society*, 10 vols. (Wilmington, NC: Broadfoot Publishing Co., 1993), vol. 5, 77–78; Hewitt, ed. *Supplement to the Official Records*, pt. II, vol. 77, 497–503; Berlin, *Wartime Genesis of Free Labor*, 426–35.

40. *OR*, ser. I, vol. 32, pt. 1, 155–56; Durham, *Rebellion Revisited*, 189; Alice Williamson Diary, 19 February 1864, Manuscript Division, Perkins Library, Duke University, Durham, NC.

41. *OR*, ser. I, vol. 32, pt. 3, 532; *Southern Bivouac*, vol. 4, 668; Daniel E. Sutherland, *A Savage Conflict: The Decisive Role of Guerrillas in the American Civil War* (Chapel Hill: University of North Carolina Press, 2009), 223; *Sycamore True Republican* (Sycamore, IL), March 12, 1884; Alice Williamson Diary, 30 April 1864. The author, J.A. Trousdale, claims "a man of mature age, intelligence and professional reputation" overheard Paine say that he had killed his "one hundred and sixth man" just prior to his departure from Gallatin. Trousdale wrote that he personally had the names, dates and places of ten of the executed.

42. *OR*, ser. I, vol. 38, pt. 4, 167–168; *OR*, ser. I, vol. 39, pt. 1, 18–19; *Milwaukee Daily Sentinel*, June 30, 1864; *Memphis Daily Appeal*, July 1, 1864; *Macon Daily Telegraph* (Macon, GA), July 18, 1864; Robert H. Milroy to Mary Milroy, 19 June 1864, General Robert H. Milroy Papers, Jasper County Public Library, Rensselaer, IN; Noyas, "My Will is Absolute Law," 143–144; Henry Newton Comey, *A Lagacy of Honor: The Memoirs and Letters of Captain Henry Newton Comey, 2nd Massachusetts Infantry* (Knoxville: University Press of Tennessee, 2004), 173–174; Explanations of E.A. Paine, *Records*. Paine received Special Field Orders no. 177, Department of the Cumberland, Major General George H. Thomas, to report to Major General Cadwallader C. Washburn, District of West Tennessee, at Memphis, Tennessee. A copy of the order was attached to Paine's explanation submitted prior to his court-martial.

43. Abraham Lincoln to Edwin M. Stanton, 18 June 1864, Lincoln Papers; *OR*, ser. I, vol. 39, pt. 2, 144; Explanations of E.A. Paine, *Records*. The adjutant general's office issued the order to Major General William T. Sherman on June 24, 1864 and later the same day Sherman issued Special Orders No. 90 removing Paine from the Department of the Cumberland and reassigning him to the Department of the Tennessee; Explanations of E.A. Paine, *Records*. Paine wrote of his conversation with Washburn in his explanation.

Chapter Two

1. Andrew Lucas Hunt to Edwin Hunt, 12 and 14 August 1864, Andrew Lucas Hunt Papers, University of North Carolina at Chapel Hill; Jennie Fyfe to Nell, 31 March 1864, Fyfe Family Papers, University of Michigan, Bentley Historical Library; Steven L. Wright, *Kentucky Soldiers and their Regiments in the Civil War: Abstracts from the Pages of Contemporary Kentucky Newspapers* (Utica, KY: McDowell Publications, 2009), vol. 2 (1862), 203; *OR*, Ser. I, vol. 39, pt. 2, 171.

2. Testimony of John T. Bolinger, *Letters Received by the Office of the Adjutant General (Main Series), 1861–1870*, RG94, M619, roll 242, file 1394 B 1864, National Archives and Records Administration, Washington, DC. Hereafter cited as *Letters*; Battle, Perrin and Kniffen, *Kentucky*, pt. II, 53, 76–77. Bolinger is sometimes cited as John F. or John J. Bolinger in the census records and court-martial records; *Miscellaneous Documents*, vol. 1, doc. no. 14, *Symes vs. Trimble*.

3. *Grant Papers*, vol. 8, 66–77. Colonel Dougherty's name is misspelled as Daugherty; *OR*, Ser. I, vol. 17, pt. 2, 249; *OR*, Ser. I, vol. 24, pt. 3, 255; *OR*, Ser. I, vol. 30, pt. 1, 732; *OR*, Ser. I, vol. 30, pt. 3, 844; *OR*, Ser. I, vol. 30, pt. 4, 471; *Returns from U.S. Military Posts, 1806–1916*, RG94, M617, roll 895, National Archives and Records Administration, Washington, DC; Newton Bateman and Paul Selby, *Historical Encyclopedia of Illinois* (Chicago: Munsell Publishing Company, 1916), Vol. I, 232; Thomas Mears Eddy, *The Patriotism of Illinois* (Chicago: Clark & Company, 1865), Vol. I, 325; George Washington Smith, *A History of Southern Illinois: A Narrative Account of Its Historical Progress, Its People, and Its Principle Interests* (Chicago: Lewis Publishing Company, 1912), 231. The list of post commanders include: General Ulysses S. Grant (September 6, 1861), General Eleazer A. Paine (September 6, 1861–September 8, 1861), General Charles F. Smith (September 8, 1861–February 5, 1862), General Eleazer A. Paine (February 11, 1862–February 13, 1862), General William T. Sherman (February 13, 1862–March 8, 1862), Colonel Silas Noble (March 8, 1862–May, 1862), Lieutenant Colonel John Olney (June–August, 1862), Colonel Thomas E.G. Ransom (September–December 31, 1862), Colonel Henry Dougherty (January 1, 1863–April 14, 1863), Col-

onel James S. Martin (Late April, 1863–October 25, 1864), and Colonel Stephen G. Hicks (October 25, 1864–July 19, 1864).

4. *Grant Papers*, vol. 8, 297; Thomas A. Duke to Abraham Lincoln, 6 July 1863, Lincoln Papers; Unknown, Note [Thomas Redd and others to Thomas E. Bramlette], 28 April 1864 and 10 May 1864, Adjutant General Letter Book—No. 3 ; 9 April–25 May 1864, Kentucky Department of Military Affairs. *Miscellaneous Documents*, vol. 1, doc. no. 14, *Symes vs. Trimble*, 27–28; *Louisville Weekly Journal*, June 21, 1864; M.A. Payne to Thomas E. Bramlette, 30 July 1864, Active Militia Records—Capital Guards, North Cumberland Btn., and Three Forks Btn., Box 76, Folder 864 1st Regt. Capital Guards Paducah Bn. Logistics, Kentucky Department of Military Affairs. Colonel Tice reported to the Inspector of the state that he had printed and plastered posters about Mayfield only a few days before General Nathan Bedford Forrest's raid into the Jackson Purchase in late March.

5. *Evansville Daily Journal*, August 12, 1864; *Frankfort Commonwealth*, April 4, 1865; George W. Reardon to [Judge A.R. Boone], 21 August 1861, Office of the Governor, Beriah Magoffin: Governor's Official Correspondence File, Requisitions for the Return of Fugitives from Justice, 1859–1861, Kentucky Department for Libraries and Archives; Pat Record, *Graves County, Ky. Census of 1860* (Melber, KY: Simons Historical Publications, 1979), 167; *Report of the Adjutant General of the State of Kentucky* (Frankfort, KY: John H. Harney, Public Printer, 1867), vol. 2, 54, 765; Wright, *Kentucky Soldiers*, vol. 4 (1864), 188; Scrapbook, United Daughters of the Confederacy, Graves County Chapter Records, MS03–01, Murray State University, Pogue Library, Historians Book, 1917–1919; Berry Craig and Dieter C. Ullrich, *Unconditional Unionist: The Hazardous Life of Lucian Anderson, Kentucky Congressman* (Jefferson, NC: MacFarland & Co., 2016), 122–123. Mayfield's Home Guard became Company A, 1st Regiment Capital Guards, Paducah Battalion on June 24, 1864.

6. *Grant Papers*, vol. 9, 380; *OR*, Ser. I, vol. 31, pt. 3, 263; *Grant Papers*, Vol. 9, 462–64.

7. *American Annual Cyclopaedia and Register of Important Events of the Year* (New York: D. Appleton & Co., 1864), vol. 4 (1864), 447–48; Albert Bradshaw to Thomas E. Bramlette, 9 February 1864, Governor Thomas E. Bramlette Papers, Kentucky Department of Library and Archives, State Archives Collection. Bradshaw wrote "not infrequently a squad of these semi-baboons driving a gov[ernment] wagon up to some house either in the city or county and in the most insolent manner proceed to pack up whatever they may choose to claim as theirs and return in triumph to the rendezvous of the nation's defenders"; S.P. Cope to Thomas E. Bramlette, 8 July 1864, Governor Thomas E. Bramlette Papers, Kentucky Department of Library and Archives, State Archives Collection.

8. Explanations of E.A. Paine, *Records*; Final Report of the Judge Advocate General Joseph Holt, *Records*: Craig, *Kentucky Confederates*, 231–245.

9. *OR*, Ser. I, vol. 39, pt. 2, 171. The organizations title, as noted by the author, was the Paducah Council, No. 3, Union League of America.

10. Ira Berlin, ed., *The Black Military* Experience (New York: Cambridge University Press, 1982), 262. *Chicago Tribune*, July 20, 1864; *Daily Missouri Democrat* (St. Louis, MO), July 20, 1864; Explanations of E.A. Paine, *Records*. Paine described his first day in command in his written explanation to the court.

11. *The Reports of the Committees of the House of Representatives made during the Second Session Thirty-eighth Congress, 1864–1865* (Washington, D.C.: Government Printing Office, 1865), Report No. 29; Explanations of E.A. Paine, *Records*; Affidavit of Warren Thornberry, September 19, 1864, *Letters*. Thornberry refused to pay the port fees for several weeks and when he did pay it was with a bad check. Colonel Outlaw was most likely Lieutenant Colonel Drew A. Outlaw of Moscow, Hickman County, Kentucky who served as an officer with the 12th Tennessee Infantry Regiment and the Third Kentucky Mounted Infantry Regiment earlier in the war (see Berry Craig, "Jackson Purchase Confederate Troops in the Civil War," *Journal of the Jackson Purchase Historical Society*, Vol. 2, 5).

12. General Order No. 3, July 20, 1864, *Letters*; *Chicago Tribune*, September 4, 1864; Military Order of the Loyal Legion of the United States. *War Papers: Being Papers Read Before the Commandery of the State of Wisconsin, Military Order of the Loyal Legion of the United States*, 4 vols. (Wilmington, NC: Broadfoot Publishing Co., 1993), vol. 1, 333. The author, Willis Danforth, was a surgeon with the 134th Illinois Infantry and served as his personal doctor during Paine's command. He first wrote of Paine's early days at Paducah as a correspondent for the *Chicago Tribune*. Years later, in 1886, he retold the story to Wisconsin veterans.

13. Testimony of John T. Bolinger and Special Orders, *Letters*.

14. Berlin, *The Black Military Experience*, 262; *The Reports of the Committees of the House of Representatives made during the Second Session Thirty-eighth Congress, 1864–1865* (Washington: Government Printing Office, 1865), Report No. 29; Explanations of E.A. Paine, *Records*.

15. Testimony of Henry Bartling, *Letters*; Robert H. Behrens, *From Salt Fork to Chickamauga: Champaign County Soldiers in the Civil War* (Urbana, IL: Urbana Free Library, 1988), 245–246; Testimony of William Bell, *Records*.

16. *Reports of Committees of the Senate of the United States for the Second Session of the Forty-second Congress, 1871–1872*, 4 vols. (Washington, D.C.: Government Printing Office, 1876), vol. 1, report No. 51; Affidavits of Lyman D. Olin and Edward B. Jones, *Letters*. Jones later claimed that $25,000 of inventory was taken from his store.

17. General and Special Orders and Testimony of Henry Bartling, 14 September 1864, *Letters*; *Missouri Democrat* (St. Louis, MO), July 27, 1864. Bartling testified that the following stores were taken in possession and assessed by Paine: Jones & Co., Davy, Lauchan, Endres & Co., Soule's Drug Store, Kinkaid & Sweatman's Drug Store, J.W. Shearer & Co., Cope's Drug Store, Ashbrook, Ryan & Co. and Prince & Dodd's Grocery Store. The last two were returned to owners and reopened.

18. Testimonies of V.S. Gillespie and W.P. Caldwell, *Records*. Several other witnesses testified at Paine's Court-Martial to have heard him call Halleck a "damned coward." Paine declared he may have "used the words hastily" in his concluding statement.

19. Berlin, *The Black Military Experience*, 262; *Missouri Democrat* (St. Louis, MO), July 27, 1864; *Chicago Tribune*, July 27, 1864.

20. Affidavit of W.A. Bell, *Letters*; Testimonies of William Bell, J.E. Woodward, Henry Bartling, Thomas M. Redd and R.M. Humble, *Records*.

21. "Civil War Soldiers & Sailors Database," National Park Service, accessed February 3, 2012, http://www.nps.gov/civilwar/soldiers-and-sailors-database.htm; Testimonies of M.G. Milan, Henry Bartling, W.P. Cummingham and Charles M. Kilgore, *Records*; Testimonies of Marian G. Milan and William Burgess affidavits of John F. Davis, *Letters*.

22. Affidavit of I.B. Overall, *Letters*; Final Report of Judge Advocate General Joseph Holt, *Records*; *Louisville Daily Journal*, March 31, 1864; Andrew Lucas Hunt to his mother, 12 August 1864, Andrew Lucas Hunt Papers; Testimony of James Johnson,

Letters; Fred G. Neuman, *The Story of Paducah* (Paducah, KY: Young Printing Company, 1927), 90; *Missouri Democrat* (St. Louis, MO), July 27, 1864; Berry F. Craig, "The Jackson Purchase Considers Secession: The Mayfield Convention," *Register of the Kentucky Historical Society* 99, no. 4 (2001): 339-61; *OR*, Ser. I, vol. 7, 897-98; Craig, *Kentucky Confederates*, 83-87, 91.

23. Statement of Bank Officers at Paducah to General Solomon Meredith and the testimony of Thomas M. Redd, *Letters*; Cashiers of Paducah Banks to Solomon Meredith, 19 September 1864, *Records*. On August 5, 1864, the cashiers of the three banks at Paducah sent a list of requests to Paine regarding transfers and packages from outside the district. All requests were denied.

24. *OR*, Ser. I, vol. 39, pt. 1, 365-66.

25. Testimony of T.L. Jacobs, *Letters*; *War Papers: Being Papers Read Before the Commandery of the State of Wisconsin*, vol. 1, 331.

26. *OR*, Ser. I, vol. 39, pt. 1, 355; Explanations of E.A. Paine, *Records*; *Evansville Daily Journal*, February 29, 1864; *Louisville Weekly Journal*, March 1, 1864; Affidavits of Donnell Higgins, Edgar H. Andress, Henry B. Aldrich, Harry Post and Samuel Beers, *Letters*; Patricia Ann Hoskins, "The Old First is with the South: The Civil War, Reconstruction, and Memory in the Jackson Purchase Region of Kentucky," (Ph.D. diss., Auburn University, 2008), 208; Craig, *Kentucky Confederates*, 226.

27. Final Report of Judge Advocate General Joseph Holt, *Records*; Affidavits of A.B. Kinkead and A.S. Jones and the testimonies of Gustavus A. Flournoy and Braxton Small, *Letters*.; Paducah City Council Minutes, 4 and 11 August 1864, Records of the City Council of Paducah, 1860-1870, MF242, reel 7, McCracken County Public Library; *Paducah Sun-Democrat*, July 24, 1956; Fred G. Neuman, *Paducahans in History* (Paducah, KY: Young Printing Company, 1922), 102-04. Jones later sought reimbursement for $300 that he paid on May 30, 1864 for a substitute who was found to have committed a felony. Paine's attempt to remove the mayor may have stemmed from Fisher being a prominent brewer in the city.

28. *Daily True Delta* (New Orleans, LA), August 9 and 16, 1864; Andrew Lucas Hunt to his mother, 2 August 1864, Andrew Lucus Hunt Papers, University of North Carolina at Chapel Hill; Dieter C. Ullrich, "Civil War Diary of Private Hawley V. Needham, 134th Illinois Volunteer Infantry Regiment, June 10 to October 2, 1864," *Journal of the Jackson Purchase Historical Society*, Vol. 43, 147-195; "Excerpts Journal of Sergeant Eugene B. Read," Jackson Purchase Historical Society, accessed December 31, 2012, http://www.jacksonpurchasehistory.org/jackson-purchase-during-the-civil-war/. Needham wrote in his diary that he arrived at Paducah on the morning of August 2, but the timeline seems to indicate that the 134th Illinois arrived at about 8:00 a.m. on August 1.

29. Plum, *The Military Telegraph*, vol. 2, 205; Russell B. Griffin, "The Military Telegrapher in the Civil War," *Telegraph Age*: 26 (November 16, 1909), 787. John Price may have been John Marshall Price of Ballard County, who served with the Seventh Kentucky Infantry.

30. Testimonies of Henry Bartling, R.J. Barber, Lyman D. Olin, William Burgess, *Letters*; Final Report of Judge Advocate General Joseph Holt, *Records*.

31. Explanations of E.A. Paine, Testimonies of J.E. Woodward, G.T. Rabb and Final Summation of E.A. Paine, *Records*. Testimonies of W.F. Swift and Affidavit of G.T. Rabb, *Letters*.

32. *OR*, Ser. 1, vol. 39, pt. 2, 260-61. *Evansville Daily Journal*, August 12, 1864; *Louisville Daily Journal*, August 16, 1864; "Civil War Soldiers & Sailors Database"; "Bryan Family History," accessed February 27, 2012, http://www.rcasey.net/bryan/brysam11.htm#_VPINDEXENTRY_2301. General Prince wrote Grant from Columbus reporting that Gregory was receiving direct orders from Paine. However, no connection between Paine and Gregory appears to be evident until Paine arrived in Mayfield on August 11, 1864. The Bryan family may have likely been involved in the Gregory family home being torched earlier in the war. Private Hawley V. Needham mentions in his diary on August 12, 1864 that three bullets were deeply lodged into the walls of the courthouse and left there after "passing though the body of a noted scoundrel" two weeks earlier.

33. *Evansville Daily Journal*, August 12, 1864.

34. *OR*, Ser. III, vol. 4, 708-709; *OR*, Ser. III, vol. 4, 573; Andrew Lucas Hunt to his parents, 14 August 1864, Andrew Lucus Hunt Papers, University of North Carolina at Chapel Hill.

35. Testimony of Roland H. Hall, *Letters*; Final Report of Judge Advocate General Joseph Holt, *Records*; Battle, Perrin and Kniffen, *Kentucky*, pt. II, 285-286, 314. Letter from David G. Bainitz to T.M. Redd, 12 August 1864, *Letters*. It was noted in the commission's investigation that all but one of those on the committee had filed claims to be reimbursed for losses occurred during the Battle of Paducah.

Chapter Three

1. *American Annual Cyclopaedia and Register of Important Events of the Year* (New York: D. Appleton & Co., 1864), vol. 4 (1864), 451-52; Explanations of E.A. Paine, *Records*; Affidavits of Thomas J. Pickett, Hiram R. Enoch and J.M. Thompson, *Letters*; *National Unionist* (Lexington, KY), August 5, 1864.

2. Order of E.A. Paine to Henry Prince and Final Report of Judge Advocate General Joseph Holt, *Records*; John E.L. Robertson, *Paducah: Frontier to the Atomic Age* (Charleston, SC: Arcadia Press, 2002), 54; Don Simmons, *Hickman County, Kentucky Census of 1860* (Melber, KY: Simmons Historical Publications, 1987); *Daily Missouri Democrat* (St. Louis, MO), August 10, 1864; *Louisville Weekly Journal*, August 16, 1864; Wright, *Kentucky Soldiers*, vol. 4 (1864), 183-185; Craig, *Kentucky Confederates*, 264. The *Daily Missouri Democrat* on August 10 reported the following persons being exiled from Columbus to Canada: McKean Hubbard, T.M. Horn, James Morton, Pembroke Walker, James Walker, S.M. Moore, R.E. Cook, N. Cook, G.B. Moss, Mr. McGowan, Mrs. Carroll and Mr. Malone. Place under arrest were Thomas H. Reike, Mr. Yantis, Judge Vance, Edward Smedley, Mr. Doughty, the Cook brothers, Mr. Harriott and Mr. Jarvis.

3. James W. Raab, *Confederate General Lloyd Tilghman: A Biography* Jefferson, NC: McFarland, 2006), 22; Neuman, *The Story of Paducah*, 135; *Grant Papers*, vol. 4, 189. Testimony of R.O. Woolfolk and Thomas M. Redd, *Records*; Testimony of W.F. Swift, *Letters*; *Paducah News Democrat*, February 15, 1903; Craig, *Kentucky Confederates*, 164-165.

4. *Paducah News Democrat*, February 15, 1903; *Paducah Sun*, April 3, 1905; Don Simmons, *1850 Census of McCracken County, Kentucky* (Murray, KY: Don Simmons Press, 1974); Virginia Jewell, *Lick Skillet and Other Tales of Hickman County* (Union City, TN: Lanzer Printing Co., 1986), 45.

5. *Paducah Daily Register*, July 26, 1907; *Paducah Evening Sun*, July 27, 1907; Rebel C. Forrester, *Glory and Tears: Obion County, Tennessee, 1860-1870* (Union City, TN: H.A. Lanzer Co., 1970), 80; *Paducah News Democrat*, February 15, 1903.

6. *Evansville Daily Journal*, August 16, 1864; *Louisville Weekly Journal*, August 23, 1864.

7. Affidavit of S.P. Cope, *Letters*; Explanation of E.A. Paine, *Records*;

S.P. Cope to Thomas E. Bramlette, 8 February 1864, Office of the Governor, Thomas E. Bramlette: Governor's Official Correspondence File, Military Correspondence, 1863-1867, Kentucky Department for Libraries and Archives.

8. E.A. Paine to Richard Yates, 8 August 1864, Yates Family Papers; Arthur Charles Cole, *The Centennial History of Illinois: The Era of the Civil War, 1848-1870* (Springfield IL: Illinois Centennial Commission, 1919), 290-311; Thomas Bahde, "Our Cause Is a Common One: Home Guards, Union Leagues, and Republican Citizenship in Illinois, 1861-1863," *Civil War History*, Vol. 56 (March 2010), 66-98.

9. Explanation of E.A. Paine and Testimonies of G.F. Rabb and J.E. Woodward, *Records*. The agreement between J.L. Allard and H.F. Given was that Allard borrowed funds to purchase cheap cotton in Humbolt, Tennessee, after Union occupation. The cotton was shipped to New Orleans then to New York for a considerable profit. Given wished to pay some of the profits to Allard with Confederate currency, but Allard refused be part of laundering money and kept the profits and did not repay the loan.

10. Andrew Lucas Hunt to his mother, 12 August 1864, Andrew Lucas Hunt Papers; Ullrich, "Civil War Diary of Private Hawley V. Needham," 147-195; Affidavit of William W. Tice, *Letters*; "Journal of Sergeant Eugene B. Read."

11. *Chicago Tribune*, August 19, 1864; *Documents of the Assembly of the State of New York, Eighty Ninth Session, 1866* (Albany, NY: C. Wendell Legislative Printer, 1866), vol. 4, nos. 61-85, 101-02; *Annual Report of the Adjutant General of the State of New York for the Year 1899* (Albany, NY: James B. Lyon State Printer, 1900), vol. 2, 951; J. Seymour Currey, *Chicago: Its History and Its Builders: A Century of Marvelous Growth* (Chicago: S.J. Clark Publishing Co., 1912), vol. 2, 34; New York National Zouaves at Fort Monroe, 15 August 1861, 10th Infantry Regiment New York Civil War Newspaper Clippings, New York State Military Museum and Veterans Research Center; Charles W. Cowtan, *Services of the Tenth New York Volunteers (National Zouaves) in the War of the Rebellion* (New York: Charles H. Ludwig Publisher, 1882), 37. McChesney's name has been misspelled in numerous documents and publications as Walter W. McChesney.

12. *Chicago Tribune*, September 22, 1864; Andrew Lucas Hunt to his mother, 13 June 1864 and 14 July 1864, Andrew Lucas Hunt Papers; Ullrich, "Civil War Diary of Private Hawley V. Needham," 147-195.

13. Battle, Perrin and Kniffen, *Kentucky*, pt. II, 53; Frazar Kirkland, *The Pictorial Book of Anecdotes and Incidents of the War of the Rebellion* (Toledo, OH: W.E. Bliss & Co., 1873), 122-23; *Chicago Tribune*, August 19, 1864.

14. Kirkland, *Pictorial Book of Anecdotes*, 122-23; *Chicago Tribune*, August 19, 1864; Explanation of E.A. Paine, *Records*.

15. Affidavits of William H. Miller, D.M. Galloway, Amos Smith, William Hall, Charles McDonald, A.B. Carter and James A. McNutt, *Letters*; Ullrich, "Civil War Diary of Private Hawley V. Needham," 147-195.

16. *Chicago Tribune*, August 13, 1864; Telegraph submitted as part of E.A. Paine's defense, *Records*; Affidavits of William H. Miller, Amos Smith, William Hall, Charles McDonald, A.B. Carter and James A. McNutt, *Letters*.

17. Ullrich, "Civil War Diary of Private Hawley V. Needham," 147-195; *New York Times*, August 26, 1864; Affidavits of T.J. Ashbrook and J.P. Prince, *Letters*; Explanation of E.A. Paine, *Reports*; Berry Craig, *Hidden History of Kentucky in the Civil War* (Charleston, S.C.: The History Press, 2010), 53-58.

18. *Chicago Tribune*, August 19, 1864.

19. Jennie Fyfe to Ellen Mott (Nell), 4 August 1864, Fyfe Family Papers; Testimonies of W.H. Starks, William H. Philips, Henry W. Berry and Henry Bartling, *Reports*.

20. Testimony of Henry W. Berry, *Reports*.

21. Andrew Lucas Hunt to his mother, 6 and 14 August 1864, Andrew Lucas Hunt Papers.

22. *Philadelphia Inquirer*, August 19, 1864; *OR*, ser. I, vol. 39, pt. 2, 260-61.

23. *Philadelphia Inquirer*, August 19, 1864.

24. Peeples & Ridgeway to Richard Yates, 16 August 1864, Yates Family Papers; *Official Records of the Union and Confederate Navies in the War of the Rebellion* (Washington, D.C.: Government Printing Office, 1894-1922), Ser. I, vol. 26, 509-15; *Daily Missouri Democrat* (St. Louis, MO), August 16 and 18, 1864; *New York Times*, August 26, 1864; *OR*, Ser. I, vol. 39, pt. 2, 257-58, 286; Andrew Lucas Hunt to his mother, 15 August 1864, Andrew Lucas Hunt Papers; Ullrich, "Civil War Diary of Private Hawley V. Needham," 147-195; Petition of Samuel Fels and E.A. Lindsay, *Letters*.

25. Peeples & Ridgeway to Richard Yates, 16 August 1864, Yates Family Papers.

26. *OR*, Ser. I, vol. 39, pt. 2, 263, 286; *OR*, ser. I, vol. 39, 465-67; *Explanations* of E.A. Paine and the testimonies of Catherine Greathouse and Robert William Greathouse, *Records*; Petition of Catherine R. Greathouse, Letter of S.M. Semont to G.W. Wamack and Affidavit of William Greathouse, *Letters*; *Daily Missouri Democrat* (St. Louis, MO), August 22, 1864; *Philadelphia Inquirer* (Philadelphia, PA), August 26, 1864; *New York Times*, August 26, 1864.

27. Affidavit of D.C. James, *Letters*.

28. *Chicago Tribune*, August 26, 1864; *Daily Missouri Democrat* (St. Louis, MO), August 22, 1864; *OR*, Ser. I, vol. 39, pt. 2, 386; Testimony of Willis W. Gardner and Affidavit of John W. Hammock, *Letters*.

29. Kentucky Writers' Project, *Union County Past and Present* (Louisville: Schuhmann Printing Co., 1941), 48-50, 169; *OR*, Ser. I, vol. 39, pt. 1, 359-60; *Official Records of the Union and Confederate Navies*, Ser. I, vol. 23, 309-11, 322, 434-45, 440; Testimonies of Joseph Gerrish and Thomas L. Sturgeon, *Records*. Gerrish declared that it was a "very dark and rainy night" when Paine's troops entered the village.

30. Testimonies of Joseph Gerrish, Peter Acker and Phillip Snow, *Records*.

31. Testimonies of Peter Acker and Phillip Snow, *Records*; Affidavit of James T. Pierson, *Letters*.

32. Affidavits of Thomas L. Sturgeon and D.O. Conn, *Letters*; Testimonies of Thomas L. Sturgeon and G.L. Tombelle, *Records*. While imprisoned at Paducah Conn contracted a disease and died not long after his return to Caseyville.

33. *Chicago Tribune*, August 26, 1864.

34. *History of Union County, Kentucky* (Evansville, IN: Courier Co., 1886), 571-72, 605-07; Testimonies of L.L. Talbot, Thomas H. Welch, Peter Davidson, W.P. Tucker and William Gregg, *Records*; Affidavits of A.J.M. Thompson and Thomas L. Sturgeon, *Letters*.

35. *OR*, Ser. I, vol. 39, pt. 2, 286; *Chicago Tribune*, August 26, 1864; *Wisconsin Daily Patriot* (Madison, WI), August 22, 1864; *Daily Missouri Democrat* (St. Louis, MO), August 22 and 29, 1864; Peyton Heady, *Union County, Kentucky in the Civil War, 1861-1865* (Morganfield, KY: Peyton Heady, 1985), 93; Wright, *Kentucky Soldiers*, vol. 4 (1864), 212; "Civil War Soldiers & Sailors Database"; Testimony of J.T. Bolinger and Special Order No. 5, *Records*; Testimony of John T. Bolinger, *Letters*.

36. *OR*, Ser. I, vol. 38, pt. 5, 743-44 and Ser. I, vol. 39, pt. 2, 330; *Reports*

of the *Committees of the House of Representatives made during the Second Session Thirty-eighth Congress, 1864–1865* (Washington, D.C.: Government Printing Office, 1865), report no. 29, 1. The *Chicago Tribune* refers to those captured as "Richard W. Taylor and A.W.S. Mathene guerrillas." Abstract returns for August of 1864 have Paine serving with the District of West Tennessee and also the District of Kentucky. Paine in his explanation to the charges against him questioned Burbridge's authority over his command and was noted to have disregarded orders issued by him before the expedition to Union County. No orders appear in the *Official Records* that place Paine under Burbridge's command.

37. E.A. Paine to J. Bates Dickson, 30 August 1864 and Exhibit given by James A. Finley, 30 August 1864, *Letters*; *Chicago Tribune*, August 26, 1864.

38. *OR*, Ser. I, vol. 39, pt. 1, 463; "Journal of Sergeant Eugene B. Read."

39. Ullrich, "Civil War Diary of Private Hawley V. Needham," 147–195; "Journal of Sergeant Eugene B. Read,."

40. Statement of Samuel L. Andrews, *Letters*; Andrew Lucas Hunt to his brother Hamilton, 15 July 1864, and to his parents, 20 June 1864 and 19 August 1864, Andrew Lucas Hunt Papers.

41. Statement of Samuel L. Andrews, *Letters*; Final Report of Judge Advocate General Joseph Holt, Charges against Colonel W.W. McChesney, W.W. McChesney Special Order No. 2, Statement of W.W. Tice and List of men that worked on the fortifications at Mayfield, *Reports*.

42. Affidavits of William Enoch, James Bradshaw, E. Moore, John S. Wilkinson, Levi Wimberly, Stephen Beasley, and Mrs. Frances Morse, *Letters*; Ullrich, "Civil War Diary of Private Hawley V. Needham," 147–195; Andrew Lucas Hunt to his mother, 18 August 1864 and 19 August 1864, Andrew Lucas Hunt Papers; Statement of W.W. Tice, *Records*.

43. Statement of W.W. Tice, *Records*: Statements made by Robert Beasley and Stephen Beasley, *Letters*. Tice stated that the incident occurred on August 25 but Robert and Stephen Beasley recalled it occurring on either the August 16 or 17. The 17th seems to fit the timeline.

44. "Journal of Sergeant Eugene B. Read."; Ullrich, "Civil War Diary of Private Hawley V. Needham," 147–195; "Civil War Soldiers & Sailors Database."

45. Andrew Lucas Hunt to his mother, 23 August 1864, Andrew Lucas Hunt Papers; Ullrich, "Civil War Diary of Private Hawley V. Needham," 147–195.

46. Andrew Lucas Hunt to his brother William, 25 August 1864, Andrew Lucas Hunt Papers; *Daily Missouri Democrat* (St. Louis, MO), August 29, 1864; Edwin H. Rennolds, *A History of the Henry County Commands which served in the Confederate States Army* (Kennesaw, GA: Continental Book Co., 1961), 257–69; "20th Tennessee Cavalry, CSA: Biographical Information," accessed November 20, 2012, http://home.olemiss.edu/~cmprice/cavalry/bio_w.html. The *Daily Missouri Democrat* reported the name as "Walters." Hunt refers to him as "Waters." A Robert A. Walters of Henry County, Tennessee, is listed as having deserted from Company E of the 20th Tennessee Cavalry Regiment on May 23, 1864. The 20th Tennessee Cavalry Regiment was at Fort Pillow on April 12, 1864.

47. Andrew Lucas Hunt to his brother William, 25 August 1864, Andrew Lucas Hunt Papers; Ullrich, "Civil War Diary of Private Hawley V. Needham," 147–195.

48. Affidavits of William Hall and James Fanning, *Letters*.

49. Affidavits of James Fanning, Edward D. Luxton and Charles E. Sinclair, *Letters*; Statement of W.W. Tice and Charges to be brought against Colonel W.W. McChesney, *Records*; Andrew Lucas Hunt to his mother, 30 August 1864, Andrew Lucus Hunt Papers, University of North Carolina at Chapel Hill.

50. Affidavit of Samuel Hinton, *Letters*.

51. *Daily Constitutional Union* (Washington, DC), September 17, 1864.

52. *Chicago Tribune*, August 29, 1864; Affidavits of Donnell Higgins, Robert L. Jenkins, Joseph A. Ghromsby, Charles W. Van Vliet, and Daniel Merriman, *Letters*; *Report of the Adjutant General of the State of Illinois* (Springfield, IL :Journal Company, Printers and Binders, 1867), vol. VII, 4–6.

53. *OR*, Ser. I, vol. 39, pt. 2, 300, 311; Andrew Lucas Hunt to his father, 29 August 1864, Andrew Lucas Hunt Papers; General Orders No. 11, 25 August 1864, *Letters*.

54. Andrew Lucas Hunt to his father, 29 August 1864, Andrew Lucas Hunt Papers; Affidavit and interrogation of Charles E. Sinclair, *Letters*; Ullrich, "Civil War Diary of Private Hawley V. Needham," 147–195; "Journal of Sergeant Eugene B. Read." Captain Lucien L. Lambert was also an officer in Company D, Eighth United States Colored Heavy Artillery Regiment, see "Civil War Soldiers & Sailors Database."

55. Ullrich, "Civil War Diary of Private Hawley V. Needham," 147–195; "Journal of Sergeant Eugene B. Read"; Lon Carter Barton, "The Reign of Terror in Graves County," *Register of the Kentucky Historical Society* 46, No. 154 (January 1948), 490–91; Record, *Graves County, Ky. Census*, 58; Stephen Douglas Lynn, *Confederate Pensioners of Kentucky: Pension Applications of the Veterans and Widows* (Baltimore: Gateway Press, Inc., 2000), 117. The 1860 Graves County census lists a "Henry B. Hicks" age fourteen. His older brother David J. Hicks served as a First Lieutenant in the Seventh Kentucky Infantry Regiment. His eldest brother W. Boon Hicks does not appear on any roster of Confederate units from Kentucky, however Barton claims that he had served in the Confederate Army. Barton's article states that Hicks was to be executed at two o'clock, but Needham wrote in his diary claims that Hicks was shot at three o'clock.

56. Barton, "The Reign of Terror in Graves County," 490–91; "Journal of Sergeant Eugene B. Read."

57. Affidavits of John C. Steele and William F. Norton, *Letters*; Final Report of Judge Advocate General Joseph Holt and Charges against Henry W. Barry, *Records*.

58. *OR*, Ser. I, vol. 38, pt. 5, 744–45; *Report of the Adjutant General*, vol. 2, 769–770; Testimonies of Phillip Snow, Charles M. Kilgore and R. Branham and Explanations of E.A. Paine, *Records*; *Philadelphia Inquirer* (Philadelphia, PA), September 9, 1864; *Chicago Tribune*, September 9, 1864. The men recruited at Mayfield became Company D of the First Regiment Capital Guards, Paducah Battalion. Only forty-nine men enlisted during the first few weeks of September of 1864. They mustered out on February 18, 1865.

59. "Journal of Sergeant Eugene B. Read"; *Chicago Tribune*, September 9, 1864; *Report of the Adjutant General of the State of Illinois* (Springfield, IL: Journal Company, Printers and Binders, 1900), vol. VII, 21, 54, 89, 174); Andrew Lucas Hunt to his mother, 4 September 1864, Andrew Lucas Hunt Papers; Ullrich, "Civil War Diary of Private Hawley V. Needham," 147–195. The regiments requested to remain the extra fifteen days by Paine were the 132nd, 134th, 136th and 141st Illinois Infantry Regiments. All the regiments remained in service for almost a month after their term of service had expired, including the 134th Illinois. None of the regiments would receive a medal or extra pay as promised by Paine.

60. Andrew Lucas Hunt to his mother, 4 September 1864, Andrew Lucas Hunt Papers; Affidavit of James Fanning, *Letters*; Edward D. Luxton to W.W. Chesney, 14 November 1864

and W.W. McChesney to E.A. Paine, 15 December 1864, *Records*.

61. *American Annual Cyclopedia and Register of Important Events of the Year 1864* (New York: D. Appleton & Co., 1865), 449; *Digest of Election Cases: Cases of Contested Election in the House of Representatives from 1865 to 1871* (Washington D.C.: U.S. Government Printing Office, 1870), 336; *OR*, Ser. II, vol. 4, 688–690; *OR*, Ser. I, vol. 39, pt. 2, 342–345; Explanations of E.A. Paine, *Records*. A copy of the letter Governor Bramlette wrote to President Lincoln was used as evidence in the disloyalty case against L.S. Trimble after the 1867 election. It was dated September 2, 1864. Bramlette later wrote that it was September 3.

62. *Reports of the Committees of the House of Representatives made during the Second Session Thirty-eighth Congress, 1864-1865* (Washington, D.C.: Government Printing Office, 1865), report no. 29, 2; *OR*, Ser. I, vol. 39, pt. 2, 349; Lucien Anderson to Green Adams, 10 September 1864, Lincoln Papers; Lucien Anderson to Abraham Lincoln, 10 September 1864, Lincoln Papers.

63. Affidavits of Donnell Higgins, James O. Tullis, James Baroff, Charles Varges and Herbert E. Brown, *Letters*. The surname of Hess could not be located in any of the 1850 or 1860 county census indices from the Jackson Purchase area.

64. Andrew Lucas Hunt to his parents, 12 September 1864, Andrew Lucas Hunt Papers; "Journal of Sergeant Eugene B. Read"; Ullrich, "Civil War Diary of Private Hawley V. Needham," 147–195; *Mayfield Messenger* (Mayfield, KY), October 4, 1932. Robert F. Wright recalled in 1932 that the man executed was John Johnson and that he had believed served with Forrest's cavalry and worked earlier upon the fortification alongside his father.

65. Ullrich, "Civil War Diary of Private Hawley V. Needham," 147–195.

66. *Ibid.*; H.N. Revelle to A.D. Revelle, 23 September 1864. Norville Hardie Revelle Letters, Filson Historical Society.

67. Surgeon's Certificate by Robert F. Baker, 10 September 1864 and Eleazer A. Paine to Lorenzo Thomas, 12 September 1864, *Letters Received by the Commission Branch of the Adjutants General's Office*.

68. *Daily Missouri Democrat* (St. Louis, MO), September 12, 1864; *OR*, Ser. I, vol. 39, pt. 2, 362; "Journal of Sergeant Eugene B. Read"; Andrew Lucas Hunt to his parents, 12 September 1864, Andrew Lucas Hunt Papers.

69. General Orders, *Letters*; Explanations of E.A. Paine, *Records*; *Louisville Daily Journal*, September 15, 1864; *Macon Telegraph* (Macon, GA), September 25, 1864; Don Simmons, *1850 Census of McCracken County, Kentucky* (Murray, KY: Don Simmons Press, 1974), 11; Battle, Perrin and Kniffen, *Kentucky*, pt. II, 76.

70. Warner, *Generals in Blue*, 319–320.

71. Andrew Lucas Hunt to his mother, 14 September 1864, Andrew Lucas Hunt Papers; W.W. McChesney to E.A. Paine, 15 December 1864, *Records*.

72. Ullrich, "Civil War Diary of Private Hawley V. Needham," 147–195.

73. Andrew Lucas Hunt to his mother, 14 September 1864 and Andrew Lucas Hunt to his brother Willie, 16 September 1864, Andrew Lucas Hunt Papers; Edwin Hunt to Richard Yates, 19 September 1864, Yates Family Papers.

Chapter Four

1. *Louisville Weekly Journal*, October 4, 1864; Final Report of Judge Advocate General Joseph Holt, *Records*; *Encyclopedia of the American Civil War: A Political, Social and Military History*, comp. David Stephen Heidler (Santa Barbara, CA: ABC-CLIO, 2000), s.v. "Fry, Speed Smith"; Marion B. Lucas, "Camp Nelson, Kentucky, during the Civil War: Cradle of Liberty or Refugee Death Camp?" *Filson Club History Quarterly* 63, no. 4 (1989): 439–452. Special Order No. 2, Part II, Headquarters Military District of Kentucky assigned a "committee of investigation" to look into affairs of the "West District of Kentucky under the command of Brigadier General E.A. Paine." The first correspondence between Burbridge and Fry relating to the investigation is dated September 9. See Report Submitted by S.S. Fry to Captain J. Bates Dickson and Letter from Captain J. Bates Dickson to General S.S. Fry, 9 September 1864, *Letters*. Paine and Fry may have met in late 1862 or early 1863 when they both served in the Department of the Cumberland. They certainly would have known of each other's exploits before Fry was selected for the Board of Investigation. However, no evidence exists that they actually met.

2. John J. McAfee, *Kentucky Politicians: Sketches of Representative Corn-Crackers and Other Miscellany* (Louisville: Courier-Journal Job Printing Co., 1886), 32–35; H. Levin, ed., *Lawyers and Lawmakers of Kentucky* (Chicago: Lewis Publishing Co., 1897): 209; Thomas Speed, *Union Regiments of Kentucky* (Louisville: Courier-Journal Printing Co., 1897): 216–18, 624–625; *OR*, Ser. I, vol. 32, pt. 3, 572.

3. *Journal of the Adjourned Session of 1863-4 of the House of Representatives of the Commonwealth of Kentucky* (Frankfort, KY: State Printing Office, 1865), 836; Speed, *Union Regiments of Kentucky*, 121–132; Elizabeth Shelby Kinkead, *A History of Kentucky* (New York: American Book Co., 1909), 206, 758–759. Craddock ran for various offices on the Conservative Union Party ticket following the war.

4. *OR*, Ser. 1, vol. 39, pt. 2, 389; *Wisconsin Daily Patriot* (Madison, WI), September 20, 1864; Report submitted by S.S. Fry to J. Bates Dickson, *Letters*; David J. Eicher, *The Longest Night: A Military History of the Civil War* (New York: Simon & Schuster, 2001), 731–32. Fry reports to Dickson that Paine departed Paducah the evening of the Board's arrival.

5. List of those testifying in the case against Paine, Testimony of Major Henry Bartling (September 14, 1864) and Jeremiah T. Boyle to Stephen G. Burbridge, 8 September 1864, *Letters*.

6. John E. Kleber, ed., *Kentucky Encyclopedia* (Lexington: University Press of Kentucky, 1992), s.v. "Boyle, Jeremiah T."; John Boyle, comp., *Boyle Genealogy: John Boyle of Virginia and Kentucky* (St. Louis, MO: Perrin & Smith Printing Co., 1909), 63–71; Jeremiah T. Boyle to Stephen G. Burbridge, 8 September 1864 and Affidavit of Samuel Hinton, *Letters*.

7. Letter to Brigadier General S.S. Fry and Colonel Mason Brown from Captain H.B. Grant, September 17, 1864, *Letters*; *Daily Patriot* (Madison, WI), September 20, 1864; John Mason Brown to Daniel W. Lindsey, 16 September 1864, Guerrilla Letters, Document Box 1, Folder G.L. 1864, Kentucky Department of Military Affairs; Explanations of E.A. Paine and Final Report of Judge Advocate General Joseph Holt, *Records*.

8. Affidavits of W.H. Covington, J.E. Rudolph, Francis Grief, M.W. Stroad, Samuel Hinton, Charles F. Phillips, S.B. Ferrell, John F. Davis, Abe Adams, Peter Acker, Mrs. Francis Morse, John H. Neale, John F. Drane, Eli Smith, L.G. Mason, J.M. Mahan, W.O. Mahan, Z.B. Thomas, Jacob Kiebler, Will S. Pierson, L.L. Talboth, John M. Young and A.S. Jones, Petitions from Samuel Fels and Catherine R. Greathouse, *Letters*. The estimate of $100,000 is very conservative since many of affidavits did not list the total number of items or their value. The cost would be roughly about $1.5 million in 2012 (see http://www.measuringworth.com).

9. Letter to Solomon Meredith from Henry Bartling, 16 September 1864, Letter from Edward D. Luxton to W.W. McChesney, 14 November

1864, Letter from Solomon Meredith to Allen C. Fuller, 20 September 1864, *Records*; Letter to S.S. Fry and Mason Brown from H.G. Grant, September 17, 1864, Affidavit of Edward D. Luxton, *Letters*.

10. *Wisconsin Daily Patriot* (Madison, WI), September 20, 1864; *Monmouth Review* (Monmouth, IL), September 23, 1864; *Louisville Daily Journal*, September 22, 1864. The *St. Louis Republican*, despite its name, and *Chicago Times* was well renowned as being one of President Lincoln's strongest critics and a leader in the anti-war movement. See *Encyclopedia of Media and Propaganda in Wartime*, comp. Martin J. Manning and Clarence R. Wyatt (Santa Barbara, CA: ABC-CLIO, 2011), s.v. "Copperhead Press."

11. Explanations of E.A. Paine, *Records*; Eicher, *The Longest Night*, 731–32; E.A. Paine to Lorenzo Thomas, 30 September 1864 and J.A. Campbell to G.M. Bascom, 30 September 1864, *Letters Received by the Commission Branch of the Adjutants General's Office*.

12. Affidavits of Donnell Higgins, Edgar H. Andress, Henry B. Aldrich, Harry Post, Samuel Beers, James O. Tullis, James H. Baroff, Charles Varges, Herbert E. Brown, Robert H. Jenkins, Joseph A. Ghormsby, Charles W. Van Vliet, W.P. Tucker, James T. Pierson, Will S. Pierson, L.L. Talboth, A.J.M. Thompson, Hiram Smith, Allen Omer, Joshua W. Collins, John W. Hammock, Davis Collins, Thomas L. Sturgeon, D.O. Conn, William H. Kirby, John H. Wright, D.C. James, Samuel M. Taylor, John M. Young and William Greathouse, *Letters*. The movements of the Board of Investigation can be theorized by the dates and locations listed on the affidavits. The last affiant sent his statement to the Board on October 3, a week after they arrived at Louisville (see affidavit of Peter Acker, *Letters*).

13. *Louisville Journal*, September 27, 1864; E. Merton Coulter, *The Civil War and Readjustment in Kentucky* (Chapel Hill: University of North Carolina Press, 1926), 182, 202–3; Craig, *Kentucky Confederates*, 276; Craig and Ullrich, *Unconditional Unionist*, 140–146; Kleber, *Kentucky Encyclopedia*, s.v. "Prentice, George Dennison."

14. *Louisville Journal*, September 27, 1864.

15. Craig and Ullrich, *Unconditional Unionist*, 137.

16. *Ibid.*, 137–138.

17. Andrew Lucas Hunt to his mother, 18 September 1864, Andrew Lucas Hunt Papers; *OR*, Ser. I, vol. 39, pt. 2, 561–3; *OR*, ser. I, vol. 38, pt. 5, 318; *OR*, Ser. I, vol. 39, pt. 2, 542–3.

18. *Chicago Tribune*, September 27, 1864; Jennie Fyfe to Nell, 27 September 1864, Fyfe Family Papers.

19. "Journal of Sergeant Eugene B. Read" Jackson Purchase Historical Society, accessed December 31, 2012, http://www.jacksonpurchasehistory.org/jackson-purchase-during-the-civil-war/; *Chicago Tribune*, October 7 and 23, 1864; *OR*, ser. I, vol. 39, pt. 3, 264; *New York Times*, October 23, 1864.

20. "Journal of Sergeant Eugene B. Read"; *Chicago Tribune*, October 23, 1864; *OR*, ser. I, vol. 39, pt. 3, 343.

21. *Chicago Tribune*, October 23, 1864; Jennie Fyfe to Nell, [20] October 1864, Fyfe Family Papers; Battle, Perrin and Kniffen, *Kentucky*, pt. II, 53; Lucien Anderson to Abraham Lincoln, 17 October 1854, Lincoln Papers; Solomon Meredith to Abraham Lincoln, 17 October 1854, Lincoln Papers. Marshall and Bullock were Circuit County Judges from Graves County appointed during the war.

22. *Cleveland Morning Leader*, October 24, 1864; Jennie Fyfe to Nell, [20] October 1864, Fyfe Family Papers; "Journal of Sergeant Eugene B. Read"; *Chicago Tribune*, November 1, 2, and 3, 1864; Affidavit of Amos Smith, *Letters*. Amos Smith filed an affidavit a month earlier that Union troops broke into his grocery store and destroyed property worth $550 and raided his farm confiscating $2,500 worth of chickens, oats and corn.

23. *OR*, Ser. I, vol. 39, pt. 3, 437 and 549; *Chicago Tribune*, October 29, 1864; *Daily True Delta* (New Orleans, LA), November 5 and 17, 1864; *Daily Ohio Statesman* (Columbus, OH), November 3, 1864; Craig, *Kentucky Confederates*, 282–284; "Journal of Sergeant Eugene B. Read."

24. Eleazer A. Paine to John M. Schofield, 25 October 1864, *Letters Received by the Commission Branch of the Adjutants General's Office*; *Louisville Daily Journal*, October 27, 1864; *Louisville Weekly Journal*, November 1, 1864. Craddock never published the declaration, which would have implicated him as Governor Bramlette's spy and Prentice's correspondent at Paducah.

25. Eleazer A. Paine to John M. Schofield, 25 October 1864, *Letters Received by the Commission Branch of the Adjutants General's Office*; *OR*, Ser. I, vol. 39, pt. 2, 423.

26. *Louisville Weekly Journal*, October 4, 1864; *Louisville Daily Journal*, October 27, 1864; *Louisville Weekly Journal*, November 1, 1864.

27. *Louisville Press*, October 24, 1864; *Louisville Daily Journal*, October 27, 1864.

28. Solomon Meredith to Allen C. Fuller, 20 September 1864, *Records*; *Chicago Tribune*, September 22, 1864; Telegram from James Oakes to Solomon Meredith, [31 October 1864], *Records*; W.W. McChesney to E.A. Paine, 15 December 1864, *Records*; James Oakes to Lorenzo Thomas, 15 December 1864, *Records*.

29. Telegraph from Paducah to the Adjutant General's Office in Springfield, IL, 25 September 1864, *Records*; Telegram from Solomon Meredith to James Oakes, 1 November 1864, *Records*; James Oakes to Lorenzo Thomas, 15 December 1864, *Records*.

30. Edward D. Luxton to W.W. McChesney, 14 November 1864, *Records*; W.W. McChesney to E.A. Paine, 15 December 1864, *Records*. Lieutenant Luxton wrote Colonel McChesney that the government agent was named "Captain Whiteside" but no record exists of such an officer in the ranks of either Meredith or Burbridge. Luxton turned over McChesney's belt and sword to Assistant Adjutant General at Paducah Captain James Graham.

31. L. Jansens to W.W. McChesney, 30 October 1864, *Records*; W.W. McChesney to E.A. Paine, 15 December 1864, *Records*; L. Jansens to W.W. McChesney, 22 November 1864, *Records*; Joseph Hooker to E.D. Townsend, 15 November 1864, *Records*.

32. Joseph Hooker to E.D. Townsend, 15 November 1864, *Records*; James Oakes to Lorenzo Thomas, 15 December 1864, *Records*; W.W. McChesney to E.A. Paine, 15 December 1864, *Records*.

33. W.W. McChesney to E.A. Paine, 15 December 1864, *Records*; Note attached to cover document from the Adjutants General's Office, 17 December 1869, *Letters Received by the Commission Branch of the Adjutants General's Office*; *Evening Union* (Washington, DC), December 2, 1864; Final Report of Judge Advocate General Joseph Holt, 1 December 1864, *Records*.

34. Final Report of Judge Advocate General Joseph Holt, 1 December 1864, *Records*.

35. *Journal of the Senate of the United States of America, being the Second Session of the Thirty-Eighth Congress* (Washington, D.C.: Government Printing Office, 1864), 17, 22; *Official Proceedings of the Democratic National Convention, held in 1864* (Chicago: Times Steam Book and Job Printing House, 1864), 29, 54; *Biographical Sketch of the Hon. Lazarus W. Powell (of Henderson, Ky.), Governor of the State of Kentucky from 1851–1855, Senator in Congress from 1859–1865* (Frankfort, KY: Kentucky Yeoman Office, 1868), 53–90.

36. *Congressional Globe: The Debates and Proceedings of the Second*

Session of the Thirty-Eighth Congress, 38th Congress also, of the Special Session of the Senate (Washington, D.C.: F & J Rives, 1865), 9–10; *Baltimore Sun* (Baltimore, MD), December 9, 1864; *Southern Bivouac*, vol. 4, 668. J.A. Trousdale wrote over twenty years after the war that he sent an affidavit to General Fry with charges that Paine murdered ten prisoners at Gallatin and mailed a copy to Colonel Charles D. Pennebaker of the 27th Kentucky Infantry Regiment. Pennebaker delivered the affidavit to Senator Powell in Washington. No affidavit from Trousdale can be found in the Letters received by the Office of the Adjutant General relating to the command of General Paine.

37. *Ibid.*, 14; G.T. Allen to Lyman Trumbull, 19 December 1864, Lyman Trumbull Papers, Manuscripts Division, Library of Congress. Allen's letter included a newspaper clipping from the *Cairo Morning News* from December 16, 1864 describing Trumbull's debate with Powell.

38. Explanations of Brigadier General E.A. Paine, 24 December 1864, *Records*.

39. *Ibid.*

40. *Ibid.*; Lowell H. Harrison and James C. Klotter, *A New History of Kentucky* (Lexington: University Press of Kentucky, 1997), 205–7.

41. *Ibid.*; E.A. Paine to Lorenzo Thomas, 28 December 1864, *Letters Received by the Commission Branch of the Adjutants General's Office*.

42. *Journal of the Adjourned Session of 1863-4, of the House of Representatives of the Commonwealth of Kentucky* (Frankfort, KY: George D. Prentice, State Printer, 1865), 15–70; *Louisville Weekly Journal*, January 10, 1865.

43. *Journal of the Senate of the Commonwealth of Kentucky* (Frankfort, KY: Wm. E. Hughes, State Printer, 1863), 237–9; *Louisville Daily Journal*, January 7, 1865; *Louisville Weekly Journal*, January 10, 1865. Prentice was elected by the Legislature as the Public Printer of the Commonwealth of Kentucky on January 27, 1864.

44. *Congressional Globe: Official Proceedings of Congress, 38th Congress, 2nd Session* (Washington, D.C.: F & J Rives, 1864), 269, 308; *Journal of the United States Senate of the United States of America being the Second Session of the Thirty-Eighth Congress* (Washington, D.C.: Government Printing Office, 1864), 74.

45. *Congressional Globe: The Debates and Proceedings of the Second Session of the Thirty-Eighth Congress, 38th Congress also, of the Special Session of the Senate* (Washington, D.C.: F & J Rives, 1865), 308–311.

46. *Ibid.*

47. *Ibid.*; *Biographical Sketch of the Hon. Lazarus W. Powell (of Henderson, Ky.), Governor of the State of Kentucky from 1851–1855, Senator in Congress from 1859–1865* (Frankfort, KY: Kentucky Yeoman Office, 1868), 82–86; *Congressional Globe: The Debates and Proceedings of the Second Session of the Thirty-Eighth Congress, 38th Congress also, of the Special Session of the Senate* (Washington, D.C.: F & J Rives, 1865), 308–311. Powell's biographer wrote that the debate against Trumbull and Conness was one of Powell's most memorable moments of his political career.

48. *Ibid.*

49. *Ibid.*, 360, 468, 488; Senate Resolution to transmit evidence, 23 January 1865, *Records*; E.D. Townsend to J. Holt, 25 January 1865, *Records*; *Letters of the Secretary of War* (Washington, D.C.: Government Printing Office, 1865) Serial Set Vol. No. 1209, Session Vol. No. 1, 38th Congress, 2nd Session, Senate Document (Executive) No. 12; *Journal of the Adjourned Session of 1863-4, of the Senate of the Commonwealth of Kentucky* (Frankfort, KY: George D. Prentice, State Printer, 1865), 232.

Chapter Five

1. Trial Proceedings, Special Orders No. 51, *Records*; E.D. Townsend to J. Holt, 30 January 1865, *Records*; *OR*, Ser. III, Vol. 4, 500; Warner, *Generals in Blue*, 378–380.

2. *Journal of the House of Representatives of the United States of America being the Second Session of the Thirty-Eighth Congress* (Washington, D.C.: Government Printing Office, 1865), 111–2, 116, 123, 143, 172; *Congressional Globe: Official Proceedings of Congress, 38th Congress, 2nd Session* (Washington, D.C.: F & J Rives, 1864), 316, 337, 369; *The Reports of the Committees of the House of Representatives made during the Second Session Thirty-Eighth Congress, 1864–1865* (Washington, D.C.: Government Printing Office, 1864), Report No. 29, 1–3.

3. Notes on trial proceedings, 8 February to February, 1865, *Records*; *War Eagle* (Cairo, IL), February 9, 1864; *Cincinnati Daily Enquirer*, February 10, 1865; *Daily Dispatch* (Richmond, VA), February 17, 1865; Special Orders No. 64, 9 February 1865, *Records*; Draft of telegraph from W.M. Dunn to William Holt, 9 February 1865, *Records*.

4. Notes on trial proceedings, 10 February 1865, *Records*; Draft of telegraph from E.D. Townsend to Joseph Holt, 10 February 1865, *Records*.

5. Telegraph from E.D. Townsend to David Hunter, 13 February 1864, *Records*; Notes on trial proceedings, 14 February 1865, *Records*; *New Orleans Picayune*, February 24, 1865; Barton, "The Reign of Terror in Graves County," 493.

6. Notes on trial proceedings, 16 February 1865, *Records*; Jennie Fyfe to Nell, 15 February 1865, Fyfe Family Papers.

7. *Chicago Tribune*, February 11, 1865; *OR*, Ser. I, vol. 49, pt. 1, 801–803; *New York Herald*, February 15, 1865; *Chicago Tribune*, February 10, 1865. The aggregate strength of the District of Western Kentucky in February of 1865 was 3,071. The total troop strength for the district at the end of August of 1864 was 4,550. See *OR*, Ser. I, vol. 38, pt. 5, 744–745.

8. Charges against Colonel James W.M. McArthur and Charges against Colonel Henry W. Barry, *Records*; *OR*, Ser. I, Vol. 48, pt. 1, 666–668; *War Eagle* (Cairo, IL), January 26, 1865; "General Sol Meredith" (newspaper clipping), 24 May 1865, Papers and Diaries of Solomon Meredith and Family, Indiana Historical Society; G.T. Allen to Lyman Trumbull, 19 December 1864, Lyman Trumbull Papers, Manuscripts Division, Library of Congress; *War Eagle* (Cairo, IL), March 3, 1865.

9. "General Sol Meredith" (newspaper clipping), 24 May 1865, Papers and Diaries of Solomon Meredith.

10. Notes on trial proceedings and Court transcripts of trial proceedings, 17 February 1865, *Records*.

11. General Court-Martial Orders No. 567, 13 October 1865, *Records*; Report to the President (Lincoln), 28 March 1865, *Records*.

12. Final Report of the Judge Advocate General Joseph Holt, *Records*; "Proclamation 113: Declaring Martial Law and a Further Writ of Habeas Corpus in Kentucky, July 5, 1864," American Presidency Project, Proclamation 113—Declaring Martial Law and a Further Suspension of the Writ of Habeas Corpus in Kentucky, accessed April 4, 2017, http://www.presidency.ucsb.edu/; Halleck, H.W., *International Law; or, Rules Regulating the Intercourse of States in Peace and War* (New York: D. Van Nostrand, 1861), 373; Benet, S.V., *A Treatise on Military Law and the Practice of Courts-Martial* (New York: D. Van Nostrand, 1864), 14; *OR*, Ser. III, Vol. 3, 148–164.

13. Hubbell, John T., ed., *Biographical Dictionary of the Union: Northern Leaders of the Civil War* (Westport, CT: Greenwood Press, 1995), 155–156; Eicher, *Civil War High*, 218.

14. Court transcripts, 17 February 1865, Testimony of V.S. Gillespie, *Records*.

15. *Ibid.*, 17 February 1865, Testimony of John Sinnott, *Records*.

16. *Ibid.*, 17 February 1865, Testimony of James R. Alexander, *Records*.
17. *Ibid.*, 17 February 1865, Testimony of R.O. Woolfolk, *Records*.
18. *Ibid.* Woolfolk's brother George W. Woolfolk served as a private with the Third Kentucky Mounted Infantry Regiment.
19. *Ibid.* The two Union officers who overheard Woolfolk were Captain Lucius B. Church of the 105th Illinois Infantry Regiment and Second Lieutenant Duncan C. McIver of the 122nd Illinois Infantry Regiment.
20. *Ibid.*, 17 February 1865, Testimony of V.S. Gillespie, *Records*.
21. *Ibid.*, 18 February 1865, Testimony of W.P. Caldwell, *Records*.
22. *Ibid.*, 18 February 1865, Testimony of G.F. Rabb, *Records*.
23. *Ibid.*, 18 February 1865, Testimony of J.E. Woodward, *Records*.
24. *Ibid.*, 19 February 1865, Testimony of J.E. Woodward, *Records*.
25. *Ibid.*, 20–21 February 1865, Testimonies of J.A. Bracken, P.D. Yeiser, J.B. Husbands and L.H. Edrington.
26. *Ibid.*; Explanations of E.A. Paine, *Records*. Yeiser was appointed the Commonwealth Attorney for the First Judicial District in January of 1862, see Battle, Perrin and Kniffen, *Kentucky*, pt. II, 332.
27. *Ibid.*; Charles F. Smith to Eleazer A. Paine, 16 November 1861, *Records*.
28. *Ibid.*, 21 February 1865, Testimony of J. Scott Ford, *Records*.
29. *Ibid.*, 21 February 1865, Testimonies of R.M. Humble and William Bell, *Records*.
30. *Ibid.*
31. *Ibid.*, 21–22 February 1865, Testimony of W.L. Mayes. Mayes son-in-law may have been Jesse Comperry who briefly served as a private in Company G, 3rd Kentucky Mounted Infantry before he deserted on December 31, 1862. See *Report of the Adjutant General of the State of Kentucky, Confederate Volunteers, War 1861–65* (Owensboro, KY: McDowell Publications, 1979), vol. 1, 116.
32. *Ibid.*, 22 February 1865, Testimony of D.Y. Craig, *Records*.
33. *Ibid.*, 22 February 1865, Testimony of W.P. Tucker; Affidavit of W.P. Tucker, *Letters*.
34. *Ibid.*, 22 February 1865, Testimony of J.W. Hammock, *Records*; Affidavit of John W. Hammock, *Letters*; *History of Union County*, 468–469.
35. *Ibid.*, 22 February 1865, Testimony of Allen Omer, *Records*; Affidavit of Allen Omar, *Letters*.
36. *Ibid.*, 23 February 1865, Testimony of W.S. Buckner, *Records*.
37. *Ibid.*, 23 February 1865, Testimonies of James T. Pierson, Will S. Pierson and W.W. Pierson, *Records*; Affidavits of James T. Pierson and Will S. Pierson, *Letters*; *History of Union County, Kentucky*, 596–597.
38. *Ibid.*, 23 February 1865, Testimonies of Thomas H. Welch, William Gregg and Caleb Tucker, *Records;* Affidavit of W.P. Tucker, *Letters*. When asked by the judge advocate if he was a loyal citizen of the United States, Caleb Tucker responded "I think so, if I know what loyalty is?"
39. *Ibid.*, 23–24 February 1865, Testimonies of Catherine Greathouse and Robert William Greathouse, *Records;* Petition from Catherine R. Greathouse to Major General Burbridge, 6 September 1864, *Letters*; Affidavit of William Greathouse, *Letters*.
40. *Ibid.*, 24 February 1865, Testimony of Robert William Greathouse, *Records*; Affidavit of William Greathouse, *Letters*.
41. *Ibid.*, 24 February 1865, Testimony of Henry Parsons, *Records*; Affidavit of W.P. Tucker, *Letters*.
42. *Ibid.*, 24 February 1865, Testimony of W.P. Tucker (recalled to testify), *Records*.
43. *Ibid.*, 24 February 1865, Testimony of James D. Moss, *Records*; 28 February 1865, Testimony of Henry Bartling, *Records*; Explanations of E.A. Paine, *Records*; Complaint of James D. Moss to General Meredith, 12 September 1864, *Letters*.
44. *Ibid.*, 24 February 1865, Testimony of James D. Moss, *Records*.
45. *Ibid.*, 24 February 1865, Testimony of L.L. Talbot, *Records*; Affidavit of L.L. Talbot, *Letters*; *History of Union County, Kentucky*, 605–607.
46. *Ibid.*, 25 February 1865, Testimony of T.H. Mayes, *Records*.
47. *Ibid.*, 25 February 1865, Testimony of Lewis T. Bradley, *Records*; Affidavit of L.T. Bradley, *Letters*.
48. *Ibid.*, 25 February 1865, Testimony of J.T. Bolinger, *Records*; Testimony of James Johnson, *Letters*; Battle, Perrin and Kniffen, *Kentucky*, pt. II, 283–284. Bigger was elected judge in the First Judicial District of Kentucky prior to the war. After the war he was elected to the Kentucky State Senate in 1866, served as a city councilman in Paducah and later as Speaker of the Kentucky House of Representatives from 1877 to 1881.
49. *Ibid.*, 25 February 1865, Testimony of J.T. Bolinger, *Records*; Affidavit of Joseph M. Bigger, *Letters*.
50. *Ibid.*, 25 February 1865, Testimony of J.T. Bolinger, *Records*.
51. *Ibid.*, 25 February 1865, Testimony of Toussaint C. Buntin, *Records*.
52. *Ibid.*, 25 February 1865, Testimony of Marian G. Milan, *Records*; 15 September 1864, Testimony of Marian G. Milan, *Letters*. Milan was interviewed by the Board of Investigation at Paducah soon after their arrival. His earlier testimony was believed to have been taken by Colonel Brown.
53. *Ibid.*, 25 February 1865, Testimonies of Mary Crutchfield, E.R. Jett and Frederick T. Whitworth, *Records*;
54. *Ibid.*, 27 February 1865, Testimony of Captain Phelps Paine, *Records*.
55. *Ibid.*, 27 February 1865, Testimony of Peter Davidson, *Records*.
56. *Ibid.*, 27 February 1865, Testimony of Peter Davidson, *Records*.
57. *Ibid.*, 27 February 1865, Testimony of J.C. Brooks, *Records*; Affidavit of J.C. Brooks, *Letters*.
58. *Ibid.*, 27 February 1865, Remarks of Judge Advocate William M. Dunn, *Records*.

Chapter Six

1. *Ibid.*, 27 February 1865, Evidence submitted by Eleazer A. Paine, *Records*.
2. *Ibid.*, 27 February 1865, Testimony of Henry W. Barry, *Records*.
3. *Ibid.*, 27–28 February 1865, Testimony of Henry W. Barry, *Records*.
4. *Ibid.*, 28 February 1865, Testimony of G.L. Tombelle, *Records*. No record of Tombelle's service in the State Militia or Home Guards could be located by the author, see *Report of the Adjutant General of the State of Kentucky* (Frankfort, KY: John H. Harney, Public Printer, 1867).
5. *Ibid.* 28 February 1865, Testimony of Henry Bartling, *Records*.
6. *Ibid.*
7. *Ibid.*
8. *Ibid.*, 28 February 1865, Testimony of Elijah Rudolph, *Records*.
9. *Ibid.*, 28 February 1865, Testimony of W.M. Starks, *Records*; *Grant Papers*, vol. 9, 149, 314, 633 & vol. 10, 181; Explanations of E.A. Paine, *Records*; *Acts of the General Assembly of the Commonwealth of Kentucky* (Frankfort, KY: Wm. E. Hughes, State Printer, 1864), 120–1.
10. *Ibid.*, 28 February 1865, Testimony of W.M. Starks, *Records*.
11. *Ibid.*, 1 March 1865, Testimonies of C.Y. Craig, J.H. Hines, J.W. Caldwell, Roland H. Hall and Robert Glover, *Records*.
12. *Ibid.*, 1 March 1865, Testimony of P.H. Hall, *Records*. The author could not locate a Major P.H. Hall that served in the Union Army from either the State of Tennessee or Kentucky. See Hewett, Janet B., ed., *The Roster of Union Soldiers, 1861–1865* (Wilmington, NC: Broadfoot Publishing Co., 2000), Civil War Centennial Commission of Tennessee, *Tennesseans in the Civil War: A Military History of Confederate and Union Units with Available Rosters of Personnel* (Nashville, TN: Civil War Centennial Commission, 1965)

13. *Ibid.*, 1 March 1865, Testimony of Ila M. Davis, *Records*.
14. *Ibid.*, 1 March 1865, Testimony of Thomas L. Sturgeon, *Records*.
15. *Ibid.*, 1 March 1865, Testimony of J.E. Woodward, *Records*.
16. *Ibid.*, 1 March 1865, Testimony of John S. Greathouse, *Records*.
17. *Ibid.*, 1 March 1865, Testimony of Richard Branham, *Records*.
18. *Ibid.*, 2 March 1865, Testimonies of Bettie Barbour Hughes and Joshua D. Hughes, *Records*; *History of Union County, Kentucky*, 196–7; *Official Army Register of the Volunteer Force of the United States Army for the Years 1861–1865* (Washington, D.C.: Adjutant-General's Office, 1865), Part II (New York and New Jersey), 745. No affidavit was found from Bettie Barbour Hughes, see *Letters*.
19. *Ibid.*, 2 March 1865, Testimony of Peter Acker, *Records*.
20. *Ibid.*
21. *Ibid.*, 2 March 1865, Testimony of Phillip Snow, *Records*.
22. *Ibid.*, 2 March 1865, Testimony of Joseph Garrish, *Records*.
23. *Ibid.*, Remarks of Judge Advocate William M. Dunn and Charges and Specifications preferred against E.A. Paine, *Records*.
24. *Ibid.*, 2 March 1865, Testimony of S.M. Purcell, *Records*. Purcell served as a captain in the Fifteenth Kentucky Volunteer Cavalry, Company B, from October of 1862 to October of 1863 (see Battle, Perrin and Kniffen, *Kentucky*, pt. II, 107).
25. *Ibid.*, 2–3 March 1865, Testimony of Thomas M. Redd, *Records*.
26. *Ibid.*, 3 March 1865, Testimony of James T. Pierson and Specifications preferred against E.A. Paine, *Records*.
27. *Ibid.*; *General Orders, Adjutant General's Office for 1863 with an Index* (Washington, D.C.: Government Printing Office, 1864), General Order No. 143, May 22, 1863.
28. *Ibid.*, 3 March 1865, Testimony of James T. Pierson, *Records*.
29. *Ibid.*, 3 March 1865, Testimonies of G.L. Tombelle, R. Branham, G.W. Price, Francis H. Shouse, H.B. Eaty, H. Munchhoff and James Kerney, *Records*. Pierson won the election by only sixteen votes over James A. Turner in 1862, see *History of Union County, Kentucky*, 679.
30. *Ibid.*, 3 March 1865, Testimony of William W. Phillips, *Records*; Robertson, John, *Michigan in the War*, revised ed. (Lansing, MI: W.S. George & Co., State Printers and Binders, 1882), 993.
31. *Ibid.*, 4 March 1865, Testimony of Henry Bartling, *Records*.
32. *Ibid.*, 4 March 1865, Testimony of W.P. Cunningham, *Records*.
33. *Ibid.*, 4 March 1865, Testimony of Thomas Atherton, *Records*. Atherton temporarily relocated to Metropolis, Illinois in 1863 after receiving threats from guerrillas. He did not return to Kentucky until after the war.
34. *Ibid.*, 4 March 1865, Testimony of P.H. Hall, *Records*.
35. *Ibid.*, 4 March 1865, Testimony of Charles M. Kilgore, *Records*.
36. *Ibid.*, 4 March 1865, Summation of E.A. Paine, *Records*; Testimonies of James T. Pierson, G.L. Tombelle, G.W. Price, James Kerney, Francis H. Shouse, H.B. Eaty, H. Munchhoff and R. Branham, *Records*.
37. *Ibid.*, 4 March 1865, Summation of E.A. Paine, *Records*; Testimonies of V.S. Gillespie, John Sinnott, James R. Alexander, R.O. Woolfolk, W.P. Caldwell, T.M. Redd and P.H. Hall, *Records*.
38. *Ibid.*, 4 March 1865, Summation of E.A. Paine, *Records*; Testimonies of G.F. Rabb, T.M. Redd and J.E. Wooward, *Records*; Birkhimer, William E., *Military Government and Martial Law*, 2nd ed. (Kansas City: Franklin Hudson Publishing Co., 1904), 57.
39. *Ibid.*, 4 March 1865, Summation of E.A. Paine, *Records*; Testimonies of P.D. Yeiser, Frederick T. Whitworth, J.H. Hines and Thomas Atherton, *Records*; C.F. Smith to E.A. Paine, 16 November 1861, *Records*.
40. *Ibid.*, 4 March 1865, Summation of E.A. Paine, *Records*; Testimonies of C.Y. Craig, J.H. Hines, J.W. Caldwell, Roland H. Hall, Robert Glover, Henry Bartling, T.M. Redd, W.M. Starks, S.M. Purcell and William Bell, *Records*.
41. *Ibid.*, 4 March 1865, Summation of E.A. Paine, *Records*; Testimonies of Toussaint C. Buntin, J.T. Bolinger and Lewis T. Bradley, *Records*.
42. *Ibid.*, 4 March 1865, Summation of E.A. Paine, *Records;* Testimonies of Peter Acker, Peter Davison and Phillip Snow, *Records*.
43. *Ibid.*, 4 March 1865, Summation of E.A. Paine, *Records*.
44. *Ibid.*, 4 March 1865, Summation of W.M. Dunn, *Records;* "Proclamation 113: Declaring Martial Law and a Further Writ of Habeas Corpus in Kentucky, July 5, 1864," The American Presidency Project, accessed April 4, 2017, http://www.presidency.ucsb.edu/; Final Report of Judge Advocate General Joseph Holt, *Records*.
45. *Ibid.*, 4 March 1865, Summation of W.M. Dunn, *Records*.
46. *Ibid.*, 6 March 1865, Verdict, *Records*.
47. *Ibid.*
48. *Ibid.*, 7 March 1865, Review, *Records*.
49. *Louisville Daily Journal*, March 2, 1864; Craig, *Kentucky Confederates*, 288–289.
50. *War Eagle* (Cairo, IL), March 9, 1865; *Chicago Tribune*, March 14, 1865.
51. *Ibid.*
52. *Ibid.*
53. Eleazer A. Paine to Lorenzo Thomas, 8 March 1865, *Letters Received by the Commission Branch of the Adjutants General's Office*.
54. *Chicago Tribune*, March 9, 1865; *Louisville Daily Journal*, March 10, 1864.
55. Report to the President (Lincoln), 28 March 1865, *Records*; Eleazer A. Paine to Lorenzo Thomas, 28 March 1865 and Report of December 17, 1869, *Letters Received by the Commission Branch of the Adjutants General's Office*. The report of December 17, 1869 that Paine "again tendered his resignation to date April 1, 1865 and on the 5th of that month it was accepted."

Chapter Seven

1. *Chicago Tribune*, March 14, 1865.
2. *Frankfort Commonwealth*, April 4, 1865; *New York Herald*, March 27, 1865; *Report of the Adjutant General of the State of Kentucky* (Frankfort, KY: John H. Harney, Public Printer, 1867), vol. 2, 825–826; Jennie Fyfe to Nell, 23 March 1865, Fyfe Family Papers. Captain McDougal may have been one of the brothers that reportedly murdered the partisan leader Colonel William W. Faulkner at Dresden, Tennessee, the month before. See Henry George, *History of the 3d, 7th, 8th and 12th Kentucky C.S.A.* (Louisville: C.T. Dearing, 1911), 139. McDougal's men were at the home of George Thomas Hayden who resided south of Fancy Farm and not far from ruins of the Gregory family homestead at Dublin.
3. *Federal Union* (Paducah, KY), April 6, 1865. Lieutenant M.L. Smith took over command of the company following his death.
4. *Federal Union* (Paducah, KY), April 6, 1865; *War Eagle* (Cairo, IL), April 7, 1865.
5. Proclamation on Lee's Surrender, April 14, 1865, Solomon Meredith Papers, Indiana Historical Society, Indianapolis.
6. Edward C. Slater, *The Nation's Loss: A Sermon upon the Death of Abraham Lincoln, sixteenth President of the United States* (Paducah, KY: Blelock & Co., 1865); *Federal Union* (Paducah, KY), April 25, 1865; *Paducah Evening Sun*, February 8, 1909. Pastor Slater was the preacher in the Paducah District of the Memphis Conference of the Methodist Episcopal Church in the spring of 1865. From 1860 to 1862 he was president of

Andrew College. He was assigned to the Broadway United Methodist Church at Paducah in 1863. See *Minutes of the Annual Conference of the Methodist Episcopal Church, South, 1858–1865* (Nashville, TN: Southern Methodist Publishing House, 1859–1870), 224, 382, 438, 596.

7. *Ibid.* The residence of Mr. Givens' may be H.F. Given, the bank owner of Watts, Given and Company.

8. *Ibid.*

9. *Federal Union* (Paducah, KY), April 25, 1865.

10. OR, ser. I, vol. 49, pt. 2, 466, 549, 564, 568; Lucian Anderson to Solomon Meredith, June 7, 1865 and February 1, 1866, Solomon Meredith Papers; Henry Clay Fox, *Memoirs of Wayne County and the City of Richmond, Indiana* (Madison, WS: Western Historical Association, 1912), vol. I, 213. On November 27, 1865, Meredith reportedly beat Julian unconscious with a whip at the railroad depot in Richmond, Indiana for having made public statements accusing him of sympathizing with rebels and traitors at Paducah. See *Richmond Weekly Telegram* (Richmond, IN), December 2, 1865.

11. OR, ser. I, vol. 49, pt. 2, 823, 852; *Louisville Weekly Journal*, May 23, 1865; Mass Meetings at Mayfield and Woodville, May 20, 1865 and Special Orders No. 248, May 22, 1865, Solomon Meredith Papers; *Federal Union* (Paducah, KY), May 24, 1865.

12. William M. Starks to Thomas E. Bramlette, 10 May 1865, Guerrilla Letters, Document Box 1, Folder G.L. 1865, Kentucky Department of Military Affairs.

13. Craig, *Kentucky Confederates*, 291; *Frankfort Commonwealth*, August 15, 18 and 22, 1865; *Federal Union* (Paducah, KY), August 8, 1865.

14. Frederick H. Dyer, *A Compendium of the War of the Rebellion* (Des Moines IA: Dyer Publishing Company, 1908), 540, 1068, 1640, 1721, 1722; George Q. Langstaff, ed., *The Life and Times of Quintus Quincy Quigley, 1828–1910: His Personal Journal 1859–1908* (Brentwood, TN: Talent Group, 1999), 81; Patricia Ann Hoskins, "'The Old First Is with the South': The Civil War, Reconstruction, and Memory in the Jackson Purchase Region of Kentucky" (Ph.D. diss., Auburn University, 2008), 262–263.

15. Hoskins, "The Old First Is with the South," 248–249; *Louisville Weekly Courier*, April 25, 1866.

16. *Ibid.*; Patricia Ann Hoskins, "The Freedmen's Bureau in the Jackson Purchase Region of Kentucky, 1866–1868," *Register of the Kentucky Historical Society* 110, Nos. 3 and 4 (Summer/Autumn 2012), 503–531.

17. Langstaff, *The Life and times of Quintus Quincy Quigley*, 259; Jennie Fyfe to Nell, 15 June 1865, Fyfe Family Papers.

18. *Woodward vs. Fels*, Court of Appeals of Kentucky, 1 Bush 162 (64 Ky. 162), *WestlawNext*; *J.E. Woodward vs. H. & S.C. Hook*, Court of Appeals of Kentucky, 1867 WL 6973 (1 Ky. Op. 94), *WestlawNext*; *John E. Woodward vs. McDonald & Roberts*, Court of Appeals of Kentucky, 1867 WL 6957 (1 Ky. Op. 71), *WestlawNext*; *L.A. Edrington vs. J.A. Bracken*, Court of Appeals of Kentucky, 1867 WL 7087 (1 Ky. Op. 600), *WestlawNext*; *Rau & Ricke vs. Boyle & Boyle*, Court of Appeals of Kentucky, 5 Bush 253 (68 Ky. 253), *WestlawNext*. It is interesting to note that Paine was mentioned in the United States Supreme Court decision of *De Arnaud vs. United States* in 1894. Grant had referred Charles De Arnaud, a Union spy, to Paine for payment for his services.

19. *Reports of Committees of the Senate of the United States for the Third Session of the Forty-second Congress, 1872–1873* (Washington, D.C.: Government Printing Office, 1872), Report No. 414; *Journal of the Senate of the United States of America being the Second Session of the Forty-fourth Congress* (Washington, D.C.: Government Printing Office, 1876), 73; *Congressional Record, First Session, Forty-fifth Congress* (Washington, D.C.: Government Printing Office, 1877), 373 (November 13, 1877); *Reports of Committees of the House of Representatives for the Second Session of the Fifty-third Congress, 1893–1894* (Washington, D.C.: Government Printing Office, 1894), Report No. 297; *Reports of Committees of the House of Representatives for the First Session of the Fifty-first Congress, 1889–1890* (Washington, D.C.: Government Printing Office, 1891), Report No. 2954; *Reports of Committees of the House of Representatives for the First Session of the Fifty-second Congress, 1889–1890* (Washington, D.C.: Government Printing Office, 1892), Report No. 305; *Guide to the Records of the U.S. House of Representatives at the National Archives, 1789–1989 Record Group 233* (College Park, MD : The U.S. National Archives and Records Administration, [1999]), 6.85.

20. *Senate Documents* (Washington, D.C.: Government Printing Office, 1914), vol. 30, Document No. 448; *Louisville Courier-Journal*, March 18, 1914.

Chapter Eight

1. *Monmouth Atlas* (Monmouth, IL), April 21, 1865.

2. E.A. Paine to James A. Hardie, Assistant Inspector General, 15 May 1865, *Records*; E.A. Paine to Joseph Holt, 10 October 1865, *Records*.

3. *Journal of the House of Representatives of the Commonwealth of Kentucky* (Frankfort, KY: State Printing Office, 1865), 349–350; *Louisville Daily Democrat*, January 28, 1866; *Louisville Weekly Courier* (Louisville, KY), January 31, 1866.

4. *Flakes's Bulletin* (Galveston, TX), February 21, 1866. *Flakes Bulletin* republished the article. The article in the *Frankfort Yeoman* could not be located.

5. *Congressional Globe: Containing the Debates and Proceedings of the First Session of the Thirty-Ninth Congress* (Washington, D.C.: F & J Rives, 1866), Appendix, 269–272.

6. *Public Ledger* (Memphis, TN), May 9, 1867; *Pulaski Citizen* (Pulaski, TN), May 24, 1867.

7. *Nashville Union and Dispatch*, April 13, 1867; *Home Journal* (Winchester, TN), April 27, 1867.

8. *Congressional Globe: Containing the Debates and Proceedings of the Second Session of the Thirty-Ninth Congress* (Washington, D.C.: F & J Rives, 1867), 1388–1390.

9. *Louisville Weekly Courier*, July 24, 1867; *Miscellaneous Documents*, vol. 1, doc. no. 14, *Symes vs. Trimble*.

10. E.A. Paine to John M. Schofield, Secretary of War, 14 February 1869, *Records*; Richard H. Collins, *Collins' Historical Sketches of Kentucky: History of Kentucky* (Covington, KY: Collins & Co., 1874), vol. I, 136, 140–141, 157, 164.

11. *Jersey Journal* (Jersey City, NJ), December 18, 1882; *The Sun* (New York, NY), December 18, 1882; *Inter Ocean* (Chicago), April 21, 1880; *Wisconsin State Journal* (Madison, WI), April 27, 1880; *14th Annual Reunion of the Association of the Graduates of the United States Military Academy*, 73–75; "Pat Thomas Gedcom: Eleazer Arthur Paine," Rootsweb, accessed January 31, 2015, http://wc.rootsweb.ancestry.com/cgi-bin/igm.cgi?op=GET&db=tyrilla&id=I2104; *St. Paul Daily Globe* (St. Paul, MN), May 21, 1893; "Eleazer Arthur Paine," Find A Grave, accessed January 31, 2015, http://www.findagrave.com/. Pat Thomas Gedcom is the great, great, great, great grandnephew of E.A. Paine and has done extensive research on the genealogy of the Paine family. Paine was first buried at what is currently Old Bergen Church Cemetery. His headstone at Oakland Cemetery has been vandalized and now lies level with the earth half buried.

12. *14th Annual Reunion of the Association of the Graduates of the United States Military Academy*, 74–75.

13. Nathaniel Southgate Shaler,

Kentucky: A Pioneer Commonwealth (New York : Houghton, Mifflin, and Company, 1885), 350–351; Zachariah Frederick Smith, *School History of Kentucky, from the earliest Discoveries and Settlements to the end of the year 1888* (Louisville: Courier-Journal Job Printing Co., 1889), 200, 206; Emma M. Connelly, *Story of Kentucky* (Boston: D. Lothrop Co., 1890), 242; Kinkead, *A History of Kentucky*, 199–202; Edward Porter Thompson, *A Young People's History of Kentucky for Schools and General Reading* (St. Louis, MO: A.R. Fleming Publishing, 1897), 262; E. Polk Johnson, *A History of Kentucky and Kentuckians* (Chicago: Lewis Publishing Co., 1912), 372, 393; William Elsey Connelley and Ellis Merton Coulter, *History of Kentucky* (New York: The American Historical Society, 1922), vol. 2, 879–880; Federal Writers' Project of the Work Projects Administration for the State of Kentucky, *Military History of Kentucky, Chronologically Arranged* (Frankfort, KY: State Journal, 1939, 211–212); Lowell H. Harrison, *The Civil War in Kentucky* (Lexington, KY; University Press of Kentucky, 1975), Chapt. 5; Richard G. Stone, *A Brittle Sword: The Kentucky Militia, 1776–1912* (Lexington: University Press of Kentucky, 1977), 73. Thompson was the author of a monumental study on Kentucky's Confederate First Brigade and the Orphan Brigade.

14. Kleber, *The Kentucky Encyclopedia*), 619; Lowell Hayes Harrison, *A New History of Kentucky* (Lexington: University Press of Kentucky, 1997), 206–207; Darrel E. Bigham, *On Jordan's Banks: Emancipation and Its Aftermath in the Ohio River Valley* (Lexington: University Press of Kentucky, 2006), 73; Sutherland, *Savage Conflict*, 223–224; Dan Lee, *The Civil War in the Jackson Purchase, 1861–1862* (Jefferson, NC: McFarland and Company, 2014), 203–206; John Philip Cashon, *Paducah and the Civil War* (Charleston, SC: History Press, 2016), chapter titled "Guerrilla Warfare and the Reign of Terror under General Eleazer Paine"; Neuman, *The Story of Paducah*, 45; D. Trabue Davis, *Story of Mayfield through a Century, 1823–1923* (Paducah, KY: Billings Printing Co., 1923), 15–16; John E.L. Robertson, *Paducah, 1830–1980: A Sesquicentennial History* (Paducah, KY: Image Graphics, 1980), 62–64; John E.L. Robertson, *Paducah: Frontier to the Atomic Age* (Charleston, SC: Arcadia Publishing Co., 2002), 53–54.

15. Barton, "The Reign of Terror in Graves County," 484–495; "Interview with Lon Carter Barton, November 29, 1990," Louie B. Nunn Center for Oral History, University of Kentucky Libraries, accessed February 28, 2015, http://nyx.uky.edu/oh/render.php?cachefile=1990OH306_LEG021_Barton.xml; *Murray Ledger Times* (Murray, KY), March 31, 2006.

16. *Paducah News-Democrat*, February 15, 1903.

17. John Allison, ed., *Notable Men of Tennessee: Personal and Genealogical, with Portraits* (Atlanta: Southern Historical Association, 1905), vol. 2, 45–51; Mary Wooldridge Latham, *Mrs. T. J. Latham's Refutation of H. A. Tyler's Charges* (Memphis: Wills & Crumpton printers, 1907), 28–35; "United Daughters of the Confederacy: Annual Convention at Montgomery, Ala.," *Confederate Veteran* 8, no. 12 (December, 1900): 521–523. Mrs. Latham claimed that President Lincoln had been a hired laborer on her father's farm in Kentucky and that she often road upon his shoulders as a little girl. It was this early personal relationship, she declared, that gained her access to the president who granted her request to have Paine removed from Paducah and the exiles returned home. All, of course, were completely fabricated by Mrs. Latham.

18. "Forrest's Men to Meet at Memphis," *Confederate Veteran* 14, no. 10 (October, 1906): 441; *Evening Star* (Washington, DC), July 22, 1907. Also referred to as the Latham-Tyler Controversy.

19. *Hickman Courier*, July 19 and 26 and August 16, 1907; *Evening Star* (Washington, DC), July 22, 1907; Henry Ashburn Tyler, *A Review of the Tyler-Latham Controversy* (Memphis: privately printed, [1907]), 25–31. It is interesting to note that General Tyler wrote in his review of the controversy that Mrs. Tyler frequently told a tale that "President Abraham Lincoln was a hired laborer upon her father's farm in Kentucky, and often carried her around upon his shoulders, and upon her reminding him of this early intimacy and acquaintance, he granted her request and had Gen. Payne removed."

20. *Paducah Evening Sun*, July 24 and 27, 1907; *Paducah Daily Register*, July 26, 1907. Josephine Horne Overall was the daughter of T.M. Horne, Sarah L. Malone Breyard was the daughter of W.G. Malone and Joseph L. Rollston the son Mary Jane Rollston.

21. *Ibid.*; *Evening Star* (Washington, DC), July 22, 1907.

22. *Mayfield Messenger*, October 4, 1932; "Henry Bascom Hicks," Find A Grave, accessed February 16, 2015, http://www.findagrave.com/. Robert's brother James Andrew Wright pointed out to the author of the *Messenger* article where the bodies of Hicks and Johnson were first buried. It is interesting to note Hicks was shot on August 30, 1864 and Johnson on August 24, 1864. One could also question whether the body reinterred at Maplewood Cemetery was Johnson's rather than Hicks.'

23. "Jeff Davis Toast Won a Guerrilla Yankee Mercy," *Louisville Courier-Journal Sunday Magazine*, June 15, 1941.

24. Paul Twitchell, "Kentucky Lovers in Exile," *Louisville Courier-Journal Sunday Magazine*, January 18, 1942.

25. W. Craig Gaines, *Encyclopedia of Civil War Shipwrecks* (Baton Rouge: LA: Louisiana State University Press, 2008), 162.

26. "Outlaws Before the World: The Story of General Orders Number Eleven: also known as The Jewish Eviction of Paducah," Market House Museum, accessed February 21, 2015, http://www.markethousemuseum.com/node/178; "Mayfield," Graves County Government, accessed February 21, 2015, http://www.gravescountyky.com/Mayfield.html. Lon Carter Barton taught at Mayfield High School for over three decades and some his former students are teachers today retelling his version of the "reign of terror."

Epilogue

1. *The Reports of the Committees of the House of Representatives made during the Second Session Thirty-eighth Congress, 1864–65* (Washington, D.C.: Government Printing Office, 1865), Report No. 29; *Congressional Globe: Containing the Debates and Proceedings of the Second Session of the Thirty-Eighth Congress, Also, of the Special Session of the Senate* (Washington, D.C.: F & J Rives, 1865), 1411–1412; *Daily Ohio Statesman* (Columbus, OH), March 30, 1865; Battle, Perrin and Kniffen, *Kentucky*, pt. II, 220.

2. *Kentucky Opinions containing the Unreported Opinions of the Court of Appeals* (Lexington, KY: Central Law Book Company, 1906), 62–64; *Hickman Courier*, August 1, 1879; *The South Kentuckian* (Hopkinsville, KY), March 21, 1882; *Hickman Courier*, June 10, 1887; "Obituary," *The Hub* (New York, NY), 36 (March, 1895): 925; *Hickman Courier*, August 12, 1892.

3. *Biographical Dictionary: Kansas Volume* (Chicago: S. Lewis & Co. Publishers, 1879), 276–278; *Los Angeles Daily Herald*, October 5, 1887; *Daily Alta California* (San Francisco, CA), November 29, 1889.

4. Dennis W. Belcher, *The 10th Kentucky Volunteer Infantry in the Civil War* (Jefferson, NC: McFarland & Company, 2009), 56; Benjamin

Perley Poore, *The Political Register and Congressional Directory: A Statistical Record of the Federal Officials, Legislative, Executive and Judicial, of the United States of America, 1776–1878* (Boston: Houghton, Osgood and Company, 1878), 272–273; "Barry, Henry W.," Biographical Directory of the United States Congress, accessed February 3, 2015, http://bioguide.congress.gov/.

5. Alfred Theodore Andreas, *History of Chicago: From 1857 until the Fire of 1871* (Chicago: A.T. Andreas Co., 1885), 545; Jason Emerson, *The Madness of Mary Lincoln* (Carbondale: Southern Illinois University Press, 2007), 40–60; Egbert Cleave, *Cleave's Biographical Cyclopaedia of Homeopathic Physicians and Surgeons* (Philadelphia: Galaxy Publishing Company, 1893), 90; Louis Frederick Frank, *The Medical History of Milwaukee: 1834–1914* (Milwaukee: Germania Publishing Company, 1915), 60–61.

6. *Chicago Tribune*, April 20, 1865 and April 22, 1865; *Troy Daily Times* (Troy, NY), May 28, 1885.

7. Warner, *Generals in Blue*, 163–164; Jack D. Welsh, *Medical Histories of Union Generals* (Kent, OH: Kent State University Press, 1996), 121–122; Hamilton Tapp and James C. Klotter, *Kentucky: Decades of Discord, 1865–1900* (Frankfort, KY: Kentucky Historical Society, 1977), 215, 239; *Acts of the General Assembly of the Commonwealth of Kentucky* (Frankfort, KY: E. Polk Johnson Public Printer, 1890), vol. 2, 776–777.

8. McAfee, *Kentucky Politicians*, 32–35; J. Stoddard Johnson, *Memorial History of Louisville from Its First Settlement to the Year 1896* (Chicago: American Biographical Pub. Co., 1896), 611–613.

9. Warner, *Generals in Blue*, 319–320; *History of Wayne County, Indiana* (Chicago: Inter-state Publishing Company, 1884), vol. I, 663–666; Andrew W. Young, *History of Wayne County, Indiana, from Its Settlement to the Present Time* (Cincinnati, OH: Robert Clark & Company, 1872), 112–113.

10. Victor B. Howard, *Black Liberation in Kentucky: Emancipation and Freedom, 1862–1884* (Lexington: University Press of Kentucky, 1983), 88–94; John E. Kleber, *Encyclopedia of Louisville* (Lexington: University Press of Kentucky, 2001), 722–723.

11. "Trimble, Lawrence Strother," Biographical Directory of the United States Congress, accessed February 6, 2015, http://bioguide.congress.gov/; *Paducah Sun*, September 24, 1904; L. Bradford Prince, *A Concise History of New Mexico* (Cedar Rapids, IA: Torch Press, 1912), 234–235.

Works Cited

Archives

Abraham Lincoln Papers. Washington, D.C.: Manuscripts Division, Library of Congress.

Active Militia Records—Capital Guards, North Cumberland Btn., and Three Forks Btn., Box 76, Folder 864 1st Regt. Capital Guards Paducah Bn. Logistics, Kentucky Department of Military Affairs. Frankfort: Kentucky Historical Society.

Adjutant General Letter Book—No. 3; 9 April-25 May 1864, Kentucky Department of Military Affairs. Frankfort: Kentucky Historical Society.

Alice Williamson Diary. Durham, NC: Manuscript Division, Perkins Library, Duke University.

Andrew Lucas Hunt Papers. Chapel Hill: University of North Carolina.

Excerpts from the Journal of Sergeant Eugene B. Read. July 13, 2012. Murray, KY: Murray State University, Forrest Pogue Library.

Fyfe Family Papers. Ann Arbor: University of Michigan, Bentley Historical Library.

General Robert H. Milroy Papers. Rensselaer, IN: Jasper County Public Library.

Governor Thomas E. Bramlette Papers. Frankfort: Kentucky Department of Library and Archives.

Guerilla Letters, Document Box 1, Folder G. L. 1864. Affairs, Kentucky Department of Military. Frankfort: Kentucky Historical Society.

Letters Received by the Commission Branch of the Adjutants General's Office, 1863-1879, Microfilm Publication M1064. Washington, D.C.: National Archives Record Administration.

Letters Received by the Office of the Adjutant General (Main Series), 1861-1870, RG94, M619, Roll 242, File 1394 B 1864. Washington, D.C.: National Archives and Records Administration.

Lyman Trumbull Papers. Washington, D.C.: Manuscripts Division, Library of Congress.

New York National Zouaves at Fort Monroe, 10th Infantry Regiment New York Civil War Newspaper Clippings. New York State Military Museum and Veterans Research Center.

Norville Hardie Revelle Letters. Louisville, KY: Filson Historical Society.

Office of the Governor, Beriah Magoffin: Governor's Official Correspondence File, Requisitions for the Return of Fugitives from Justice, 1859-1861. Frankfort: Kentucky Department for Libraries and Archives.

Office of the Governor, Thomas E. Bramlette: Governor's Official Correspondence File, Military Correspondence, 1863-1867. Frankfort: Kentucky Department for Libraries and Archives.

Paducah City Council Minutes, Records of the City Council of Paducah, 1860-1870, MF242. Paducah, KY: McCracken County Public Library.

Papers and Diaries of Solomon Meredith and Family. Indianapolis, IN : Indiana Historical Society,

Records of the Judge Advocate General's Office (Army), Entry 15, Court-Martial Case Files, 1809-1894, RG153, File No. MM1609, Boxes 1032-1033. Washington, D.C.: National Archives and Records Administration.

Returns from U.S. Military Posts, 1806-1916, RG94, M617, Roll 895. Washington, D.C.: National Archives and Records Administration.

Scrapbook, United Daughters of the Confederacy, Graves County Chapter Records, MS03-01, 1917-1919. Murray, KY: Murray State University, Pogue Library.

Solomon Meredith Papers. Indianapolis: Indiana Historical Society.

Yates Family Papers. Springfield, IL: Abraham Lincoln Presidential Library.

Newspapers

Baltimore Sun
Cairo Morning News
Chattanooga Daily Gazette
Chicago Tribune
Cincinnati Daily Enquirer
Cleveland Morning Leader
Cleveland Paine Dealer
The Crisis (Columbus, OH)
Daily Alta California (San Francisco, CA)
Daily Constitutional Union (Washington, D.C.)
Daily Dispatch (Richmond, VA)
Daily Illinois State Journal (Springfield, IL)
Daily Louisville Democrat
Daily Louisville Democrat
Daily Missouri Democrat (St. Louis, MO)
Daily Missouri Republican (Saint Louis, MO)
Daily Ohio Statesman (Columbus, OH)
Daily Patriot (Madison, WI)
Daily True Delta (New Orleans, LA)
Dayton Journal
Evansville Daily Journal
Evening Star (Washington, D.C.)
Evening Union (Washington, D.C.)
Federal Union (Paducah, KY)

Flakes's Bulletin (Galveston, TX)
Frankfort Commonwealth
Frankfort Yeoman
Hickman Courier
Home Journal (Winchester, TN)
The Hub (New York, NY)
Inter Ocean (Chicago, IL)
Jersey Journal (Jersey City, NJ)
Los Angeles Daily Herald
Louisville Courier-Journal
Louisville Daily Democrat
Louisville Daily Journal
Louisville Press
Louisville Weekly Courier
Louisville Weekly Journal
Macon Daily Telegraph
Mayfield Messenger
Memphis Daily Appeal
Milwaukee Daily Sentinel
Missouri Democrat (St. Louis, MO)
Monmouth Atlas
Monmouth Review
Morning Louisville Democrat
Murray Ledger Times
Nashville Union and Dispatch
National Unionist (Lexington, KY)
New Orleans Picayune
New York Herald
New York Times
Omaha World Herald
Ottawa Free Trader
Paducah Daily Register
Paducah Evening Sun
Paducah News-Democrat
Paducah Sun
Paducah Sun-Democrat
Philadelphia Inquirer
Public Ledger (Memphis, TN)
Public Ledger (Philadelphia, PA)
Pulaski Citizen (Pulaski, TN)
Richmond Weekly Telegram (Richmond, IN)
St. Louis Republican
The South Kentuckian (Hopkinsville, KY)
The Sun (New York, NY)
Sycamore True Republican (Sycamore, IL)
Troy Daily Times (Troy, NY)
War Eagle (Cairo, IL)
Weekly Patriot and Union (Harrisburg, PA)
Weekly Wisconsin Patriot (Madison, WI)
Wisconsin Daily Patriot (Madison, WI)
Wisconsin State Journal (Madison, WI)

Primary Sources

Acts of the General Assembly of the Commonwealth of Kentucky. Frankfort, KY: Wm. E. Hughes, State Printer, 1864.

Acts of the General Assembly of the Commonwealth of Kentucky. Frankfort, KY: E. Polk Johnson Public Printer, 1890

American Annual Cyclopaedia and Register of Important Events of the Year. New York: D. Appleton & Co., 1864.

Annual Report of the Adjutant General of the State of New York for the Year 1899. Albany, NY: James B. Lyon State Printer, 1900.

Campbell, John Quincy Adams. *The Union Must Stand: The Civil War Diary of John Quincy Adams Campbell, Fifth Iowa Volunteer Infantry.* Knoxville: University Press of Tennessee, 2000.

Congressional Globe: Containing the Debates and Proceedings of the First Session of the Thirty-Ninth Congress. Washington, D.C.: F & J Rives, 1866.

Congressional Globe: Containing the Debates and Proceedings of the Second Session of the Thirty-Eighth Congress, Also, of the Special Session of the Senate. Washington, D.C.: F & J Rives, 1865.

Congressional Globe: Containing the Debates and Proceedings of the Second Session of the Thirty-Ninth Congress. Washington, D.C.: F & J Rives, 1867.

Congressional Globe: Official Proceedings of Congress, 38th Congress, 2nd Session. Washington, D.C.: F & J Rives, 1864.

Congressional Globe: The Debates and Proceedings of the Second Session of the Thirty-Eighth Congress, 38th Congress Also, of the Special Session of the Senate. Washington, D.C.: F & J Rives, 1865.

Congressional Record, First Session, Forty-Fifth Congress. Washington, D.C.: Government Printing Office, 1877.

DeRosier, Jr., Arthur H. *Through the South with a Union Soldier.* Johnson City, TN: East Tennessee State University Research Advisory Council, 1969.

Digest of Election Cases: Cases of Contested Election in the House of Representatives from 1865 to 1871. Washington, D.C.: Government Printing Office, 1870.

Documents of the Assembly of the State of New York, Eighty Ninth Session. Albany, NY: C. Wendell Legislative Printer, 1866.

14th Annual Reunion of the Association of the Graduates of the United States Military Academy at West Point, New York, June 12, 1883. East Saginaw, MI: Courier Printing Co., 1883.

General Orders, Adjutant General's Office for 1863 with an Index. Washington, D.C.: Government Printing Office, 1864.

Graf, Leroy P., and Ralph W. Haskins. *The Papers of Andrew Johnson.* Knoxville: University Press of Tennessee, 1983.

Griffin, Russell B. "The Military Telegrapher in the Civil War." *Telegraph Age*, 1909: 787.

Hewitt, Janet B. *Supplement to the Official Records of the Union and Confederate Armies.* Wilmington, NC: Broadfoot Publishing Co., 1994–2001.

Journal of the Adjourned Session of 1863-4 of the House of Representatives of the Commonwealth of Kentucky. Frankfort, KY: State Printing Office, 1865.

Journal of the House of Representatives of the Commonwealth of Kentucky. Frankfort, KY: State Printing Office, 1865.

Journal of the House of Representatives of the United States of America Being the Second Session of the Thirty-Eighth Congress. Washington, D.C.: Government Printing Office, 1865.

Journal of the Senate of the United States of America Being the Second Session of the Forty-Fourth Congress. Washington, D.C.: Government Printing Office, 1876.

Journal of the United States Senate of the United States of America Being the Second Session of the Thirty-Eighth Congress. Washington, D.C.: Government Printing Office, 1864.

Kentucky Opinions Containing the Unreported Opinions

of the Court of Appeals. Lexington, KY: Central Law Book Company, 1906.

Langstaff, George Q. *The Life and Times of Quintus Quincy Quigley, 1828–1910: His Personal Journal 1859–1908*. Brentwood, TN: Talent Group, 1999.

Latham, Mary Wooldridge. *Mrs. T. J. Latham's Refutation of H. A. Tyler's Charges*. Memphis: Wills & Crumpton printers, 1907.

Letters of the Secretary of War. Washington, D.C.: Government Printing Office, 1865.

Lynn, Stephen Douglas. *Confederate Pensioners of Kentucky: Pension Applications of the Veterans and Widows*. Baltimore: Gateway Press, Inc., 2000.

McCormick, Thomas J. *Memoirs of Gustave Koerner, 1809–1896*. Cedar Rapids, IA: Torch Press, 1909.

Military Order of the Loyal Legion of the United States. *Personal Narratives of Events in the War of the Rebellion, Being Papers Read Before the Rhode Island Soldiers and Sailors Historical Society*. Wilmington, NC: Broadfoot Publishing Co., 1993.

_____. *War Papers: Being Papers Read Before the Commandery of the District of Columbia, Military Order of the Loyal Legion of the United States*. Wilmington, NC: Broadfoot Publishing Co., 1993.

_____. *War Papers: Being Papers Read Before the Commandery of the State of Wisconsin, Military Order of the Loyal Legion of the United States*. Wilmington, NC: Broadfoot Publishing Co., 1993.

Minutes of the Annual Conference of the Methodist Episcopal Church, South, 1858–1865. Nashville, TN: Southern Methodist Publishing House, 1859–1870.

Miscellaneous Documents of the House of Representatives for the Second Session of the Fortieth Congress, 1867–1868. Washington, D.C.: Government Printing Office, 1868.

Official Army Register of the Volunteer Force of the United States Army for the Years 1861–1865. Washington, D.C.: Adjutant-General's Office, 1865.

Official Proceedings of the Democratic National Convention. Chicago: Times Steam Book and Job Printing House, 1864.

Official Records of the Union and Confederate Navies in the War of the Rebellion. Washington, D.C.: Government Printing Office, 1894–1922.

Plum, William R. *The Military Telegraph During the Civil War in the United States*. Chicago: Jansen, McClurg & Co., 1882.

Rebellion Record: A Diary of American Events. New York: Arno Press, 1977.

Report of the Adjutant General of the State of Illinois. Springfield, IL: Journal Company, Printers and Binders, 1867.

Report of the Adjutant General of the State of Kentucky. Frankfort, KY: John H. Harney, Public Printer, 1867.

Report of the Adjutant General of the State of Kentucky, Confederate Volunteers, War 1861–65. Owensboro, KY: McDowell Publications, 1979.

Reports of Committees of the House of Representatives for the First Session of the Fifty-First Congress, 1889–1890. Washington, D.C.: Government Printing Office, 1891.

Reports of Committees of the House of Representatives for the First Session of the Fifty-Second Congress, 1889–1890. Washington, D.C.: Government Printing Office, 1892.

Reports of Committees of the House of Representatives for the Second Session of the Fifty-Third Congress, 1893–1894. Washington, D.C.: Government Printing Office, 1894.

Reports of Committees of the Senate of the United States for the First Session of the Forty-Fourth Congress, 1875–1876. Washington, D.C.: Government Printing Office, 1876.

Reports of Committees of the Senate of the United States for the First Session of the Forty-Fourth Congress, 1875–1876. Government Printing Office: Washington, D.C., 1876.

Reports of Committees of the Senate of the United States for the Second Session of the Forty-Second Congress, 1871–1872. Washington, D.C.: Government Printing Office, 1876.

Reports of Committees of the Senate of the United States for the Third Session of the Forty-Second Congress, 1872–1873. Washington, D.C.: Government Printing Office, 1872.

Reports of the Committees of the House of Representatives Made During the Second Session Thirty-Eighth Congress, 1864–1865. Washington, D.C.: Government Printing Office, 1865.

Reports of the Committees of the Senate of the United States for the Second Session of the Forty-First Congress, 1869–1870. Washington, D.C.: Government Printing Office, 1870.

Senate Documents. Washington, D.C.: Government Printing Office, 1914.

Simon, John Y. *The Papers of Ulysses S. Grant*. Carbondale: Southern Illinois University Press, 1967.

Slater, Edward C. *The Nation's Loss: A Sermon Upon the Death of Abraham Lincoln, Sixteenth President of the United States*. Paducah, KY: Blelock & Co., 1865.

Tyler, Henry Ashburn. *A Review of the Tyler-Latham Controversy*. Memphis: privately printed, [1907].

Ullrich, Dieter C. "Civil War Diary of Private Hawley V. Needham, 134th Illinois Volunteer Infantry Regiment, June 10 to October 2, 1864." *Journal of the Jackson Purchase Historical Society*, 2016: 144–195.

U.S. War Department. *The War of the Rebellion: A Compilation of the Official Records of the Union and Confederate Armies*. Washington, D.C.: Government Printing Office, 1880–1901.

Secondary Sources

Allison, John. *Notable Men of Tennessee: Personal and Genealogical, with Portraits*. Atlanta: Southern Historical Association, 1905.

Andreas, Alfred Theodore. *History of Chicago: From 1857 Until the Fire of 1871*. Chicago: A.T. Andreas Co., 1885.

Bahde, Thomas. "Our Cause Is a Common One: Home Guards, Union Leagues, and Republican Citizenship in Illinois, 1861–1863." *Civil War History*, 2010: 66–98.

Barton, Lon Carter. "The Reign of Terror in Graves County." *Register of the Kentucky Historical Society*, 1948: 490–91.

Bateman, Newton, and Paul Selby. *Historical Encyclopedia of Illinois*. Chicago: Munsell Publishing Company, 1916.

Battle, J.H., W.H. Perrin, and G.C. Kniffen. *Kentucky: A History of the State, 1st Ed*. Louisville, KY: F.A. Battey Publishing Co., 1885.

Works Cited

Behrens, Robert H. *From Salt Fork to Chickamauga: Champaign County Soldiers in the Civil War.* Urbana, IL: Urbana Free Library, 1988.

Belcher, Dennis W. *The 10th Kentucky Volunteer Infantry in the Civil War.* Jefferson, NC: McFarland, 2009.

Benet, S.V. *A Treatise on Military Law and the Practice of Courts-Martial.* New York: D. Van Nostrand, 1864.

Berlin, Ira. *The Black Military Experience.* New York: Cambridge University Press, 1982.

_____. *Wartime Genesis of Free Labor: The Upper South.* New York: Cambridge University Press, 1993.

Bigham, Darrel E. *On Jordan's Banks: Emancipation and Its Aftermath in the Ohio River Valley.* Lexington: University Press of Kentucky, 2006.

Biographical Dictionary: Kansas Volume. Chicago: S. Lewis & Co. Publishers, 1879.

Biographical Sketch of the Hon. Lazarus W. Powell (Of Henderson, Ky.), Governor of the State of Kentucky from 1851–1855, Senator in Congress from 1859–1865. Frankfort: Kentucky Yeoman Office, 1868.

Birkhimer, William E. *Military Government and Martial Law, 2nd Ed.* Kansas City: Franklin Hudson Publishing Co., 1904.

Boyle, John. *Boyle Genealogy: John Boyle of Virginia and Kentucky.* St. Louis, MO: Perrin & Smith Printing Co., 1909.

Cashon, John Philip. *Paducah and the Civil War.* Charleston, SC: History Press, 2016.

Civil War Centennial Commission of Tennessee. *Tennesseans in the Civil War: A Military History of Confederate and Union Units with Available Rosters of Personnel.* Nashville, TN: Civil War Centennial Commission, 1965.

Cleave, Egbert. *Cleave's Biographical Cyclopaedia of Homoeopathic Physicians and Surgeons.* Philadelphia: Galaxy Publishing Company, 1893.

Cole, Arthur Charles. *The Centennial History of Illinois: The Era of the Civil War, 1848–1870.* Springfield IL: Illinois Centennial Commission, 1919.

Collins, Richard H. *Collins' Historical Sketches of Kentucky: History of Kentucky.* Covington, KY: Collins & Co., 1874.

Comey, Henry Newton. *A Legacy of Honor: The Memoirs and Letters of Captain, 2nd Massachusetts Infantry.* Knoxville: University Press of Tennessee, 2004.

Connelley, William Elsey, and Ellis Merton Coulter. *History of Kentucky.* New York: The American Historical Society, 1922.

Connelly, Emma M. *Story of Kentucky.* Boston: D. Lothrop Co., 1890.

Coulter, E. Merton. *The Civil War and Readjustment in Kentucky.* Chapel Hill: University of North Carolina Press, 1926.

Cowtan, Charles W. *Services of the Tenth New York Volunteers (National Zouaves) in the War of the Rebellion.* New York: Charles H. Ludwig Publisher, 1882.

Cozzens, Peter. "Roadblock on the Mississippi." *Civil War Times Illustrated,* 2002: 429–459.

Craig, Berry. *Hidden History of Kentucky in the Civil War.* Charleston, S.C.: The History Press, 2010.

_____. "Jackson Purchase Confederate Troops in the Civil War." *Journal of the Jackson Purchase Historical Society,* 1974: 5.

_____. "The Jackson Purchase Considers Secession: The Mayfield Convention." *Register of the Kentucky Historical Society,* 2001: 339–361.

_____. *Kentucky Confederates: Secession, Civil War, and the Jackson Purchase.* Lexington: University Press of Kentucky, 2014.

Craig, Berry, and Dieter C. Ullrich. *Unconditional Unionist: The Hazardous Life of Lucian Anderson, Kentucky Congressman.* Jefferson, NC: McFarland, 2016.

Cullum, George W. *Biographical Register of the Officers and Graduates of the U.S. Military Academy at West Point, N.Y. from Its Establishment in 1802 to 1890.* Boston: Houghton, Mifflin and Co., 1891.

Currey, J. Seymour. *Chicago: Its History and Its Builders: A Century of Marvelous Growth.* Chicago: S.J. Clark Publishing Co., 1912.

Daniel, Larry J., and Lynn N. Bock. *Island No. 10: Struggle for the Mississippi Valley.* Tuscaloosa: University of Alabama Press, 1996.

Davis, D. Trabue. *Story of Mayfield Through a Century, 1823–1923.* Paducah, KY: Billings Printing Co., 1923.

Durham, Walter D. *Rebellion Revisited: A History of Sumner County, Tennessee from 1861 to 1870.* Nashville, TN: Parthenon Press, 1982.

Dyer, Frederick H. *A Compendium of the War of the Rebellion.* Des Moines, IA: Dyer Publishing Company, 1908.

Eddy, Thomas Mears. *The Patriotism of Illinois.* Clark & Company: Chicago, 1865.

Eicher, David J. *The Longest Night: A Military History of the Civil War.* New York: Simon & Schuster, 2001.

Eicher, John H., and David J. Eicher. *Civil War High Commands.* Stanford, CA: Stanford University Press, 2011.

Emerson, Jason. *The Madness of Mary Lincoln.* Carbondale: Southern Illinois University Press, 2007.

Federal Writers' Project of the Work Projects Administration for the State of Kentucky, Military History of Kentucky, Chronologically Arranged. Frankfort, KY: State Journal, 1939.

Fleharty, S.F. *Our Regiment: A History of the 102d Illinois Infantry Volunteers.* Chicago: Brewster & Hanscom, 1865.

"Forrest's Men to Meet at Memphis." *Confederate Veteran,* 1906: 441.

Forrester, Rebel C. *Glory and Tears: Obion County, Tennessee, 1860–1870.* Union City, TN: H.A. Lanzer Co., 1970.

Fox, Henry Clay. *Memoirs of Wayne County and the City of Richmond, Indiana.* Madison, WI: Western Historical Association, 1912.

Frank, Louis Frederick. *The Medical History of Milwaukee: 1834–1914.* Milwaukee: Germania Publishing Company, 1915.

Gaines, W. Craig. *Encyclopedia of Civil War Shipwrecks.* Baton Rouge: LA: Louisiana State University Press, 2008.

George, Henry. *History of the 3d, 7th, 8th and 12th Kentucky C.S.A.* Louisville, KY: C.T. Dearing, 1911.

Guide to the Records of the U.S. House of Representatives at the National Archives, 1789–1989 Record Group 233. College Park, MD: National Archives and Records Administration, [1999].

Hackemer, Kurt H. *To Rescue My Native Land: The*

Civil War Letters of William T. Shepherd, First Illinois Light Artillery. Knoxville: University Press of Tennessee, 2005.

Halleck, H.W. *International Law; Or, Rules Regulating the Intercourse of States in Peace and War.* New York: D. Van Nostrand, 1861.

Harrison, Lowell H. *The Civil War in Kentucky.* Lexington: University Press of Kentucky, 1975.

Heady, Peyton. *Union County, Kentucky in the Civil War, 1861–1865.* Morganfield, KY: Peyton Heady, 1985.

Heidler, David Stephen. *Encyclopedia of the American Civil War: A Political, Social and Military History.* Santa Barbara, CA: ABC-CLIO, 2000.

Hewett, Janet B. *The Roster of Union Soldiers, 1861–1865.* Wilmington, NC: Broadfoot Publishing Co., 2000.

History of Union County, Kentucky. Evansville, IN: Courier Co., 1886.

History of Wayne County, Indiana. Chicago: Inter-state Publishing Company, 1884.

Hoskins, Patricia Ann. "The Freedmen's Bureau in the Jackson Purchase Region of Kentucky, 1866–1868." *Register of the Kentucky Historical Society,* 2012: 503–531.

_____. *The Old First Is with the South: The Civil War, Reconstruction, and Memory in the Jackson Purchase Region of Kentucky* (PhD Diss.). Auburn, AL: Auburn University, 2008.

Howard, Victor B. *Black Liberation in Kentucky: Emancipation and Freedom, 1862–1884.* Lexington: University Press of Kentucky, 1983.

Hubbell, John T. *Biographical Dictionary of the Union: Northern Leaders of the Civil War.* Westport, CT: Greenwood Press, 1995.

"Jeff Davis Toast Won a Guerrilla Yankee Mercy." *Louisville Courier-Journal Sunday Magazine,* June 15, 1941.

Jewell, Virginia. *Lick Skillet and Other Tales of Hickman County.* Union City, TN: Lanzer Printing Co., 1986.

Johnson, E. Polk. *A History of Kentucky and Kentuckians.* Chicago: Lewis Publishing Co., 1912.

Johnson, J. Stoddard. *Memorial History of Louisville from Its First Settlement to the Year 1896.* Chicago: American Biographical Pub. Co., 1896.

Kentucky Writers' Project. *Union County Past and Present.* Louisville, KY: Schuhmann Printing Co., 1941.

Kinkead, Elizabeth Shelby. *A History of Kentucky.* New York: American Book Co., 1896.

_____. *A History of Kentucky.* New York: American Book Co., 1909.

Kirkland, Frazar. *The Pictorial Book of Anecdotes and Incidents of the War of the Rebellion.* Toledo, OH: W.E. Bliss & Co., 1873.

Kleber, John E. *Encyclopedia of Louisville.* Lexington: University Press of Kentucky, 2001.

_____. *Kentucky Encyclopedia.* Lexington: University Press of Kentucky, 1992.

Klotter, James C. *A New History of Kentucky.* Lexington: University Press of Kentucky, 1997.

Lee, Dan. *The Civil War in the Jackson Purchase, 1861–1862.* Jefferson, NC: McFarland, 2014.

Levin, H. *Lawyers and Lawmakers of Kentucky.* Chicago: Lewis Publishing Co., 1897.

Lucas, Marion B. "Camp Nelson, Kentucky, During the Civil War: Cradle of Liberty or Refugee Death Camp?" *Filson Club History Quarterly,* 1989: 439–452.

Manning, Martin J., and Clarence R. Wyatt. *Encyclopedia of Media and Propaganda in Wartime.* Santa Barbara, CA: ABC-CLIO, 2011.

McAfee, John J. *Kentucky Politicians: Sketches of Representative Corn-Carckers.* Louisville, KY: Courier-Journal Job Printing Company, 1886.

Mesch, Allen H. *Teacher of Civil War Generals: Major General Charles Ferguson Smith, Soldier and West Point Commandant.* Jefferson, NC: McFarland, 2015.

Monmouth College During the War of the Rebellion. Monmouth, IL: Monmouth College Oracle, 1911.

Morris, Marion. *A History of the Ninth Regiment Illinois Volunteer Infantry.* Monmouth, IL: John S. Clark, 1864.

Neuman, Fred G. *Paducahans in History.* Paducah, KY: Young Printing Company, 1922.

_____. *The Story of Paducah.* Paducah, KY: Young Printing Company, 1927.

Noyas, Jonathon A. *"My Will Is Absolute Law": A Biography of Union General Robert H. Milroy.* Jefferson, NC: McFarland, 2006.

Paine, E.A. *Military Instructions: Designed for the Militia and Volunteers with Particular Directions to Commissioned Officers, Respecting Their Duties at the Officer Musters.* Painesville, OH: Office of the Northern Ohio Freeman, 1843.

Phelps, Oliver Seymour. *The Phelps Family of America.* Pittsfield, MA: Eagle Publishing Co., 1899.

Poore, Benjamin Perley. *The Political Register and Congressional Directory: A Statistical Record of the Federal Officials, Legislative, Executive and Judicial, of the United States of America, 1776–1878.* Boston: Houghton, Osgood and Company, 1878.

Prince, L. Bradford. *A Concise History of New Mexico.* Cedar Rapids, IA: Torch Press, 1912.

Raab, James W. *Confederate General Lloyd Tilghman: A Biography.* Jefferson, NC: McFarland, 2006.

Record, Pat. *Graves County, Ky. Census of 1860.* Melber, KY: Simons Historical Publications, 1979.

Rennolds, Edwin H. *A History of the Henry County Commands Which Served in the Confederate States Army.* Kennesaw, GA: Continental Book Co., 1961.

Robertson, John. *Michigan in the War, Revised Ed.* Lansing, MI: W.S. George & Co., State Printers and Binders, 1882.

Robertson, John E.L. *Paducah, 1830–1980: A Sesquicentennial History.* Paducah, KY: Image Graphics, 1980.

_____. *Paducah: Frontier to the Atomic Age.* Charleston, SC: Arcadia Press, 2002.

Shaler, Nathaniel Southgate. *Kentucky: A Pioneer Commonwealth.* New York: Houghton, Mifflin, and Company, 1885.

Sifakis, Stewart. *Who Was Who in the Civil War.* New York: Facts on File Pub., 1988.

Simmons, Don. *1850 Census of McCracken County, Kentucky.* Murray, KY: Don Simmons Press, 1974.

_____. *1850 Census of McCracken County, Kentucky.* Murray, KY: Don Simmons Press, 1974.

_____. *Hickman County, Kentucky Census of 1860.* Melber, KY: Simmons Historical Publications, 1987.

Smith, George Washington. *A History of Southern Illinois: A Narrative Account of Its Historical Progress, Its People, and Its Principle Interests.* Lewis Publishing Company: Chicago, 1912.

Smith, Zachariah Frederick. *School History of Kentucky, from the Earliest Discoveries and Settlements to the End of the Year 1888*. Louisville, KY: Courier-Journal Job Printing Co., 1889.

Southern Bivouac. Wilmington, NC: Broadfoot Publishing Co., 1992.

Sparks, Edwin Erle. *Collections of the Illinois State Historical Library: Lincoln Series*. Springfield, IL: Illinois State Historical Library, 1908.

Speed, Thomas. *Union Regiments of Kentucky*. Louisville, KY: Courier-Journal Printing Co., 1897.

Stone, Richard G. *A Brittle Sword: The Kentucky Militia, 1776–1912*. Lexington: University Press of Kentucky, 1977.

Sutherland, Daniel E. *A Savage Conflict: The Decisive Role of Guerrillas in the American Civil War*. Chapel Hill: University of North Carolina Press, 2009.

Tapp, Hamilton, and James C. Klotter. *Kentucky: Decades of Discord, 1865–1900*. Frankfort: Kentucky Historical Society, 1977.

Thompson, Edward Porter. *A Young People's History of Kentucky for Schools and General Reading*. St. Louis, MO: A.R. Fleming Publishing, 1897.

Twitchell, Paul. "Kentucky Lovers in Exile." *Louisville Courier-Journal Sunday Magazine*, January 18, 1942.

"United Daughters of the Confederacy: Annual Convention at Montgomery, Ala." *Confederate Veteran*, 1900: 521–523.

United States Military Academy. *Register of the Officers and Cadets of the U.S. Military Academy*. West Point, NY: United States Military Academy Printing Office, June, 1839.

Unites States Military Academy. *14th Annual Reunion of the Association of the Graduates of the United States Military Academy at West Point, New York, June 12, 1883*. East Saginaw, MI: Courier Printing Co., 1883.

Upton, Harriet Taylor. *History of the Western Reserve*. Chicago: Lewis Publishing Co., 1910.

Urban, William. "The Temperance Movement in Monmouth, 1857–1859." *Western Illinois Regional Studies*, 1990: 32–45.

Warner, Ezra J. *Generals in Blue: Lives of the Union Commanders*. Baton Rouge: Louisiana State University Press, 1964.

Welsh, Jack D. *Medical Histories of Union Generals*. Kent, OH: Kent State University Press, 1996.

Wilson, James Grant. *Biographical Sketches of Illinois Officers Engaged in the War Against the Rebellion of 1861*. Chicago: James Barnet, 1862,

Wright, Steven L. *Kentucky Soldiers and Their Regiments in the Civil War: Abstracts from the Pages of Contemporary Kentucky Newspapers*. Utica, KY: McDowell Publications, 2009.

Young, Andrew W. *History of Wayne County, Indiana, from Its Settlement to the Present Time*. Cincinnati, OH: Robert Clark & Company, 1872.

Websites

American Presidency Project. *Proclamation 113—Declaring Martial Law and a Further Suspension of the Writ of Habeas Corpus in Kentucky*. http://www.presidency.ucsb.edu/ (accessed April 4, 2017).

Biographical Directory of the United States Congress. Barry, Henry W. http://bioguide.congress.gov/ (accessed February 3, 2015).

_____. Trimble, Lawrence Strother. http://bioguide.congress.gov/ (accessed February 6, 2015).

Bryan Family History. http://www.rcasey.net/bryan/brysaml1.htm (accessed April 4, 2016).

Civil War Soldiers & Sailors Database. August 4, 2012. http://www.nps.gov/civilwar/soldiers-and-sailors-database.htm.

Find a Grave. *Eleazer Arthur Paine*. http://www.findagrave.com/ (accessed January 31, 2015).

Graves County Government. *Mayfield*. http://www.gravescountyky.com/Mayfield.html (accessed February 21, 2015).

Louie B. Nunn Center for Oral History, University of Kentucky Libraries. *Interview with Lon Carter Barton, November 29, 1990*. http://nyx.uky.edu/oh/render.php?cachefile=1990OH306_LEG021_Barton.xml. (accessed February 28, 2015).

National Park Service. *Civil War Soldiers & Sailors Database*. http://www.nps.gov/civilwar/soldiers-and-sailors-database.htm (accessed February 3, 2012).

Paducah Market House Museum. *Outlaws Before the World: The Story of General Orders Number Eleven: Also Known as the Jewish Eviction of Paducah*. http://www.markethousemuseum.com/node/178 (accessed February 21, 2015).

Person Sheet: Eleazer Paine. December 14, 1999. http://stevepayne.home.mindspring.com/ps03/ps03_459.htm (accessed April 4, 2016).

Person Sheet: Gen. Eleazer Arthur Paine. May 28, 2001. http://stevepayne.home.mindspring.com/ps03/ps03_407.htm (accessed April 4, 2016).

Person Sheet: Hendrick Ellsworth Paine. June 6, 1999. http://stevepayne.home.mindspring.com/ps03/ps03_398.htm (accessed April 4, 2016).

Price, R.M. *20th Tennessee Cavalry, CSA: Biographical Information*. 1999. http://home.olemiss.edu/~cmprice/cavalry/bio_w.html (accessed November 20, 2012).

Rootsweb. *Pat Thomas Gedcom: Eleazer Arthur Paine*. http://wc.rootsweb.ancestry.com/cgi-bin/igm.cgi?op=GET&db=tyrilla&id=I2104 (accessed January 31, 2015).

United States Department of Health and Human Resources, National Digestive Diseases Information Clearinghouse. *Irritable Bowel Syndrome*. http://www.digestive.niddk.nih.gov/ddiseases/pub/ibs (accessed December 16, 2011).

Database

WestlawNext

Index

Numbers in **_bold italics_** indicate pages with illustrations

Abner, Aaron 52
Acker, Peter 48, 103–104, 108, 140, 145–146
Adams, Green 58
African American soldiers 28–29, 32, 37–38, 41, 62–63, 83, 99, 104–105, 116, 123
Albuquerque, N.M. 130
Alexander, James R. 85, 100, 104, 107, 110–111, 139–140, 143
Allard, C.O. 41, 87–88, 107, 109
Allard, J.L. 41, 87–88, 118, 143
Allard & Crozier Mill Co. 118
Allen, George T. 74
Allen, Hall 2
Allen, James C. 80
Alloway, John F. 49
Anderson, Lucian 3–4, 15, **_24_**, 26–28, 30, 41, 44, 66, 121, 128, 149; accused in Paine investigation 69–71, 76; Congressional investigation 79–81; election of 1865 115–116; at Mayfield 50–51, 58; timeline 131–140
Andrews, Samuel L. 51
Arcola 46
Army of the Mississippi 17, 132
Ashbrook, T.J. 44
Ashbrook, Ryan & Co. 44
Associated Charities Commission 128
Association of the Graduates of the United States Military Academy 121–122
Atchison, Topeka & Santa Fe Railroad 128
Atherton, Thomas 106, 140
Atkins, Thomas J. 124
Aurora, Ky. 34
Australia 35

Baker, Robert F. 59
Baldwin, Miss Hester 35
Ballard County, Ky. 64, 67, 88, 97–98, 119
Baltimore Union Convention 133
banishment 1, 23, 38, 40, 66, 72, 84, 122–124
Bank of Mayfield 128
Barry, Henry W. 34, 42, 54, **_67_**, 72, 74, 83, 99; arrested by Hicks 29–32; May Kerr incident 56; post-war career 128–129; removed as post commander at Fort Anderson 62–63; timeline 133–134, 139–140
Bartling, Henry **_31_**, 37, 41, 45, 50, 72, 94, 97; Bell's drugstore 89–90; board of investigation 63–66, charges against 144–145; Paine's court martial 99–100, 106; post-war career; Provost Marshal at Paducah 32–35; timeline 128, 134, 137–138, 140
Barton, Lon Carter 122
Beasley, Robert 52
Belden, Thomas W.E. 51
Bell, William E. 32–33, 89–90, 94–95, 100–101, 104, 108, 139, 144
Bellevue Cemetery (Danville, Ky.) 129
Belmont, Mo. 14
Benet, Stephen Vincent 84
Big Bethel, battle of 42
Bigelow, John C. 53, 57
Bigger, Joseph M. 95
Bigger, W.W. 100
Bird's Point, Mo. 15, **_16_**, 17, 29, 132
Birmingham, Ellen 36, 87, 107, 109
Birmingham, Thomas 143
Birmingham, Ala. 123
Blandville, Ky. 35
Bloomfield, Mo. 17
Blount, W.G. 51
Blue, Solomon 118
Bolinger, John T. 66, 75, 108, 121, 145; attacks made by Prentice 70–71; government steamer to Hickman 49–51; Paine's court martial 95–96; post-war career 128; seeking removal of Grant 26–28; timeline 132, 135
Bolinger, Casey & Co. 26–27
Boydsville, Ky. 59, 70, 136
Boyle, Jeremiah T. 63, 75, 118, 133, 136
Boyle, John 63
Boyle County, Ky. 129
Bracken, John A. 88–89, 97, 106–108, 118, 132, 139, 144

Bradley, Lewis T. 95–96, 139, 145
Bradshaw, Albert 37
Bramlette, Thomas E. 4, 27, **_28_**, 29, 58, 84, 115, 121; board of investigation 62–63; charges against Anderson 79–80, charges against Paine 143; message to Kentucky Legislature on Paine 76; Paine's court martial 104–105, 107, 109; timeline 133, 136–138
Branham, Richard 103, 105, 140
Breyard, Sarah L. Malone 123
Brittle Sword: The Kentucky Militia (Stone) 122
Brooks, J.C. 97–98, 139, 145
Brown, Benjamin Grazt 62, 77
Brown, James 62
Brown, James S. 80
Brown, John Mason 62–63, **_64_**, 65, 72–77, 121, 129, 136, 140
Brown, Joseph F. 114
Brownfield, Empson 145
Bryan, John Tate 36
Bryan, William Shelby 36, 135
Buckner, W.S. 91, 93, 139, 148
Buford, Abraham 38, 54, 68
Bull Run, first battle of 12
Bull Run, second battle of 60
Buntin, Toussaint C. 96, 108, 139
Burbridge, Stephen 27, **_39_**, 46, 50, 54, 58, 69, 71, 75–76, 92; banishment of Sothern sympathizers 38; board of investigation 62–63, 65; timeline 134–137
Bureau of Military Justice 134
Burnett, Henry C. 12, 15, 26
bushwhackers 21–22, 24, 34, 52–53, 61, 112
Butler, Benjamin F. 2

Cairo, Ill. 2, 25, 28, 35, 38, 40, 46, 57–58, 60, 65, 67, 70, 111, 113, 124, 145; Bolinger at 94–96; Paine at 9, 11, 13–16; Paine's court martial 79, 81, 83; timeline 131–132, 135, 137–139
Cairo News 28
Cairo riot 81
Caldwell, J.W. 101

184   Index

Caldwell, W.P. 87, 100, 104, 106–107, 139–140, 143
Calloway County, Ky. 45, 64, 70, 100
Cambridge City, Ind. 129
Cambridge City District Agricultural Society 129
Camp Butler, Ill. 42
Camp Dick Robinson, Ky. 62
Camp Douglas, Ill. 125
Camp Nelson, Ky. 62
Campbell, James 33, 110–111, 116
Canada 1, 35, 38, 40, 46, 66, 72, 75, 84, 86, 123–125
Canby, Edward 9
Carlton, Caleb H. 115
Carpenter, Charles 84
Carrington, Henry B. 79, 81, **82**
Carter, A.B. 43–44
Casey, Silas 79, **80**, 81
Caseyville 46–49, 64–65, 84, 91–92, 94, 102–105, 135, 143, 145–148
Cave Hill Cemetery (Louisville) 129
Cedar Bluff, Ala. 70
Center of Conflict: A Factual Story of the War Between the States in Western Kentucky and Tennessee 2
Centre College 62
Champion (steamer) 83, 139
Chancellorsville, battle of 60
Chapman, Edward L. 110–111
Charleston, Mo. 16
Chattanooga, Tenn. 70
Chicago, Ill. 2, 40, 42, 44, 58, 71, 129, 131, 137, 140, 150
Chicago Academy of Medicine 129
Chicago Homeopathic Medical Society 129
Chicago Times 65
Chicago Tribune 18, 57, 71, 83, 111, 129
Chickamauga, battle of 62
Cincinnati, Ohio 37, 85
Cincinnati Commercial 83
Cincinnati Enquirer 13
Civil Rights Act 116–117
Civil War in Kentucky (Harrison) 122
Civil War in the Jackson Purchase (Lee) 122
Cleveland Plain Dealer 17
Clinton, Ky. 34, 50, 83, 133–134, 138–139
Clois, B.H. 54
Cole 138
Colfax, Schuler 79
Collier, W.A. 124
Collins' Historical Sketches of Kentucky (Richard H. Collins) 1–4, 121–122, 127
Colossus (steamer) 46
Columbian College 128
Columbus, Ky. 1, 6, 25, **36**, 42, 46, 50, 54–55, 57, 66–68, 83, 86, 101, 106, 112, 116; Confederate troops at 11–15; exiles to Canada 38, 40; Kesterson captured 34–35; mentioned at Paine's court martial 88–89, 95–96; timeline 132–135, 138; Tyler-Latham Controversy 124
Columbus, Miss. 128
Commercial Bank (Paducah, Ky.) 33, 110, 134
Commercial Point, Ky. 49, 94
Confederate Veteran 123
Conn, David O. 49, 102, 146
Connell, John 79, 81
Conness, John 77
Continental Hotel (Paducah, Ky.) 29–30, 33, 134
Convoy (steamer) 35, 50, 95–96, 145
Cook, Richard E. 38
Cook, William 38
Cookville, Tenn. 23
Cope, S.P. 41
Copperheads 28, 32–33, 61, 90
Corbett, Thomas H. 119
Corinth, Miss. 6, 18, 32, 68, 132
contraband 6, 24, 26, 31–33, 41, 44, 75, 87
cotton 26, 30–31, 33, 49–50, 66, 75, 88, 95–96, 108, 134, 145
court-martial 2, 4, 6, 17, 27, 32, 78–79, 90, 104, 120
Craddock, Jesse J. 58, 62–63, 65–66, 70
Craig, D.Y. 90, 101, 139–140
Crozier, William 118
Crutchfield, Mary 96, 139, 148
Cullum, George W. 17
Cumberland River 13, 16, 44
Cumberland Valley 23
Cunningham, William P. 106, 140
Curlew Mines (Caseyville, Ky.) 49
Cynthiana, Ky. 62

Daily Illinois State Journal (Springfield. Ill.) 11
Daily Milwaukee News 66
Danforth, Willis 42, 57, 71, 129
Danville, Ky. 62, 129
Davidson, Peter 49, 65, 93, 97, 108, 137, 139
Davis, D. Trabue 122
Davis, Garrett 74, 121
Davis, Henry W. 111
Davis, Ila M. 102, 140, 147
Davis, Jefferson 13, 38, 125
Davis, John F. 33
Davis, Richard E. 121
Democrats 4, 6–7, 41, 46, 62, 66, 68, 116–117, 121
Department of Cumberland 23, 25, 79, 99, 110, 133–134, 139
Department of Missouri 15–16, 85
Department of Tennessee 25, 27, 99, 133
Department of the Ohio 136
Detroit, Mich. 40
Dicus, Wiley 35
District of Kentucky 25, 38, 50, 54, 62–64
District of Nashville 23
District of Western Kentucky 1, 67, 83, 88, 110–111, 119, 135; formation of 5; troops serving in 25, 30, 55–56, 116
District of West Tennessee 25, 27, 50

Dougherty, Henry 27, 88
Doughty, J.W. 38
Dover, Tenn. 16
Dresden, Tenn. 34, 134
Dublin, Ky. 28, 36
Duck River 24
Duke of Wellington 107
Dunn, William McKee 79, **81**, 83–87, 91, 93–100, 102–107, 109, 139
Dustin, Daniel 24

Eaker, John 42–43, 53–55
Eastern Division of Kentucky 62
Eaty, H.B. 140
Edrington, Leonidas H. 88–89, 107–108, 118, 139
Eighth United States Colored Artillery Regiment 29, 30, 34, 40, 44–46, 50, 54, 58, 65, 67, 106, 116, 135, 144
Eighty Ninth Ohio Volunteer Infantry 115
Elk River 24
emancipation 5–6, 41, 50, 63, 73, 104–105, 115, 135, 149
Emancipation Proclamation 32, 49, 115, 133
Enders, Robert 40
Enoch, Eli 52, 58, 135
Etheridge, Emerson 32, **33**, 66, 85, 87, 107, 110, 134
Evansville, Ind. 2, 40, 50, 111

Fairview Cemetery (Albuquerque, N.M.) 130
Fancy Farm, Ky. 112, 133
Fanning, James 57–58
Farmington, Ky. 56, 132
Farmington, Miss. 18
Faulkner, W.W. 132
Fayetteville, Tenn. 23–24
"Federal salvation" 30, 117
Federal Union (Paducah, Ky.) 112, 116
Feliciana, Ky. 50, 135
Fels, Samuel 118
Fifth Tennessee Volunteer Infantry Regiment (Confederate) 33
Filson Club Historical Society 129
fines 35, 54
First Alabama Infantry Regiment (Confederate) 18–19
First Brigade of the District of Cairo 14
First Regiment Capital Guards 58, 62
Fisher (steamer) 46
Fisher, John G. 35
Fitch, Le Roy 48
Flournoy, Gustavus A. 35, 116
Flournoy, Lawrence M. 33, 54
Ford, J. Scott 96–97, 100, 104, 139, 144, 147–148
Forrest, Nathan Bedford 6, 53–54, 57, 59, 75, 102, 113; attacks Paducah 14, 26, 29, 31–33, 38, 41, 48; threatens to invade Jackson Purchase 68–70; timeline 133, 137
Forrest Cavalry Corps 123
Fort Anderson (Ky.) 14, 29, 31–32, 34, 37, 54, **55**, 58, 65, 72, 83, 106, 114, 135–136

Index

Fort Donelson (Tenn.) 16
Fort Heiman (Ky.) 70
Fort Henry (Tenn.) 16
Fort Pillow (Tenn.) Massacre 53
Fort Pleasant (Fla.) 9
Fort Sumter (S.C.) 11, 14, 60
Forty Fourth Wisconsin Volunteer Infantry 114, 116
Foster, Stephen 1
Fourteenth United States Colored Infantry 23
Fourth United States Colored Heavy Artillery 67
Frankfort, Ky. 2, 26, 28, 46, 58, 62–63
Frankfort Yeoman 119–120
Freedmen's Bureau 116–117, 120
Freemont, John C. 132
Fry, Speed Smith 62–63, **64**, 65–66, 72–76, 121, 129, 136–138
Fyfe, Jennie 67, 83, 117

Gainesboro, Tenn. 23
Gallatin, Tenn. 20, **21**, 22–24, 29, 74, 88, 132–133
Galloway, D.M. 43
Gardner, Willis W. 143
Garland, Parson 138
Geauga County, Ohio 9, 131
General Lawrence (steamer) 46
Gerrish, Joseph 104, 140, 145
Gettysburg, battle of 60
Gillespie, V.S. 85, 87, 109, 139, 143
Glover, Robert 101–102, 140
Graham (steamer) 35
Grand Army of the Republic 128
Grant, Henry B. 64–65
Grant, Ulysses S. 3, 5–6, 9, 12, **13**, 14–16, 18, 20, 27–28, 39, 46, 58, 85, 101, 115, 127, 131–133, 136, 138, 140
Graves County, Ky. 26, 28, 34, 36, 43, 50–51, 56, 64, 69, 94, 100, 116, 118, 122, 127–128, 135, 141, 149–150
Graves County Courthouse 28, 36, 43, 50–53, 55, 60, 64, 66–67, 69–70, 75, 118, 125, 127, 135, 137, 141
Graves County Public Library 1
Greathouse, Catherine R. 92–93, 139, 146
Greathouse, John S. 92, 102–103, 140
Greathouse, Robert William 92–93, 139, 146
Greenback Clubs 128
Greenback Party 128
Gregg, William 92, 99, 139, 148
Gregory, Jasper 28
Gregory, Jonathan Franklin 28
Gregory, Mary 28
Gregory, Thomas Jones 27–28, 36, 46, 51–53, 55–56, 59–61, 112, **113**, 125, 134–135, 140
Gregory's Avengers 112
Griffie, George 35
guerrilla warfare 6, 27–28, 31, 77, 112, 115, 118, 120, 146, 149–150; at Bird's Point 16; at Gallatin 20–24; in Jackson Purchase 34–36, 38, 41, 43–44, 50–53, 55–59, 67–71, 74–75; mentioned at Paine's court martial 83, 89–93, 97–99, 101–104; timeline 132–136, 138, 140; in Union County 46, 48–49

Haddix's Ferry, Ky. 34, 134
Hahnemann Medical College 129
Haldeman, Walter N. 129
Hall, P.H. 102, 106, 140
Hall, Roland H. 37, 72, 90, 101–102, 135, 140, 144
Hall, William 43–44, 53–54
Halleck, Henry W. 4, 9, 18, 27, 58, 60, 69, **108**; called coward by Paine 32, 66; and Paine at Bird's Point 15–17; Paine's court martial 84–87, 107, 109–110, 150; timeline 134, 136, 143
Hammock, John William 49, 91, 99, 139, 147
Happy, James B. 34, 43, 100–101, 133
Harrow, William 79, **80**, 81
Hart County, Ky. 62
Hartsville, Tenn. 21
Hatfield, John 52
Hayden, Thomas 112
Heintzelman, Samuel P. 79, **80**, 81
Henderson, Ky. 49, 103
Hendricks, J.T. 114–115
Hendricks, Thomas A. 77, 120–121
Herrington, John M. 114
Hess (execution) 58–59, 136
Hickman, Ky. 28, 64, 67, 112, 123, 145; Bolinger at 49–50; Confederate troops at 12–13; mentioned in Paine's court martial 95–96, 108; timeline 133, 135, 138
Hickman County, Ky. 67
Hicks, Henry Bascom 1, 56, 125, **126**, 136
Hicks, Stephen G. 27, 29, **30**, 32, 63, 74, 83, 101, 115
Hillyer, William S. 13
Hines, J.H. 101, 140
Hinton, Samuel 54
History of Kentucky (Connelley & Coulter) 122
History of Kentucky (Kinkead) 122
History of Kentucky and Kentuckians (Johnson) 122
Hobbs, Clementine 40
Holt, Joseph 72, **73**, 75–76, 79, 81, 84, 110–111, 119, 134, 138
Home Guard 27, 36, 52–53, 56, 60, 69, 112, 134
Hood, John Bell 70
Hooker, Joseph 72
Horne, T.M. 38
Hoskins, Patricia Ann 3
Hovey, Alvin P. 47
Hubbard, John H. 80
Hubbard, William McKeene 38
Hughes, Bettie B. 103, 140, 147
Hughes, Joshua 103
Hughes, Sam 125
Hughes, Willis 103
Humble, R.M. 89–90, 139, 144
Hunt, Andrew Lucas 45, 52–53, 61
Hunter, Charles 42
Hunter, David 79, 81, 83–84, 109
Husbands, James B. 89, 139
Husbands, Lorenzo Dow 123

Illinois artillery regiments: 1st 14; 2nd 67, 114
Illinois cavalry regiments: 2nd 31; 3rd 35, 42, 50–52, 59–60, 67, 69, 135–137, 149
Illinois Central Railroad Company 31
Illinois infantry regiments: 9th 9, 11, 14, 131; 12th 9; 17th 11; 49th 114, 116; 105th 24; 111th 145; 132nd 34, 46, 54, 59, 65, 67; 134th 35, 42, 50–53, 55, 57–58, 61, 66, **68**, 71, 129, 135, 137, 149; 136th 44, 46, 50, 67, 135, 149–150; 139th 49, 97; 141st 46, 67
Illinois State Homeopathic Society 129
Illinois State Legislature 5, 10, 115, 131
International Law; or, Rules Regulating the Intercourse of States in Peace and War (Halleck) 84
Island No. 10 6, 17, 32

Jackson Purchase, Ky. 1–3, 5–6, 27–28, 41, 56, 67–68, 75, 83, 112–113, 116–117, 128
Jacobs, T.L. 34, 134
James, Alexander 139
James, David C. 47
Jansens, L. 72
Jefferson Davis Monument Association 123
Jersey City, N.J. 121
Jett, E.R. 97–98, 139, 145
Jim Crow South 117
Johnson, Adam R. 44, 46, **47**, 48–49, 91–93, 97, 135
Johnson, Andrew 115, **116**, 117
Johnson, John 59
Johnson, Samuel F.
Johnsonville, Tenn. 70
Jones, A.S. 35
Jones, Edward B. 32
Jones, Henry 40
Jones, W.H. 60
Julian, George W. 115

Kelley, D.C. 123
Kenesaw Mountain, Ga. 133
Kentucky: A Pioneer Commonwealth (Shaler) 122
Kentucky cavalry regiments: 2nd 62; 10th 62; 15th 26, 56; 16th 27
Kentucky Confederates: Civil War, Secession, and the Jackson Purchase 3
Kentucky Encyclopedia 122
Kentucky General Assembly 29, 104, 116, 129, 133, 138
Kentucky infantry regiments: 20th 27; 42nd 27; 45th 62; 48th 44; 52nd 48
Kerney, James 140
Kerr, May 56
Kesterson, James 34, 46, 75, 101–102, 134
Kibby, W.H. 104, 147
Kidd, W. Henry 37
Kilgore, Charles M. 33, 106–107, 140

Kinkead, A.B. 34–35
Ku Klux Klan 117

Lambert, Lucien L. 55
Lansing, Mich. 44
Latham, Mary **123**, 124, 141
Latham, Thomas J. 123–124
Lawrence, William H. 59, 68–69
Lawton, Alexander 9
Lee, Robert E. 113, 119
Lexington, Ky. 2, 62, 65, 69, 129
Lieber Code 84
Lincoln, Abraham 3–6, 35, 66, 69, 71, 105–106, 111, 120–121, 149; assassination and death 114–115, assessments 25–26, 29–30; emancipation 32, 49; and Paine 9–11, 58, 60, 75–76; *Proclamation 113* 84, 109; 119; timeline 131, 133–140
Lincoln, Mary Todd 129
Lindsey, Daniel W. 63
Livingston County, Ky. 64
Los Angeles Panorama Co. 128
Louisville, Ky. 2, 38, 62–65, 70, 79, 119, 129–130, 137
Louisville Courier 129
Louisville Courier Journal 129
Louisville Democrat 15
Louisville Journal 4, 40, 65–66, 70–71, 76, 85, 108, 110–111, 120–121
Louisville Press 71
Lovelaceville, Ky. 15, 88–89, 106, 132
Lucas, Samuel T. 57
Luxton, Edward D. 58, 64, 71–72
Lynchburg, Tenn. 23–24
Lyon, H.F. 37

Mackall, William W. 18
Madisonville, Ky. 47
Malone, Sarah L. 124
Malone, W.G. 38
Manassas, Va. 12, 113
Maplewood Cemetery (Mayfield, Ky.) 1, 125, 128
Marion, Ky. 49
Market House (Paducah, Ky.) 30, 69, 134
martial law 41, 73, 84, 107, 109
Martin, James S. 27
Masonic Gem (steamer) 30, 40
Matheny, E.W.S. 49, 54, 136
Maurous, E.A. 40
Mayes, Chapel 54
Mayes, T.H. 89–90, 94–95, 139
Mayes, William L. 90, 100–102, 108, 139, 144
Mayfield, Ky. 1, 3, 25–26, 34, 83, 89, 115, 122, 124–125, 128–129; board of investigation 64–66, 71–72, 75; courthouse burned 69; executions 36, 46, 59; fortifications at 149–150; Home Guard 27–28; mentioned in Paine's court martial 101; occupation 41–44, 50–60, 66–72; timeline 132–133, 135–138, 141
Mayfield Creek, Ky. 14
McArthur, James N. 54, 83, 95
McChesney, Robert 71–72
McChesney, Waters W. **43**; charges and arrest 61, 65–66, 71–72; death 129; earlier in the war 42; fortifications at Mayfield 149–150; at Mayfield 43–44, 50–59; timeline 131, 135–137, 140–141
McChesney's Zouaves 42
McClellan, George B. 11, 68, 85, 106
McConnell, Henry K. 23
McConnell, James B. 121
McCracken County, Ky. 13, 35, 44, 60, 90, 97, 100–101, 116
McDonald, Charles 43–44
McDougal, Captain 112
McIntosh, John B. 79, **81**
McKinney, Charles 38
McNutt, James A. 43–44
Memphis, Tenn. 24–25, 60, 69, 123–124, 136
Memphis Water Co. 123
Meredith, Solomon 3, **69**, 94, 97; at Cairo 25, 35, 46, 58; at Mayfield 61, 150; at Paducah 60, 64–68, 70–72, 83–84, 110–115; post-war career 129; timeline 137–140
Mexican-American War 27, 62
Milam, Marian G. 33, 96, 100, 106–107, 139, 145
Milburn, Ky. 14, 35, 132
Military History of Kentucky (Federal Writers' Project) 122
Mill Springs, battle of 62
Miller, William H. 43–44
Milroy, Robert H. 24
Milwaukee, Wis. 129
Mississippi River 14, 17, 27, 37, 111
Mitchellville, Tenn. 20, 132
Monmouth, Ill. 5, 10, **11**, 19, 21, 46, 63, 65, 111, 119, 121, 131, 137, 140
Monmouth Presbyterian Church 5
Monmouth Republican Party 10
Monmouth Review 65
Monmouth Temperance League 10, 131
Montgomery, Alex 125
Montreal, Quebec 125
Moore, Joseph M. 38
Moore, Timothy 103
Morgan, J.E.D. 37
Morgan, John 37
Morgan, John Hunt 62, 123, 125
Morganfield, Ky. 47, 64, 92–93, 99, 103–104
Morton, James 38
Moscow, Ky. 55, 112
Moss, George B. 38
Moss, James Dickey 94, 99–100, 139, 144
Mound City, Ill. 132
Mt. Sterling, Ky. 62
Munchhuff, H. 140
Murray State University 1, 3

Nashville, Tenn. 6, 20, 23–24, 28, 70, 72, 132–133, 137
Nathan Bedford Forrest Monument (Memphis, Tenn.) 123
National Unionist (Lexington, Ky.) 38
Needham, Hawley V. 53, 57, 59, 61
Nero 123

New History of Kentucky (Harrison & Klotter) 122
New Madrid, Mo. 17, 132
New Orleans, La. 2, 35, 43, 88
Nineteenth Indiana Volunteer Infantry 60
Noble, Silas 27
Norton, Harlow B. 40, 54
Norton, William F. 56
Norton Brothers Bank (Paducah, Ky.) 56

Oak Hill Cemetery (Washington, D.C.) 129
Oakes, James 72
Oakland Cemetery (St. Paul, Minn.) 121
Oakwood Cemetery (Troy, N.Y.) 129
Ohio infantry regiments: 71st 23; 89th 115
Ohio River **12**, 14, 32, 34, 37, 44, 46, 54, 58, 83, 99, 135–137
Ohio State Militia 5, 10, 131
Omer, Allen 49, 91, 99, 139, 147
On Jordan's Banks: Emancipation and Its Aftermath in the Ohio River Valley (Bigham) 122
Ord, Edward 9
Ottawa, Ill. 21
Outlaw, Drew A. 30
Overall, Josephine Horne 123
Owens, Reverend 34

Paducah, Ky. 1, 4, **12**, 79–90, 93–102, 104–107, 110–120, 123–130; after the war 115–118; board of investigation at 62–65; charges against Paine at 143–145, 148; earlier in the war 4–6, 9, 12–16, 22, 24–29; exiles to Canada 40; Grant at 12–13; Lincoln's funeral at 114–115; and Meredith at 60–77, 79–115; Paine at 9–15; Paine's court martial at 81–111; Paine's return 29–41, 43–46, 48–50, 53–60; timeline 131–140; Tyler-Latham Controversy 123–124
Paducah and the Civil War (Cashon) 122
Paducah Daily Register 124
Paducah, 1830-1980 (Robertson) 122
Paducah Evening Sun 124
Paducah: Frontier to the Atomic Age (Robertson) 122
Paducah Herald 120
Paducah News Democrat 122
Paducah Sun Democrat 2
Paine, Charlotte Phelps 10, 63, 65, 121
Paine, Edward 10
Paine, Eleazer Arthur: and Anderson 15, 25, 30, 58; at Bird's Point 15–17; birth and early life 9–10; board of investigation 58, 62–63, 65–66, 71–73, 76–77, 96, 120; at Cairo 9, 11, 16; charges against 72, 84, 143–148; court martial 78–111; and employment of former slaves 23; exiles to Canada 38–40; at

Gallatin 20–24; and Grant and 9, 12–16, 58; and Halleck 9, 17, 32, 58, 66, 84–87, 109; at Island No. 10 and Tiptonville 17–18; legacy and folklore 121–127; and Lincoln 9–11, 58, 60, 75–76; at Mayfield 42–44, 55; and McChesney 42–44, 72; and military enlistments of African Americans 23, 29, 37, 99; at Paducah (1861) 12–15; post-war career and death 119–121; and Prentice 65–66, 70; return to Paducah (1864) 26–42, 50–54, 56–60; at Siege of Corinth 18–19; and Smith 9, 14–15; timeline 131–141; at Tullahoma 24–25; at Tuscumbia 19–20; Union County campaign 46–49
Paine, Halbert Eleazer 60
Paine, Harriet Phelps 9
Paine, Hendrick Ellsworth 9
Paine, Phelps 38, 40, 50, 66, 89, 97, 100, 124, 139, 145
Painesville, Ohio 9–10, 131
Paris, Tenn. 94
Parkman, Ohio 9, 131
Parsons, Henry 49, 93, 99, 139, 148
Payne, M.A. 27
Peck, John H. 34
Peck, Joseph F. 56
Peoria Democrat 120
Perry, Ohio 10
Perryville, battle of 62
Phelps, Samuel W. 10
Philips, William H. 140
Phillips, William W. 106
Pierce, Liston H. 54
Pierson, James T. 92, 104–107, 139–140, 143, 145, 148
Pierson, Will S. 92, 139, 143, 148
Pierson, William Wright 92, 139, 148
Pope, John F. 6, 17, *18*, 19, 132
Porter, Fitz John 79
Portsmouth Daily Times 66
Powell, Lazarus W. *73*, 74, 76–78, 120
Prentice, George D. 4, 65–66, *67*, 70–71, 76, 105, 129
Price, G.W. 140
Price, John 35
Prince, Henry 25, 35, 38, *45*, 46, 54
Prince, J.P. 44
Prince & Dodd Co. 44
Proclamation 113 84, 109, 134
Purcell, Samuel M. 104, 140
Puryear, J.R. 124

Quigley, Quintus Q. *117*, 124

Rabb, G.F. 41, 87–88, 100, 104, 139, 143–144
Ramsey, John T. 112
Redd, Thomas M. 32, 34, 37, 44, 101, 104, 140
Reelfoot Lake 17
Republicans 6–7, 10, 17, 74, 115, 120
Revelle, Hardie N. 59
Riley, Albert T. 52
Riverside Cemetery (Cambridge, Ind.) 129

Rollins, James S. 80
Rollston, Joseph L. 124
Rollston, Mary Jane 40
Rosecrans, William S. 19, *20*, 21
Rousseau, Lovell H. 23
Rowland, Fannie E. 124
Rudolph, Elijah 100, 140
Russell, Susan 125

St. Charles Hotel (Cairo, Ill.) 81
St. Francis Hotel (Paducah, Ky.) 13
St. Louis, Mo. 2, 17, 62–63, 65, 111, 137
St. Louis Republican 65
St. Martinsville, La. 123
St. Paul, Minn. 121
Salem, Ky. 49
Saline Landing, Ill. 44, 135
Samuel B. Orr (steamer) 125
San Francisco, Ca. 128
San Francisco New City Hall Commission 128
Sanders, Catherine L. 40
Savage Conflict (Sutherland) 122
Scammon Hospital (Chicago) 129
Schofield, John M. 65, 70, 136–137
Schofield, Richard 58–59
School History of Kentucky (Smith) 122
Scofield, Glenni W. 80
secessionists 4, 6, 12, 14, 20, 28, 38, 43, 49, 54, 83–85, 101, 116, 119
Second Seminole War 9
Selma, Ky. 44
Seventh Tennessee Volunteer Cavalry Regiment 55, 67, 114, 116
Shanklin, Robert H. 40
Shawneetown, Ill. 46–47
Sheridan, Philip 3
Sherman, William T. 3, 20, 38, 133
Shields, John 13
Shiloh, battle of 18, 27, 62
Shouse, Francis H. 140, 146
Sikeston, Mo. 17, 132
Sinclair, Charles E. 53, 55, 136
Sinnott, John 85, 109, 139, 143
Slater, Edward C. *114*, 115
slavery 3–4, 10, 23, 65, 76, 117
Small, Braxton 35
Smedley, Edward S. 38
Smith, Amos 43–44, 70, 138
Smith, Andrew Jackson 100, *101*
Smith, Charles F. 6, 9, 14, *15*, 39, 85, 89, 107, 132
Smith, Green Clay 79–80
Smith, M.L. 113
Smithland, Ky. 13, 44, 49, 135
Smith's Chicago Artillery 9
Snow, Phillip 103–104, 140
Soldier's Home (Louisville) 129
Sons of Confederate Veterans 4, 122, 124, 127
Sons of Liberty 54
specifications of court martial 6, 84, 104, 107–109
Spencer's Chapel (Mayfield, Ky.) 52
Springfield, Ill. 11, 19, 42, 57–58, 60
Stanton, Edwin 28, 37, 58, 72, 74, 76, 78–79, 84, 115, 133, 136, 138, 140
Starks, William M. 100–101, 115–116, 140

Steele, John B. 80
Steele, John C. 56
Story of Kentucky (Connelly) 122
Story of Mayfield Through a Century (Davis) 122
Story of Paducah (Neuman) 22
Stuart, William M. 80
Sturgeon, Thomas L. 102, 140, 146
Swift, W.F. 36, 135
Symes, George G. 121

Talbott, Louis L. 49, 139, 146
Taylor, Richard W. 49, 54, 136
Taylor, Zachary 9
Tennessee River 3, 12, 16, 25, 32, 34, 70, 83
Tenth Kentucky Cavalry Regiment (Confederate) 49
Tenth New York Volunteer Infantry Regiment 42, 131
Terrell, Martha Grungy 124
Third Kentucky Mounted Infantry Regiment (Confederate) 49
Thirteenth Amendment 3
Thirty Fourth New Jersey Volunteer Infantry 46, 55, 59–60, 67, 103
Thomas, George H. 23, 134
Thomas, Lorenzo 15, 23, 30, 32, *37*, 60, 65, 72, 111, 135, 137, 140
Thompson, D.D. 75
Tice, William W. 27
Tilghman, Lloyd 39
Tiptonville, Tenn. 6, 17–18, *19*, 132
tobacco 26, 30–31, 43, 46, 49–50, 53–54, 63, 66, 75, 95–96, 118, 134, 145
Tombelle, G.L. 49, 99, 105, 107, 140
Topeka, Kan. 128
Topeka & Southwestern Railway 128
Townsend, Edward D. 72, 75
trade restrictions 26, 37, 44, 63, 75
Tradewater Mill (Caseyville, Ky.) 49
Tradewater River 49
Treatise of Military Law and the Practice of Courts Martial (Benet) 84
Trimble, Lawrence Strother 12, *26*, 27–28, 32, 56, 116–117, 120–121, 130
Trimble, Duke & Co. 26–27
Trumbull, Lyman 73, *74*, 77, 120–121
Tucker, Caleb 49, 92–94, 99, 139, 148
Tucker, W.P. 91–93, 139, 146
Tullahoma, Tenn. 24, 29, 120, 122
Tullis, Amos K. 53
Tuscumbia, Ala. 19–20, 29, 70, 132
Twelfth Kentucky Cavalry Regiment (Confederate) 36
Tylor, Henry A. *57*, 123–124, 141

Unconditional Unionist: The Hazardous Life of Lucian Anderson, Kentucky Congressman 3
Unconditional Unionists 4, 49, 69, 77, 93, 101, 103–108, 133–134
Union City, Tenn. 28, 57, 124, 133
Union County, Ky. 47–49, 54, 57,

64–65, 84, 90–95, 97, 99, 102–106, 118, 125, 135–136
Union Democrats 4, 62–63, 104
Union League of America (Paducah, Ky.) 29–30, 37, 41, 69, 83, 114
Uniontown, Ky. 44, 46–47, 50, 64, 92–93, 99, 102, 108, 125
United Daughters of the Confederacy 122–124, 127
United States Congress 4, 15, 24, 29, 73, 76, 105, 116, 118, 128, 133–134
United States infantry regiments: 1st 9
United States Marine Hospital (Paducah, Ky.) 12, 14, 44, 67
United States Medical and Surgical Journal 129
United States Military Academy 5, 9, *10*, 121, 131
United States Senate 73–78, 120–121
United States Senate, Committee on Military Affairs 74, 76–78
United States Treasury Department 37, 58, 106, 131
United States War Department 28, 60, 69, 71–74, 76, 81, 83, 133, 138–140
University of Tennessee at Martin 1

Vance, W.R. 38
Vicksburg, Miss. 20, 27
Vincennes, Ind. 40, 70

Wadesboro, Ky. 42
Walker, Burns M. 38
Walker, James Pembroke 38
Wallace, Lew 39
Walters, Robert A. 52–53, 136
War Eagle (Cairo, Ill.) 111
Wartham 138
Washburn, Cadwallader C. 25, 29, 30, 46, 50, 57, 69, 75, 133–134
Washington, D.C. 26, 28–29, 50, 58, 72–73, 79, 81, 110–111, 129
Watson's Landing, Ky. 17
Watts, Given & Co. 36, 41, 87, 107, 109, 143
Weakley County, Tenn. 33, 96, 102, 106
Webster, Joseph D. 14, 132
Welch, Thomas H. 92, 139, 148
Whig Party 10, 37, 103
Whitfield, Kate Woolfolk 40, 124, 140
Whitworth, Frederick T. 97–98, 139
Willard Hotel (Washington) 72
William Clark Market Museum House 127
Williams, Rufus King 25, 114–115, 133

Williamson, Alice 23–24
Wilson, Henry 76
Wilson, John A. 51
Wilson County, Tenn. 21–22
Windsor, Ontario 38, 40
Wisconsin Homeopathic Society 129
Woodward, John E. 35, 41, 46, 66, 87–88, 102, 118, 139–140, 143–144
Wooldridge Monuments (Mayfield, Ky.) 1
Woolfolk, George 39
Woolfolk, Mary 123
Woolfolk, Robert O. 39–40, 85–86, 100, 104, 107, 117, 122, 139–140, 143
Woolfolk, Roberta 123
Wortham, Peter 70

Yale University 51, 62
Yantis, James A. 38
Yates, Richard *11*, 19, 21, 41, 47, 57, 61
Yeiser, Philip D. 88–89, 107, 139–140, 144
Young People's History of Kentucky for Schools and General Reading (Thompson) 122

Zollicofer, Felix K. 62

www.ingramcontent.com/pod-product-compliance
Lightning Source LLC
Chambersburg PA
CBHW081559300426
44116CB00015B/2940